ESSENTIALS OF
ORGANIZATIONAL BEHAVIOR

ESSENTIALS OF ORGANIZATIONAL BEHAVIOR

ninth edition

Stephen P. Robbins

San Diego State University

Timothy A. Judge

University of Florida

PEARSON

Prentice
Hall

Upper Saddle River, NJ 07458

Cataloging for this publication can be obtained from the Library of Congress.

Editor-in-Chief: David Parker
Senior Acquisitions Editor: Mike Ablassmeir
Product Development Manager: Ashley Santora
Project Manager: Claudia Fernandes
Editorial Assistant: Kristen Varina
Media Project Manager: Ashley Lulling
Marketing Manager: Anne Howard
Marketing Assistant: Susan Osterlitz
Associate Director, Production Editorial: Judy Leale
Managing Editor: Renata Butera
Production Editor: Kelly Warsak
Permissions Coordinator: Charles Morris
Associate Director, Manufacturing: Vinnie Scelta
Manufacturing Buyer: Diane Peirano
Design/Composition Manager: Christy Mahon
Composition Liaison: Suzanne Duda
Designer: Steve Frim
Interior Design: Janet Slowik/Steve Frim
Cover Design: Steve Frim
Illustration (Interior): GGS Book Services
Composition: GGS Book Services
Full-Service Project Management: GGS Book Services
Printer/Binder: Courier-Westford
Cover Printer: Lehigh Press
Typeface: 10/12 Janson Text

Credits and acknowledgments borrowed from other sources and reproduced, with permission, in this textbook appear on appropriate page within text.

Pearson Education LTD.
Pearson Education Singapore, Pte. Ltd
Pearson Education, Canada, Ltd
Pearson Education–Japan

Pearson Education Australia PTY, Limited
Pearson Education North Asia Ltd
Pearson Educación de Mexico, S.A. de C.V.
Pearson Education Malaysia, Pte. Ltd

10 9 8 7 6 5 4 3 2 1
ISBN-13: 978-0-13-243152-1
ISBN-10: 0-13-243152-1

This book is dedicated to our friends and colleagues in

The Organizational Behavior Teaching Society,

who, through their teaching research and commitment

to the learning process, have significantly

improved the ability of students

to understand and apply OB concepts.

Brief Contents

Contents

Preface

This book was created as an alternative to the 600- or 700-page comprehensive textbook in organizational behavior (OB). It attempts to provide balanced coverage of all the key elements comprising the discipline of OB, in a style that readers will find both informative and interesting. We're pleased to say that this text has achieved a wide following in short courses and executive programs, as well as in traditional courses as a companion volume with experiential, skill development, case, and readings books. It is currently used at more than 500 colleges and universities in the United States, Canada, Latin America, Europe, Australia, and Asia. It's also been translated into Spanish, Portuguese, Japanese, Chinese, Dutch, Polish, Turkish, Danish, and Bahasa Indonesian.

RETAINED FROM THE PREVIOUS EDITION

What do people like about this book? Surveys of users have found general agreement about the following features. Needless to say, they've all been retained in this edition.

- Length. Since its inception in 1984, we've tried diligently to keep this book in the range of 325–350 pages. Users tell me this length allows them considerable flexibility in assigning supporting materials and projects.

- *Balanced topic coverage.* Although short in length, this book continues to provide balanced coverage of all the key concepts in OB. This includes not only traditional topics, such as personality, motivation, and leadership, but also cutting-edge issues such as emotions, trust, negotiation, and knowledge management.

- *Writing style.* This book is frequently singled out for its fluid writing style and extensive use of examples. Users regularly tell us that they find this book "conversational," "interesting," "student friendly," and "very clear and understandable."

- *Practicality.* This book has never been solely about theory. It's about *using* theory to better explain and predict the behavior of people in organizations. In each edition of this book, we have focused on making sure that readers see the link between OB theories, research, and implications for practice.

- *Absence of pedagogy.* Part of the reason we've been able to keep this book short in length is that it doesn't include review questions, cases, exercises, or similar teaching/learning aids. It continues to provide only the basic core of OB

EXHIBIT A   Integrative Topics

Chapter	Globalization and Cross-Cultural Differences	Diversity	Ethics
1	7–8, 10	8–9	11–12
2			20
3	39–41, 45–47	42–44	44–45
4	65–66		66
5	77, 79, 86–87		
6	95–99, 105	95	
7	115–116	114	122
8	129, 132–133	132	
9	143, 154–155	149–151, 157	
10	160, 163, 169, 171–173	170–171	
11			187, 191–192
12	201, 205		209
13	215, 225–226	224–225	
14		233	
15	250	252	259–260
16	265, 279–280	265	265, 277

knowledge, allowing instructors the maximum flexibility in designing and shaping their courses.

■ *Integration of globalization, diversity, and ethics.* As shown in Exhibit A, the topics of globalization and cross-cultural differences, diversity, and ethics are discussed throughout this book. Rather than being presented in stand-alone chapters, these topics have been woven into the context of relevant issues. Users tell us they find that this integrative approach makes these topics more fully part of OB and reinforces their importance.

■ *Comprehensive supplements.* While this book may be short in length, it's not short on supplements. It comes with a complete, high-tech support package for both faculty and students. This includes a comprehensive Instructor's Manual and Test Item File; a dedicated Web site (www.prenhall.com/robbins); an Instructor's Resource CD-ROM, including the computerized Test Item File, Instructor's Manual, and PowerPoint slides; and the Self-Assessment Library, which provides students with insights into their skills, abilities, and interests. These supplements are described in detail later in this Preface.

New to the Ninth Edition

This ninth edition has been updated in terms of research, examples, and topic coverage. New material in this edition includes:

- New chapter on mood and emotions to reflect the managerial implications of cutting edge research in this area (Chapter 7)

- Updated research on personality, including the Big Five personality traits (Chapter 3)

- New research on managerial decision making and what we can do to avoid decision-making errors and biases (Chapter 4)

- Expansion of material on goal-setting theory, which has been argued to be the most practically useful motivation theory ever (Chapter 5)

- More material on job design and telecommuting, which continue to be cutting-edge issues for organizations today (Chapter 6)

- Coverage of emotional labor and how employees and managers can better manage their and others' emotions in the workplace (Chapter 7)

- Some of the latest research on group behavior, including research showing the dark side of groups (Chapter 8)

- New research on how to compose the best work teams (Chapter 9)

- The latest research on communication barriers between men and women and across cultures (Chapter 10)

- Significantly expanded treatment of the latest and most exciting theory in leadership research—transformational/charismatic leadership—and what organizations can do to improve leadership (Chapter 11)

- New research on influence tactics, which suggests that the most widely used ways of influencing people are the *least* effective in organizations (Chapter 12)

- The latest research on conflict and negotiation, which suggests many practical ways that individuals can improve their abilities to resolve conflicts and better negotiate desired outcomes (Chapter 13)

- Updated material on the virtual organization, which continues to evolve with ever-changing information technology (Chapter 14)

- Increased coverage on how to create an ethical culture (Chapter 15)

- More material on barriers to change and how to overcome them (Chapter 16)

- New research on work stress that shows not all stress is bad (Chapter 16)

SUPPLEMENTS PACKAGE

Essentials of Organizational Behavior continues to be supported with an extensive supplement package for both students and faculty.

FACULTY RESOURCES

Instructor's Resource Center

Register. Redeem. Login.

At www.prenhall.com/irc instructors can access a variety of print, media, and presentation resources available with this text in downloadable, digital format.

It gets better.   Once you register, you will not have additional forms to fill out, or multiple usernames and passwords to remember, to access new titles and/or editions. As a registered faculty member, you can log in directly to download resource files and to receive immediate access and instructions for installing Course Management content to your campus server.

Need help?   Our dedicated Technical Support team is ready to assist instructors with questions about the media supplements that accompany this text. Visit www.247.prenhall.com for answers to frequently asked questions and toll-free user-support phone numbers. The following supplements are available to adopting instructors.

For detailed descriptions of all the supplements listed here, please visit www.prenhall.com/irc.

Instructor's Resource Center (IRC) on CD-ROM: ISBN 0-13-243154-8
Printed Instructor's Manual with Test Item File: ISBN 0-13-243153-X
TestGen test-generating software: Visit the IRC (both online and on CD-Rom) for this text.
PowerPoints: Visit the IRC (both online and on CD-Rom) for this text.
Videos on DVD: ISBN 0-13-186411-4

STUDENT RESOURCES

Prentice Hall's Self-Assessment Library (S.A.L.)

The Self-Assessment Library is available with this text in print, on CD-ROM, or online (stand-alone site or within your OneKey course management course). It contains more than 50 self-scoring exercises that provide insights into your skills, abilities, and interests.

Companion Website

www.prenhall.com/robbins contains valuable resources for both students and professors, including an online study guide with multiple-choice, true/false, and short-answer questions.

VangoNotes.com

Study on the go with VangoNotes—chapter reviews from your text in downloadable mp3 format. Now wherever you are—whatever you're doing—you can study by listening to the following for each chapter of your textbook:

- *Big Ideas:* Your "need to know" for each chapter.
- *Practice Test:* A gut check for the Big Ideas—tells you if you need to keep studying.
- *Key Terms:* Audio drill to help you review key concepts and terms.
- *Rapid Review:* A quick drill session—use it right before your test.

VangoNotes are **flexible.** You can download all the material directly to your player, or only the chapters you need. And they're **efficient.** Use them in your car, at the gym, walking to class, wherever. So get yours today. And get studying.

SafariX eTextbooks Online

The Largest eTextbook Store on the Internet!

Developed for students looking to save money on required or recommended textbooks, SafariX eTextbooks Online saves students up to 50 percent off the suggested list price of the print text. Students simply select their eText by title or author and purchase immediate access to the content for the duration of the course using any major credit card. With a SafariX eText, students can search for specific keywords or page numbers, make notes online, print out reading assignments that incorporate lecture notes, and bookmark important passages for later review. For more information, or to purchase a SafariX eTextbook, visit www.safarix.com.

OneKey Online Course Management Materials

OneKey means all your resources are in one place for maximum convenience, simplicity, and success.

What's Key for Students?
- *Learning Modules:* Every section of all 16 chapters is supported by section-level pretest, content summary for review, learning application exercise, and post-test. Learning modules are a great way to study for exams and are not connected to the instructor grade book, offering unlimited practice.
- *Prentice Hall's Self-Assessment Library (S.A.L)*
- *Research Navigator™:* The easiest way for students to start a research assignment or research paper. Complete with extensive help on the research process and four exclusive databases of credible and reliable source material, including the EBSCO Academic Journal and Abstract Database, New York Times Article Archive, and Company Financials.

Research navigator helps students quickly and efficiently make the most of their research time.

What's Key for Instructors?

- *Instructor Resource Center:* Faculty can access all instructor resources in one place.

FEEDBACK

The author and product team would appreciate hearing from you! Let us know what you think about this textbook by writing to college_marketing@prenhall.com. Please include "Feedback About Robbins/Judge 9e" in the subject line.

If you have questions related to this product, please contact our customer service department online at www.247.prenhall.com.

Acknowledgements

A number of people played critical roles in helping to produce this revision. Special thanks are extended to the following reviewers for their helpful comments and suggestions through previous editions: Professors Bryan Bonner, University of Utah; Jason Duan, Midwestern State University; Karen Eickhoff, University of Tennessee; Kamala Gollakota, University of San Diego; Don Mosley, University of Southern Alabama; Marcella Norwood, University of Houston; Marian Orr, Waynesburg College; Aysar Philip Sussan, University of Central Florida; and David Vequist, University of the Incarnate Word.

At Prentice Hall, we want to thank Michael Ablassmeir, Claudia Fernandes, and Judy Leale for overseeing the production and marketing of this book. Also, we'd like to thank other editors at Prentice Hall: Jeff Shelstad, Jen Simon, and David Parker.

About the Authors

Stephen P. Robbins
Ph.D. University of Arizona

Stephen P. Robbins has held academic positions at San Diego State University, Southern Illinois University at Edwardsville, University of Baltimore, Concordia University in Montreal, and University of Nebraska at Omaha. His research interests have focused on conflict, power, and politics in organizations, behavioral decision making, and the development of effective interpersonal skills. He has published several books in both management and organizational behavior including *Management*, 9th ed. with Mary Coulter, *Organizational Behavior*, 12th ed. with Timothy Judge, and *Fundamentals of Management*, 5th ed., with David DeCenzo. His books are used at more than a thousand U.S. colleges and universities, have been translated into 16 languages, and have adapted editions for Canada, Australia, South Africa, and India. In his "other life," Dr. Robbins actively participates in masters' track competition. Since turning 50 in 1993, he's won 14 national championships, nine world titles, and set numerous U.S. and world age-group records at 60, 100, 200, and 400 meters.

Timothy A. Judge
Ph.D. University of Illinois at Urbana-Champaign

Timothy A. Judge is currently the Matherly-McKethan Eminent Scholar in Management at the Warrington College of Business Administration at the University of Florida. He has held academic positions at the University of Iowa, Cornell University, Charles University in Czech Republic, Comenius University in Slovakia, and University of Illinois at Urbana-Champaign. Dr. Judge's primary research interests are in (1) personality, moods, and emotions, (2) job attitudes, (3) leadership and influence behaviors, and (4) careers (person-organization fit, career success). Dr. Judge published more than 90 articles in these and other major topics in journals such as *Academy of Management Journal and Journal of Applied Psychology*. He is a fellow of several organizations, including the American Psychological Association and the Academy of Management. In 1995, Dr. Judge received the Distinguished Early Career Contributions Award from the Society for Industrial and Organizational Psychology, and in 2001, he received the Larry L. Cummings Award for midcareer contributions from the Organizational Behavior Division of the Academy of Management. He is a co-author of *Organizational Behavior*, 12th ed. with Stephen P. Robbins and *Staffing Organizations*, 5th ed. with Herbert G. Heneman III. He is married and has three children, who range in age from an 18 year old daughter who is a freshman at Florida State University to a four year old son.

ESSENTIALS OF ORGANIZATIONAL BEHAVIOR

CHAPTER 1

Introduction to Organizational Behavior

After studying this chapter, you should be able to:

1. Define organizational behavior (OB).
2. Explain the value of the systematic study of OB.
3. Identify the contributions made to OB by major behavioral science disciplines.
4. Describe how OB concepts can help make organizations more productive.
5. List the major challenges and opportunities for managers to use OB concepts.
6. Identify the three levels of analysis in OB.

If you ask managers to describe their most frequent or troublesome problems, the answers you get tend to exhibit a common theme. The managers most often describe *people* problems. They talk about their bosses' poor communication skills, employees' lack of motivation, conflicts between team members, overcoming employee resistance to a company reorganization, and similar concerns. It may surprise you to learn, therefore, that it's only recently that courses in *people skills* have become an important part of business school programs.

Although practicing managers have long understood the importance of interpersonal skills to managerial effectiveness, business schools have been slower to get the message. Until the late 1980s, business school curricula emphasized the technical aspects of management, specifically focusing on economics, accounting, finance, and quantitative techniques. Course work in human behavior and people skills received minimal attention relative to the technical aspects of management. Over the past two decades, however, business faculty have come to realize the importance that an understanding of human behavior plays in determining a manager's effectiveness, and required courses on people skills have been added to many curricula. As the director of leadership at the Massachusetts Institute of Technology (MIT) Sloan School of Management recently put it, "M.B.A. students may get by on their technical and quantitative skills the first couple of years out of school. But soon, leadership and communication skills come to the fore in distinguishing the managers whose careers really take off."[1]

To get and keep high-performing employees, organizations recognize the importance of developing managers' interpersonal skills. Regardless of labor market conditions, outstanding employees are always in short supply. Companies with reputations as good places to work—such as Starbucks, Adobe Systems, Cisco, Whole Foods, American Express, Amgen, Goldman Sachs, Pfizer, and Marriott—have a big advantage. A national study of the U.S. workforce found that wages and fringe benefits are not the main reasons people like their jobs or stay with an employer. Far more important is the quality of the employee's job and the supportiveness of the work environment.[2] So having managers with good interpersonal skills is likely to make the workplace more pleasant, which, in turn, makes it easier to hire and keep qualified people. In addition, creating a pleasant workplace appears to make good economic sense. For instance, companies with reputations as good places to work (such as the companies that are included among the "100 Best Companies to Work for in America") can generate superior financial performance.[3]

Technical skills are necessary, but they are not enough to succeed in management. In today's increasingly competitive and demanding workplace, managers can't succeed on their technical skills alone. They also have to have good people skills. This book has been written to help both managers and potential managers develop those people skills.

THE FIELD OF ORGANIZATIONAL BEHAVIOR

The study of people at work is generally referred to as the study of organizational behavior. Let's begin, then, by defining the term *organizational behavior* and briefly reviewing its origins.

Organizational behavior (often abbreviated as OB) studies the influence that individuals, groups, and structure have on behavior within organizations. The chief goal of OB is to apply that knowledge toward improving an organization's effectiveness. And because OB is concerned specifically with employment-related situations, it emphasizes behavior related to jobs, work, absenteeism, employment turnover, productivity, human performance, and management.

OB focuses on the three determinants of behavior in organizations: individuals, groups, and structure. While scholars increasingly agree on what topics constitute the subject area of OB, they continue to debate the relative importance of each. In this book, we focus on the following core topics:

- Motivation
- Leader behavior and power
- Interpersonal communication

- Group structure and processes
- Learning
- Attitude development and perception
- Change processes
- Conflict
- Work design[4]

COMPLEMENTING INTUITION WITH SYSTEMATIC STUDY

Each of us is a student of behavior. Since our earliest years, we've watched the actions of others and have attempted to interpret what we see. Whether or not you've explicitly thought about it before, you've been *reading* people almost all your life. You watch what others do, trying to understand why they engage in their behavior and perhaps attempting to predict what they might do under different sets of conditions. Unfortunately, a casual or commonsense approach to reading others often leads to erroneous predictions. To improve your predictive ability, you can supplement your intuitive opinions with a more systematic approach, as informed by the study of OB.

Using the systematic approach in this book, we will uncover important facts and relationships that will enable you to make more accurate predictions of behavior. Underlying this systematic approach is the belief that behavior is not random. Rather, certain fundamental consistencies underlie the behavior of all individuals, and these fundamental consistencies can be identified and then modified to reflect individual differences.

—Behavior is not random. Rather, certain fundamental consistencies underlie the behavior of all individuals.

Without these fundamental consistencies, we would have great difficulty predicting behavior. For example, when you get into your car, you make some definite and, usually, highly accurate predictions about how other people will behave. In North America, you would predict that other drivers will stop at stop signs and red lights, drive on the right side of the road, and pass on your left. Can you imagine what would happen if driving behaviors were unpredictable?

Obviously, the rules of driving make predictions about driving behavior fairly easy. What may be less obvious are the rules (written and unwritten) that exist in almost every setting. For instance, do you turn around and face the doors when you get into an elevator? Almost everyone does. But did you ever read that you're supposed to do this? Probably not! We would argue that it's possible to predict behavior (undoubtedly, not always with 100 percent accuracy) in supermarkets, classrooms, doctors' offices, elevators, and in most structured situations. Just as we make predictions about automobile drivers (for which there are definite rules), we can make predictions about the behavior of people in elevators (for which there are few written rules).

In short, behavior is generally predictable, and the *systematic study* of behavior is a means to making reasonably accurate predictions. By **systematic study**, we mean the following:

- Examining relationships.
- Attempting to attribute causes and effects.

■ Basing our conclusions on scientific evidence—that is, on data gathered under controlled conditions and measured and interpreted in a reasonably rigorous manner.

Systematic study augments **intuition**, those "gut feelings" about "what makes others tick." Of course, a systematic approach does not disprove things you have come to believe in an unsystematic way. Some of the conclusions we make in this text, based on reasonably substantive research findings, will only support what you already considered true, but some research evidence may run counter to what you thought was common sense. We hope that you can enhance your intuitive views of behavior and improve your accuracy in explaining and predicting behavior by practicing systematic analysis.

CONTRIBUTING DISCIPLINES TO THE OB FIELD

OB is an applied behavioral science built on contributions from a number of behavioral disciplines, including psychology and social psychology, sociology, and anthropology. Psychology's contributions have informed analysis mainly at the individual (micro level), while the other disciplines have contributed to our understanding of group processes and organizations (macro levels), as illustrated in Exhibit 1-1.

Psychology

Psychology is the science that seeks to measure, explain, and sometimes change the behavior of humans and other animals. Psychologists concern themselves with studying and attempting to understand individual behavior. Those who have contributed and continue to add to the knowledge of OB are learning theorists, personality theorists, counseling psychologists, and, most important, industrial and organizational psychologists.

Early industrial/organizational psychologists concerned themselves with the problems of fatigue, boredom, and other factors relevant to working conditions that could impede efficient work performance. More recently, psychologists' contributions have expanded to include learning, perception, personality, emotions, training, leadership effectiveness, needs and motivational forces, job satisfaction, decision-making processes, performance appraisals, attitude measurement, employee-selection techniques, work design, and job stress.

Social Psychology

Social psychology blends concepts from both psychology and sociology, though it is generally considered a branch of psychology. It focuses on people's influences on one another. One major area receiving considerable investigation from social psychologists has been *change*—how to implement it and how to reduce barriers to its acceptance. In addition, we find social psychologists making significant contributions in the areas of measuring, understanding, and changing attitudes; communication patterns; and building trust. Social psychologists also have made important contributions to our study of group behavior, power, and conflict.

EXHIBIT 1-1   Toward an OB Discipline

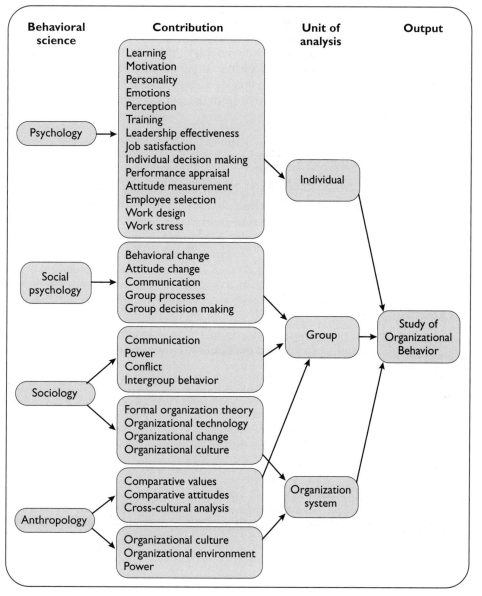

Sociology

While psychology focuses on the individual, **sociology** is the study of people in relation to their social environment or culture. Sociologists have contributed to OB through their study of group behavior in organizations, particularly formal and complex organizations. Perhaps most importantly, sociologists have contributed to research on organizational culture, formal organization theory and structure, organizational technology, communications, power, and conflict.

Anthropology

Anthropology is the study of societies for the purpose of learning about human beings and their activities. Anthropologists' work on cultures and environments has helped us understand differences in fundamental values, attitudes, and behavior among people in different countries and within different organizations. Much of our current understanding of organizational culture, organizational environments, and differences among national cultures comes from the work of anthropologists or those using their methods.

FEW ABSOLUTES IN OB

Few, if any, simple and universal principles explain OB. The physical sciences—chemistry, astronomy, physics—have laws that are consistent and apply in a wide range of situations. They allow scientists to generalize about the pull of gravity or to be confident about sending astronauts into space to repair satellites. But as a noted behavioral researcher aptly concluded, "God gave all the easy problems to the physicists." Human beings are complex and diverse, limiting our ability to make simple, accurate, and sweeping generalizations. Two people often act very differently in the same situation, and one person's behavior changes in different situations, say at church on Sunday and at a party that night.

That doesn't mean, of course, that we can't offer reasonably accurate explanations of human behavior or make valid predictions. However, it does mean that OB concepts must reflect situational, or contingency, conditions. We can say that x leads to y, but only under conditions specified in z—the **contingency variables**. The science of OB was developed by taking general concepts and applying them to a particular situation, person, or group. For example, OB scholars avoid stating that everyone likes complex and challenging work (the general concept) because not everyone wants a challenging job and some people prefer the simple over the complex. In other words, a job that is appealing to one person may not appeal to another, so the attraction of the job is contingent on the person who holds it.

As you proceed through this book, you'll encounter a wealth of research-based theories about how people behave in organizations. But don't expect to find a lot of straightforward cause-and-effect relationships. There aren't many! OB theories mirror the subject matter they address. People are complex and complicated, and so too must be the theories developed to explain their actions.

CHALLENGES AND OPPORTUNITIES FOR OB

Understanding OB has never been more important for managers. Consider some of the dramatic changes now taking place in organizations:

- Workers represent a large range of cultures, races, and ethnic groups.
- The "war on terror" has brought to the forefront the challenges of working with and managing people during uncertain times.
- The typical employee is older.
- More women are in the workplace.

- Global competition requires employees to become more flexible and to learn to cope with rapid change.
- Corporate downsizing and the heavy use of temporary workers are severing the bonds of loyalty that historically tied many employees to their employers.

In short, today's challenges offer managers many opportunities to use OB concepts. Let's review some of the more critical issues confronting managers for which OB offers solutions—or at least some meaningful insights toward solutions.

Responding to Globalization

Organizations are no longer constrained by national borders. A British firm owns Burger King, and McDonald's sells hamburgers in Moscow. ExxonMobil, a so-called U.S. company, receives almost 75 percent of its revenues from sales outside the United States. New employees at Finland-based phone maker Nokia are increasingly being recruited from India, China, and other developing countries—with non-Finns now outnumbering Finns at Nokia's renowned research center in Helsinki. And all major automobile manufacturers now build cars outside their home country's borders—Honda in Ohio, Ford in Brazil, Volkswagen in Mexico, and both Mercedes and BMW in South Africa.

As the world becomes a global village, the manager's job is changing.

Increased Foreign Assignments   If you're a manager, you are increasingly likely to find yourself in a foreign assignment—transferred to your employer's operating division or subsidiary in another country. Once there, you'll have to manage a workforce that is likely to be very different in needs, aspirations, and attitudes from those you were used to back home.

Working with People from Different Cultures   Even in your own country, you're going to find yourself working with bosses, peers, and other employees who were born and raised in different cultures. What motivates you may not motivate them. To work effectively with people from different cultures, you will have to understand how their culture, geography, and religion have shaped them and how to adapt your management style to their differences.

Coping with Anticapitalism Backlash   Capitalism's focus on efficiency, growth, and profits may be generally accepted in the United States, Australia, and Hong Kong, but these capitalistic values aren't nearly as popular in places such as France, the Middle East, and the Scandinavian countries. Managers at such global companies as McDonald's, Disney, and Coca-Cola have come to realize that economic values are not universally transferable. Management practices must be modified to reflect the values of the different countries in which an organization operates.

—Management practices must be modified to reflect the values of the different countries in which an organization operates.

Overseeing Movement of Jobs to Countries with Low-Cost Labor   It's increasingly difficult for managers in advanced nations, where minimum wages are typically $6 or more an hour, to compete against firms relying on workers from China and other developing nations where labor is available for $.30 an hour. The exportation of jobs, however, often comes with strong criticism from labor groups, politicians, local community leaders, and others who see such practices as undermining the job markets in developed countries. Managers must deal with the difficult task of balancing the interests of their organizations with their responsibilities to the communities in which they operate.

Managing People During the War on Terror   Surveys suggest that fear of terrorism is the number-one reason business travelers have cut back on their trips. But travel isn't the only concern. Increasingly, organizations must find ways to deal with employee fears about security precautions (in most cities, you can't get into an office building without passing through several layers of airport-like security) and assignments abroad (How would you feel about an assignment in a country with substantial sentiments against people from your country?).[5] An understanding of such OB topics as emotions, motivation, communication, and leadership can help managers to deal more effectively with their employees' fears about terrorism.

Managing Workforce Diversity

One of the most important and broad-based challenges currently facing organizations is adapting to people who are different. The term we use for describing this challenge is *workforce diversity*. While globalization focuses on differences among people *from* different countries, workforce diversity addresses differences among people *within* given countries.

Workforce diversity means that organizations are becoming a more heterogeneous mix of people in terms of gender, age, race, ethnicity, and sexual orientation. A diverse workforce, for instance, includes women, people of color, the physically disabled, senior citizens, and gays and lesbians (see Exhibit 1-2). Managing this diversity has become a global concern. It's an issue not just in the United States but also in Canada, Australia, South Africa, Japan, and Europe. For instance, managers in Canada and Australia are finding it necessary to adjust to large influxes of Asian workers. The "new" South Africa is increasingly characterized by blacks' holding important technical and managerial jobs. Women in Japan, long confined to low-paying temporary jobs, are moving into managerial positions. And the European Union cooperative trade arrangement, which opened up borders throughout much of Western Europe, has increased workforce diversity in organizations that operate in countries such as Germany, Portugal, Italy, and France.

Workforce diversity has important implications for management practice. Managers have to shift their philosophy from treating everyone alike to recognizing differences and responding to those differences in ways that ensure employee retention and greater productivity while, at the same time, not discriminating. This shift includes, for instance, providing diversity training and revamping benefits programs to accommodate the different needs of different employees. Diversity, if positively managed, can increase creativity and innovation in organizations and improve decision making by providing different perspectives on problems.[6] When diversity is not managed properly, the potential for higher turnover, more difficult communication, and more interpersonal conflicts increases.

EXHIBIT 1-2   Major Workforce Diversity Categories

Gender
Nearly half of the U.S. workforce is now made up of women, and women are a growing percentage of the workforce in most countries throughout the world. Organizations need to ensure that hiring and employment policies create equal access and opportunities to individuals, regardless of gender.

Race
The percentage of Hispanics, blacks, and Asians in the U.S. workforce continues to increase. Organizations need to ensure that policies provide equal access and opportunities, regardless of race.

National Origin
A growing percentage of U.S. workers are immigrants or come from homes where English is not the primary language spoken. Because employers in the United States have the right to demand that English be spoken at the workplace during job-related activities, communication problems can occur when employees' English-language skills are weak.

Age
The U.S. workforce is aging, and recent polls indicate that an increasing percentage of employees expect to work past the traditional retirement age of 65. Organizations cannot discriminate on the basis of age and need to make accommodations to the needs of older workers.

Disability
Organizations need to ensure that jobs and workplaces are accessible to the mentally, physically, and health challenged.

Domestic Partners
An increasing number of gay and lesbian employees, as well as employees with live-in partners of the opposite sex, are demanding the same rights and benefits for their partners that organizations have provided for traditional married couples.

Non-Christian
Organizations need to be sensitive to the customs, rituals, and holidays, as well as the appearance and attire, of individuals of non-Christian faiths such as Judaism, Islam, Hinduism, Buddhism, and Sikhism, and they need to ensure that these individuals suffer no adverse impact as a result of their appearance or practices.

Improving Quality and Productivity

Today's managers understand that the success of any effort made to improve quality and productivity must include their employees. These employees not only will be a major force in carrying out changes but increasingly will actively participate in planning those changes. OB offers important insights into helping managers work through these changes.

Improving Customer Service

Today, the majority of employees in developed countries work in service jobs. For instance, 80 percent of the U.S. labor force is employed in service industries. In the United Kingdom, Germany, and Japan the percentages are 69, 68, and 65, respectively. Examples of these service jobs include technical support representatives, fast-food counter workers, sales clerks, waiters or waitresses, nurses, automobile repair technicians, consultants, credit representatives, financial planners, and flight attendants. The common characteristic of these jobs is that they require substantial interaction with an organization's customers. Many an organization has failed because its employees failed

—Management needs to create a customer-responsive culture.

to please the customer. Thus, management must create a customer-responsive culture. OB can provide considerable guidance in helping managers create such cultures—cultures in which employees exhibit these qualities:

- Friendly and courteous
- Accessible
- Knowledgeable
- Prompt in responding to customer needs
- Willing to do what's necessary to please the customer[7]

Improving People Skills

We opened this chapter by demonstrating how important people skills are to managerial effectiveness. We said that "this book has been written to help both managers and potential managers develop those people skills."

As you proceed through the chapters, you'll find relevant concepts and theories that can help you explain and predict the behavior of people at work. In addition, you'll gain insights into specific people skills that you can use on the job. Specifically, you'll learn ways to design motivating jobs, techniques for improving your listening skills, and ideas about how to create more effective teams.

Stimulating Innovation and Change

Whatever happened to Montgomery Ward, Woolworth, Smith Corona, Eastern Airlines, Enron, Bethlehem Steel, and WorldCom? All these giants went bust. Why have other giants, such as Sears, Boeing, and Lucent Technologies, implemented huge cost-cutting programs and eliminated thousands of jobs? To avoid going broke.

Today's successful organizations must foster innovation and master the art of change or they'll become candidates for extinction. Victory will go to the organizations that maintain their flexibility, continually improve their quality, and beat their competition to the marketplace with a constant stream of innovative products and services. Domino's single-handedly brought on the demise of thousands of small pizza parlors whose managers thought they could continue doing what they had been doing for years. Amazon.com is putting a lot of independent bookstores out of business as it proves you can successfully sell books from an Internet Web site. Dell has become the world's largest seller of computers by continually reinventing itself and outsmarting its competition.

An organization's employees can be the impetus for innovation and change or they can be a major stumbling block. The challenge for managers is to stimulate their employees' creativity and tolerance for change. The field of OB provides a wealth of ideas and techniques to aid in realizing these goals.

Coping with Temporariness

With change comes temporariness. Globalization, expanded capacity, and advances in technology have combined in recent years to make it imperative that organizations be fast and flexible if they are to survive. The result is that most managers and employees today work in a climate best characterized as *temporary*.

Evidence of temporariness is everywhere in organizations. Jobs are continually being redesigned; tasks are increasingly being done by flexible teams rather than individuals; companies are relying more on temporary workers; jobs are being subcontracted out to other firms; and pensions are being redesigned to move with people as they change jobs.

Workers must continually update their knowledge and skills to perform new job requirements. For example, production employees at companies such as Caterpillar, Ford, and Alcoa now need to know how to operate computerized production equipment. That was not part of their job descriptions 20 years ago. Work groups are also increasingly in a state of flux. In the past, each employee was assigned to a specific work group, and that assignment was relatively permanent. Employees enjoyed a considerable amount of security in working with the same people day in and day out. That predictability has been replaced by temporary work groups, teams that include members from different departments and whose members change all the time, and the increased use of employee rotation to fill constantly changing work assignments. In addition, organizations themselves are in a state of flux. They continually reorganize their various divisions, sell off poorly performing businesses, downsize operations, subcontract noncritical services and operations to other organizations, and replace permanent employees with temporary workers.

Today's managers and employees must learn to cope with temporariness. They must learn to live with flexibility, spontaneity, and unpredictability. The study of OB can provide important insights into helping you better understand a work world of continual change, how to overcome resistance to change, and how best to create an organizational culture that thrives on change.

—Today's managers and employees must learn to cope with temporariness.

Helping Employees Balance Work–Life Conflicts

In the 1960s and 1970s, employees typically showed up at the workplace Monday through Friday and did their job in eight- or nine-hour chunks of time. The workplace and hours were clearly specified. That's no longer true for a large segment of today's workforce. Employees are increasingly complaining that the line between work and nonwork time has become blurred, creating personal conflicts and stress.[8] At the same time, however, today's workplace presents opportunities for workers to create and structure their work roles.

The field of OB offers a number of suggestions to guide managers in designing workplaces and jobs that can help employees deal with work–life conflicts.

Improving Ethical Behavior

In an organizational world characterized by cutbacks, expectations of increasing worker productivity, and tough competition in the marketplace, it's not altogether surprising that many employees feel pressured to cut corners, break rules, and engage in other forms of questionable practices.

Members of organizations increasingly find themselves facing **ethical dilemmas**, situations in which they are required to define right and wrong conduct. For example, should they "blow the whistle" if they uncover illegal activities taking place in their company? Should they follow orders with which they don't personally agree?

Do they give an inflated performance evaluation to an employee they like, knowing that such an evaluation could save that employee's job? Do they allow themselves to play politics in the organization if it will help their career advancement?

What constitutes good ethical behavior has never been clearly defined, and, in recent years, the line differentiating right from wrong has become even more blurred. Employees see people all around them engaging in unethical practices: elected officials are indicted for padding their expense accounts or taking bribes; corporate executives inflate their companies' profits so they can cash in lucrative stock options; and university administrators "look the other way" when winning coaches encourage scholarship athletes to stay eligible by taking easy courses in place of those needed for graduation. When caught, these people may give excuses such as "Everyone does it" or "You have to seize every advantage nowadays." Is it any wonder that employees are expressing decreased confidence and trust in management and that they're increasingly uncertain about what constitutes appropriate ethical behavior in their organizations?[9]

Today's manager needs to create an ethically healthy climate for his or her employees, in which employees can work productively and confront a minimal degree of ambiguity regarding what constitutes right and wrong behaviors. In upcoming chapters, we'll discuss the kinds of actions managers can take to create an ethically healthy climate and to help employees sort through ethically ambiguous situations.

THE PLAN OF THIS BOOK

How is this book going to help you better explain, predict, and control behavior? Our approach uses a building-block process. As illustrated in Exhibit 1-3, OB is characterized by three levels of analysis. As we move from the individual level to the organization system level, we increase in an additive fashion our understanding of behavior in organizations.

Chapter 2 through 7 deal with the individual in the organization. We begin by looking at such foundations of individual behavior as demographic characteristics, attitudes, personality, and values. Then we consider the role of motivation and perception and decision making in individual behavior. We conclude this section with a discussion of moods and emotions.

EXHIBIT 1-3   Levels of OB Analysis

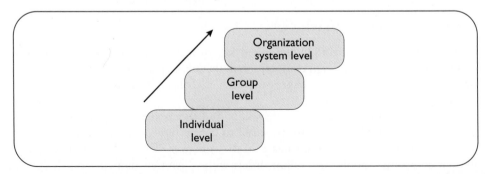

The behavior of people in groups is something more than the sum total of each individual acting in his or her own way. People's behavior in groups is different from their behavior when they are alone. Chapter 8 through 13 address group behavior. We introduce basic group concepts, discuss ways to make teams more effective, consider communication issues and group decision making, and then investigate the important topics of leadership, power, politics, conflict, and negotiation.

OB reaches its highest level of sophistication when we add the formal organization system to our knowledge of individual and group behavior. Just as groups are more than the sum of their individual members, organizations are not necessarily merely the summation of the behavior of a number of groups. In Chapter 14 through 16, we discuss how an organization's structure affects behavior, how each organization has its own culture that acts to shape the behavior of its members, and the various organizational change and development techniques that managers can use to affect behavior for the organization's benefit.

IMPLICATIONS FOR MANAGERS

Managers need to develop their interpersonal or people skills if they are going to be effective in their jobs. OB is a field of study that investigates the impact that individuals, groups, and structure have on behavior within organizations, for the purpose of applying such knowledge toward improving an organization's effectiveness.

We all hold generalizations about the behavior of people. Some of our generalizations may provide valid insights into human behavior, but many are erroneous. OB uses systematic study to improve predictions of behavior that would be made from intuition alone. You can achieve your potential as a manager by enhancing your intuitive views of behavior with systematic analysis, in the belief that such analysis will improve your accuracy in explaining and predicting behavior.

OB offers both challenges and opportunities for managers:

- It offers specific insights to improve a manager's people skills.
- It recognizes differences and helps managers to see the value of workforce diversity and practices that may need to be changed when managing in different countries.
- It can improve quality and employee productivity by showing managers how to empower their people, design and implement change programs, improve customer service, and help employees balance work–life conflicts.
- It provides suggestions for helping managers meet chronic labor shortages.
- It can help managers to cope in a world of temporariness and to learn ways to stimulate innovation.
- It can offer managers guidance in creating an ethically healthy work climate.

CHAPTER 2

Foundations of Individual Behavior

In this chapter, we examine three foundations of individual behavior in organizations: ability, attitudes, and learning. Specifically, we discuss how intellectual ability contributes to job performance, how employees' attitudes about their jobs affect the workplace, how people learn behaviors, and what management can do to shape those behaviors. We also pay special attention to a particular attitude—job satisfaction—that has important implications for organizational behavior.

ABILITY

Ability refers to an individual's capacity to perform the various tasks in a job. It is a current assessment of what one can do. Managers are less interested in whether people differ in terms of their abilities and more interested in knowing *how* people differ in abilities and using that knowledge to increase the likelihood that an employee will perform his or her job well.

Intellectual Ability

Intellectual ability—which ecompasses mental activies such as thinking, reasoning, and problem solving—is one of the best predictors of performance across all sorts of jobs.[1] Of course, jobs differ in the demands they place on incumbents to use their intellectual abilities. The more complex a job is in terms of information-processing demands, the more general intelligence and verbal abilities will be necessary to perform the job successfully.[2] One reason intelligent people are better job performers is that they are more creative. Smart people learn jobs more quickly, are more adaptable to changing circumstances, and are better at inventing solutions that improve performance.[3]

Interestingly, while intelligence is a big help in performing a job well, it doesn't make people happier or more satisfied with their jobs. The correlation between intelligence and job satisfaction is about zero. Why? Research suggests that although intelligent people perform better and tend to have more interesting jobs, they also are more critical in evaluating their job conditions. Thus, smart people have it better, but they also expect more.[4]

—While intelligence is a big help in performing a job well, it doesn't make people happier or more satisfied with their jobs.

Ability and Job Fit

Employee performance is enhanced when an employee and position are well matched—what we call a high ability–job fit. If we focus only on the employee's abilities or the ability requirements of the job, we ignore the fact that employee performance depends on the interaction of the two.

What predictions can we make when the fit is poor? If employees lack the required abilities, they are likely to fail. If you're hired as a word processor and you can't meet the job's basic keyboard typing requirements, your performance is going to be poor in spite of your positive attitude or your high level of motivation. When an employee has abilities that far exceed the requirements of the job, our predictions would be very different. The employee's performance may be adequate, but it may be accompanied by organizational inefficiencies and possible declines in employee satisfaction because the employee is frustrated by the limitations of the job. Additionally, given that pay tends to reflect the highest skill level that employees possess, if an employee's abilities far exceed those necessary to do the job, management will be paying more than it needs to pay.

ATTITUDES

Attitudes are evaluative statements—either favorable or unfavorable—concerning objects, people, or events. They reflect how one feels about something. When I say "I like my job," I am expressing my attitude about work. To fully understand attitudes, we need to consider their fundamental properties. Let's examine four questions about attitudes:

1. What are the main components of attitudes?
2. How consistent are attitudes?

3. Does behavior always follow from attitudes?

4. What are the major job attitudes?

What Are the Main Components of Attitudes?

Typically, researchers have assumed that attitudes have three components: cognition, affect, and behavior.[5] Let's look at each of these components.

The statement that "discrimination is wrong" is evaluative. Such an opinion is the **cognitive component** of an attitude. It sets the stage for the more critical part of an attitude: its **affective component**. Affect is the emotional or feeling segment of an attitude and is reflected in the statement "I don't like Jon because he discriminates against minorities." Finally, and we'll discuss this issue at considerable length later in this section, affect can lead to behavioral outcomes. The **behavioral component** of an attitude refers to an intention to behave in a certain way toward someone or something. So, to continue our example, I might choose to avoid Jon because of my feelings about him.

Viewing attitudes as made up of three components—cognition, affect, and behavior—is helpful in understanding their complexity and the potential relationship between attitudes and behavior. Keep in mind that these components are closely related. In particular, in many ways cognition and affect are inseparable. For example, imagine that you concluded that someone had just treated you unfairly. Aren't you likely to have feelings about that, occurring virtually instantaneously with the thought? Thus, cognition and affect are intertwined.

Exhibit 2-1 illustrates how the three components of an attitude are related. In this example, an employee didn't get a promotion he thought he deserved; a coworker got it instead. The employee's attitude toward his supervisor is illustrated as follows: cognition (the employee thought he deserved the promotion), affect (the employee strongly dislikes his supervisor), and behavior (the employee is looking for another job). As we previously noted, although we often think that cognition causes affect which then causes behavior, in reality these components are often difficult to separate.

How Consistent Are Attitudes?

Did you ever notice how people change what they say so it doesn't contradict what they do? Perhaps a friend of yours has consistently argued that the quality of American cars isn't up to that of the import brands and that he'd never own anything but a Japanese or German car. Then his dad gives him a late-model Ford Mustang, and suddenly American cars aren't so bad. Or when going through sorority rush, a new freshman believes that sororities are good and that pledging a sorority is important. If she fails to make a sorority, however, she may say, "I recognized that sorority life isn't all it's cracked up to be, anyway."

Research has generally concluded that people seek consistency among their attitudes and between their attitudes and their behavior.[6] In other words, individuals try to reconcile divergent attitudes and align their attitudes to their behavior so they appear rational and consistent. When there is an inconsistency, the individual may alter either the attitudes or the behavior or may develop a rationalization for the discrepancy. Tobacco executives provide an example.[7] How, you might wonder, do these

EXHIBIT 2-1   The Components of an Attitude

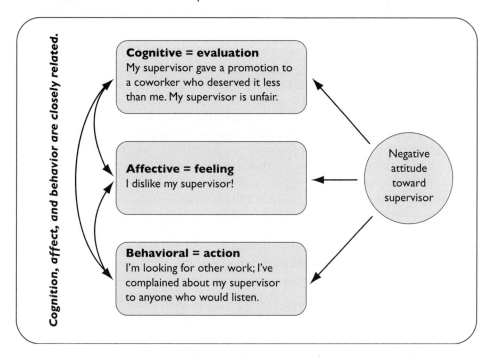

people cope with the ongoing barrage of data linking cigarette smoking and negative health outcomes? Following are some possibilities:

- They can deny that any clear causation between smoking and cancer, for instance, has been established.
- They can brainwash themselves by continually articulating the benefits of tobacco.
- They can acknowledge the negative consequences of smoking but rationalize that people are going to smoke and that tobacco companies merely promote freedom of choice.
- They can accept the research evidence and begin actively working to make more healthy cigarettes or at least reduce their availability to more vulnerable groups, such as teenagers.
- They can quit their job because the inconsistency is too great.

In the late 1950s, Leon Festinger proposed the theory of **cognitive dissonance** to explain the linkage between attitudes and behavior.[8] *Cognitive dissonance* refers to any inconsistency that an individual might perceive between two or more attitudes, or between behavior and attitudes. Festinger argued that any form of inconsistency is uncomfortable and that individuals will attempt to reduce the dissonance and, hence, the discomfort. Therefore, individuals will seek a stable state in which there is a minimum of dissonance.

No individual, of course, can completely avoid dissonance. You know that cheating on your income tax is wrong, but you fudge the numbers a bit every year and hope you're not audited. Or you tell your children to floss their teeth every day, but *you* don't. So how do people cope? Festinger would propose that the desire to reduce dissonance would be determined by three attributes:

- The *importance* of the elements creating the dissonance. If the elements creating the dissonance are relatively unimportant, the pressure to correct this imbalance will be low.

- The *degree of influence* the individual believes he or she has over the elements. The degree of influence individuals believe they have over the elements will affect how they react to the dissonance. If they perceive the dissonance to be caused by something over which they have no control, they are less likely to be receptive to attitude change. For example, if the dissonance-producing behavior is required as a result of a boss's directive, the pressure to reduce dissonance would be less than if the behavior was performed voluntarily.

- The *rewards* that may be involved in dissonance. Rewards also influence the degree to which individuals are motivated to reduce dissonance. High rewards accompanying high dissonance tend to reduce the tension inherent in the dissonance. The rewards act to reduce dissonance by increasing the consistency side of the individual's balance sheet. These moderating factors suggest that individuals will not necessarily move directly toward reducing dissonance just because they experience it.

What are the organizational implications of the theory of cognitive dissonance? It can help managers to predict the propensity of employees to engage in attitude and behavioral change. In addition, the greater the dissonance—after it has been moderated by importance, choice, and reward factors—the greater the pressures to reduce it.

Does Behavior Always Follow from Attitudes?

Early research on attitudes assumed that they were causally related to behavior; that is, the attitudes that people hold determine what they do. Common sense, too, suggests a relationship. However, in the late 1960s, a review of research challenged this intrepretation of the relationship between attitudes and behavior, concluding that attitudes were unrelated to behavior or, at best, only slightly related.[9] However, more recent research has demonstrated that attitudes significantly predict future behavior and confirmed Festinger's original belief that the relationship can be enhanced by taking moderating variables into account.[10]

Moderating Variables   The most powerful moderators of the attitude–behavior relationship are these:

- *Importance* of the attitude. Important attitudes reflect fundamental values, self-interest, or identification with individuals or groups that a person values. Attitudes that individuals consider important tend to show a strong relationship to behavior.

- Its *specificity*. The more specific the attitude and the more specific the behavior, the stronger the link between the two. For instance, asking someone specifically about her intention to stay with the organization for the next six months is likely to better predict turnover for that person than if you asked her how satisfied she was with her pay.

- Its *accessibility*. Attitudes that are easily remembered are more likely to predict behavior than attitudes that are not accessible in memory. Interestingly, you're more likely to remember attitudes that are frequently expressed. So the more you talk about your attitude on a subject, the more you're likely to remember it, and the more likely it is to shape your behavior.

- The existence of *social pressures*. Discrepancies between attitudes and behavior are more likely to occur when social pressures to behave in certain ways hold exceptional power. This tends to characterize behavior in organizations. This may explain why an employee who holds strong anti-union attitudes attends pro-union organizing meetings or why tobacco executives, who are not smokers themselves and who tend to believe the research linking smoking and cancer, don't actively discourage others from smoking in their offices.

- A person's *direct experience* with the attitude. The attitude–behavior relationship is likely to be much stronger if an attitude refers to something with which the individual has direct personal experience. Asking college students with no significant work experience how they would respond to working for an authoritarian supervisor is far less likely to predict actual behavior than asking that same question of employees who have actually worked for such an individual.

Self-Perception Theory Although most attitude–behavior studies yield positive results, researchers have achieved still higher correlations by pursuing another direction: looking at whether behavior influences attitudes. This view, called **self-perception theory**, has generated some encouraging findings. Let's briefly review the theory.[11]

When asked about an attitude toward some object, individuals often recall their behavior relevant to that object and then infer their attitude from their past behavior. So if an employee was asked her feelings about being a training specialist at Marriott, she would likely think, "I've had this same job with Marriott as a trainer for 10 years. Nobody forced me to stay on this job. So I must like it!" Self-perception theory, therefore, argues that attitudes are used, after the fact, to make sense out of an action that has already occurred rather than as devices that precede and guide action. When people are asked about their attitudes and they don't have strong convictions or feelings, self-perception theory says they tend to create plausible answers.

Self-perception theory has been well supported by research.[12] While the traditional attitude–behavior relationship is generally positive, the behavior–attitude relationship is just as strong. This is particularly true when attitudes are vague and ambiguous. When you have had few experiences regarding an attitude issue or have given little previous thought to it, you'll tend to infer your attitudes from your behavior. However, when your attitudes have been established for a while and are well defined, those attitudes are likely to guide your behavior.

> *—Self-perception theory argues that attitudes are used, after the fact, to make sense out of an action that has already occurred rather than as devices that precede and guide action.*

What Are the Major Job Attitudes?

A person can have thousands of attitudes, but OB focuses our attention on a very limited number of work-related attitudes. These work-related attitudes tap positive or negative evaluations that employees hold about aspects of their work environment.

Most OB research has been concerned with three attitudes: job satisfaction, job involvement, and organizational commitment. We'll examine these three, as well as two other attitudes that are attracting attention from researchers: perceived organizational support and employee engagement.

Job Satisfaction   The term **job satisfaction** can be defined as a positive feeling about one's job resulting from an evaluation of its characteristics. A person with a high level of job satisfaction holds positive feelings about the job, while a person who is dissatisfied holds negative feelings about the job. When people speak of employee attitudes, more often than not they mean job satisfaction. In fact, the two are frequently used interchangeably. Because of the high importance OB researchers have given to job satisfaction, we'll review this attitude in considerable detail later in this chapter.

Job Involvement   Although much less studied than job satisfaction, **job involvement** measures the degree to which people identify psychologically with their job and consider their perceived performance level important to self-worth.[13] Employees with a high level of job involvement strongly identify with and really care about the kind of work they do. A closely related concept is **psychological empowerment**, which is employees' beliefs in the degree to which they affect their work environments, their competence, the meaningfulness of their jobs, and the perceived autonomy in their work.[14] For example, one study of nursing managers in Singapore found that good leaders empower their employees by involving them in decisions, making them feel that their work is important, and giving them discretion to "do their own thing."[15]

High levels of job involvement and psychological empowerment are positively related to organizational citizenship and job performance.[16] In addition, high job involvement is related to fewer absences and lower resignation rates.[17]

Organizational Commitment   The state in which an employee identifies with a particular organization and its goals and wishes to maintain membership in the organization is referred to as **organizational commitment**.[18] So, high job involvement means identifying with one's specific job, whereas high organizational commitment means identifying with one's employing organization. Let's examine the three separate dimensions of organizational commitment:[19]

1. **Affective commitment**: an emotional attachment to the organization and a belief in its values. For example, a Petco employee may be affectively committed to the company because of its involvement with animals.
2. **Continuance commitment**: the perceived economic value of remaining with an organization compared to leaving it. An employee may be committed to an employer because she is paid well and feels it would hurt her family to quit.
3. **Normative commitment**: an obligation to remain with the organization for moral or ethical reasons. An employee who is spearheading a new initiative may remain with an employer because he feels it would "leave the employer in a lurch" if he left.

A positive relationship between organizational commitment and job productivity appears to exist, but the relationship is modest.[20] And, as with job involvement, the research evidence demonstrates negative relationships between organizational commitment and both absenteeism and turnover.[21] In general, it seems that affective commitment is more strongly related to organizational outcomes such as performance and turnover than are the other two commitment dimensions. One study found that affective commitment was a significant predictor of various outcomes (perception of task characteristics, career satisfaction, intent to leave) for 72 percent of the cases, compared to only 36 percent for normative commitment and 7 percent for continuance commitment.[22] The weak results for continuance commitment make sense in that it doesn't really represent a strong commitment. Rather than an allegiance (affective commitment) or an obligation (normative commitment) to an employer, a continuance commitment describes an employee who is "tethered" to an employer simply because there isn't anything better available.

The concept of commitment may be less important to employers and employees than it once was. The unwritten loyalty contract that existed 30 years ago between employees and employers has been seriously damaged, and the notion of employees staying with a single organization for most of their careers has become increasingly obsolete. As such, "measures of employee–firm attachment, such as commitment, are problematic for new employment relations."[23] This suggests that *organizational commitment* is probably less important as a work-related attitude than it once was. In its place we might expect something akin to *occupational commitment* to become a more relevant variable because it better reflects today's fluid workforce.[24]

Other Job Attitudes   **Perceived organizational support (POS)** is the degree to which employees believe the organization values their contributions and cares about their well-being. For example, an employee believes that his organization would accommodate him if he had a child-care problem or would forgive an honest mistake on his part. Research shows that people perceive their organization as supportive when the following are true:

- Rewards are deemed fair.
- Employees have a voice in decisions.
- Their supervisors are seen as supportive.[25]

A very new concept is **employee engagement**, which can be defined as individuals' involvement with, satisfaction with, and enthusiasm for, the work they do. To assess employee engagement, one might ask employees about these:

- The availability of resources and the opportunities to learn new skills
- Whether they feel their work is important and meaningful
- Whether their interactions with their coworkers and supervisors were rewarding[26]

A recent study of nearly 8,000 business units in 36 companies found that business units whose employees had high-average levels of engagement had higher levels of customer satisfaction, were more productive, had higher profits, and had lower levels of turnover and accidents.[27] Because the concept is so new, we don't know how engagement relates to other concepts, such as job satisfaction, organizational commitment, job involvement, or intrinsic motivation to do one's job well. Engagement may be broad enough that it captures the intersection of these variables. In other words, engagement may be what these attitudes have in common.

> —*A recent study found that business units whose employees had high-average levels of engagement had higher levels of customer satisfaction and lower levels of turnover and accidents.*

Are These Job Attitudes Really All That Distinct?   You might wonder whether these job attitudes are really distinct. After all, if people feel deeply involved in their job (high job involvement), isn't it probable that they like it (high job satisfaction)? Similarly, won't people who think their organization is supportive (high perceived organizational support) also feel committed to it (strong organizational commitment)? Evidence suggests that these attitudes are highly related, perhaps to a troubling degree. For example, the correlation between perceived organizational support and affective commitment is very strong.[28] The problem for researchers is that a strong correlation means that the variables may be redundant. For example, if you know someone's affective commitment, you basically know her perceived organizational support. But why is this redundancy so troubling? Well, why have two steering wheels on a car when you only need one? Why have two concepts—going by different labels—when you only need one? This redundancy is inefficient and confusing.

Although we OB researchers like proposing new attitudes, often we haven't been good at showing how each attitude compares and contrasts to the others. While there is some measure of distinctiveness among these attitudes, they do overlap greatly. The overlap may exist for various reasons, including the employee's personality. Some people are predisposed to be positive or negative about almost everything. If someone tells you she loves her company, it may not mean a lot if she is positive about everything else in her life. Or the overlap may mean that some organizations are just all around better places to work than others. This may mean that if you as a manager know someone's level of job satisfaction, you know most of what you need to know about how the person sees the organization.

JOB SATISFACTION

To make a closer examination of job satisfaction, a concept introduced earlier in this chapter, let's consider several questions relevant to managers:

- How satisfied are employees in their jobs?
- What causes an employee to have a high level of job satisfaction?
- How do dissatisfied and satisfied employees affect an organization?

How Satisfied Are People in Their Jobs?

Are most people satisfied with their jobs? The answer seems to be a qualified "Yes" in the United States and in most developed countries. Independent studies, conducted among U.S. workers over the past 30 years, generally indicate that the majority of workers are satisfied with their jobs.[29] Although the percentage range is wide, more people report that they're satisfied than not. Moreover, these results generally apply to other developed countries. For instance, comparable studies among workers in Canada, Mexico, and Europe indicate more positive than negative results.[30]

Research shows that satisfaction levels vary a lot depending on which facet of job satisfaction you're talking about. As shown in Exhibit 2-2, people are, on average, satisfied with their jobs overall, with the work itself, and with their supervisors and coworkers. However, they tend to be less satisfied with their pay and with promotion opportunities. It's not really clear why people dislike their pay and promotion possibilities more than other aspects of their jobs.[31]

EXHIBIT 2-2   Average Job Satisfaction Levels by Facet

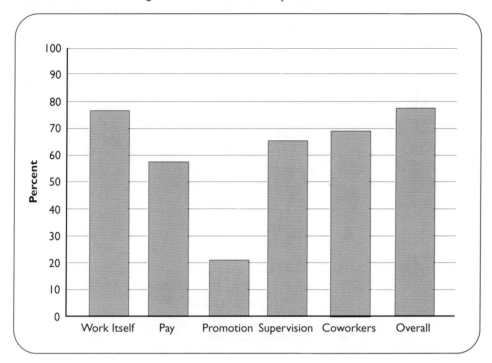

What Causes Job Satisfaction?

Think about the best job you ever had. What made it so? Chances are you probably liked the work you did. In fact, of the major job-satisfaction facets—work itself, pay, advancement opportunities, supervision, coworkers—enjoying the work itself almost always has the strongest correlation to high levels of overall job satisfaction. In other words, most people prefer work that is challenging and stimulating over work that is predictable and routine.

As you have probably noticed, discussions of job satisfaction often focus on pay. Let's explore the interesting relationship between salary and job satisfaction. For people who are poor (for example, living below the poverty line) or who live in poor countries, pay does correlate with job satisfaction and with overall happiness. But once an individual reaches a level of comfortable living (in the United States, that occurs at about $40,000 a year, depending on the region and family size), the relationship virtually disappears. In other words, people who earn $80,000 are, on average, no happier with their jobs than those who earn close to $40,000. Take a look at Exhibit 2-3, which shows the relationship between the average pay for a job and the average level of job satisfaction. As you can see, there isn't much of a relationship between them. Jobs that are compensated handsomely have average job-satisfaction levels no higher than those that are paid much less.

Job satisfaction is also affected by an individual's personality. Some people are predisposed to like almost anything, and others are unhappy even in the seemingly greatest jobs. Research has shown that people who have a negative personality (those

EXHIBIT 2-3   Relationship Between Average Pay in a Job and Job Satisfaction of Employees in That Job

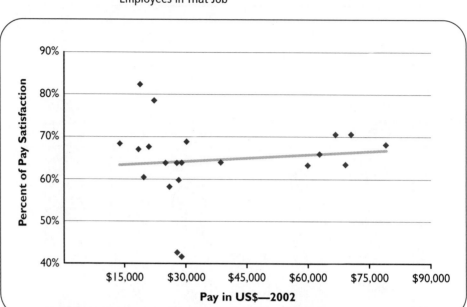

Source: T. A. Judge, R. F. Piccolo, N. P. Podsakoff, J. C. Shaw, and B. L. Rich, "Can Happiness Be 'Earned'? The Relationship Between Pay and Job Satisfaction," working paper, University of Florida, 2005.

who tend to be grumpy, critical, and negative) are usually less satisfied with their jobs. The Neutral Objects Satisfaction Questionnaire (see Exhibit 2-4) is a measure for understanding the link between personality and job satisfaction. One study showed that nurses who were dissatisfied with the majority of the items on the list were also dissatisfied with their jobs. This isn't surprising. After all, if someone dislikes his first name, his telephone service, and even 8½″ × 11″ paper, you'd expect him to dislike most things in his life—including his job.

The Effects of Satisfied and Dissatisfied Employees on the Workplace

Consequences manifest when employees like their jobs and when they don't. The following text focuses on more specific outcomes of job satisfaction and dissatisfaction in the workplace.

Job Satisfaction and Job Performance   Are happy workers more productive workers? Some researchers used to believe that the relationship between job satisfaction and job performance was nonexistent, but a review of 300 studies suggested that the correlation is pretty strong.[32] Moreover, as we move from the individual level to the organization level, we also find support for the satisfaction–performance relationship.[33] When satisfaction and productivity data are gathered for the organization as a whole, we find that organizations with more satisfied employees tend to be more effective than organizations with fewer satisfied employees.

EXHIBIT 2-4   Neutral Objects Satisfaction Questionnaire

Instructions: Circle whether you are on average satisfied, neutral, or dissatisfied with each of the following items.

The city in which you live	Satisfied	Neutral	Dissatisfied
The neighbors you have	Satisfied	Neutral	Dissatisfied
The high school you attended	Satisfied	Neutral	Dissatisfied
The climate where you live	Satisfied	Neutral	Dissatisfied
Movies being produced today	Satisfied	Neutral	Dissatisfied
The quality of food you buy	Satisfied	Neutral	Dissatisfied
Today's cars	Satisfied	Neutral	Dissatisfied
Local newspapers	Satisfied	Neutral	Dissatisfied
Your first name	Satisfied	Neutral	Dissatisfied
The people you know	Satisfied	Neutral	Dissatisfied
Telephone service	Satisfied	Neutral	Dissatisfied
8 ½″ × 11″ paper	Satisfied	Neutral	Dissatisfied
Restaurant food	Satisfied	Neutral	Dissatisfied
Modern art	Satisfied	Neutral	Dissatisfied

Source: T. A. Judge and C. L. Hulin, "Job Satisfaction as a Reflection of Disposition: A Multiple-Source Causal Analysis," *Organizational Behavior and Human Decision Processes,* 1993, Vol. 56, pp. 388–421.

Job Satisfaction and OCB   It seems logical to assume that job satisfaction should be a major determinant of an employee's **organizational citizenship behavior (OCB)** or discretionary behaviors that contribute to organizational effectiveness (like helping coworkers) but are not part of an employee's formal job description. Satisfied employees would seem more likely to talk positively about the organization, help others, and go beyond the normal expectations in their job. Moreover, satisfied employees might be more prone to go beyond the call of duty because they want to reciprocate their positive experiences. Consistent with this thinking, early discussions of OCB assumed that it was closely linked with satisfaction.[34] More recent evidence, however, suggests that satisfaction influences OCB, but through perceptions of fairness.

—Satisfied employees might be more prone to go beyond the call of duty because they want to reciprocate their positive experiences.

A modest overall relationship exists between job satisfaction and OCB.[35] But satisfaction is unrelated to OCB when fairness is controlled for.[36] What does this mean? Basically, job satisfaction comes down to conceptions of fair outcomes, treatment, and procedures. If you don't feel that your supervisor, the organization's procedures, or pay policies are fair, your job satisfaction is likely to suffer significantly. However, when you perceive organizational processes and outcomes to be fair, you develop trust. And when you trust your employer, you're more willing to voluntarily engage in behaviors that go beyond your formal job requirements.

Job Satisfaction and Customer Satisfaction   Employees in service jobs often interact with customers. Since the management of service organizations should be concerned with pleasing those customers, it is reasonable to ask "Is employee satisfaction related to positive customer outcomes?" For frontline employees who have regular contact with customers, the answer is "Yes."

The evidence indicates that satisfied employees increase customer satisfaction and loyalty.[37] Why? In service organizations, customer retention and defection are highly dependent on how frontline employees deal with customers. Satisfied employees are more likely to be friendly, upbeat, and responsive—which customers appreciate. And because satisfied employees are less prone to turnover, customers are more likely to encounter familiar faces and receive experienced service. These qualities build customer satisfaction and loyalty. In addition, the relationship seems mutual: Dissatisfied customers can increase an employee's job dissatisfaction. Employees who have regular contact with customers report that rude, thoughtless, or unreasonably demanding customers adversely affect the employees' job satisfaction.[38]

Job Satisfaction and Absenteeism   We find a consistent negative relationship between satisfaction and absenteeism, but the correlation is moderate to weak.[39] While it certainly makes sense that dissatisfied employees are more likely to miss work, other factors affect the relationship and reduce the correlation coefficient. For example, organizations that provide liberal sick leave benefits are encouraging all their employees—including those who are highly satisfied—to take days off. Assuming that you have a reasonable number of varied interests, you can find work satisfying and yet still take off work to enjoy a three-day weekend or tan yourself on a warm summer day if those days come free with no penalties.

A study done at Sears, Roebuck provides an excellent illustration of how satisfaction directly leads to attendance, when there is minimal influence from other factors.[40] A freak April 2 snowstorm in Chicago created the opportunity to compare employee attendance at the Chicago office with attendance in the New York office, where the weather was quite nice. The snowstorm gave the Chicago employees a built-in excuse not to come to work. The storm crippled the city's transportation, and individuals knew they could miss work this day with no penalty. Sears's policy did not permit employees to be absent from work for avoidable reasons without penalty.

Satisfaction data were available on employees in Chicago and New York, enabling managers to compare attendance records for satisfied and dissatisfied employees at the two locations: one where employees were expected to be at work (with normal pressures for attendance) and the other where employees were free to choose with no penalty involved. If satisfaction leads to attendance, when there is an absence of outside factors, the more satisfied employees should have come to work in Chicago, while dissatisfied employees should have stayed home. The study found that on this particular April 2, absenteeism rates in New York were just as high for satisfied groups of workers as for dissatisfied groups. But in Chicago, the workers with high satisfaction scores had much higher attendance than did those with lower satisfaction levels. These findings are exactly what we expected if satisfaction is negatively correlated with absenteeism.

Job Satisfaction and Turnover   Satisfaction is also negatively related to turnover, but the correlation is stronger than what we found for absenteeism.[41] Yet again, other factors such as labor-market conditions, expectations about alternative job opportunities, and length of tenure with the organization are important constraints on the actual decision to leave one's current job.[42]

Evidence indicates that an important moderator of the satisfaction–turnover relationship is the employee's level of performance.[43] Specifically, level of satisfaction is less important in predicting turnover for superior performers. Why? The organization typically makes considerable efforts to keep these people. They get pay raises, praise, recognition, increased promotional opportunities, and so forth. Regardless of level of satisfaction, the high performers are more likely to remain with the organization because the receipt of recognition, praise, and other rewards gives them more reasons for staying. Just the opposite tends to apply to poor performers. Organizations make few attempts to retain them and may even apply subtle pressures to encourage them to quit. We would expect, therefore, that job satisfaction has greater influence on poor performers than superior performers.

Job Satisfaction and Workplace Deviance   Job dissatisfaction predicts a lot of specific behaviors, including unionization attempts, substance abuse, stealing at work, undue socializing, and tardiness. Researchers argue that these behaviors are indicators of a broader syndrome that we would term *deviant behavior* in the workplace (or employee withdrawal).[44] The key is that if employees don't like their work environment, they'll respond somehow. It is not always easy to forecast exactly *how* they'll respond. One worker's response might be to quit. But another may respond by taking work time to surf the Internet, taking work supplies home for personal use, and so on. If employers want to control the undesirable consequences of job dissatisfaction, they had best attack the source of the problem—the dissatisfaction—rather than trying to control the different responses.

LEARNING

All complex behavior is learned. If we want to explain and predict behavior, we need to understand how people learn. Let's examine a definition of learning, three popular learning theories, and ways that managers can facilitate employee learning.

A Definition of Learning

A generally accepted definition of **learning** is *any relatively permanent change in behavior that occurs as a result of experience.*[45] Several components of this definition deserve clarification:

1. Learning involves change. Change may be good or bad. People can learn unfavorable behaviors—to hold prejudices or to shirk their responsibilities, for example—as well as favorable behaviors.
2. The change must become ingrained. Immediate changes may be only reflexive or a result of fatigue (or a sudden burst of energy) and thus may not represent learning.
3. Some form of experience is necessary for learning. Experience may be acquired directly through observation or practice, or it may be acquired indirectly, as through reading.

Theories of Learning

How do we learn? Two popular theories are used here to explain the process by which we acquire patterns of behavior: *operant conditioning* and *social learning*.

Operant Conditioning   Behavior is a function of its consequences, according to the theory of **operant conditioning**.[46] People learn to behave to get something they want or to avoid something they don't want. The developer of operant conditioning, Harvard psychologist B. F. Skinner, argued that creating pleasing consequences to follow specific forms of behavior would increase the frequency of that behavior.

—People learn to behave to get something they want or to avoid something they don't want.

He demonstrated that people will most likely engage in desired behaviors if they are positively reinforced for doing so; that rewards are most effective if they immediately follow the desired response; and that behavior that is not rewarded, or is punished, is less likely to be repeated. The concept of operant conditioning was part of Skinner's broader concept of *behaviorism*, which argues that behavior follows stimuli in a relatively unthinking manner. In Skinner's form of radical behaviorism, concepts such as feelings, thoughts, and other states of mind are rejected as causes of behavior. In short, people learn to associate stimulus and response, but their conscious awareness of this association is irrelevant.[47]

Any situation in which it is either explicitly stated or implicitly suggested that reinforcements are contingent on some action on your part involves the use of operant learning. Your instructor says that if you want a high grade in the course you must supply correct answers on the test. A commissioned salesperson wanting to earn a sizable income finds that doing so is contingent on generating high sales in her territory. Of course, the linkage can also work to teach the individual to engage in behaviors that work against the best interests of the organization. Assume that your boss tells you that you'll be compensated at your next performance appraisal if you will work overtime during the next three-week busy season. However, when performance-appraisal time comes, you find that you are given no positive reinforcement for your overtime work. The next time your boss asks you to work overtime, what will you do? You'll probably decline! Your behavior can be explained by operant conditioning: If a behavior fails to be positively reinforced, the probability that the behavior will be repeated declines.

Social Learning   Individuals can also learn by observing what happens to other people and just by being told about something, as well as by direct experiences. This view that we can learn through both observation and direct experience is called the theory of **social learning**.[48]

Although social learning theory is an extension of operant conditioning—that is, it assumes that behavior is a function of consequences—it also acknowledges the existence of observational learning and the importance of perception in learning. People respond to how they perceive and define consequences, not to the objective consequences themselves.

The influence of models is central to the social learning viewpoint. Four processes have been found to determine the influence that a model will have on an individual:

1. *Attentional processes.* People learn from a model only when they recognize and pay attention to its critical features. We tend to be most influenced by models that are attractive, repeatedly available, important to us, or similar to us in our estimation.
2. *Retention processes.* A model's influence will depend on how well the individual remembers the model's action after the model is no longer readily available.
3. *Motor reproduction processes.* After a person has seen a new behavior by observing the model, the watching must be converted to doing. This process then demonstrates that the individual can perform the modeled activities.
4. *Reinforcement processes.* Individuals will be motivated to exhibit the modeled behavior if positive incentives or rewards are provided. Behaviors that are positively reinforced will be given more attention, learned better, and performed more often.

Shaping: A Managerial Tool

Because learning takes place on the job as well as prior to it, managers will be concerned with how they can teach employees to behave in ways that most benefit the organization. When we attempt to mold individuals by guiding their learning in graduated steps, we are **shaping behavior**. We *shape* behavior by systematically reinforcing each successive step that moves the individual closer to the desired response.

Methods of Shaping Behavior Behavior can be shaped in four ways:

1. Following a response with something pleasant is called *positive reinforcement*. This would describe, for instance, the boss who praises an employee for a job well done.

2. Following a response by removing something unpleasant is called *negative reinforcement*. If your college instructor asks a question and you don't know the answer, the instructor may stop calling on you. This is a negative reinforcement because the instructor has concluded that calling on you does not produce the desired response.

3. When a behavior leads to an unpleasant response, that's called *punishment*, which is an attempt to eliminate an undesirable behavior. Giving an employee a two-day suspension from work without pay for showing up drunk is an example of punishment.

4. Eliminating any reinforcement of a behavior is called *extinction*. When the behavior is not reinforced, it tends to be gradually extinguished. College instructors who wish to discourage students from asking questions in class can eliminate this behavior in their students by ignoring those who raise their hands to ask questions. Hand raising will become extinct when it is invariably met with an absence of reinforcement.

Both positive and negative reinforcement result in learning. They strengthen a response and increase the probability of repetition. However, both punishment and extinction weaken behavior and tend to decrease its subsequent frequency.

Schedules of Reinforcement In shaping behavior, a critical issue is the timing of reinforcements. The two major types of reinforcement schedules are *continuous* and *intermittent*. A **continuous reinforcement** schedule reinforces the desired behavior each and every time it is demonstrated. Take, for example, the case of someone who historically has had trouble arriving at work on time. Every time he is not tardy his manager might compliment him on his desirable behavior. In an **intermittent reinforcement** schedule, on the other hand, not every instance of the desirable behavior is reinforced, but reinforcement is given often enough to make the behavior worth repeating. This latter schedule can be compared to the workings of a slot machine, which people will continue to play even when they know that it is adjusted to give a considerable return to the casino. The intermittent payoffs occur just often enough to reinforce the behavior of slipping in coins and pulling the handle. Evidence indicates that the intermittent, or varied, form of reinforcement tends to promote more resistance to extinction than does the continuous form.[49]

Intermittent reinforcement can be a *ratio* or *interval* type. **Ratio schedules** depend on how many responses the subject makes. The individual is reinforced after giving a certain number of specific types of behavior. **Interval schedules** depend on how much time has passed since the previous reinforcement. With interval schedules, the individual is reinforced on the first appropriate behavior after a particular time has elapsed.

A reinforcement can also be classified as *fixed* or *variable*. When rewards are spaced at uniform time intervals, the reinforcement schedule is of the **fixed-interval** type. The critical variable is time, and it is held constant. When you get your paycheck on a weekly, semimonthly, monthly, or other predetermined time basis, you're rewarded on a fixed-interval reinforcement schedule. If rewards are distributed in time so that reinforcements are unpredictable, the schedule is of the **variable-interval** type. A series of randomly timed unannounced visits to a company office by the corporate audit staff is an example of a variable-interval schedule.

In a **fixed-ratio** schedule, after a fixed or constant number of responses are given, a reward is initiated. A piece-rate incentive plan for which an employee in a dressmaking factory is paid $5.00 for every zipper installed is an example of a fixed-ratio schedule. When the reward varies relative to the behavior of the individual, he or she is said to be reinforced on a **variable-ratio** schedule. Salespeople on commission are examples of individuals on such a reinforcement schedule. On some occasions, they may make a sale after only two calls on a potential customer. On other occasions, they might need to make 20 or more calls to secure a sale. Exhibit 2-5 summarizes the schedules of reinforcement.

Reinforcement Schedules and Behavior   Continuous reinforcement schedules can lead to early satiation, and under this schedule behavior tends to weaken rapidly when reinforcers are withheld. However, continuous reinforcers are appropriate for newly emitted, unstable, or low-frequency responses (e.g., getting a reward for a perfect score on an exam). In contrast, intermittent reinforcers preclude early satiation because they don't follow every response. They are appropriate for stable or high-frequency responses (e.g., getting a reward for a passing grade on an exam).

In general, variable schedules tend to lead to higher performance than fixed schedules. For example, as noted previously, most employees in organizations are paid on fixed-interval schedules. But such a schedule does not clearly link performance and rewards. The reward is given for time spent on the job rather than for a specific

EXHIBIT 2-5   Schedules of Reinforcement

Reinforcement Schedule	Nature of Reinforcement	Effect on Behavior	Example
Continuous	Reward given after each desired behavior	Fast learning of new behavior but rapid extinction	Compliments
Fixed-interval	Reward given at fixed time intervals	Average and irregular performance with rapid extinction	Weekly paychecks
Variable-interval	Reward given at variable time intervals	Moderately high and stable performance with slow extinction	Pop quizzes
Fixed ratio	Reward given at fixed amounts of output	High and stable performance attained quickly but also with rapid extinction	Piece-rate pay
Variable-ratio	Reward given at variable amounts of output	Very high performance with slow extinction	Commissioned sales

response (performance). In contrast, variable-interval schedules generate high rates of response and more stable and consistent behavior because of a high correlation between performance and reward and because of the uncertainty involved: The employee tends to be more alert because of the surprise factor.

Problems with Reinforcement Theory   Although the effectiveness of reinforcements in the form of rewards and punishments has a lot of support in the literature, that doesn't necessarily mean that Skinner was right. What if the power of reinforcements isn't due to operant conditioning or behaviorism? One problem with behaviorism is research showing that thoughts and feelings immediately follow environmental stimuli, even those explicitly meant to shape behavior. This is contrary to the assumptions of behaviorism, which assume that people's innermost thoughts and feelings in response to the environment are irrelevant.

Also, is it really shaping if the compliment was given without an intention of molding behavior? Isn't it perhaps overly restrictive to view all stimuli as motivated to obtain a particular response? Is the only reason we tell someone we love them because we wish to obtain a reward or to mold their behavior?

Because of these problems, among others, operant conditioning and behaviorism have been superseded by other approaches that emphasize cognitive processes.[50] However, the contribution of these theories to our understanding of human behavior cannot be denied.

IMPLICATIONS FOR MANAGERS

This chapter looked at three major influences on individual behavior in organizations: ability, attitudes, and learning.

Ability   Ability directly influences an employee's level of performance and satisfaction through the ability–job fit. Given management's desire to get a compatible fit, what can be done?

1. An effective selection process will improve the fit. Jobs can be analyzed to determine the abilities required. Applicants can then be tested, interviewed, and evaluated on the degree to which they possess those abilities.
2. Promotion and transfer decisions affecting individuals already in the organization's employ should reflect the abilities of candidates.
3. The fit can be improved by fine-tuning the job to better match an incumbent's abilities. Examples include changing some of the equipment used or reorganizing tasks within a group of employees.

Attitudes   Managers should be interested in their employees' attitudes because attitudes give warnings of potential problems and because they influence behavior. Satisfied and committed employees, for instance, have lower rates of turnover, absenteeism, and withdrawal behaviors. They also perform better on the job. Given that managers want to keep resignations and absences down—especially among their more productive employees—they will want to do the things that will generate positive job attitudes.

The most important action managers can take to raise employee satisfaction is to focus on the intrinsic parts of the job, such as making the work challenging and interesting. Although paying employees poorly will likely not attract high-quality employees to or keep high performers in the organization, managers should realize that high pay alone is unlikely to create a satisfying work environment. Managers should also be aware that employees' cognitive dissonance can be managed. If employees are required to engage in activities that appear inconsistent to them or are at odds with their attitudes, the pressures to reduce the resulting dissonance will be lessened when employees perceive that the dissonance is externally imposed and beyond their control or that the rewards are significant enough to offset the dissonance.

Learning   Positive reinforcement is a powerful tool for modifying behavior. By identifying and rewarding performance-enhancing behaviors, management increases the likelihood that such behaviors will be repeated. Our knowledge about learning further suggests that reinforcement is a more effective tool than punishment. Although punishment eliminates undesired behavior more quickly than negative reinforcement does, punished behavior tends to be only temporarily suppressed rather than permanently changed and may produce unpleasant side effects, such as lower morale and higher absenteeism or turnover. In addition, the recipients of punishment tend to become resentful of the punisher. Managers, therefore, are advised to use reinforcement rather than punishment.

CHAPTER 3

Personality and Values

> **After studying this chapter, you should be able to:**
>
> 1. Explain the factors that determine an individual's personality.
> 2. Describe the Myers–Briggs Type Indicator personality framework.
> 3. Identify the key traits in the Big Five personality model.
> 4. Explain how the major personality attributes predict behavior at work.
> 5. Contrast terminal and instrumental values.
> 6. List the dominant values in today's workforce.
> 7. Identify Hofstede's five value dimensions of national culture.

Our personality shapes our behavior, so if we want to better understand the behavior of someone in an organization, it helps if we know something about his or her personality. In the first half of this chapter, we review the research on personality and its relationship to behavior. In the latter half, we look at how values shape many of our work-related behaviors.

PERSONALITY

Why are some people quiet and passive, whereas others are loud and aggressive? Are certain personality types better adapted for certain job types? Before we can answer these questions, we must address a more basic one: What is personality?

What Is Personality?

Personality can be thought of as the sum total of ways in which an individual reacts to and interacts with others. It is most often described in terms of measurable traits that a person exhibits.

Personality Traits

The early research on the structure of personality revolved around attempts to identify and label enduring characteristics that describe an individual's behavior. Popular characteristics include shy, aggressive, submissive, lazy, ambitious, loyal, and timid. Those characteristics, when they're exhibited in a large number of situations, are called **personality traits**.

Much attention has been paid to personality traits because researchers have long believed that these traits could help in employee selection, matching people to jobs, and in guiding career development decisions. For instance, if certain personality types perform better on specific jobs, management could use personality tests to screen job candidates and improve employee job performance. However, early efforts to identify the primary traits that govern behavior resulted in long lists of traits that provided little practical guidance to organizational decision makers. Two exceptions are the Myers–Briggs Type Indicator and the Big Five model. Over the past 20 years, these two approaches have become the dominant frameworks for identifying and classifying traits.

The Myers–Briggs Type Indicator   The **Myers–Briggs Type Indicator (MBTI)**[1] is the most widely used personality-assessment instrument in the world. It's a 100-question personality test that asks people how they usually feel or act in particular situations. On the basis of the answers individuals give to the test questions, they are classified as extroverted or introverted (E or I), sensing or intuitive (S or N), thinking or feeling (T or F), and judging or perceiving (J or P). These terms are defined as follows:

- *Extroverted Versus Introverted*—Extroverted individuals are outgoing, sociable, and assertive. Introverts are quiet and shy.
- *Sensing Versus Intuitive*—Sensing types are practical and prefer routine and order. They focus on details. Intuitives rely on unconscious processes and look at the big picture.
- *Thinking Versus Feeling*—Thinking types use reason and logic to handle problems. Feeling types rely on their personal values and emotions.
- *Judging Versus Perceiving*—Judging types want control and prefer their world to be ordered and structured. Perceiving types are flexible and spontaneous.

These classifications are then combined into 16 personality types. Let's take two examples. INTJs are visionaries. They usually have original minds and great drive for their own ideas and purposes. They are characterized as skeptical, critical, independent, determined, and often stubborn. ESTJs are organizers. They are realistic, logical, analytical, and decisive and have a natural head for business or mechanics. They like to organize and run activities.

The MBTI is widely used by such organizations as Apple Computer, AT&T, GE, and the U.S. Armed Forces. In spite of its popularity, the evidence is mixed as to whether the MBTI is a valid measure of personality—with most of the evidence suggesting it isn't.[2] The best we can say is that it can be a valuable tool for increasing self-awareness and for providing career guidance. But because MBTI results tend to be unrelated to job performance, it probably should not be used as a selection test for choosing among job candidates.

The Big Five Model In contrast to the MBTI, the five-factor model of personality—more typically called the *Big Five*—has received strong supporting evidence. An impressive body of research, accumulated in recent years, supports that five basic dimensions underlie all others and encompass most of the significant variation in human personality.[3] The following are the Big Five factors:

- *Extroversion*—This dimension captures one's comfort level with relationships. Extroverts tend to be gregarious, assertive, and sociable. Introverts tend to be reserved, timid, and quiet.
- *Agreeableness*—This dimension refers to an individual's propensity to defer to others. Highly agreeable people are cooperative, warm, and trusting. People who score low on agreeableness are cold, disagreeable, and antagonistic.
- *Conscientiousness*—This dimension is a measure of reliability. A highly conscientious person is responsible, organized, dependable, and persistent. Those who score low on this dimension are easily distracted, disorganized, and unreliable.
- *Emotional stability* (often labeled by its converse, *neuroticism*)—This dimension taps a person's ability to withstand stress. People with positive emotional stability tend to be calm, self-confident, and secure. Those with high negative scores tend to be nervous, anxious, depressed, and insecure.
- *Openness to experience*—This dimension addresses one's range of interests and fascination with novelty. Extremely open people are creative, curious, and artistically sensitive. Those at the other end of the openness category are conventional and find comfort in the familiar.

In addition to providing a unifying personality framework, research on the Big Five also has found relationships between these personality dimensions and job performance.[4] Researchers examined a broad spectrum of occupations: professionals (including engineers, architects, accountants, attorneys), police, managers, salespeople, and semiskilled and skilled employees. The results showed that conscientiousness predicted job performance for all occupational groups. Evidence also finds a relatively strong and consistent relationship between conscientiousness and organizational citizenship behavior.[5] This, however, seems to be the only Big Five personality dimension that predicts OCB.

For the other personality dimensions, predictability depended on both the performance criterion and the occupational group. For instance, extroversion predicted performance in managerial and sales positions. This finding makes sense because those occupations involve high social interaction. Similarly, openness to experience was found to be important in predicting training proficiency, which also seems logical. What wasn't so clear was why positive emotional stability wasn't related to job performance. Intuitively, it would seem that people who are calm and secure would perform better in almost all jobs than people who are nervous and depressed. The answer might be that some aspects of negative emotional stability—such as nervousness—might actually help job performance. Consider a stock trader at a Wall Street firm. If she fails to research all her options thoroughly and is never nervous about making the wrong transaction, she may fail to see the danger in, say, purchasing stock in a volatile young company. The other aspect of negative emotional stability—a depressive outlook—is bad for every job because when you're depressed, it's difficult to motivate yourself, to make a decision, or to take a risk. So, it may be that negative emotional stability has aspects that both help and hinder performance.

You may be interested to know that the Big Five have other implications for work and for life. Let's look at the implications of these traits one at a time.

Compared to introverts, extroverts tend to be happier in their jobs and in their lives as a whole. They usually have more friends and spend more time in social situations than introverts. But they also appear to be more impulsive, as evidenced by the fact that extroverts are more likely to be absent from work and engage in risky behavior such as unprotected sex, drinking, and other impulsive or sensation-seeking behavior.[6]

You might expect agreeable people to be happier than disagreeable people, and they are, but only slightly. When people choose romantic partners, friends, or organizational team members, agreeable individuals are usually their first choice. Agreeable children do better in school and as adults are less likely to get involved in drugs or excessive drinking.[7]

Interestingly, conscientious people live longer because they tend to take better care of themselves (eat better, exercise more) and engage in fewer risky behaviors (smoking, drinking/drugs, risky sexual or driving behavior).[8] Still, conscientiousness has its downside. It appears that conscientious people, probably because they're so organized and structured, don't adapt as well to changing contexts. Conscientious people are generally performance oriented. They have more trouble than less conscientious people learning complex skills early on because their focus is on performing well rather than on learning.

—Of the Big Five, emotional stability is most strongly related to life satisfaction, job satisfaction, and low stress levels.

People who score high on emotional stability are happier than those who score low on emotional stability. Of the Big Five, emotional stability is most strongly related to life satisfaction, to job satisfaction, and to low stress levels. High scores on emotional stability also are associated with fewer health complaints. One upside for low emotional stability: When in a bad mood, such people make faster and better decisions compared to emotionally stable people in bad moods.[9]

Finally, individuals who score high on openness to experience are more creative in science and in art, tend to be less religious, and are more likely to be politically liberal than those who score lower on openness to experience. Open people cope better with organizational change and are more adaptable in changing contexts.

Major Personality Attributes Influencing OB

Let's evaluate several additional personality attributes that can be powerful predictors of behavior in organizations:

- Core self-evaluation
- Machiavellianism
- Narcissism
- Self-monitoring
- Risk taking
- Type A and proactive personalities

Core Self-Evaluation   People who have a positive **core self-evaluation** like themselves and see themselves as effective, capable, and in control of their environments. Those with a negative core self-evaluation tend to dislike themselves, question their capabilities, and view themselves as powerless over their environments.[10]

Two main elements determine an individual's core self-evaluation:

1. **Self-esteem** is defined as individuals' degree of liking or disliking themselves and the degree to which they think they are worthy or unworthy as people. People who have a positive view of themselves and their capabilities tend to like themselves and see themselves as valuable. People with low self-esteem, however, are more susceptible to external influences, suggesting that individuals with low self-esteem depend on the receipt of positive evaluations from others. As a result, people with low self-esteem are more likely to seek approval from others and are more prone to conform to the beliefs and behaviors of those they respect than are people who believe in themselves. Studies have shown that people with low self-esteem may benefit more from training programs because their self-concept is more influenced by such interventions.[11]

2. **Locus of control** is the degree to which people believe they are masters of their own fate. **Internals** are individuals who believe that they control what happens to them. **Externals** are individuals who believe that what happens to them is controlled by outside forces, such as luck or chance.[12] Locus of control is an indicator of core self-evaluation because people who think they lack control over their lives tend to lack confidence in themselves. For example, if you think your success in school is determined by the whim of the professor or by blind luck, you probably don't have a lot of confidence in your ability to get straight A's; you would have an external locus of control, and most likely this would reflect a negative core self-evaluation.

How is the concept of core self-evaluations related to job satisfaction and job performance? On the issue of job satisfaction, people with positive core self-evaluations see more challenge in their jobs, which results in more satisfaction. Individuals with positive core self-evaluations also tend to obtain more complex and challenging jobs, perceive themselves as having control over their jobs, and tend to attribute positive outcomes to their own actions.[13] Related to job performance, people with positive core self-evaluations perform better because they set more ambitious goals, are more committed to their goals, and persist longer when attempting to reach these goals. For example, one study of life insurance agents found that the majority of the successful salespersons had positive core self-evaluations.[14]

You might wonder whether someone can be *too* positive. In other words, what happens when someone thinks he is capable but is actually incompetent? One study of *Fortune* 500 CEOs, for example, showed that many CEOs are overconfident and that this self-perceived infallibility often causes them to make bad decisions.[15] Though overconfidence surely exists, very often we sell ourselves short and are less effective. If I decide I can't do something, for example, I won't try, and not doing it only reinforces my self-doubts.

Machiavellianism   The personality characteristic of **Machiavellianism** (Mach) is named after Niccolo Machiavelli, who wrote in the sixteenth century on how to gain and use power. An individual high in Machiavellianism is pragmatic, maintains emotional distance, and believes that ends can justify means. "If it works, use it" is consistent with a high-Mach perspective. A considerable amount of research has been directed toward relating high- and low-Mach personalities to certain behavioral outcomes.[16] High Machs manipulate more, win more, are persuaded less, and persuade others more than do low Machs.[17] Yet these high-Mach outcomes are moderated by situational factors. It has been found that high Machs flourish (1) when they interact face to face with others rather than indirectly; (2) when the situation has a minimum number of rules and regulations, thus allowing latitude for improvisation; and (3) when emotional involvement with details irrelevant to winning distracts low Machs.[18]

Should we conclude that high Machs make good employees? That answer depends on the type of job and whether you consider ethical implications in evaluating performance. In jobs that require bargaining skills (such as labor negotiation) or that offer substantial rewards for winning (as in commissioned sales), high Machs will be productive. But if ends can't justify the means, if absolute standards of behavior exist, or if the three situational factors noted in the preceding paragraph are absent, our ability to predict a high-Mach's performance will be severely curtailed.

Narcissism   A person high in **narcissism** has a grandiose sense of self-importance, requires excessive admiration, has a sense of entitlement, and is arrogant. The term *narcissist* comes from the Greek myth of Narcissus, the story of a man so vain and proud that he fell in love with his own image.

In terms of the workplace, one study found that while narcissists thought they were *better* leaders than their colleagues, their supervisors actually rated them as *worse* leaders. For example, an Oracle executive described that company's CEO Larry Ellison as follows: "The difference between God and Larry is that God does not believe he is Larry."[19] Because narcissists often want to gain the admiration of others and receive affirmation of their superiority, they tend to talk down (to treat others as if they were inferior) to those who threaten them. Narcissists also tend to be selfish and exploitive, and they often carry the attitude that others exist for their benefit.[20] Studies indicate that narcissists are rated by their bosses as less effective at their jobs, particularly when it comes to helping other people.[21]

> —One study found that while narcissists thought they were better leaders than their colleagues, their supervisors actually rated them as worse leaders.

Self-Monitoring   Individuals high in **self-monitoring** show considerable adaptability in adjusting their behavior to external, situational factors. They are highly sensitive to external cues and can behave differently in different situations. High self-monitors are capable of presenting striking contradictions between their public persona and their private self. Low self-monitors can't disguise themselves in that way. They tend to display their true dispositions and attitudes in every situation; hence, who they are and what they do display high behavioral consistency.

The evidence indicates that high self-monitors tend to pay closer attention to the behavior of others and are more capable of conforming than are low self-monitors.[22] They also receive better performance ratings, are more likely to emerge as leaders, and show less commitment to their organizations.[23] In addition, high self-monitoring managers tend to be more mobile in their careers, receive more promotions (both internal and cross-organizational), and are more likely to occupy central positions in an organization.[24]

Risk Taking   People differ in their willingness to take chances. This propensity to assume or avoid risk affects how long it takes managers to make a decision and how much information they require before making a choice. For instance, 79 managers worked on simulated personnel exercises that required them to make hiring deci-sions.[25] High risk-taking managers made more rapid decisions and used less informa-tion in making their choices than did the low risk-taking managers. Interestingly, the decision accuracy was the same for both groups.

Although previous studies have shown managers in large organizations to be more risk averse than are growth-oriented entrepreneurs who actively manage small businesses, recent findings suggest that managers in large organizations may actually be more willing to take a risk than entrepreneurs.[26] The work population as a whole also exhibits differences in risk propensity.[27] As a result, it makes sense to recognize these differences and even to consider aligning risk-taking propensity with specific job demands. For instance, a high risk-taking propensity may lead to more effective per-formance for a stock trader in a brokerage firm because that type of job demands rapid decision making. On the other hand, a willingness to take risks might prove a major obstacle to an accountant who performs auditing activities. The latter job might be better filled by someone with a low risk-taking propensity.

Type A Personality   Do you know people who are excessively competitive and always seem to be experiencing a sense of time urgency? If you do, it's a good bet that those people have a **Type A personality**. A person with a Type A personality is "aggressively involved in a chronic, incessant struggle to achieve more and more in less and less time, and, if required to do so, against the opposing efforts of other things or other persons."[28] In the North American culture, such characteristics tend to be highly prized and positively associated with ambition and the successful acquisition of material goods. Type A's:

1. are always moving, walking, and eating rapidly;
2. feel impatient with the rate at which most events take place;
3. strive to think or do two or more things at once;
4. cannot cope with leisure time;
5. are obsessed with numbers, measuring their success in terms of how many or how much of everything they acquire.

Type A's operate under moderate to high levels of stress. They subject them-selves to more or less continuous time pressure, creating for themselves a life of dead-lines. These characteristics result in some rather specific behavioral outcomes. For example, Type A's are fast workers, because they emphasize quantity over quality. In managerial positions, Type A's demonstrate their competitiveness by working long hours and, not infrequently, making poor decisions because they make them too fast. Type A's are also rarely creative. Because of their concern with quantity and speed, they rely on past experiences when faced with problems. They will not allocate the time necessary to develop unique solutions to new problems.

In contrast to the Type A personality is the Type B, who is exactly opposite. Type B's are "rarely harried by the desire to obtain a wildly increasing number of things or participate in an endless growing series of events in an ever-decreasing amount of time."[29] Type B's:

1. never suffer from a sense of time urgency with its accompanying impatience;
2. feel no need to display or discuss either their achievements or accomplishments unless such exposure is demanded by the situation;

3. play for fun and relaxation, rather than to exhibit their superiority at any cost;

4. can relax without guilt.

Do Type A's differ from Type B's in their ability to get hired? The answer appears to be "Yes."[30] Type A's do better in job interviews because they are more likely to be judged as having desirable traits such as high drive, competence, aggressiveness, and success motivation.

Proactive Personality   Individuals with a **proactive personality** identify opportunities, show initiative, take action, and persevere until meaningful change occurs. They create positive change in their environment, regardless or even in spite of constraints or obstacles.[31] Not surprisingly, proactives have many desirable behaviors that organizations covet. For instance, the evidence indicates that proactives are more likely to be seen as leaders and more likely to act as change agents within the organization.[32] Other actions of proactives can be positive or negative, depending on the organization and the situation. For example, proactives are more likely to challenge the status quo or voice their displeasure when situations aren't to their liking.[33] As individuals, proactives are more likely to achieve career success.[34] This is because they select, create, and influence work situations in their favor. Proactives are more likely to seek out job and organizational information, develop contacts in high places, engage in career planning, and demonstrate persistence in the face of career obstacles.

Personality and National Culture

Do personality frameworks, like the Big Five model, transfer across cultures? Are dimensions like locus of control and the Type A personality relevant in all cultures? Let's try to answer these questions.

The five personality factors identified in the Big Five model appear in almost all cross-cultural studies.[35] This includes a wide variety of diverse cultures, such as China, Israel, Germany, Japan, Spain, Nigeria, Norway, Pakistan, and the United States. Most differences appear related to which dimensions are emphasized and whether countries are predominantly individualistic—meaning that people prefer to act as individuals rather than as members of groups—or collectivistic—where there's a tight social framework in which people expect others in groups of which they are a part to look after them and protect them. Chinese companies, for example, use the category of conscientiousness more often and the category of agreeableness less often than do U.S. firms. And the Big Five appear to predict a bit better in individualistic cultures than in collectivist ones.[36] But there is a surprisingly high amount of agreement, especially among individuals from developed countries. A comprehensive review of studies covering people from the 15-nation European Community found that conscientiousness was a valid predictor of performance across jobs and occupational groups.[37] This is exactly what U.S. studies have found.

No common personality types dominate any given country, as high and low risk takers are found in almost all cultures. However, a country's culture influences the dominant personality characteristics of its population. We can see this by looking at locus of control and the Type A personality. Evidence indicates that cultures differ in terms of people's relationships to their environments. In some cultures, such as those in North America, people believe that they can dominate their environments. People in other societies, such as

—A country's culture influences the dominant personality characteristics of its population.

Middle Eastern countries, believe that life is essentially preordained. Note the close parallel to internal and external locus of control.[38] We should expect, therefore, a larger proportion of internals in U.S. and Canadian workforces than in the Saudi Arabian or Iranian workforces.

The prevalence of Type A personalities will be influenced somewhat by the culture in which a person grows up. Type A's reside in every country, but more are found in capitalistic countries, where achievement and material success are highly valued. It is estimated that about 50 percent of the North American population is Type A.[39] This percentage shouldn't be too surprising. The United States and Canada both have a high emphasis on time management and efficiency. Both have cultures that stress accomplishments and acquisition of money and material goods. In cultures such as Sweden and France, where materialism is less revered, we would predict a smaller proportion of Type A personalities.

Values

While personality and values are related, they're not the same. Values are often very specific, describing belief systems rather than behavioral tendencies. Some beliefs or values don't say much about a person's personality, and people don't always act in ways consistent with their values.

Values represent basic, enduring convictions that "a specific mode of conduct or end-state of existence is personally or socially preferable to an opposite or converse mode of conduct or end-state of existence."[40] Values involve judgment because they represent an individual's ideas about what is right, good, or desirable. All of us have a hierarchy of values that form our value system. This system is identified by the relative importance we assign to values such as freedom, pleasure, self-respect, honesty, obedience, and equality. We can evaluate values in relation to two attributes:

1. The *content attribute*, which says that a mode of conduct or end-state of existence is *important*.
2. The *intensity attribute*, which specifies *how important* it is. When we rank an individual's values in terms of their intensity, we obtain that person's **value system**.

Types of Values

Can we classify values? Yes we can, and two approaches help us to develop value typologies.

Rokeach Value Survey   Milton Rokeach created the Rokeach Value Survey (RVS).[41] The RVS consists of two sets of values, with each set containing 18 individual value items. One set, called **terminal values**, refers to desirable end-states. These are the goals that a person would like to achieve during his or her lifetime. The other set, called **instrumental values**, refers to preferable modes of behavior, or means of achieving the terminal values. Exhibit 3-1 gives common examples for each of these sets.

Several studies confirm that the RVS values vary among groups.[42] People in the same occupations or categories (for example, corporate managers, union members, parents, students) tend to hold similar values. For instance, one study compared corporate executives, members of the steelworkers' union, and members of a community activist group. Although a good deal of overlap was found among the three groups,

EXHIBIT 3-1   Terminal and Instrumental Values in Rokeach Value Survey

Terminal Values	Instrumental Values
A comfortable life (a prosperous life)	Ambitious (hardworking, aspiring)
An exciting life (a stimulating, active life)	Broad-minded (open-minded)
A sense of accomplishment (lasting contribution)	Capable (competent, efficient)
A world at peace (free of war and conflict)	Cheerful (lighthearted, joyful)
A world of beauty (beauty of nature and the arts)	Clean (neat, tidy)
Equality (brotherhood, equal opportunity for all)	Courageous (standing up for your beliefs)
Family security (taking care of loved ones)	Forgiving (willing to pardon others)
Freedom (independence, free choice)	Helpful (working for the welfare of others)
Happiness (contentedness)	Honest (sincere, truthful)
Inner harmony (freedom from inner conflict)	Imaginative (daring, creative)
Mature love (sexual and spiritual intimacy)	Independent (self-reliant, self-sufficient)
National security (protection from attack)	Intellectual (intelligent, reflective)
Pleasure (an enjoyable, leisurely life)	Logical (consistent, rational)
Salvation (saved, eternal life)	Loving (affectionate, tender)
Self-respect (self-esteem)	Obedient (dutiful, respectful)
Social recognition (respect, admiration)	Polite (courteous, well-mannered)
True friendship (close companionship)	Responsible (dependable, reliable)
Wisdom (a mature understanding of life)	Self-controlled (restrained, self-disciplined)

Source: Reprinted with the permission of The Free Press, a Division of Simon & Schuster Adult Publishing Group, from *The Nature of Human Values* by Milton Rokeach. Copyright © 1973 by The Free Press. Copyright renewed © 2001 by Sandra J. Ball-Rokeach. All rights reserved.

there were also some very significant differences (see Exhibit 3-2).[43] The activists had value preferences that were quite different from those of the other two groups. They ranked *equality* as their most important terminal value; executives and union members ranked this value 12 and 13, respectively. Activists ranked *helpful* as their second-highest instrumental value. The other two groups both ranked it 14. These differences are important because executives, union members, and activists all have a vested interest in what corporations do. These differences make it difficult when these groups have to negotiate with each other, and they can create serious conflicts when they contend with each other over an organization's economic and social policies.

Contemporary Work Cohorts   We have integrated several recent analyses of work values into four groups that attempt to capture the unique values of different cohorts or generations in the U.S. workforce.[44] Exhibit 3-3 proposes that employees can be segmented by the era in which they entered the workforce. Because most people start work between the ages of 18 and 23, the eras also correlate closely with the chronological age of employees.

Before going any further, let's acknowledge some limitations of this analysis:

1. We make no assumption that this framework applies universally across all cultures.
2. Very little rigorous research on generational values exists, so we have to rely on an intuitive framework.
3. These categories are imprecise. No law states that someone born in 1985 can't have values similar to those of someone born in 1955.

Despite these limitations, values do change over generations, and some useful insights can be gained from analyzing values chronologically.

EXHIBIT 3-2   Mean Value Ranking of Executives, Union Members, and Activists (Top Five Only)

Executives		Union Members		Activists	
Terminal	**Instrumental**	**Terminal**	**Instrumental**	**Terminal**	**Instrumental**
1. Self-respect	1. Honest	1. Family security	1. Responsible	1. Equality	1. Honest
2. Family security	2. Responsible	2. Freedom	2. Honest	2. A world of peace	2. Helpful
3. Freedom	3. Capable	3. Happiness	3. Courageous	3. Family security	3. Courageous
4. A sense of accomplishment	4. Ambitious	4. Self-respect	4. Independent	4. Self-respect	4. Responsible
5. Happiness	5. Independent	5. Mature love	5. Capable	5. Freedom	5. Capable

Source: Based on W. C. Frederick and J. Weber, "The Values of Corporate Managers and Their Critics: An Empirical Description and Normative Implications," in W. C. Frederick and L. E. Preston (eds.), *Business Ethics: Research Issues and Empirical Studies* (Greenwich, CT: JAI Press, 1990), pp. 123–44.

EXHIBIT 3-3   Dominant Work Values in Today's Workforce

Cohort	Entered the Workforce	Approximate Current Age	Dominant Work Values
Veterans	1950s or early 1960s	65+	Hard-working, conservative, conforming; loyalty to the organization
Boomers	1965–1985	Early 40s to mid-60s	Success, achievement, ambition, dislike of authority; loyalty to career
Xers	1985–2000	Late 20s to early 40s	Work/life balance, team-oriented, dislike of rules; loyalty to relationships
Nexters	2000 to present	Under 30	Confident, financial success, self-reliant but team-oriented; loyalty to both self and relationships

Workers who grew up influenced by the Great Depression, World War II, the Andrews Sisters, and the Berlin blockade entered the workforce through the 1950s and early 1960s believing in hard work, the status quo, and authority figures. We call them *Veterans* (some use the label *Traditionalists*). Once hired, Veterans tended to be loyal to their employers and respectful of authority. They tend to be hardworking and practical. In terms of the terminal values on the RVS, these employees are likely to place the greatest importance on a comfortable life and family security.

Boomers (Baby Boomers) are a large cohort born after World War II when military veterans returned to their families and times were good. Boomers entered the workforce from the mid-1960s through the mid-1980s. This cohort was influenced heavily by the civil rights movement, women's lib, the Beatles, the Vietnam War, and baby-boom competition. They brought with them a large measure of the "hippie ethic" and distrust of authority, but they place a great deal of emphasis on achievement and material success. They work hard and want to enjoy the fruits of their labors. They're pragmatists who believe that ends can justify means. Boomers see the organizations that employ them merely as vehicles for their careers. Terminal values such as a sense of accomplishment and social recognition rank high with them.

Xers (*Generation X*) lives have been shaped by globalization, two-career parents, MTV, AIDS, and computers. They value flexibility, life options, and the achievement of job satisfaction. Family and relationships are very important to this cohort. Unlike Veterans, Xers are skeptical, particularly of authority. They also enjoy team-oriented work. Money is important as an indicator of career performance, but Xers are willing to trade off salary increases, titles, security, and promotions for increased leisure time and expanded lifestyle options. In search of balance in their lives, Xers are less willing to make personal sacrifices for the sake of their employer than previous generations were. On the RVS, they rate high on true friendship, happiness, and pleasure.

The most recent entrants to the workforce, the *Nexters* (also called *Neters*, *Millennials*, *Generation Y*, and *Generation Next*) grew up during prosperous times but find themselves entering a post-boom economy. Though they face insecurity about their jobs and careers, they have high expectations and seek meaning in their work. Nexters are at ease with diversity and are the first generation to take technology for granted. They've lived much of their lives with ATMs, DVDs, cell phones, laptops, and the Internet. This generation tends to be money oriented and desirous of the things that money can buy. They seek financial success. Like Xers, they enjoy team-work, but they're also highly self-reliant. They tend to emphasize terminal values such as freedom and a comfortable life.

An understanding that individuals' values differ but tend to reflect the societal values of the period in which they grew up can be a valuable aid in explaining and pre-dicting behavior. Employees in their late sixties, for instance, are more likely to accept authority than their coworkers who are 10 or 15 years younger. And workers in their thirties are more likely than their parents to balk at having to work weekends and more prone to leave a job in mid-career to pursue another that provides more leisure time.

Values, Loyalty, and Ethical Behavior

Has there been a decline in business ethics? Although the issue is debatable, a lot of people think ethical standards began to erode in the late 1970s.[45] If ethical standards have declined, perhaps we should look to our work cohorts model (see Exhibit 3-3) for a possible explanation. After all, managers consistently report that the action of their bosses is the most important factor influencing ethical and unethical behavior in their organizations.[46] Given this fact, the values of those in middle and upper management should have a significant bearing on the entire ethical climate within an organization.

Through the mid-1970s, the managerial ranks were dominated by Veterans, whose loyalties were to their employers. When faced with ethical dilemmas, their decisions were made in terms of what was best for their organizations. Beginning in the mid- to late 1970s, Boomers began to rise into the upper levels of management. By the early 1990s, Boomers held a large portion of middle and top management posi-tions in business organizations. The loyalty of Boomers is to their careers. Their focus is inward, and their primary concern is with looking out for themselves. Such self-centered values would be consistent with a decline in ethical standards. Could this help explain the alleged decline in business ethics beginning in the late 1970s?

The potential good news in this analysis is that Xers are now in the process of moving into middle-management slots and soon will be rising into top management.

Since their loyalty is to relationships, they are more likely to consider the ethical implications of their actions on others around them. The result? We might look forward to an uplifting of ethical standards in business over the next decade or two merely as a result of changing values within the managerial ranks.

Values Across Cultures

Because values differ across cultures, an understanding of these differences should be helpful in explaining and predicting behavior of employees from different countries.

Hofstede's Framework for Assessing Cultures   One of the most widely referenced approaches for analyzing variations among cultures was done in the late 1970s by Geert Hofstede.[47] He surveyed more than 116,000 IBM employees in 40 countries about their work-related values. He found that managers and employees vary on five value dimensions of national culture. They are listed and defined as follows:

- **High power distance** versus **low power distance**: Power distance is the degree to which people in a country accept that power in institutions and organizations is distributed unequally. A high-power-distance rating means that large inequalities of power and wealth exist and are tolerated in the culture. Such cultures are more likely to follow a class or caste system that discourages upward mobility of its citizens. A low-power-distance ranking indicates the culture discourages differences between power and wealth. These societies stress equality and opportunity.

- **Individualism** versus **collectivism**: Individualism is the degree to which people prefer to act as individuals rather than as members of groups and believe in individual rights above all else. Collectivism emphasizes a tight social framework in which people expect others in groups of which they are a part to look after them and protect them.

- **Masculinity** versus **femininity**: These dimensions reflect the degree to which the culture favors traditional masculine roles such as achievement, power, and control versus a culture that views men and women as equals. A high-masculinity rating indicates the culture has separate roles for men and women, with men dominating the society. A high-femininity rating means that the culture has little differentiation between male and female roles. High femininity does not mean that the culture emphasizes feminine roles; rather, it emphasizes equality between men and women.

- **Uncertainty avoidance**: This is the degree to which people in a country prefer structured over unstructured situations. In cultures that score high on uncertainty avoidance, people have an increased level of anxiety about uncertainty and ambiguity. Such cultures tend to emphasize laws, regulations, and controls that are designed to reduce uncertainty. In cultures that score low on uncertainty avoidance, individuals are less dismayed by ambiguity and uncertainty and have a greater tolerance for a variety of opinions. Such cultures are less rule oriented, take more risks, and more readily accept change.

- **Long-term orientation** versus **short-term orientation**: This newest addition to Hofstede's typology focuses on the degree of a society's long-term devotion to traditional values. People in cultures with long-term orientations look to the future and value thrift, persistence, and tradition. In a short-term orientation, people value the here and now, change is accepted more readily, and commitments do not represent impediments to change.

How does the United States score on Hofstede's dimensions? The United States is very individualistic. In fact, it's the most individualistic nation of all (closely followed by Australia and Great Britain). The United States also tends to be short term in its orientation and low in power distance (people in the United States tend not to accept built-in class differences between people). The United States is also relatively low on uncertainty avoidance, meaning that most Americans are relatively tolerant of uncertainty and ambiguity. In addition, the United States scores relatively high on masculinity, meaning that most Americans emphasize traditional gender roles (at least relative to such other countries as Denmark, Finland, Norway, and Sweden).

While Hofstede's culture dimensions influenced OB researchers and managers enormously, critics point out several weaknesses:

- Although the data have since been updated, the original data are from 30 years ago and were based on a single company (IBM).

- Few researchers have read the details of Hofstede's methodology closely and therefore are unaware of the many decisions and judgment calls he had to make (for example, reducing the cultural values to just five).

- Some of Hofstede's results are unexpected. For example, Japan, which is often considered a highly collectivist nation, is considered only average on collectivism under Hofstede's dimensions.[48]

Despite these concerns, Hofstede has been one of the most widely cited social scientists ever, and his framework has left a lasting mark on OB.

The GLOBE Framework for Assessing Cultures   Begun in 1993, the Global Leadership and Organizational Behavior Effectiveness (GLOBE) research program is an ongoing cross-cultural investigation of leadership and national culture. Using data from 825 organizations in 62 countries, the GLOBE team identified nine dimensions on which national cultures differ (see Exhibit 3-4 for examples of country ratings on each of the dimensions).[49]

- *Assertiveness:* The extent to which a society encourages people to be tough, confrontational, assertive, and competitive versus modest and tender.

- *Future orientation:* The extent to which a society encourages and rewards future-oriented behaviors such as planning, investing in the future, and delaying gratification. This is essentially equivalent to Hofstede's long-term/short-term orientation.

- *Gender differentiation:* The extent to which a society maximizes gender role differences. This is equivalent to Hofstede's masculinity/femininity dimension.

- *Uncertainty avoidance:* As identified by Hofstede, the GLOBE team defined this term as a society's reliance on social norms and procedures to alleviate the unpredictability of future events.

- *Power distance:* As did Hofstede, the GLOBE team defined this as the degree to which members of a society expect power to be unequally shared.

- *Individualism/collectivism:* Again, this term was defined—as was Hofstede's—as the degree to which individuals are encouraged by societal institutions to be integrated into groups within organizations and society.

- *In-group collectivism:* In contrast to focusing on societal institutions, this dimension encompasses the extent to which members of a society take pride in membership in

EXHIBIT 3-4   GLOBE Highlights

Dimension	Countries Rating Low	Countries Rating Moderate	Countries Rating High
Assertiveness	Sweden New Zealand Switzerland	Egypt Ireland Philippines	Spain United States Greece
Future orientation	Russia Argentina Poland	Slovenia Egypt Ireland	Denmark Canada Netherlands
Gender differentiation	Sweden Denmark Slovenia	Italy Brazil Argentina	South Korea Egypt Morocco
Uncertainty avoidance	Russia Hungary Bolivia	Israel United States Mexico	Austria Denmark Germany
Power distance	Denmark Netherlands South Africa	England France Brazil	Russia Spain Thailand
Individualism/collectivism*	Denmark Singapore Japan	Hong Kong United States Egypt	Greece Hungary Germany
In-group collectivism	Denmark Sweden New Zealand	Japan Israel Qatar	Egypt China Morocco
Performance orientation	Russia Argentina Greece	Sweden Israel Spain	United States Taiwan New Zealand
Humane orientation	Germany Spain France	Hong Kong Sweden Taiwan	Indonesia Egypt Malaysia

*A low score is synonymous with collectivism.
Source: M. Javidan and R. J. House, "Cultural Acumen for the Global Manager: Lessons from Project GLOBE," *Organizational Dynamics,* Spring 2001, pp. 289–305. Copyright © 2001. Reprinted with permission from Elsevier.

small groups, such as their family and circle of close friends and the organizations in which they are employed.

■ *Performance orientation:* This refers to the degree to which a society encourages and rewards group members for performance improvement and excellence.

■ *Humane orientation:* This is defined as the degree to which a society encourages and rewards individuals for being fair, altruistic, generous, caring, and kind to others.

A comparison of the GLOBE dimensions against those identified by Hofstede suggests that the former has extended Hofstede's work rather than replaced it. The GLOBE project confirms that Hofstede's five dimensions are still valid while adding some dimensions and providing us with an updated measure of where countries rate on each dimension. As generations evolve and immigrants enter a nation, a country's cultural values can change. For instance, the GLOBE survey suggests that the United States has become somewhat less individualist over time. We can expect future cross-cultural studies of human behavior and organizational practices to increasingly use the GLOBE dimensions to assess differences between countries.

LINKING AN INDIVIDUAL'S PERSONALITY AND VALUES TO THE WORKPLACE

Because managers today are less interested in an applicant's ability to perform a *specific* job than with the *flexibility* to meet changing situations and commitment to the organization, in recent years managers have become interested in determining how well an employee's personality *and* values match the *organization*. We'll now discuss person–job fit and person–organization fit in more detail.

Person–Job Fit

Matching job requirements with personality characteristics is best articulated in John Holland's **personality–job fit theory**.[50] The theory is based on the notion of fit between an individual's personality characteristics and the job. Holland presents six personality types and proposes that satisfaction and the propensity to leave a position depend on the degree to which individuals successfully match their personalities to a job. Each one of the six personality types has a congruent occupation. Exhibit 3-5 describes the six types and their personality characteristics and gives examples of congruent occupations.

Holland has developed a Vocational Preference Inventory questionnaire that contains 160 occupational titles. Respondents indicate which of these occupations they like or dislike, and their answers are used to form personality profiles. Using this procedure, research strongly supports the hexagonal diagram shown in Exhibit 3-6.[51] This figure shows that the closer two fields or orientations are in the hexagon, the

EXHIBIT 3-5   Holland's Typology of Personality and Congruent Occupations

Type	Personality Characteristics	Congruent Occupations
Realistic: Prefers physical activities that require skill, strength, and coordination	Shy, genuine, persistent, stable, conforming, practical	Mechanic, drill press operator, assembly-line worker, farmer
Investigative: Prefers activities that involve thinking, organizing, and understanding	Analytical, original, curious, independent	Biologist, economist, mathematician, news reporter
Social: Prefers activities that involve helping and developing others	Sociable, friendly, cooperative, understanding	Social worker, teacher, counselor, clinical psychologist
Conventional: Prefers rule-regulated, orderly, and unambiguous activities	Conforming, efficient, practical, unimaginative, inflexible	Accountant, corporate manager, bank teller, file clerk
Enterprising: Prefers verbal activities in which there are opportunities to influence others and attain power	Self-confident, ambitious, energetic, domineering	Lawyer, real estate agent, public relations specialist, small business manager
Artistic: Prefers ambiguity and activities that allow creative expression	Imaginative, disorderly, idealistic, emotional, impractical	Painter, musician, writer, interior unsystematic decorator

EXHIBIT 3-6   Relationships Among Occupational Personality Types

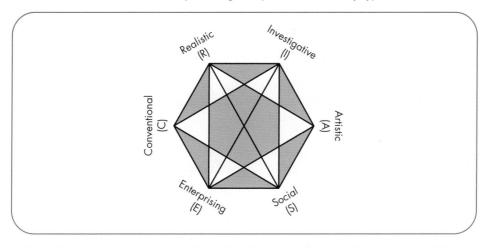

more compatible they are. Adjacent categories are quite similar, whereas those diagonally opposite are highly dissimilar.

What does all this mean? The theory argues that satisfaction is highest and turnover lowest when personality and occupation are in agreement. Social individuals should be in social jobs, conventional people in conventional jobs, and so forth. The key points of this model are as follows:

1. There do appear to be intrinsic differences in personality among individuals.
2. There are different types of jobs.
3. People in jobs congruent with their personalities should be more satisfied and less likely to voluntarily resign than should people in incongruent jobs.

Person–Organization Fit

Attention in recent years has expanded to include matching people to *organizations* as well as *jobs*. Because organizations face a dynamic and changing environment, they require employees who are able to readily change tasks and move easily between teams, so it's more important that employees' personalities fit with the overall organization's culture than with the characteristics of any specific job.

The person–organization fit essentially argues that people leave organizations that are not compatible with their personalities.[52] Using the Big Five terminology, we could expect that the following:

- People high on extroversion fit better with aggressive and team-oriented cultures.
- People high on agreeableness match up better with a supportive organizational climate than one that focuses on aggressiveness.
- People high on openness to experience fit better into organizations that emphasize innovation rather than standardization.[53]

—The fit of employees' values with the culture of their organization predicts job satisfaction, commitment to the organization, and low turnover.

By following these guidelines at the time of hiring, managers select new employees who fit better with the organization's culture, which, in turn, should result in higher employee satisfaction and reduced turnover.

Research on person–organization fit has also looked at people's values and whether they match the organization's culture. The fit of employees' values with the culture of their organization predicts job satisfaction, commitment to the organization, and low turnover.[54]

IMPLICATIONS FOR MANAGERS

Personality   What value, if any, does the Big Five provide to managers? Seeking employees who score high on conscientiousness, for instance, is probably sound advice. Similarly, screening candidates for managerial and sales positions to identify those high in extroversion also should pay dividends. In terms of exerting effort at work, impressive evidence suggests that people who score high on conscientiousness, extroversion, and emotional stability are likely to be highly motivated employees.[55] Of course, situational factors must be considered—job demands, the degree of required interaction with others, and the organization's culture—because they moderate the personality–job performance relationship. So, managers need to evaluate the job, the work group, and the organization to determine the optimum personality fit.

Although the Myers–Briggs Type Inventory has been widely criticized, it may have a place for use in organizations. In training and development, it can help employees to better understand themselves. It can provide aid to teams by helping members better understand each other. And it can open up communication in work groups and possibly reduce conflicts.

Values   Why is it important to know an individual's values? Although they don't have a direct *effect* on behavior, values strongly influence a person's attitudes, behaviors, and perceptions. So knowledge of an individual's value system can provide insight into what makes the person tick.

Given that people's values differ, managers can use the Rokeach Value Survey to assess potential employees and determine if their values align with the dominant values of the organization. Employees' performance and satisfaction are likely to be higher if their values fit well with the organization. A person who places high importance on imagination, independence, and freedom is likely to be poorly matched with an organization that seeks conformity from its employees. Managers are more likely to appreciate, evaluate positively, and allocate rewards to employees who fit in, and employees are more likely to be satisfied if they perceive that they do fit in. This argues for management to strive during the selection of new employees to find job candidates who not only have the ability, experience, and motivation to perform but also possess a value system that is compatible with the organization's.

CHAPTER 4

Perception and Individual Decision Making

In this chapter, we'll examine factors that influence how individuals perceive others in the workplace, as well as the various ways individuals make judgments about others. Then we'll link perception to decision making, describe how decisions should be made, and review how decisions are actually made in organizations.

WHAT IS PERCEPTION?

Perception is a process by which individuals organize and interpret their sensory impressions to give meaning to their environment. Perception is important in the study of OB simply because people's behaviors are based on their perceptions of what reality is, not on reality itself. *The world as it is perceived is the world that is behaviorally important.*

FACTORS INFLUENCING PERCEPTION

How do we explain that individuals may look at the same thing, yet perceive it differently? A number of factors resident in different sources operate to shape and sometimes distort perception:

- *Perceiver.* When an individual looks at a target and attempts to interpret what he or she sees, that interpretation is heavily influenced by the perceiver's personal characteristics, including attitudes, personality, motives, interests, past experiences, and expectations.
- *Target.* Characteristics of the target—the object being perceived—can affect how it is perceived. Loud people are more likely to be noticed in a group than quiet ones. So, too, are extremely attractive or unattractive individuals.
- *Situation.* Because targets are not looked at in isolation, the relationship of a target to its background—the context in which the perception is made (see Exhibit 4-1)—also influences perception, as does our tendency to group close things and similar things. Also, the time at which an object or event is seen can influence attention, as can location, light, heat, or any number of other situational factors.

EXHIBIT 4-1   Factors That Influence Perception

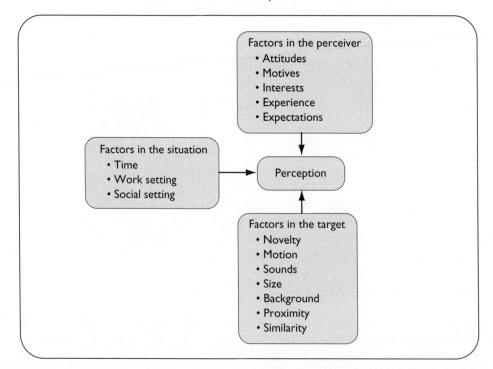

PERSON PERCEPTION: MAKING JUDGMENTS ABOUT OTHERS

Now we turn to the most relevant application of perception concepts to OB. This is the issue of *person perception*. By that, we mean the perceptions people form about each other.

Attribution Theory

Our perceptions of people differ from our perceptions of inanimate objects such as desks, machines, or buildings because we make inferences about the actions of people that we don't make about inanimate objects. Nonliving objects are subject to the laws of nature, but–unlike people—they have no beliefs, motives, or intentions. The result is that when we observe people, we attempt to develop explanations of why they behave in certain ways. Our perceptions and judgments of people's actions, therefore, will be significantly influenced by the assumptions we make about their internal states.

Attribution theory suggests that when we observe an individual's behavior, we attempt to determine whether it was internally or externally caused.[1] *Internally* caused behaviors are those that are believed to be under the personal control of the individual. *Externally* caused behaviors are seen as resulting from outside causes; that is, the person is seen as having been forced into the behavior by the situation. For example, if one of your employees is late for work, you might attribute his lateness to his partying into the wee hours of the morning and then oversleeping; this would be an internal attribution. If you attribute his arriving late to an automobile accident that tied up traffic on the road that this employee regularly uses, this would be an external attribution.

Our determination of internally and externally caused behavior depends largely on three factors:

1. *Distinctiveness.* Distinctiveness refers to whether an individual displays different behaviors in different situations. Is the employee who arrives late today also the source of complaints by coworkers for being someone who regularly blows off commitments? We want to know whether this behavior is unusual. If it is, the observer is likely to give the behavior an external attribution. If this action is not unusual, it will probably be judged as internal.

2. *Consensus.* If everyone who faces a similar situation responds in the same way, we can say the behavior shows consensus. The behavior of the tardy employee would meet this criterion if all employees who took the same route to work were also late. From an attribution perspective, if consensus is high, you would be expected to give an external attribution to the employee's tardiness, whereas if other employees who took the same route made it to work on time, your conclusion as to causation would be internal.

3. *Consistency.* Does the person respond the same way over time? Coming in 10 minutes late for work is not perceived in the same way for the employee for whom it is an unusual case (she hasn't been late for several months) as it is for the employee for whom it is part of a routine pattern (she is late two or three times a week). The more consistent the behavior, the more the observer is inclined to attribute it to internal causes. Exhibit 4-2 summarizes the key elements in attribution theory.

EXHIBIT 4-2   Attribution Theory

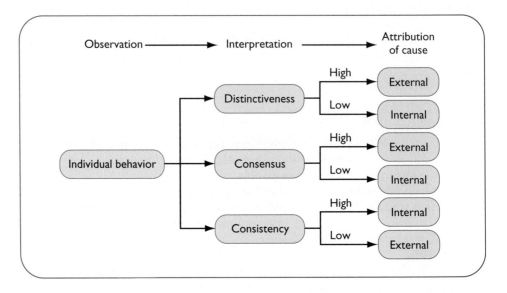

One of the more interesting findings from attribution theory is that errors or biases distort attributions. Substantial evidence suggests that when we make judgments about the behavior of other people, we have a tendency to underestimate the influence of external factors and overestimate the influence of internal or personal factors.[2] This is called the **fundamental attribution error** and can explain why a sales manager is prone to attribute the poor performance of her sales agents to laziness rather than to the innovative product line introduced by a competitor. Also, individuals and organizations have a tendency to attribute their own successes to internal factors such as ability or effort while putting the blame for failure on external factors such as bad luck or unproductive coworkers; this is called the **self-serving bias**.[3] For example, when the Iraq war appeared to go well, the White House declared "Mission Accomplished." But when it became clear that the weapons of mass destruction (WMD) were nowhere to be found and that the fighting was far from over, the White House rushed to blame intelligence failures.

Frequently Used Shortcuts in Judging Others

Perceiving and interpreting what others do is burdensome. As a result, individuals develop shortcuts for making the task more manageable. Though these shortcuts are sometimes valuable time-savers, they are not foolproof.

Selective Perception   Any characteristic that makes a person, object, or event stand out will increase the probability that it will be perceived. Because it is impossible for us to assimilate everything we see—only certain stimuli can be taken in. So, we engage in **selective perception**.

Because we cannot assimilate all that we observe, we take in bits and pieces. Those bits and pieces are not chosen randomly, though; rather, they are selectively chosen according to our interests, background, experience, and attitudes. This tendency explains why you are more likely to notice cars like your own or why some people may be reprimanded by their boss for doing something that, when done by another employee, goes unnoticed. Selective perception allows us to speed-read others, but not without the risk of drawing an inaccurate picture. Because we see what we want to see, we can draw unwarranted conclusions from an ambiguous situation.

Halo Effect   When we draw a general impression about an individual on the basis of a single characteristic, such as intelligence, sociability, or appearance, a **halo effect** is operating.[4] This phenomenon frequently occurs when students appraise their classroom instructor. Students may give prominence to a single trait, such as enthusiasm, and allow their evaluations to be tainted entirely by how they judge the instructor on that one trait. Thus, an instructor may be quiet, assured, knowledgeable, and highly qualified, but if his or her style lacks zeal, students who value zeal would probably give the instructor a low rating. The appearance of the halo effect is not random. Research suggests that it is likely to be most extreme when the traits to be perceived are ambiguous in behavioral terms (e.g., how open to new experiences someone is, which is often hard to judge), when the traits have moral overtones, and when the perceiver is judging traits with which he or she has had limited experience.[5]

Contrast Effects   An old adage among entertainers who perform in variety shows is "Never follow an act that has kids or animals in it" because the common belief is that audiences love children and animals so much that you'll look bad in comparison. This example demonstrates how **contrast effects** can distort perceptions. We don't evaluate a person in isolation. Our reaction to one person is influenced by other persons we have recently encountered. For instance, when an interviewer sees a pool of job applicants, distortions in any given candidate's evaluation can occur as a result of his or her place in the interview schedule. A candidate is likely to receive a more favorable evaluation if preceded by mediocre applicants and a less favorable evaluation if preceded by strong applicants.

Projection   It's easy to judge others if we assume they're similar to us. For instance, if you want challenge and responsibility in your job, you assume others want the same. This tendency to attribute one's own characteristics to other people—which is called **projection**—can distort perceptions made about others. People who engage in projection tend to perceive others according to what they themselves are like rather than according to what the person being observed is really like. When managers engage in projection, they compromise their ability to respond to individual differences. They tend to see people as more homogeneous than they really are.

Stereotyping   When we judge someone on the basis of our perception of the group to which he or she belongs, we are using the shortcut called **stereotyping**.[6] We sterotype because it is a means of simplifying a complex world, and it permits us to maintain consistency. Assume you're a sales manager looking to hire a salesperson who is ambitious and hardworking. You've had success in the past by hiring individuals who participated in athletics during college. So you focus your search by looking for candidates who participated in collegiate athletics. In so doing, you have cut down considerably on your search time. Furthermore, to the extent that athletes are ambitious and hardworking, the use of this stereotype can improve your decision making. The problem is, of course, when we inaccurately generalize or overgeneralize. In other words, not all college athletes are ambitious and hardworking.

In organizations, we frequently hear comments that represent stereotypes based on gender, age, race, ethnicity, and even weight: "Women won't relocate for a promotion"; "Men aren't interested in child care"; "Older workers can't learn new skills"; "Asian immigrants are hardworking and conscientious"; "Overweight people lack discipline."[7] From a perceptual standpoint, if people expect to see these stereotypes, they will, whether or not these perceptions are accurate.

THE LINK BETWEEN PERCEPTION AND INDIVIDUAL DECISION MAKING

Individuals in organizations make **decisions**, choosing from among two or more alternatives. Virtually every member of an organization, from its top managers to its nonmanagerial employees, makes decisions at some point. Individual decision making, therefore, is an important part of organizational behavior. But how individuals in organizations make decisions and the quality of their final choices are largely influenced by their perceptions.

Decision making occurs as a reaction to a **problem**. A discrepancy between some current state of affairs and some desired state requires a person to consider alternative courses of action. Unfortunately, most problems don't come neatly packaged with a *problem* label clearly displayed on them. So the awareness that a problem exists and that a decision needs to be made is a perceptual issue. Moreover, every decision requires the interpretation and evaluation of information. People typically gather data from multiple sources and then screen, process, and interpret it. Which data, for instance, are relevant to the decision and which are not? The perceptions of the decision makers will answer that question. They will develop alternatives and evaluate the strengths and weaknesses of each. Finally, throughout the entire decision process, perceptual distortions often surface that have the potential to bias analysis and conclusions.

How Should Decisions Be Made?

Let's begin by describing, at least in theory, how individuals should behave in order to maximize or optimize a certain outcome. We call this the *rational decision-making process.*

The Rational Decision-Making Process

We often think that the best decision maker is **rational**, someone who makes consistent, value-maximizing choices within specified constraints.[8] These choices are made following a six-step **rational decision-making model**.[9]

The Rational Model   The six steps in the rational decision-making model are listed in Exhibit 4-3.

1. The model begins by *defining the problem*. If you calculate your monthly expenses and find you're spending $100 more than you allocated in your budget, you have defined a problem. Many poor decisions can be traced to the decision maker overlooking a problem or defining the wrong problem.

EXHIBIT 4-3 Steps in the Rational Decision-Making Model

1. Define the problem.
2. Identify the decision criteria.
3. Allocate weights to the criteria.
4. Develop the alternatives.
5. Evaluate the alternatives.
6. Select the best alternative.

2. Once a decision maker has defined the problem, he or she needs to *identify the decision criteria* that will be important in solving the problem. In this step, the decision maker determines what is relevant in making the decision. This step brings the decision maker's interests, values, and similar personal preferences into the process.

3. The criteria identified are rarely all equal in importance. So the third step requires the decision maker to *weight the previously identified criteria* to give them the correct priority in the decision.

4. The fourth step requires the decision maker to *generate possible alternatives* that could succeed in resolving the problem. No attempt is made in this step to appraise these alternatives, only to list them.

5. Once the alternatives have been generated, the decision maker must critically analyze and evaluate each one. This is done by *rating each alternative on each criterion.* The strengths and weaknesses of each alternative become evident as they are compared with the criteria and weights established in the second and third steps.

6. The final step in this model requires *computing the optimal decision.* This is done by evaluating each alternative against the weighted criteria and selecting the alternative with the higher total score.

Assumptions of the Model   The rational decision-making model contains a number of assumptions.[10] Let's briefly outline those assumptions.

1. *Problem clarity.* The problem is clear and unambiguous. The decision maker is assumed to have complete information regarding the decision situation.

2. *Known options.* It is assumed the decision maker can identify all the relevant criteria and can list all the viable alternatives. Furthermore, the decision maker is aware of all the possible consequences of each alternative.

3. *Clear preferences.* Rationality assumes that the criteria and alternatives can be ranked and weighted to reflect their importance.

4. *Constant preferences.* It's assumed that the specific decision criteria are constant and that the weights assigned to them are stable over time.

5. *No time or cost constraints.* The rational decision maker can obtain full information about criteria and alternatives because it's assumed that there are no time or cost constraints.

6. *Maximum payoff.* The rational decision maker will choose the alternative that yields the highest perceived value.

Improving Creativity in Decision Making

Although following the steps of the rational decision-making model will often result in better decisions, the rational decision maker also needs **creativity**, the ability to produce novel and useful ideas.[11] Creativity is important to decision making because it allows the decision maker to more fully appraise and understand the problem, including seeing problems others can't see. However, creativity's most obvious value is in helping the decision maker to identify all viable alternatives, or to identify alternatives that aren't readily apparent.

—Creativity allows the decision maker to more fully appraise and understand the problem, including seeing problems others can't see.

Creative Potential   Most people have creative potential that they can use when confronted with a decision-making problem, but to unleash that potential they have to get out of the psychological ruts many of us get into and learn how to think about a problem in divergent ways.

People differ in their inherent creativity, and exceptional creativity is scarce. Albert Einstein, Emily Dickinson, Pablo Picasso, and Wolfgang Mozart were individuals of exceptional creativity. But what about the typical individual? People who score high on Openness to Experience (see Chapter 3), for example, are more likely to be creative. Intelligent people also are more likely to be creative.[12] Other traits associated with creative people include independence, self-confidence, risk taking, an internal locus of control, tolerance for ambiguity, and perseverance in the face of frustration.[13]

Three-Component Model of Creativity   What can individuals and organizations do to stimulate employee creativity? The best answer to this question lies in the **three-component model of creativity**.[14] Based on an extensive body of research, this model proposes that individual creativity essentially requires expertise, creative-thinking skills, and intrinsic task motivation (see Exhibit 4-4). Studies confirm that the higher the level of each of these three components, the higher the creativity.

EXHIBIT 4-4   The Three Components of Creativity

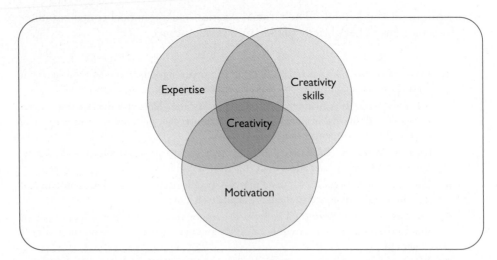

1. *Expertise* is the foundation for all creative work. The film writer, producer, and director Quentin Tarantino spent his youth working in a video rental store, where he built up an encyclopedic knowledge of movies. The potential for creativity is enhanced when individuals have abilities, knowledge, proficiencies, and similar expertise in the field of their endeavors.

2. The second component is *creative-thinking skills.* This encompasses personality characteristics associated with creativity, the ability to use analogies, as well as the talent to see the familiar in a different light. The effective use of analogies allows decision makers to apply an idea from one context to another. One of the most famous examples in which analogy resulted in a creative breakthrough was Alexander Graham Bell's observation that it might be possible to take concepts of how the ear operates and apply them to his "talking box." Some people have developed their creative skills because they are able to see problems in a new way. They're able to make the strange familiar and the familiar strange. For instance, most of us think of hens laying eggs, but how many of us have considered that a hen is only an egg's way of making another egg?

3. The final component in the three-component model of creativity is *intrinsic task motivation.* This is the desire to work on something because it's interesting, involving, exciting, satisfying, or personally challenging. This motivational component is what turns creativity *potential* into *actual* creative ideas. Importantly, an individual's work environment can have a significant effect on intrinsic motivation. Work-environment stimulants that have been found to foster creativity include a culture that encourages the flow of ideas, fair and constructive judgment of ideas, and rewards and recognition for creative work; sufficient financial, material, and information resources; freedom to decide what work is to be done and how to do it; a supervisor who communicates effectively, shows confidence in others, and supports the work group; and work-group members who support and trust each other.[15]

HOW DO ORGANIZATIONS ACTUALLY MAKE DECISIONS?

Are decision makers in organizations rational? Do they carefully assess problems, identify all relevant criteria, use their creativity to identify all viable alternatives, and painstakingly evaluate every alternative to find an optimal choice? For novice decision makers with little experience, for decision makers faced with simple problems that have few alternative courses of action, or when the cost of searching out and evaluating alternatives is low, the rational model provides a fairly accurate description of the decision process.[16] However, such situations are the exception. Most decisions in the real world don't follow the rational model. For instance, people are usually content to find an acceptable or reasonable solution to their problem rather than an optimal one. As such, decision makers generally make limited use of their creativity. Next, let's examine how most decisions in organizations are actually made.

Bounded Rationality

When you considered which college to attend, did you look at every viable alternative? Did you carefully identify all the criteria that were important in your decision? Did you evaluate each alternative against the criteria so you could find the optimal college? We expect the answers to these questions are all probably "No." Well, don't feel bad. Few people made their college choice this way. Instead of optimizing, you probably satisfied.

When faced with a complex problem, most people respond by reducing the problem to a level at which it can be readily understood. This is because the limited information-processing capability of human beings makes it impossible to assimilate and understand all the information necessary to optimize.[17] So people *satisfice*; that is, they seek solutions that are satisfactory and sufficient.

> *—The limited information-processing capability of human beings makes it impossible to assimilate and understand all the information necessary to optimize.*

Because the capacity of the human mind for formulating and solving complex problems is far too small to meet the requirements for full rationality, individuals operate within the confines of **bounded rationality**. They construct simplified models that extract the essential features from problems without capturing all their complexity.[18] Individuals can then behave rationally within the limits of the simple model.

How does bounded rationality work for the typical individual? Once a problem is identified, the search for criteria and alternatives begins, but the list of criteria is likely to be far from exhaustive. The decision maker will identify a limited list of the more conspicuous choices. These are the choices that are easy to find and that tend to be highly visible. In most cases, they will represent familiar criteria and previously tried-and-true solutions. Once this limited set of alternatives is identified, the decision maker will begin reviewing them. But the review will not be comprehensive—not all the alternatives will be carefully evaluated. Instead, the decision maker will begin with alternatives that differ only in a relatively small degree from the choice currently in effect. Following along familiar and well-worn paths, the decision maker proceeds to review alternatives only until he or she identifies an alternative that is "good enough"—one that meets an acceptable level of performance. The first alternative that meets the "good enough" criterion ends the search. So the final solution represents a satisficing choice rather than an optimal one.

One of the more interesting aspects of bounded rationality is that the order in which alternatives are considered is critical in determining which alternative is selected. Because decision makers use simple and limited models, they typically begin by identifying alternatives that are obvious, ones with which they are familiar, and those not too far from the status quo. The solutions that depart least from the status quo and meet the decision criteria are those most likely to be selected. A unique and creative alternative may present an optimizing solution to the problem; however, it's unlikely to be chosen because an acceptable solution will be identified well before the decision maker is required to search very far beyond the status quo.

Common Biases and Errors

An accumulating body of research tells us that decision makers also allow systematic biases and errors to creep into their judgments.[19] These come out of attempts to minimize effort and shortcut the decision process. In many instances, these shortcuts are helpful. However, they can lead to severe distortions from rationality. The following material highlights the most common distortions.

Overconfidence Bias   It's been said that "No problem in judgment and decision making is more prevalent and more potentially catastrophic than overconfidence."[20] When we're given factual questions and asked to judge the probability that our answers are correct, we tend to be far too optimistic. For instance, studies have found that when people say they're 65 to 70 percent confident that they're right, they are actually correct only about 50 percent of the time.[21] And when they say they're 100 percent sure, they tend to be 70 to 85 percent correct.[22]

From an organizational standpoint, one of the more interesting findings related to overconfidence is that those individuals whose intellectual and interpersonal abilities are *weakest* are most likely to overestimate their performance and ability.[23] Thus, as managers and employees become more knowledgeable about an issue, the less likely they are to display overconfidence.[24] In addition, overconfidence is most likely to surface when organizational members are considering issues or problems that are outside their area of expertise.[25]

—As managers and employees become more knowledgeable about an issue, the less likely they are to display overconfidence.

Anchoring Bias   The **anchoring bias** is a tendency to fixate on initial information. Once set, we then fail to adequately adjust for subsequent information.[26] The anchoring bias occurs because the mind appears to give a disproportionate amount of emphasis to the first information it receives. So initial impressions, ideas, prices, and estimates carry undue weight relative to information received later.

Consider the role of anchoring in negotiations and interviews. Any time a negotiation takes place, so does anchoring. As soon as someone states a number, your ability to objectively ignore that number has been compromised. For instance, when a prospective employer asks how much you were making in your prior job, your answer typically anchors the employer's offer. You may want to keep this in mind when you negotiate your salary, but remember to set the anchor only as high as you realistically can (in other words, it probably won't work to ask for as much as Donald Trump makes).

Confirmation Bias   The **confirmation bias** represents a specific case of selective perception. We seek out information that reaffirms our past choices, and we discount information that contradicts past judgments.[27] We also tend to accept information at face value that confirms our preconceived views, while being critical and skeptical of information that challenges these views. Therefore, the information we gather is typically biased toward supporting views we already hold.

Availability Bias   The **availability bias** is the tendency for people to base their judgments on information that is readily available to them.[28] Events that evoke emotions, that are particularly vivid, or that have occurred more recently tend to be more available in our memory. The availability bias explains why many more people think flying is more dangerous than driving. Although flying is indeed much safer than driving, the media gives a lot more attention to air accidents. Consequently, we tend to overstate the risk of flying and understate the risk of driving. The availability bias can also explain why managers, when doing annual performance appraisals, tend to give more weight to recent behaviors of an employee than to behaviors of six or nine months earlier.

Representative Bias   Many inner-city African-American male teenagers in the United States talk about the goal of playing basketball in the NBA.[29] In reality, these young people have a far better chance of becoming medical doctors than they do of playing in the NBA, but these kids are suffering from a **representative bias**. They tend to assess the likelihood of an occurrence by inappropriately considering the current situation as identical to past situations. They hear about a young man from their neighborhood who went on to play professional basketball 10 years ago, or they watch NBA games on television and think that those players are like them.

We are all guilty of falling into a representative bias at times. Managers, for example, frequently predict the performance of a new product by relating it to a previous product's success. Or if three graduates from the same college were hired and turned out to be poor performers, managers may predict that a current job applicant from the same college will not be a good employee.

Escalation of Commitment   Staying with a decision even when there is clear evidence that it's wrong is **escalation of commitment**. [30] It has been well documented that individuals escalate commitment to a failing course of action when they view themselves as responsible for the failure. [31] That is, they "throw good money after bad" to demonstrate that their initial decision wasn't wrong and to avoid having to admit they made a mistake. Escalation of commitment is also congruent with evidence that people try to appear consistent in what they say and do. Increasing commitment to previous actions conveys consistency.

Escalation of commitment has obvious implications for managerial decisions. Given that consistency is a characteristic often associated with effective leaders, managers—in an effort to appear effective—may be motivated to be consistent when switching to another course of action may be preferable. In actuality, effective managers are those who are able to differentiate between situations in which persistence will pay off and situations in which it will not.

Randomness Error   Human beings have a lot of difficulty dealing with chance. Most of us like to believe we have some control over our world and our destiny. Although we undoubtedly can control a good part of our future by rational decision making, the truth is that the world will always contain random events. Our tendency to believe we can predict the outcome of random events is the **randomness error**.

Decision making becomes impaired when we try to create meaning out of random events. One of the most serious impairments caused by random events is when we turn imaginary patterns into superstitions. [32] These can be completely contrived ("I never make important decisions on a Friday the 13th") or evolve from a certain pattern of behavior that has been reinforced previously ("Tiger Woods often wears a red shirt during the final round of a golf tournament because he won many junior golf tournaments while wearing red shirts"). Although many of us engage in some superstitious behavior, it can be debilitating when it affects daily judgments or biases major decisions. At the extreme, some decision makers become controlled by their superstitions—making it nearly impossible for them to change routines or process new information objectively.

Hindsight Bias   The **hindsight bias** is the tendency for us to believe falsely, after an outcome is actually known, that we would have accurately predicted the outcome. [33] When something happens and we have accurate feedback on the outcome, we seem to be pretty good at concluding that this outcome was relatively obvious. For instance, a lot more people seem to have been sure about the inevitability of who would win the Super Bowl on the day *after* the game than they were the day *before*. [34]

The hindsight bias seems to be a result of both selective memory and our ability to reconstruct earlier predictions. We apparently aren't very good at recalling the way an uncertain event appeared to us *before* we find out the actual results of that event. However, we seem to be fairly well adept at reconstructing the past by overestimating what we knew beforehand based upon what we learned later.

Intuition

Intuitive decision making is an unconscious process created out of distilled experience. It doesn't necessarily operate independently of rational analysis; rather, the two complement each other. Importantly, intuition can be a powerful force in decision making.

Research on chess playing provides an excellent illustration of how intuition works.[35] Novice chess players and grand masters were shown an actual, but unfamiliar, chess game with about 25 pieces on the board. After 5 or 10 seconds, the pieces were removed and each participant was asked to reconstruct the pieces by position. On average, the grand master could put 23 or 24 pieces in their correct squares, while the novice was able to replace only 6. Then the exercise was changed. This time the pieces were placed randomly on the board. Again, the novice got only about 6 correct, but so did the grand master! The second exercise demonstrated that the grand master didn't have any better memory than the novice. What the grand master did have was the ability, based on the experience of having played thousands of chess games, to recognize patterns and clusters of pieces that occur on chessboards in the course of games. Studies further show that chess professionals can play 50 or more games simultaneously, in which decisions often must be made in only seconds, and exhibit only a moderately lower level of skill than when playing one game under tournament conditions, where decisions take half an hour or longer. The expert's experience allows him or her to recognize the pattern in a situation and draw on previously learned information associated with that pattern to arrive at a decision choice quickly. The result is that the intuitive decision maker can decide rapidly based on what appears to be very limited information.

For most of the twentieth century, experts believed that the use of intuition by decision makers was irrational or ineffective. That's no longer the case. There is growing recognition that rational analysis has been overemphasized and that, in certain instances, relying on intuition can improve decision making.

When are people most likely to use intuitive decision making? Eight conditions have been identified: (1) when a high level of uncertainty exists; (2) when there is little precedent to draw on; (3) when variables are less scientifically predictable; (4) when "facts" are limited; (5) when facts don't clearly point the way; (6) when analytical data are of little use; (7) when there are several plausible alternative solutions from which to choose, with good arguments for each; and (8) when time is limited and there is pressure to come up with the right decision.[36]

Individual Differences

Decision making in practice is characterized by bounded rationality, common biases and errors, and the use of intuition. In addition, individual differences create deviations from the rational model. Let's examine two individual-difference variables.

Personality   Though to date little research has been done on personality and decision making, the studies that have been conducted suggest that personality does influence decision making. Some research has shown that specific facets of conscientiousness (see Chapter 3)—rather than the broad trait itself—affect escalation of commitment.[37]

Interestingly, one study revealed that the two facets of conscientiousness—achievement striving and dutifulness—actually had opposite effects on escalation of commitment. Achievement-striving people were more likely to escalate their commitment, whereas dutiful people were less likely to escalate. Why might this be the case? Generally, achievement-oriented people hate to fail, so they escalate their commitment hoping to forestall failure. Dutiful people, however, will be more inclined to do what they see as best for the organization.

Gender   Recent research on rumination—the act of contemplating or reflecting at length—offers insights into gender differences in decision making.[38] In terms of decision making, it means overthinking about problems. Twenty years of study find that women spend much more time than men in analyzing the past, present, and future. They're more likely to overanalyze problems before making a decision and rehash the decision once it has been made. Thus, women in general are more likely than men to engage in rumination. On the positive side, this is likely to lead to more careful consideration of problems and choices. However, it can make problems harder to solve, can increase regret over past decisions, and can increase depression (women are nearly twice as likely as men to develop depression).[39]

Why women ruminate more than men is not clear. Several theories have been suggested. One view is that parents encourage and reinforce the expression of sadness and anxiety more in girls than in boys. Another theory is that women, more than men, base their self-esteem and well-being on what others think of them. A third theory is that women are more empathetic and more affected by events in others' lives, so they have more to ruminate about.

This rumination tendency appears to be moderated by age. Gender differences surface early. By age 11, for instance, girls are ruminating more than boys, but this gender difference seems to lessen with age. Differences are largest during young adulthood and smallest after age 65, when both men and women ruminate the least.[40]

Organizational Constraints

Organizations can constrain decision makers, creating deviations from the rational model. Managers, for instance, shape their decisions to reflect the organization's performance evaluation and reward system, to comply with the organization's formal regulations, and to meet organizationally imposed time constraints. Previous organizational decisions also act as precedents to constrain current decisions.

Performance Evaluation   Managers are strongly influenced in their decision making by the criteria on which they are evaluated. If a division manager believes that the manufacturing plants for which he is responsible are operating best when he hears nothing negative, we shouldn't be surprised to find his plant managers spending a good part of their time ensuring that negative information doesn't reach the division boss. Similarly, if a college dean believes that an instructor should never fail more than 10 percent of her students—to fail more reflects on the instructor's ability to teach—we should expect that instructors who want to receive favorable evaluations will decide not to fail too many students.

Reward Systems   An organization's reward system influences decision makers by suggesting to them what choices are preferable in terms of personal payoff. For example, if the organization rewards risk aversion, managers are more likely to make conservative decisions. From the 1930s through the mid-1980s, General Motors consistently gave out promotions and bonuses to managers who kept a low profile, avoided controversy, and were good team players. The result was that GM managers became very adept at dodging tough issues and passing controversial decisions on to committees.

—The organization's reward system influences decision makers by suggesting to them what choices are preferable in terms of personal payoff.

Formal Regulations   David Gonzalez, a shift manager at a Taco Bell restaurant in San Antonio, Texas, describes constraints he faces on his job: "I've got rules and regulations covering almost every decision I make—from how to make a burrito to how often I need to clean the restrooms. My job doesn't come with much freedom of choice." David's situation is not unique. All but the smallest of organizations create rules, policies, procedures, and other formalized regulations to standardize the behavior of their members. By programming decisions, organizations are able to get individuals to achieve high levels of performance without paying for the years of experience that would be necessary in the absence of regulations. Of course, in so doing, they limit the decision maker's choices.

System-Imposed Time Constraints   Organizations impose deadlines on decisions, such as department budgets needing to be completed by the following Friday or the report on new-product development needing to be ready for executive committee review by the first of the month. A host of decisions must be made quickly to stay competitive and keep customers satisfied. In fact, almost all important decisions come with explicit deadlines. These conditions create time pressures on decision makers and often make it difficult, if not impossible, to gather all the information desired before making a final choice.

Historical Precedents   Decisions aren't made in a vacuum. They have a context. In fact, individual decisions are more accurately characterized as points in a stream of decisions.

Decisions made in the past are ghosts that haunt decision makers, as commitments tend to constrain current options. For example, in government budget decisions, it's common knowledge that the largest determining factor of the size of any given year's budget is the prior year's budget.[41] Choices made today, therefore, are largely a result of choices made over the years.

Cultural Differences

The cultural background of the decision maker can have significant influence on the selection of problems, depth of analysis, importance placed on logic and rationality, and whether organizational decisions should be made autocratically by an individual manager or collectively in groups.[42] Cultures, for example, differ in terms of time orientation, the importance of rationality, their belief in the ability of people to solve problems, and their preference for collective decision making. Differences in time orientation help us understand why managers in Egypt will make decisions at a much slower and more deliberate pace than their U.S. counterparts. Whereas rationality is valued in North America, that's not true everywhere in the world. A North American manager might make an important decision intuitively but knows that it's important to appear to proceed in a rational fashion because rationality is highly valued in the West. In countries such as Iran, where rationality is not deified, efforts to appear rational are not necessary.

Some cultures emphasize solving problems, while others focus on accepting situations as they are. The United States falls in the former category; Thailand and Indonesia are examples of cultures that fall into the latter category. Because problem-solving managers believe they can and should change situations to their benefit, managers in the United States might identify a problem long before their Thai or Indonesian counterparts would choose to recognize it as such. As another example, managerial decision making in Japan is much more group oriented than in the United States. The Japanese value conformity and cooperation. So before Japanese CEOs make an important decision, they collect a large amount of information, which is then used in consensus-forming group decisions.

ETHICS IN DECISION MAKING

No contemporary discussion of decision making would be complete without the inclusion of ethics because ethical considerations should be an important criterion in organizational decision making. In this chapter's final section, we present three ways to frame decisions ethically and look at how ethical standards vary across national cultures.

An individual can use three different criteria in making ethical choices:[43]

1. The *utilitarian* criterion, in which decisions are made solely on the basis of their outcomes or consequences. The goal of **utilitarianism** is to provide the greatest good for the greatest number. This view tends to dominate business decision making. It is consistent with such goals as efficiency, productivity, and high profits.

2. A focus on *rights*. This calls on individuals to make decisions consistent with fundamental liberties and privileges as set forth in documents such as the Bill of Rights. An emphasis on rights in decision making means respecting and protecting the basic rights of individuals, such as the right to privacy, to free speech, and to due process. Use of this criterion would protect **whistle-blowers**—individuals who report to the press or government agencies any unethical or illegal practices of their employers—on the grounds of their right to free speech.

3. A focus on *justice*. This requires individuals to impose and enforce rules fairly and impartially so that an equitable distribution of benefits and costs results. Union members typically favor this view. It justifies paying people the same wage for a given job, regardless of performance differences, and using seniority as the primary determination in making layoff decisions.

Each of these three criteria has advantages and liabilities. A focus on utilitarianism promotes efficiency and productivity, but it can result in ignoring the rights of some individuals, particularly those with minority representation in the organization. The use of rights as a criterion protects individuals from injury and is consistent with freedom and privacy, but it can create an overly legalistic work environment that hinders productivity and efficiency. A focus on justice protects the interests of the underrepresented and less powerful, but it can encourage a sense of entitlement that reduces risk taking, innovation, and productivity.

IMPLICATIONS FOR MANAGERS

Perception   Individuals behave in a given manner based not on the way their external environment actually is but, rather, on what they see or believe it to be. It's the employee's perception of a situation that becomes the basis for behavior. Therefore, to be able to influence productivity, it's necessary to assess how workers perceive their jobs.

Dissatisfaction with working conditions or the belief that promotion opportunities in the organization are lacking are judgments based on attempts to create meaning out of one's job. The employee's conclusion that a job is good or bad is an interpretation. Managers must spend time understanding how each individual interprets reality, and when there is a significant difference between what is seen and what exists, the managers must try to eliminate the distortions. Failure to deal with the differences when individuals perceive the job in negative terms will result in increased absenteeism and turnover and lower job satisfaction.

Individual Decision Making   What can managers do to improve their decision making? We offer five suggestions:

1. *Analyze the situation.* Adjust your decision-making approach to the national culture you're operating in and to the criteria your organization evaluates and rewards. For instance, if you're in a country that doesn't value rationality, don't feel compelled to follow the rational decision-making model or even to try to make your decisions appear rational.

2. Similarly, organizations differ in terms of the importance they place on risk, the use of groups, and the like. *Adjust your decision approach to ensure that it's compatible with the organization's culture.*

3. *Be aware of biases, then try to minimize their impact.* Exhibit 4-5 offers some suggestions.

EXHIBIT 4-5   Toward Reducing Biases and Errors

Focus on goals. Without goals, you can't be rational, you don't know what information you need, you don't know which information is relevant and which is irrelevant, you'll find it difficult to choose between alternatives, and you're far more likely to experience regret over the choices you make. Clear goals make decision making easier and help you to eliminate options that are inconsistent with your interests.

Look for information that disconfirms your beliefs. One of the most effective means for counteracting overconfidence and the confirmation and hindsight biases is to actively look for information that contradicts your beliefs and assumptions. When we overtly consider various ways we could be wrong, we challenge our tendencies to think we're smarter than we actually are.

Don't try to create meaning out of random events. The educated mind has been trained to look for cause-and-effect relationships. When something happens, we ask why. And when we can't find reasons, we often invent them. You have to accept that some events in life are outside your control. Ask yourself if patterns can be meaningfully explained or whether they are merely coincidental. Don't attempt to create meaning out of coincidence.

Increase your options. No matter how many options you've identified, your final choice can be no better than the best of the option set you've selected. This argues for increasing your decision alternatives and for using creativity in developing a wide range of diverse choices. The more alternatives you can generate, and the more diverse those alternatives, the greater your chance of finding an outstanding one.

Source: S. P. Robbins, *Decide & Conquer: Making Winning Decisions and Taking Control of Your Life* (Upper Saddle River, NJ: Financial Times/Prentice Hall, 2004), pp. 164–68.

4. *Combine rational analysis with intuition.* These are not conflicting approaches to decision making. By using both, you can actually improve your decision-making effectiveness. As you gain managerial experience, you should feel increasingly confident in imposing your intuitive processes on top of your rational analysis.

5. *Enhance your creativity.* Look for novel solutions to problems, attempt to see problems in new ways, and use analogies. In addition, try to remove work and organizational barriers that might impede your creativity.

CHAPTER 5

Motivation Concepts

After studying this chapter, you should be able to:

1. Outline the motivation process.
2. Describe Maslow's hierarchy of needs.
3. Summarize criticisms of Two-Factor Theory.
4. List the characteristics that high achievers prefer in a job.
5. Summarize the types of goals that increase performance.
6. Discuss ways self-efficacy can be increased.
7. State the impact of underrewarding employees.
8. Clarify the key relationships in expectancy theory.

Motivation is one of the most frequently researched topics in OB. One reason for its popularity is revealed in a recent Gallup poll, which found that a majority of U.S. employees—55 percent to be exact—have no enthusiasm for their work.[1] Clearly, this suggests a problem, at least in the United States. The good news is that all this research provides us with considerable insights into how to improve motivation. In this chapter, we discuss the basics of motivation and assess a number of early and contemporary theories of motivation.

DEFINING MOTIVATION

We define **motivation** as the processes that account for an individual's intensity, direction, and persistence of effort toward attaining a goal.[2] While general motivation is concerned with effort toward *any* goal, we'll narrow the focus to *organizational* goals in order to reflect our singular interest in work-related behavior.

Let's examine the three key elements in our definition:

- *Intensity* is concerned with how hard a person tries.
- However, high intensity is unlikely to lead to favorable job-performance outcomes unless the effort is channeled in a *direction* that benefits the organization.

- Finally, motivation has a *persistence* dimension. This is a measure of how long a person can maintain effort.

Early Theories of Motivation

The 1950s were a fruitful period in the development of motivation concepts. Three specific theories were formulated during this period that, although heavily attacked and now questionable in terms of validity, are probably still the best-known explanations for employee motivation: the hierarchy of needs theory, Theories X and Y, and the two-factor theory. As you'll see later in this chapter, we have since developed more valid explanations of motivation, but you should know these early theories for at least two reasons: (1) They represent a foundation from which contemporary theories have grown, and (2) practicing managers still regularly use these theories and their terminology in explaining employee motivation.

Hierarchy of Needs Theory

It's probably safe to say that the most well-known theory of motivation is Abraham Maslow's **hierarchy of needs**.[3] Maslow hypothesized that within every human being there exists a hierarchy of five needs:

1. *Physiological:* Includes hunger, thirst, shelter, sex, and other bodily needs.
2. *Safety:* Includes security and protection from physical and emotional harm.
3. *Social:* Includes affection, belongingness, acceptance, and friendship.
4. *Esteem:* Includes internal esteem factors, such as self-respect, autonomy, and achievement, and external esteem factors, such as status, recognition, and attention.
5. *Self-actualization:* The drive to become what one is capable of becoming; includes growth, achieving one's potential, and self-fulfillment.

As each of these needs becomes substantially satisfied, the next need becomes dominant. In terms of Exhibit 5-1, the individual moves up the steps of the hierarchy.

EXHIBIT 5-1   Maslow's Hierarchy of Needs

Source: A. H. Maslow, *Motivation and Personality,* 3rd ed., R. D. Frager and J. Fadiman (eds.). © 1997. Adapted by permission of Pearson Education, Inc., Upper Saddle River, New Jersey.

From the standpoint of motivation, the theory would say that although no need is ever fully gratified, a substantially satisfied need no longer motivates. If you want to motivate someone, according to Maslow, you must understand what level of the hierarchy that person is currently on and focus on satisfying the needs at or above that level.

Maslow separated the five needs into higher and lower orders. Physiological and safety needs were described as lower-order needs, and social, esteem, and self-actualization needs are categorized as higher-order needs. The differentiation between the two orders was made on the premise that higher-order needs are satisfied internally (within the person), whereas lower-order needs are predominantly satisfied externally (by things such as pay, union contracts, and tenure).

Maslow's needs theory has received wide recognition, particularly among practicing managers. Unfortunately, however, research does not validate the theory. Maslow provided no empirical substantiation, and several studies that sought to validate the theory found no support for it.[4]

Theory X and Theory Y

Douglas McGregor proposed two distinct views of human beings: one basically negative, labeled **Theory X**, and the other basically positive, labeled **Theory Y**.[5] After viewing the way in which managers dealt with employees, McGregor concluded that managers' views of the nature of human beings are based on a certain grouping of assumptions and that managers tend to mold their behavior toward employees according to these assumptions.

Under Theory X, four assumptions are held by managers:

1. Employees inherently dislike work and, whenever possible, will attempt to avoid it.
2. Since employees dislike work, they must be coerced, controlled, or threatened with punishment to achieve goals.
3. Employees will avoid responsibilities and seek formal direction whenever possible.
4. Most workers place security above all other factors associated with work and will display little ambition.

In contrast to these negative views about the nature of human beings, McGregor listed the four positive assumptions that he called Theory Y:

1. Employees can view work as being as natural as rest or play.
2. People will exercise self-direction and self-control if they are committed to the objectives.
3. The average person can learn to accept, even seek, responsibility.
4. The ability to make innovative decisions is widely dispersed throughout the population and is not necessarily the sole province of those in management positions.

What are the motivational implications if you accept McGregor's analysis? The answer is best expressed in the framework presented by Maslow. Theory X assumes that lower-order needs dominate individuals. Theory Y assumes that higher-order needs dominate individuals. McGregor himself held to the belief that Theory Y assumptions were more valid than Theory X. Therefore, he proposed such ideas as participative decision making, responsible and challenging jobs, and good group relations as approaches that would maximize an employee's job motivation.

OB theories need to have empirical support for us to accept them. Unfortunately, there is no evidence to confirm that either set of assumptions is valid or that accepting Theory Y assumptions and altering one's actions accordingly will lead to more motivated workers.

Two-Factor Theory

The **two-factor theory**—also called *motivation–hygiene theory*—was proposed by psychologist Frederick Herzberg.[6] In the belief that an individual's relation to work is basic and that one's attitude toward work can very well determine success or failure, Herzberg investigated the question "What do people want from their jobs?" He asked people to describe, in detail, situations in which they felt exceptionally *good* or *bad* about their jobs. These responses were then tabulated and categorized.

From the categorized responses, Herzberg concluded that the replies people gave when they felt good about their jobs were significantly different from the replies given when they felt bad. As seen in Exhibit 5-2, certain characteristics tend to be consistently related to job satisfaction and others to job dissatisfaction. While satisfied respondents tended to cite intrinsic factors, such as advancement, recognition, and responsibility, dissatisfied respondents tended to cite extrinsic factors, such as supervision, pay, and working conditions.

The data suggest, said Herzberg, that the opposite of satisfaction is not dissatisfaction, as was traditionally believed. Removing dissatisfying characteristics from a job does not necessarily make the job satisfying. Herzberg proposed that his findings indicated the existence of a dual continuum: The opposite of "satisfaction" is "no satisfaction," and the opposite of "dissatisfaction" is "no dissatisfaction."

According to Herzberg, the factors leading to job satisfaction are separate and distinct from those that lead to job dissatisfaction. Therefore, managers who seek to eliminate factors that can create job dissatisfaction may bring about peace but not necessarily motivation. They will be placating their workforce rather than motivating them. As a result, conditions surrounding the job, such as quality of supervision, pay, company policies, physical working conditions, relations with others, and job security, were characterized by Herzberg as **hygiene factors**. When they're adequate, people will not be dissatisfied; neither will they be satisfied. To motivate people on their jobs, Herzberg suggested emphasizing factors associated with the work itself or to outcomes directly derived from it, such as promotional opportunities, opportunities for personal growth, recognition, responsibility, and achievement. These are the characteristics that people find intrinsically rewarding.

The two-factor theory has not been well supported in the literature, and it has many detractors.[7] The criticisms of the theory include the following:

1. The procedure that Herzberg used is limited by its methodology. When things are going well, people tend to take credit themselves. Contrarily, they blame failure on the extrinsic environment.

EXHIBIT 5-2 Comparison of Satisfiers and Dissatisfiers

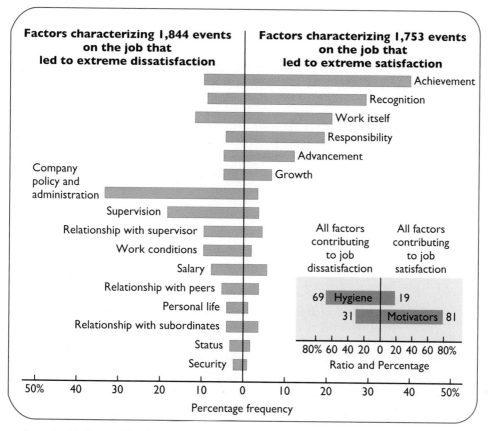

2. The reliability of Herzberg's methodology is questioned. Raters have to make interpretations, so they may contaminate the findings by interpreting one response in one manner while treating a similar response differently.

3. No overall measure of satisfaction was utilized. A person may dislike part of a job yet still think the job is acceptable overall.

4. The theory is inconsistent with previous research. The two-factor theory ignores situational variables.

5. Herzberg assumed a relationship between satisfaction and productivity, but the research methodology he used looked only at satisfaction, not at productivity. To make such research relevant, one must assume a strong relationship between satisfaction and productivity.

Regardless of criticisms, Herzberg's theory has been widely read and few managers are unfamiliar with his recommendations. It's important to realize that even though we may intuitively *like* a theory, that does not mean that we should accept it. Sometimes science backs up intuition, and sometimes it doesn't.

CONTEMPORARY THEORIES OF MOTIVATION

The previous theories are well-known but, unfortunately, have not held up well under close examination. However, all is not lost. A number of contemporary theories have one thing in common: Each has a reasonable degree of valid supporting documentation. Of course, this doesn't mean that the theories we are about to introduce are unquestionably right. We call them *contemporary theories* not because they necessarily were developed recently but because they represent the current state of thinking in explaining employee motivation.

McClelland's Theory of Needs

McClelland's theory of needs, developed by David McClelland and his associates, focuses on three needs:[8]

1. *Need for achievement:* The drive to excel, to achieve in relation to a set of standards, to strive to succeed.
2. *Need for power:* The need to make others behave in a way that they would not have behaved otherwise.
3. *Need for affiliation:* The desire for friendly and close interpersonal relationships.

Some people have a compelling drive to succeed. They're striving for personal achievement rather than the rewards of success per se. This drive is the achievement need (*nAch*). From research into the achievement need, McClelland found that high achievers differentiate themselves from others by their desire to do things better.[9] They seek situations in which they can attain personal responsibility for finding solutions to problems, in which they can receive rapid feedback on their performance so they can determine easily whether they are improving or not, and in which they can set moderately challenging goals. High achievers are not gamblers; they dislike succeeding by chance. They prefer the challenge of working at a problem and accepting the personal responsibility for success or failure rather than leaving the outcome to chance or the actions of others. Importantly, they avoid what they perceive to be very easy or very difficult tasks. They prefer tasks of intermediate difficulty.

High achievers perform best when they perceive their probability of success as being 0.5, that is, when they estimate that they have a 50–50 chance of success. They dislike gambling with high odds because they get no achievement satisfaction from happenstance success. Similarly, they dislike low odds (high probability of success) because then there is no challenge to their skills. They like to set goals that require stretching themselves a little.

The need for power (*nPow*) is the desire to have impact, to be influential, and to control others. Individuals high in nPow enjoy being in charge, strive for influence over others, prefer to be placed into competitive and status-oriented situations, and tend to be more concerned with prestige and gaining influence over others than with effective performance.

The third need isolated by McClelland is affiliation (*nAff*). This need has received the least attention from researchers. Individuals with a high affiliation motive strive for friendship, prefer cooperative situations rather than competitive ones, and desire relationships that involve a high degree of mutual understanding.

Some reasonably well-supported predictions can be made based on the relationship between achievement need and job performance. Although less research has been done on power and affiliation needs, consistent findings are found here, too. First, individuals with a high need to achieve prefer job situations with personal responsibility, feedback, and an intermediate degree of risk. When these characteristics are prevalent, high achievers will be strongly motivated. The evidence consistently demonstrates, for instance, that high achievers are successful in entrepreneurial activities such as running their own businesses and managing a self-contained unit within a large organization.[10] Second, a high need to achieve does not necessarily lead to being a good manager, especially in large organizations. People with a high achievement need are interested in how well they do personally and not in influencing others to do well. Salespeople high in nAch do not necessarily make good sales managers, and the good general manager in a large organization does not typically have a high need to achieve.[11] Third, the needs for affiliation and power tend to be closely related to managerial success. The best managers are high in the need for power and low in the need for affiliation.[12] Finally, employees have been successfully trained to stimulate their achievement needs. So, if the job calls for a high achiever, management can select a person with a high nAch or develop its own candidate through achievement training.[13]

Cognitive Evaluation Theory

Cognitive evaluation theory proposes that the introduction of extrinsic rewards, such as pay, for work effort that was previously intrinsically rewarding (due to the pleasure associated with the content of the work itself) tends to decrease overall motivation. In other words, when extrinsic rewards are given to someone for performing an interesting task, it causes intrinsic interest in the task itself to decline. Cognitive evaluation theory has been extensively researched, and a large number of studies have been supportive.[14]

Why would a decrease in intrinsic motivation occur? The popular explanation is that the individual experiences a loss of control over his or her own behavior so that the previous intrinsic motivation diminishes. Furthermore, the elimination of extrinsic rewards can produce a shift—from an external to an internal explanation—in an individual's perception of causation of why he or she works on a task. If you're reading a novel a week because your English literature instructor requires you to, you can attribute your reading behavior to an external source. However, after the course is over, if you find yourself continuing to read a novel a week, your natural inclination is to say "I must enjoy reading novels because I'm still reading one a week."

If the cognitive evaluation theory is valid, it should have major implications for managerial practices. It has been a truism among compensation specialists for years that if pay or other extrinsic rewards are to be effective motivators, they should be made contingent on an individual's performance. But, cognitive evaluation theorists would argue that this will only tend to decrease the internal satisfaction that the individual receives from doing the job. In fact, if cognitive evaluation theory is correct, it would make sense to make an individual's pay *noncontingent* on performance in order to avoid decreasing intrinsic motivation.

Although cognitive evaluation theory has received support, it has also had its share of attacks, specifically on the methodology used in these studies and in the interpretation of the findings. So can we say that when organizations use extrinsic motivators, such as pay and promotions and verbal rewards to stimulate workers' performance, they do so at the expense of reducing intrinsic interest and motivation in the work being done? The answer is not a simple "yes" or "no." Extrinsic rewards that are verbal (e.g., receiving praise from a supervisor or coworker) or tangible (e.g., money) can actually have different effects on people's intrinsic motivation. That is, verbal rewards increase intrinsic motivation, whereas tangible rewards undermine it. When people are told they will receive a tangible reward, they come to count on it and focus more on the reward than on the task. Verbal rewards, however, seem to keep people focused on the task and encourage them to do it better.

> *—Verbal rewards increase intrinsic motivation, whereas tangible rewards undermine it.*

What does all this mean? Managers need to provide intrinsic rewards in addition to extrinsic incentives, making the work interesting, providing recognition, and supporting employee growth and development. Employees who feel that what they do is within their control and a result of free choice are likely to be more motivated by their work and committed to their employers.

Goal-Setting Theory

From either a parent or a coach, you've probably heard the phrase "Just do your best. That's all anyone can ask for." But what does "do your best" mean? Do we ever know if we've achieved that vague goal? What if instead someone told you to shoot for something more specific, such as striving for 85 percent or higher in your English class? The research on **goal-setting theory** addresses these issues, and the findings, as you'll see, are impressive in terms of the effect that goal specificity, challenge, and feedback have on performance.

Specific goals produce a higher level of output than does the generalized goal of "do your best." The specificity of the goal itself seems to act as an internal stimulus. For instance, when a trucker commits to making 12 weekly round-trip hauls between Toronto and Buffalo, New York, this intention gives him a specific objective to strive to attain. We can say that, all things being equal, the trucker with a specific goal will outperform a counterpart operating with no goals or the generalized goal of "do your best."

If factors such as acceptance of the goals are held constant, we can also state that the more difficult the goal, the higher the level of performance. Of course, it's logical to assume that easier goals are more likely to be accepted. But once a hard task is accepted, the employee can be expected to exert a high level of effort to try to achieve it.

But why are people more motivated by difficult goals?[15]

- Difficult goals direct our attention to the task at hand and away from distractions.
- Difficult goals energize us because we have to work harder to attain them.
- When goals are difficult, people persist in striving to attain them.
- Difficult goals lead us to discover strategies that help us perform the job or task more effectively.

People will do better when they get feedback on how well they are progressing toward their goals because feedback helps to identify discrepancies between what they have done and what they want to do; that is, feedback acts to guide behavior. But all feedback is not equally potent. Self-generated feedback, which accrues when employees are able to monitor their own progress, has been shown to be a more powerful motivator than externally generated feedback.[16]

If employees have the opportunity to participate in the setting of their own goals, will they try harder? The evidence is mixed regarding the superiority of participative goals over assigned goals.[17] In some cases, participatively set goals elicited superior performance, while in other cases individuals performed best when assigned goals by their bosses. But a major advantage of participation may be in increasing acceptance of the goal itself as a desirable one toward which to work.[18] As we'll note shortly, commitment's important. If participation isn't used, then the purpose and importance of the goal must be explained clearly by the individual assigning the goal.[19]

Are there any contingencies in goal-setting theory, or can we take it as a universal truth that difficult and specific goals will *always* lead to higher performance? In addition to feedback, three other factors have been found to influence the goals–performance relationship: goal commitment, task characteristics, and national culture.

1. Goal-setting theory presupposes that an individual is committed to the goal. Behaviorally, this means that an individual (a) believes he or she can achieve the goal and (b) wants to achieve it. Goal commitment is most likely to occur when goals are made public, when the individual has an internal locus of control (see Chapter 3) and when the goals are self-set rather than assigned.[20]

2. Research indicates that goal-setting theory doesn't work equally well on all tasks. Instead, goals seem to have a more substantial effect on performance when tasks are simple rather than complex, well-learned rather than novel, and independent rather than interdependent.[21] On interdependent tasks, group goals are preferable.

3. Goal-setting theory is culture bound. It's well adapted to countries like the United States and Canada because its key components align reasonably well with North American cultures. It assumes that employees will be reasonably independent (not too high a score on power distance), that managers and employees will seek challenging goals (low in uncertainty avoidance), and that performance is considered important by both (high in achievement). So don't expect goal setting to lead always to higher employee performance in countries such as Portugal or Chile, where the opposite conditions exist.

Management by Objectives

Goal-setting theory has an impressive base of research support. But as a manager, how do you make goal setting operational? One answer to that question is that you install a management by objectives (MBO) program.

Management by objectives emphasizes participatively setting goals that are tangible, verifiable, and measurable. MBO's appeal lies undoubtedly in its emphasis on converting overall organizational objectives into specific objectives for organizational units and individual members. MBO operationalizes the concept of objectives by devising a process by which objectives cascade down through the organization. As depicted in Exhibit 5-3, the organization's overall objectives are translated into specific objectives for each succeeding level (that is, divisional, departmental, individual) in the organization. But because lower-unit managers jointly participate in setting

EXHIBIT 5-3   Cascading of Objectives

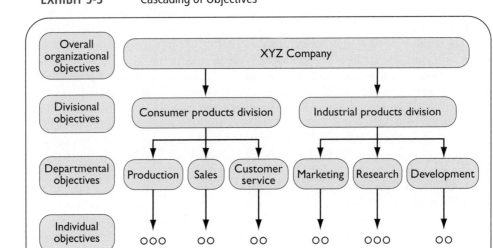

their own goals, MBO works from the *bottom up* as well as from the *top down*. The result is a hierarchy that links objectives at one level to those at the next level. For the individual employee, MBO provides specific personal performance objectives.

Four ingredients are common to MBO programs:

1. Goal specificity
2. Participation in decision making (including participation in the setting of goals or objectives)
3. An explicit time period
4. Performance feedback[22]

Many of the elements in MBO programs match goal-setting theory's propositions. For example, having an explicit time period to accomplish objectives matches goal-setting theory's emphasis on goal specificity. Similarly, feedback about goal progress is a critical element of goal-setting theory. The only area of possible disagreement between MBO and goal-setting theory relates to the issue of participation: MBO strongly advocates it, while goal-setting theory demonstrates that managers assigning goals is usually just as effective.

You'll find MBO programs in many business, health-care, educational, government, and nonprofit organizations. MBO's popularity should not be construed to mean that it always works. In a number of documented cases, MBO has been implemented but failed to meet management's expectations.[23] When MBO doesn't work, the culprits tend to be factors such as these:

- Unrealistic expectations regarding results
- Lack of commitment by top management
- An inability or unwillingness by management to allocate rewards based on goal accomplishment

Failures also can arise out of cultural incompatibilities. For instance, Fujitsu recently scrapped its MBO-type program because management found it didn't fit well with the Japanese culture's emphasis on minimizing risk and emphasizing long-term goals.

Self-Efficacy Theory

Self-efficacy theory (also known as *social cognitive theory* or *social learning theory*) refers to an individual's belief that he or she is capable of performing a task. In difficult situations, we find that people with low self-efficacy are more likely to lessen their effort or give up altogether, whereas those with high self-efficacy will try harder to master a challenge.[24] In addition, individuals high in self-efficacy seem to respond to negative feedback with increased effort and motivation, whereas those low in self-efficacy are likely to lessen their effort when given negative feedback.[25] Managers can help their employees achieve high levels of self-efficacy by bringing together goal-setting theory and self-efficacy theory.

Goal-setting theory and self-efficacy theory don't compete with one another; rather, they complement each other. See Exhibit 5-4. As the exhibit shows, when a manger sets difficult goals for employees, this leads employees to have a higher level of self-efficacy and also leads them to set higher goals for their own performances. Why is this the case? Research has shown that setting difficult goals for people communicates confidence. For example, imagine that your boss sets a high goal for you and you learn that it is higher than the goals she has set for your coworkers. How would you interpret this? As long as you don't feel you're being picked on, you probably would think "Well, I guess my boss thinks I'm capable of performing better than

EXHIBIT 5-4   Joint Effects of Goals and Self-Efficacy on Performance

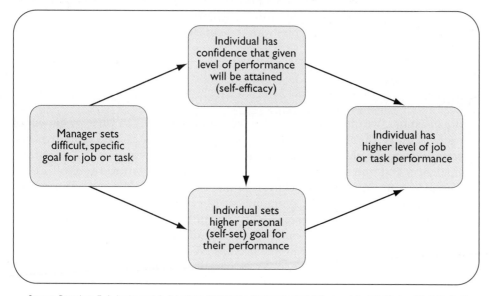

Source: Based on E. A. Locke and G. P. Latham, "Building a Practically Useful Theory of Goal Setting and Task Motivation: A 35-Year Odyssey," *American Psychologist,* September 2002, pp. 705–717.

others." This then sets into motion a psychological process in which you're more confident in yourself (higher self-efficacy) and set higher personal goals, causing you to perform better both inside and outside the workplace.

The researcher who developed self-efficacy theory, Albert Bandura, argues that self-efficacy can be increased in four ways:[26]

1. *Enactive mastery,* the most important source of increasing self-efficacy according to Bandura, is gaining relevant experience with the task or job. If I've been able to do the job successfully in the past, I'm more confident I'll be able to do it in the future.

2. *Vicarious modeling* is becoming more confident because you see someone else doing the task. Vicarious modeling is most effective when you see yourself as similar to the person you are observing (so watching Tiger Woods play a difficult golf shot is not likely to increase my confidence in being able to play the same shot).

3. *Verbal persuasion* is becoming more confident because someone convinces you that you have the skills necessary to be successful. Motivational speakers use this tactic a lot.

4. *Arousal,* Bandura argues, increases self-efficacy. Arousal leads to an energized state, which drives a person to complete the task. However, arousal doesn't always lead to better performance. If the task is something that requires a steadier, lower-key perspective (say, carefully editing a manuscript), arousal may in fact hurt performance.

Note that intelligence and personality are absent from Bandura's list. A lot of research shows that intelligence and personality (especially conscientiousness and emotional stability) can increase self-efficacy.[27] Those individual traits are so strongly related to self-efficacy (people who are intelligent, conscientious, and emotionally stable are much more likely to have high self-efficacy than those who score low on these characteristics) that some researchers would argue self-efficacy does not exist. What this means is that self-efficacy may simply be a by-product of a smart person with a confident personality and that the term *self-efficacy* is superfluous and unnecessary. Although Bandura strongly disagrees with this conclusion, more research on the issue is needed.

Equity Theory

In organizations, we often compare what we put into our jobs to what we get out of our jobs. **Equity theory** proposes that these comparisons can affect motivation. Specifically, employees compare their job inputs (effort, experience, education, competence) and outcomes (salary levels, raises, recognition) to those of others. We perceive our outcomes in relation to our inputs, and then we compare our outcome–input ratio with the outcome–input ratio of relevant others. This is shown in Exhibit 5-5. If we perceive our ratio to be equal to that of the relevant others with whom we compare ourselves, a state of equity is said to exist. We perceive our situation as fair—that justice prevails. When we see the ratio as unequal, we experience equity tension. When we see ourselves as underrewarded, the tension creates anger; when overrewarded, the tension creates guilt. J. Stacy Adams has proposed that this negative state of tension provides the motivation to do something to correct it.[28]

EXHIBIT 5-5   Equity Theory

Ratio Comparisons*	Perception
$\dfrac{O}{I_A} < \dfrac{O}{I_B}$	Inequity due to being underrewarded
$\dfrac{O}{I_A} = \dfrac{O}{I_B}$	Equity
$\dfrac{O}{I_A} > \dfrac{O}{I_B}$	Inequity due to being overrewarded

*Where $\dfrac{O}{I_A}$ represents the employee; and $\dfrac{O}{I_B}$ represents relevant others.

The referent that an employee selects adds to the complexity of equity theory. An employee can use four referent comparisons:

1. *Self-inside:* An employee's experiences in a different position inside the employee's current organization.
2. *Self-outside:* An employee's experiences in a situation or position outside the employee's current organization.
3. *Other-inside:* Another individual or group of individuals inside the employee's organization.
4. *Other-outside:* Another individual or group of individuals outside the employee's organization.

Employees might compare themselves to friends, neighbors, coworkers, or colleagues in other organizations or compare their present jobs with past jobs they themselves have had. Which referent an employee chooses will be influenced by the information the employee holds about referents, as well as by the attractiveness of the referent. This has led to focusing on four moderating variables:[29]

- *Gender.* Research shows that both men and women prefer same-sex comparisons. The research also demonstrates that women are typically paid less than men in comparable jobs and have lower pay expectations than men for the same work.[30] So a woman who uses another woman as a referent tends to calculate a lower comparative standard. This leads us to conclude that employees in jobs that are not sex segregated will make more cross-sex comparisons than those in jobs that are either male or female dominated. This also suggests that if women are tolerant of lower pay, it may be due to the comparative standard they use. Of course, employers' stereotypes about women (for example, the belief that women are less committed to the organization, or that "women's work" is less valuable) also may contribute to the pay gap.[31]
- *Length of tenure.* Employees with short tenure in their current organizations tend to have little information about others inside their organizations, so they rely on their own personal experiences. However, employees with long tenure rely more heavily on coworkers for comparison.

- *Level in the organization.* Upper-level employees, those in the professional ranks, tend to have better information about people in other organizations. Therefore, these types of employees will make more other–outside comparisons.
- *Amount of education or professionalism.* Like upper-level employees, those with higher amounts of education tend to make more other–outside comparisons.

Based on equity theory, when employees perceive inequity, they can be predicted to make one of six choices:[32]

1. *Change their inputs* (for example, don't exert as much effort).
2. *Change their outcomes* (for example, individuals paid on a piece-rate basis can increase their pay by producing a higher quantity of units of lower quality).
3. *Distort perceptions of self* (for example, "I used to think I worked at a moderate pace but now I realize that I work a lot harder than everyone else").
4. *Distort perceptions of others* (for example, "Mike's job isn't as desirable as I previously thought it was").
5. *Choose a different referent* (for example, "I may not make as much as my brother-in-law, but I'm doing a lot better than my Dad did when he was my age").
6. *Leave the field* (for example, quit the job).

The theory establishes the following propositions relating to inequitable pay:

1. *Given payment by time, overrewarded employees will produce more than will equitably paid employees.* Hourly and salaried employees will generate high quantity or quality of production in order to increase the input side of the ratio and bring about equity.
2. *Given payment by quantity of production, overrewarded employees will produce fewer but higher-quality units than will equitably paid employees.* Individuals paid on a piece-rate basis will increase their effort to achieve equity, which can result in greater quality or quantity. However, increases in quantity will only increase inequity, since every unit produced results in further overpayment. Therefore, effort is directed toward increasing quality rather than increasing quantity.
3. *Given payment by time, underrewarded employees will produce less or poorer quality of output.* Effort will be decreased, which will bring about lower productivity or poorer-quality output than equitably paid subjects.
4. *Given payment by quantity of production, underrewarded employees will produce a large number of low-quality units in comparison with equitably paid employees.* Employees on piece-rate pay plans can bring about equity because trading off quality of output for quantity will result in an increase in rewards with little or no increase in contributions.

Some of these propositions have been supported, but other ones haven't. First, inequities created by overpayment do not seem to have a very significant effect on behavior in most work situations. Apparently, people have a great deal more tolerance of overpayment inequities than of underpayment inequities or are better able to rationalize them. It's pretty damaging to a theory when one-half of the equation (how people respond to overreward) falls apart. Second, not all people are equity sensitive.[33] For example, a small part of the working population actually prefer that their outcome–input ratios be less than the referent comparison's. Predictions from equity theory are not likely to be very accurate with these benevolent types.

Recent research has been directed at expanding what is meant by equity or fairness.[34] Historically, equity theory focused on **distributive justice**, which is the employee's perceived fairness of the *amount and allocation* of rewards among individuals. But increasingly equity is thought of from the standpoint of **organizational justice**, which we define as an overall perception of what is fair in the workplace. One key element of organizational justice is that justice is a *perception*. So, fairness is subjective, and what one person may see as unfair another may see as perfectly appropriate. The other key element of organizational justice is the view that justice is multidimensional. Although how much we get paid, relative to what we think we should be paid (distributive justice) is important, *how* we get paid is just as important. Thus, **procedural justice**—the perceived fairness of the *process* used to determine the distribution of rewards—is another major dimension of justice. Two key elements of procedural justice are these:

1. *Process control:* the opportunity to present one's point of view about desired outcomes to decision makers.
2. *Explanations:* clear reasons given to a person by management for the outcome.

Thus, for employees to see a process as fair, they need to feel they have some control over the outcome and that they were given an adequate explanation about why the outcome occurred.

Research shows that the effects of procedural justice become more important when distributive justice is lacking. This makes sense. If we don't get what we want, we tend to focus on *why*. For example, if your supervisor gives a cushy office to a coworker instead of to you, you're much more focused on your supervisor's treatment of you than if you had gotten the office.

A recent addition to research on organizational justice is **interactional justice**, which is the individual's perception of the degree to which he or she is treated with dignity, concern, and respect. When people are treated in an unjust manner (at least in their own eyes), they respond by retaliating (for example, badmouthing a supervisor).[35] Because interactional justice or injustice is intimately tied to the conveyer of the information (usually one's supervisor), whereas procedural injustice often results from impersonal policies, one would expect perceptions of injustice to be more closely related to one's supervisor. Generally, that's what the evidence suggests.[36] Exhibit 5-6 shows a multidimensional model of organizational justice.

Of these three forms of justice, distributive justice is most strongly related to satisfaction with outcomes (for example, satisfaction with pay) and organizational commitment. Procedural justice relates most strongly to job satisfaction, employee trust, withdrawal from the organization, job performance, and citizenship behaviors. There is less evidence on interactional justice.[37]

To promote fairness in the workplace, managers should consider openly sharing information on how allocation decisions are made, following consistent and unbiased procedures, and engaging in similar practices to increase the perception of procedural justice. By having an increased perception of procedural fairness, employees are likely to view their bosses and the organization positively even if they are dissatisfied with pay, promotions, and other personal outcomes.

—To promote fairness in the workplace, managers should consider openly sharing information on how allocation decisions are made.

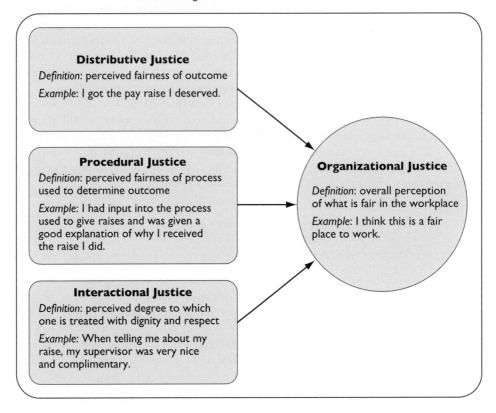

EXHIBIT 5-6   Model of Organizational Justice

Expectancy Theory

Currently, one of the most widely accepted explanations of motivation is Victor Vroom's **expectancy theory**.[38] Although it has its critics, most of the evidence is supportive of the theory.

In practical terms, expectancy theory says that employees will be motivated to exert a high level of effort when they believe:

- that effort will lead to a good performance appraisal;
- that a good appraisal will lead to organizational rewards, such as a bonus, a salary increase, or a promotion; and
- that the rewards will satisfy the employees' personal goals.

The theory, therefore, focuses on three relationships (see Exhibit 5-7):

1. *Effort–performance relationship:* the probability perceived by the individual that exerting a given amount of effort will lead to performance.
2. *Performance–reward relationship:* the degree to which the individual believes that performing at a particular level will lead to the attainment of a desired outcome.
3. *Rewards–personal goals relationship:* the degree to which organizational rewards satisfy an individual's personal goals or needs and the attractiveness of those potential rewards for the individual.[39]

EXHIBIT 5-7 Expectancy Theory

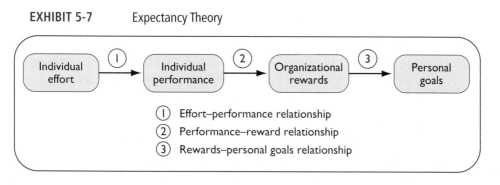

- ① Effort–performance relationship
- ② Performance–reward relationship
- ③ Rewards–personal goals relationship

Expectancy theory helps explain why a lot of workers aren't motivated on their jobs and do only the minimum necessary to get by. This is evident when we look at the theory's three relationships in a little more detail. We present them as questions employees must answer in the affirmative if their motivation is to be maximized.

First, *if I give a maximum effort, will it be recognized in my performance appraisal?* For a lot of employees, the answer is "No." Why? Their skill level may be deficient, which means that no matter how hard they try, they're not likely to be a high performer. The organization's performance appraisal system may be designed to assess nonperformance factors such as loyalty, initiative, or courage, which means more effort won't necessarily result in a higher evaluation. Still another possibility is that employees, rightly or wrongly, perceive that the boss doesn't like them. As a result, they expect to get a poor appraisal regardless of level of effort. These examples suggest that one possible source of low employee motivation is the belief by employees that no matter how hard they work, the likelihood of getting a good performance appraisal is low.

Second, *if I get a good performance appraisal, will it lead to organizational rewards?* Many employees see the performance–reward relationship in their job as weak. The reason is that organizations reward a lot of things besides just performance. For example, when pay is allocated to employees based on factors such as seniority, being cooperative, or for "kissing up" to the boss, employees are likely to see the performance–reward relationship as being weak and demotivating.

Finally, *if I'm rewarded, are the rewards ones that I find personally attractive?* The employee works hard in the hope of getting a promotion but gets a pay raise instead. Or the employee wants a more interesting and challenging job but receives only a few words of praise. Or the employee puts in extra effort to be relocated to the company's Paris office but instead is transferred to Singapore. These examples illustrate the importance of the rewards being tailored to individual employee needs. Unfortunately, many managers are limited in the rewards they can distribute, which makes it difficult to individualize rewards. Moreover, some managers incorrectly assume that all employees want the same thing, thus overlooking the motivational effects of differentiating rewards. In either case, employees are not motivated to their full potential.

—Some managers incorrectly assume that all employees want the same thing, thus overlooking the motivational effects of differentiating rewards.

Does expectancy theory work? Attempts to validate the theory have been complicated by methodological, criterion, and measurement problems. As a result, many published studies that purport to support or negate the theory must be viewed with caution. Importantly, most studies have failed to replicate the methodology as it was originally proposed. For example, the theory proposes to explain different levels of effort from the same person under different circumstances, but almost all replication studies have looked at different people. Correcting for this flaw has greatly improved support for the validity of expectancy theory.[40] Some critics suggest that the theory has only limited use, arguing that it tends to be more valid for predicting in situations in which effort–performance and performance–reward linkages are clearly perceived by the individual.[41] Because few individuals perceive a high correlation between performance and rewards in their jobs, the theory tends to be idealistic. If organizations actually rewarded individuals for performance rather than according to such criteria as seniority, effort, skill level, and job difficulty, the theory's validity might be considerably greater. However, rather than invalidating expectancy theory, this criticism can be used in support of the theory, because it explains why a significant segment of the workforce exerts low levels of effort in carrying out job responsibilities.

CAVEAT EMPTOR: MOTIVATION THEORIES ARE OFTEN CULTURE BOUND

In our discussion of goal setting, we said that managers need to take care in applying this theory because it assumes cultural characteristics that are not universal. This is true for many of the theories presented in this chapter because most current motivation theories were developed in the United States by Americans and about Americans. For instance, both goal-setting and expectancy theories emphasize goal accomplishment as well as rational and individual thought—characteristics that are consistent with American culture. Let's take a look at several motivation theories and consider their cross-cultural transferability.

Maslow's needs hierarchy argues that people start at the physiological level and then move progressively up the hierarchy in this order: physiological, safety, social, esteem, and self-actualization. This hierarchy, if it has any application at all, aligns with American culture. In countries like Japan, Greece, and Mexico, where uncertainty avoidance characteristics are strong, security needs would be on top of the need hierarchy. Countries that score high on nurturing characteristics—Denmark, Sweden, Norway, The Netherlands, and Finland—would have social needs on top.[42] We would predict, for instance, that group work will motivate employees more when the country's culture scores high on the nurturing criterion.

Another motivation concept that clearly has an American bias is the achievement need. The view that a high achievement need acts as an internal motivator presupposes two cultural characteristics:

- A willingness to accept a moderate degree of risk (which excludes countries with strong uncertainty avoidance characteristics).
- A concern with performance (which applies almost singularly to countries with strong achievement characteristics).

This combination is found in Anglo-American countries such as the United States, Canada, and Great Britain.[43] However, these characteristics are relatively absent in countries such as Chile and Portugal.

Equity theory has gained a relatively strong following in the United States. That's not surprising since U.S.-style reward systems are based on the assumption that workers are highly sensitive to equity in reward allocations. And in the United States, equity is meant to closely tie pay to performance. However, evidence suggests that in collectivist cultures, especially in the former socialist countries of Central and Eastern Europe, employees expect rewards to reflect their individual needs as well as their performance.[44] Moreover, consistent with a legacy of communism and centrally planned economies, employees exhibited an entitlement attitude—that is, they expected outcomes to be *greater* than their inputs.[45] These findings suggest that U.S.-style pay practices may need modification, especially in Russia and former communist countries, in order to be perceived as fair by employees.

But don't assume there are *no* cross-cultural consistencies. For instance, the desire for interesting work seems important to almost all workers, regardless of their national culture. In a study of seven countries, employees in Belgium, Britain, Israel, and the United States ranked "interesting work" number one among 11 work goals. And this factor was ranked either second or third in Japan, The Netherlands, and Germany.[46] Similarly, in a study comparing job-preference outcomes among graduate students in the United States, Canada, Australia, and Singapore, growth, achievement, and responsibility were rated the top three and had identical rankings.[47] Both of these studies suggest some universality to the importance of intrinsic factors in the two-factor theory.

IMPLICATIONS FOR MANAGERS

The theories we've discussed in this chapter address different outcome variables. Some are directed at explaining turnover, while others emphasize productivity. The theories also differ in their predictive strength. In this section, we:

- reviewed the most established motivation theories to determine their relevance in explaining our dependent variables, and
- assessed the predictive power of each.

Need Theories   We introduced three theories that focused on needs. These were Maslow's needs hierarchy, the two-factor theory, and McClelland's theory of needs. None of these theories has found widespread support, though the strongest of these is probably McClelland's, particularly regarding the relationship between achievement and productivity. In general, need theories are not very valid explanations of motivation, and managers would be well-advised to look to more contemporary theories of motivation.

Goal-Setting Theory   It is rarely disputed that clear and difficult goals lead to higher levels of employee productivity. This evidence leads us to conclude that goal-setting theory provides one of the more powerful explanations of this dependent variable. The theory, however, does not address absenteeism, turnover, or satisfaction.

Equity Theory/Organizational Justice   Equity theory also deals with productivity, satisfaction, absence, and turnover variables. However, its strongest legacy probably is that it provided the spark for research on organizational justice, which has more support in the literature.

Expectancy Theory   Expectancy theory has proved to offer a relatively powerful explanation of employee productivity, absenteeism, and turnover. But expectancy theory assumes that employees have few constraints on their decision discretion. It makes many of the same assumptions that the rational model makes about individual decision making (see Chapter 4). This acts to restrict its applicability.

Overall, the motivation theories with the most research, and the most recent support, probably deserve the most attention by managers. These theories are goal-setting theory, organizational justice, and, to a lesser degree, expectancy theory. Fortunately, though implementing no theory in the complexities of the workplace is simple, these theories do contain within them practical suggestions for how to make workplaces for motivating.

CHAPTER 6

Motivation: From Concepts to Applications

1. Discuss the ways in which employees can be motivated by changing the work environment.
2. Explain why managers might want to use employee involvement programs.
3. Discuss how the different types of variable-pay programs can increase employee motivation.
4. Describe the link between skill-based pay plans and motivation theories.
5. Explain how employee recognition programs affect motivation.

In this chapter, we focus on applying motivation concepts. We link motivation theories to practices such as employee involvement and skill-based pay. It's one thing to be able to know specific motivation theories; it's quite another to see how, as a manager, you can use them.

MOTIVATING BY CHANGING THE NATURE OF THE WORK ENVIRONMENT

Increasingly, research on motivation is focused on approaches that link motivational concepts to changes in the way work is structured. Research in **job design** provides evidence that the way the elements in a job are organized can act to increase or decrease effort. This research also offers detailed insights into how we identify those elements. We'll first review the job characteristics model, discuss some ways jobs can be redesigned, and then explore some alternative work arrangements.

The Job Characteristics Model

Developed by J. Richard Hackman and Greg Oldham, the **job characteristics model (JCM)** proposes that any job can be described in terms of five core job dimensions:[1]

1. *Skill variety:* The degree to which the job requires a variety of different activities so the worker can use a number of different skills and talent. A job scoring high on skill variety would be the owner–operator of a garage who does electrical repairs, rebuilds engines, does body work, and interacts with customers. A job scoring low on this dimension would be a body shop worker who sprays paint eight hours a day.
2. *Task identity:* The degree to which the job requires completion of a whole and identifiable piece of work. A job scoring high on identity would be a cabinetmaker who designs a piece of furniture, selects the wood, builds the object, and finishes it to perfection. A job scoring low on this dimension would be a worker in a furniture factory who operates a lathe solely to make table legs.
3. *Task significance:* The degree to which the job has a substantial impact on the lives or work of other people. A job scoring high on significance would be a nurse handling the diverse needs of patients in a hospital intensive care unit. A job scoring low on this dimension would be a janitor sweeping floors in the same hospital.
4. *Autonomy:* The degree to which the job provides substantial freedom, independence, and discretion to the individual in scheduling the work and in determining the procedures to be used in carrying it out. A job scoring high on autonomy is a salesperson who schedules his or her own work each day and decides on the most effective sales approach for each customer without supervision. A job scoring low on this dimension would be a salesperson who is given a set of leads each day and is required to follow a standardized sales script with each potential customer.
5. *Feedback:* The degree to which carrying out the work activities required by the job results in the individual obtaining direct and clear information about the effectiveness of his or her performance. A job with high feedback is a factory worker who assembles iPods and then tests them to see if they operate properly. A job scoring low on feedback would be that same factory worker who, after assembling the iPod, is required to route it to a quality-control inspector who tests it for proper operation and makes needed adjustments.

Exhibit 6-1 illustrates JCM. Note how the first three dimensions—skill variety, task identity, and task significance—combine to create meaningful work. If these three characteristics exist in a job, the model predicts that the incumbent will view the job as being important, valuable, and worthwhile. Jobs that possess autonomy give employees a feeling of personal responsibility for the results and, if a job provides feedback, employees will know how effectively they are performing. From a motivational standpoint, the JCM says that individuals enjoy internal rewards when they

- learn (knowledge of results) that they
- personally (experienced responsibility) have performed well on a task that they
- care about (experienced meaningfulness).

EXHIBIT 6-1   The Job Characteristics Model

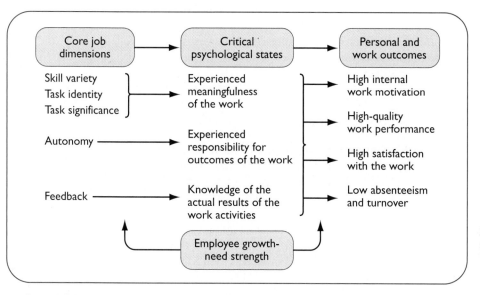

Source: J. R. Hackman and G. R. Oldham, *Work Redesign* © 1980; pp. 78–80. Adapted by permission of Pearson Education, Inc. Upper Saddle River, New Jersey.

The more that these three psychological states are present, the greater will be employees' motivation, performance, and satisfaction and the lower their absenteeism and likelihood of leaving the organization. As Exhibit 6-1 shows, the links between the job dimensions and the outcomes are moderated or adjusted by the strength of the individual's growth need—that is, by the employee's desire for self-esteem and self-actualization. Individuals with a high growth need are more likely to experience the psychological states when their jobs are enriched than are their counterparts with a low growth need. Moreover, they will respond more positively to the psychological states when they are present than will individuals with a low growth need.

The core dimensions can be combined into a single predictive index, called the **motivating potential score (MPS)**, which is calculated as follows:

$$\text{MPS} = \frac{\text{Skill variety} + \text{Task identity} + \text{Task significance}}{3} \times \text{Autonomy} \times \text{Feedback}$$

Jobs that are high on motivating potential must be high on at least one of the three factors that lead to experienced meaningfulness, and they must be high on both autonomy and feedback. If jobs score high on motivating potential, the model predicts that motivation, performance, and satisfaction will be positively affected and that the likelihood of absence and turnover will be lessened.

The JCM has been well researched, and most of the evidence supports the general framework of the theory: that these characteristics affect behavioral outcomes.[2] However, it also appears managers can bypass the complex MPS formula and better derive motivating potential by simply adding the characteristics.[3] Beyond employee growth-need strength, other variables, such as the employee's perception of his or her workload compared to others, may also moderate the link between the core job dimensions and personal and work outcomes.[4] Overall, though, it appears that jobs that have the intrinsic elements of variety, identity, significance, autonomy, and feedback are more satisfying and generate higher performance from people than do jobs that lack these characteristics.

How Can Jobs Be Redesigned?

"Every day was the same thing," Frank Greer said. "Stand on that assembly line. Wait for an instrument panel to be moved into place. Unlock the mechanism and drop the panel into the Jeep Liberty as it moved by on the line. Then I plugged in the harnessing wires. I repeated that for eight hours a day. I don't care that they were paying me twenty-four dollars an hour. I was going crazy. I did it for almost a year and a half. Finally, I just said to my wife that this isn't going to be the way I'm going to spend the rest of my life. My brain was turning to Jell-O on that Jeep assembly line. So I quit. Now I work in a print shop, and I make less than $15 an hour. But let me tell you, the work I do is really interesting. The job changes all the time, I'm continually learning new things, and the work really challenges me! I look forward every morning to going to work again."

Frank Greer's job at the Jeep plant was made up of repetitive tasks that provided him with little variety, autonomy, or motivation. In contrast, his job in the print shop is challenging and stimulating. Let's look at some of the ways that the JCM can be put into practice to make jobs more motivating.

Job Rotation   If employees suffer from monotony of their work, one alternative is to use **job rotation** (or what many now call *cross-training*). We define this practice as the periodic shifting of an employee from one task to another. When an activity is no longer challenging, the employee is rotated to another job, usually at the same level, that has similar skill requirements. Singapore Airlines, one of the best-rated airlines in the world, uses job rotation extensively. For example, a ticket agent may take on the duties of a baggage handler. Job rotation is one of the reasons Singapore Airlines is rated as a highly desirable place to work.

The strengths of job rotation are that it:

- reduces boredom,
- increases motivation through diversifying the employee's activities, and
- helps employees better understand how their work contributes to the organization.

Job rotation also has indirect benefits for the organization because employees with a wider range of skills give management more flexibility in scheduling work, adapting to changes, and filling vacancies. However, job rotation is not without its drawbacks. Training costs are increased, and productivity is reduced by moving a worker into a new position just when efficiency at the prior job is creating organizational economies. Job rotation also creates disruptions. Members of the work group have to adjust to the new employee. And supervisors may also have to spend more time answering questions and monitoring the work of recently rotated employees.

Job Enlargement   More than 35 years ago, the idea of expanding jobs horizontally, or what we call **job enlargement**, grew in popularity. Increasing the number and variety of tasks that an individual performed resulted in jobs with more diversity. Instead of only sorting the incoming mail by department, for instance, a mail sorter's job could be enlarged to include physically delivering the mail to the various departments or running outgoing letters through the postage meter. The difference between job rotation and job enlargement may seem subtle. In job rotation, jobs are not redesigned; in job enlargement, they are.

Efforts at job enlargement often meet with less than enthusiastic results.[5] As one employee who experienced such a redesign on his job remarked, "Before I had one lousy job. Now, through enlargement, I have three!" However, some applications of job enlargement have been successful. The job of housekeeper in some smaller hotels, for example, includes not only cleaning bathrooms, making beds, and vacuuming but also replacing burned-out light bulbs, providing turn-down service, and restocking mini-bars.

Job Enrichment   **Job enrichment** refers to the vertical expansion of jobs. It increases the degree to which the worker controls the planning, execution, and evaluation of the work. An enriched job organizes tasks so as to allow the worker to do a complete activity, increases the employee's freedom and independence, increases responsibility, and provides feedback, so the individual will be able to assess and correct his or her own performance. The enrichment of jobs can be traced to Herzberg's two-factor theory (from Chapter 5): By increasing the intrinsic factors in a job—such as achievement, responsibility, and growth—employees are more likely to be satisfied with the job and motivated to perform it.

How does management enrich an employee's job? Exhibit 6-2 offers suggested guidelines based on the job characteristics model:

- *Combining tasks* takes existing and fractionalized tasks and puts them together to form a new and larger module of work.

EXHIBIT 6-2   Guidelines for Enriching a Job

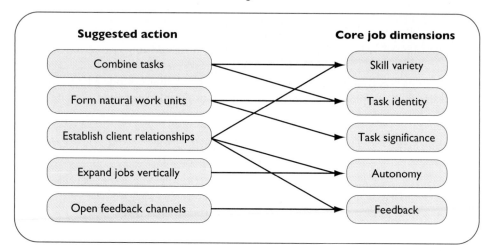

Source: J. R. Hackman and J. L. Suttle (eds.), *Improving Life at Work* (Glenview, IL: Scott Foresman, 1977), p. 138. Reprinted by permission of Richard Hackman and J. Lloyd Suttle.

- *Forming natural work units* creates an identifiable and meaningful whole for tasks done by an employee.
- *Establishing client relationships* increases the direct relationships between workers and their clients (who may be internal customers or people outside the organization).
- *Expanding jobs vertically* gives employees responsibilities and control that were formerly reserved for management.
- *Opening feedback channels* lets employees know how well they are performing their jobs and whether their performance is improving, deteriorating, or remaining at a constant level.

Evidence on job enrichment generally shows that it reduces absenteeism and turnover costs and increases satisfaction. But on the critical issue of productivity, the evidence is inconclusive.[6] In some situations, job enrichment increases productivity; in others, it decreases it. However, even when productivity goes down, there does seem to be consistently more conscientious use of resources and a higher quality of product or service.

Alternative Work Arrangements

Beyond redesigning the nature of the work itself and involving employees in decisions, another approach to making the work environment more motivating is to alter work arrangements. We'll discuss three alternative work arrangements: flextime, job sharing, and telecommuting. With the increasing advances in technology, these alternative work arrangements have become more popular.

Flextime   The term **flextime** is short for "flexible work hours." It allows employees some discretion over when they arrive at work and when they leave. Employees have to work a specific number of hours a week, but they are free to vary the hours of work within certain limits. As shown in Exhibit 6-3, each day consists of a common core, usually six hours, with a flexibility band surrounding the core. For example, exclusive of a one-hour lunch break, the core may be 9:00 A.M. to 3:00 P.M., with the office actually opening at 6:00 A.M. and closing at 6:00 P.M. All employees are required to be at their jobs during the common core period, but they are allowed to accumulate their other two hours before and/or after the core time. Some flextime programs allow extra hours to be accumulated and turned into a free day off each month.

Flextime has become an extremely popular scheduling option. The proportion of full-time U.S. employees on flextime more than doubled between the late 1980s

EXHIBIT 6-3   Example of a Flextime Schedule

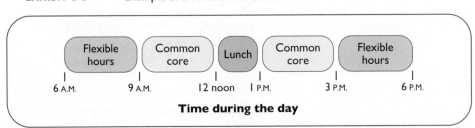

and 2005. Approximately 43 percent of the U.S. full-time workforce now has flexibility in daily arrival and departure times.[7] And this is not just a U.S. phenomenon. In Germany, for instance, 29 percent of businesses have flextime for their employees.[8]

The benefits claimed for flextime are numerous and include these:

- Reduced absenteeism
- Increased productivity
- Reduced overtime expenses
- A lessening in hostility toward management
- Reduced traffic congestion around work sites
- Elimination of tardiness
- Increased autonomy and responsibility for employees, which may increase employee job satisfaction

But beyond the claims, what's flextime's record? Most of the performance evidence stacks up favorably. Flextime tends to reduce absenteeism and frequently improves worker productivity, probably for several reasons.[9] Employees can schedule their work hours to align with personal demands, thus reducing tardiness and absences, and employees can adjust their work activities to those hours in which they are individually more productive.

Flextime's major drawback is that it's not applicable to every job. It works well with clerical tasks for which an employee's interaction with people outside his or her department is limited. It is not a viable option for receptionists, sales personnel in retail stores, or similar jobs for which comprehensive service demands that people be at their work stations at predetermined times.

Job Sharing A recent work scheduling innovation is **job sharing**. It allows two or more individuals to split a traditional 40-hour-a-week job. For example, one person might perform the job from 8:00 A.M. to noon, while another performs the same job from 1:00 P.M. to 5:00 P.M.; or the two could work full, but alternate, days. For example, Sue Manix and Charlotte Schutzman share the title of vice president of employee communications in the Philadelphia office of Verizon.[10] Schutzman works Monday and Tuesday, Manix works Thursday and Friday, and they alternate Wednesdays. The two women have job-shared for 10 years, acquiring promotions, numerous bonuses, and a 20-person staff along the way. With each having children at home, this arrangement allows them the flexibility to better balance their work and family responsibilities.

Approximately 31 percent of large organizations now offer their employees job sharing.[11] However, in spite of its availability, job sharing doesn't seem to be widely adopted by employees. This is probably because of the difficulty of finding compatible partners with whom to share a job and the negative perceptions historically held of individuals not completely committed to their jobs and employers.

Job sharing allows the organization to draw on the talents of more than one individual in a given job. It also opens up the opportunity to acquire skilled workers—for instance, women with young children and retirees—who might not be available on a full-time basis. Many Japanese

—Job sharing allows the organization to draw on the talents of more than one individual in a given job.

firms are increasingly considering job sharing—but for a very different reason.[12] Because Japanese executives are extremely reluctant to fire people, job sharing is seen as a potentially humanitarian means for avoiding layoffs due to overstaffing.

From the employee's perspective, job sharing increases flexibility. As such, it can increase motivation and satisfaction for those to whom a 40-hour-a-week job is just not practical. But the major drawback, from management's perspective, is finding compatible pairs of employees who can successfully coordinate the intricacies of one job.

Telecommuting No commuting, flexible hours, freedom to dress as you please, and few or no interruptions from colleagues: That might be close to the ideal job for many people. It's called **telecommuting** and refers to employees who do their work remotely at least two days a week using computers linked to their offices.[13] (A closely related term—*virtual office*—is increasingly being used to describe the situation for employees who work out of their homes on a relatively permanent basis.)

Recent estimates indicate that between 9 million and 24 million people telecommute in the United States, depending on exactly how the term is defined.[14] This translates to about 10 percent or more of the workforce. Well-known organizations that actively encourage telecommuting include AT&T, IBM, Merrill Lynch, American Express, Hewlett-Packard, and a number of U.S. government agencies. The concept is also catching on worldwide. In Finland, Sweden, Britain, and Germany, telecommuters represent 17, 15, 8, and 6 percent of their workforces, respectively.[15]

What kinds of jobs lend themselves to telecommuting? Three categories have been identified as most appropriate:

- Routine information-handling tasks
- Mobile activities
- Professional and other knowledge-related tasks[16]

Writers, attorneys, analysts, and employees who spend the majority of their time on computers or the telephone are natural candidates for telecommuting. Telemarketers, customer-service representatives, reservations agents, and product-support specialists spend most of their time on the phone. As telecommuters, they can access information on their computer screens at home as easily as in the company's office.

Numerous stories support telecommuting's success.[17] For instance, 3,500 Merrill Lynch employees telecommute. After that program was in place just a year, management reported an increase in productivity of between 15 and 20 percent among telecommuters, 3.5 fewer sick days a year, and a 6 percent decrease in turnover. Putnam Investments, located in Boston, has found telecommuting to be an attractive recruitment tool. The company was having difficulty attracting new hires, but after introducing telecommuting, the number of its applicants grew 20-fold. Putnam's management calculates that the 12 percent of its employees who telecommute have substantially higher productivity than in-office staff and about one-tenth the attrition rate.

The potential pluses for management of telecommuting include:

- a larger labor pool from which to select,
- higher productivity,
- less turnover,
- improved morale, and
- reduced office-space costs.

The major downside for management is less direct supervision of employees. In addition, in today's team-focused workplace, telecommuting may make it more difficult for management to coordinate teamwork. From the employee's standpoint, telecommuting offers a considerable increase in flexibility, but not without costs. For employees with a high social need, telecommuting can increase feelings of isolation and reduce job satisfaction. And all telecommuters potentially suffer from the "out of sight, out of mind" effect. Employees who aren't at their desks, who miss meetings, and who don't share in day-to-day informal workplace interactions may be at a disadvantage when it comes to raises and promotions. It's easy for bosses to overlook or undervalue the contribution of employees they see less regularly.

> *—For employees with a high social need, telecommuting can increase feelings of isolation and reduce job satisfaction.*

EMPLOYEE INVOLVEMENT

We define **employee involvement** as a participative process that uses the input of employees to increase their commitment to the organization's success. The underlying logic is that by involving workers in the decisions that affect them and by increasing their autonomy and control over their work lives, employees will become more motivated, more committed to the organization, more productive, and more satisfied with their jobs.[18]

Employee involvement programs differ among countries. A study comparing the acceptance of employee involvement programs in four countries, including the United States and India, confirmed the importance of modifying practices to reflect national culture.[19] While American employees readily accepted these programs, managers in India who tried to empower their employees through employee involvement programs were rated low by those employees. In these Indian cases, employee satisfaction also decreased. These reactions are consistent with India's high power–distance culture, which accepts and expects differences in authority.

Examples of Employee Involvement Programs

Now let's consider two major forms of employee involvement—*participative management* and *representative participation*—in more detail.

Participative Management   The distinct characteristic common to all **participative management** programs is the use of joint decision making. That is, subordinates actually share a significant degree of decision-making power with their immediate superiors. Participative management has, at times, been promoted as a panacea for poor morale and low productivity. For participative management to work, it requires the following:

- Employees are involved only in decisions that are relevant to them (i.e., employees should not be involved simply for involvement's sake).
- Employees have the competence and knowledge to make a useful contribution (i.e., employees will only be frustrated if they do not know how to make a difference).

■ Participation is not a substitute for trust—for participation to work, trust and confidence among all parties involved must be present.[20]

Dozens of studies have been conducted on the participation–performance relationship. The findings, however, are mixed.[21] When the research is reviewed carefully, it appears that participation typically has only a modest influence on variables such as employee productivity, motivation, and job satisfaction. Of course, that doesn't mean that the use of participative management can't be beneficial under the right conditions. What it says, however, is that the use of participation is not a sure means for improving employee performance.

Representative Participation   Rather than participating directly in decisions, workers are represented by a small group of employees who actually participate in **representative participation**. Almost every country in Western Europe has some type of legislation requiring companies to practice representative participation. Representative participation has been called "the most widely legislated form of employee involvement around the world."[22] The goal of representative participation is to redistribute power within an organization, putting labor on a more equal footing with the interests of management and stockholders.

The two most common forms that representative participation takes are works councils and board representatives.[23] *Works councils* are groups of nominated or elected employees who must be consulted when management makes decisions involving personnel. *Board representatives* are employees who sit on a company's board of directors and represent the interests of the firm's employees.

The overall influence of representative participation on working employees seems to be minimal.[24] For instance, the evidence suggests that works councils are dominated by management and have little impact on employees or the organization. And although this form of employee involvement might increase the motivation and satisfaction of the individuals who are doing the representing, there is little evidence that this trickles down to the operating employees represented. Overall, "the greatest value of representative participation is symbolic. If one is interested in changing employee attitudes or in improving organizational performance, representative participation would be a poor choice."[25]

REWARDING EMPLOYEES

In deciding what to pay employees and how to pay them, management must make some strategic decisions. Will the organization lead, match, or lag the market in pay? How will individual contributions be recognized? In this section, we consider four major strategic rewards decisions that need to be made:

1. What to pay employees (establishing a pay structure)
2. How to pay individual employees (choosing among variable pay plans and skill-based pay plans)
3. What benefits to offer, especially whether to offer employees choice in benefits (flexible benefits)
4. How to construct employee recognition programs

What to Pay: Establishing a Pay Structure

Employees can be paid in many ways. The process of initially setting pay levels can be rather complex and entails balancing two types of equity:

- *Internal equity:* the worth of the job to the organization (usually established through a technical process called *job evaluation*)
- *External equity:* the external competitiveness of an organization's pay relative to pay elsewhere in its industry (usually established through pay surveys)

Obviously, the best pay system pays the employee what the job is worth (internal equity) while also paying competitively relative to the labor market. But some organizations prefer to be pay leaders by paying above the market, whereas some may lag the market because they can't afford to pay market rates or they are willing to bear the costs of paying below market (namely, higher turnover as people are lured to better-paying jobs). Wal-Mart, for example, pays less than its competitors and often outsources jobs overseas. Chinese workers in Shenzhen earn $120 a month ($1,440 per year) to make stereos for Wal-Mart. Of the 6,000 factories that are worldwide suppliers to Wal-Mart, 80 percent are located in China. In fact, one-eighth of all Chinese exports to the United States go to Wal-Mart.[26]

Pay more and you may get better qualified, more highly motivated employees who will stay with the organization longer. But pay is often the highest single operating cost for an organization, which means that paying too much can make the organization's products or services too expensive and the firm itself less competitive. It's a strategic decision an organization must make, with clear trade-offs.

How to Pay: Rewarding Individual Employees Through Variable-Pay Programs

A number of organizations—business firms, as well as school districts and other government agencies—are moving away from paying people based solely on credentials or length of service and toward using variable-pay programs. Piece-rate plans, merit-based pay, bonuses, profit sharing, gain sharing, and employee stock ownership plans are all forms of **variable-pay programs**. Instead of paying a person only for time on the job or seniority, a variable-pay program bases a portion of an employee's pay on some individual and/or organizational measure of performance. Earnings therefore fluctuate up and down with the measure of performance. Variable-pay plans have long been used for compensating salespeople and executives. Recently they have begun to be applied to all employees. IBM, Wal-Mart, Pizza Hut, Cigna Corp., and John Deere are just a few examples of companies using variable pay with rank-and-file employees.[27] Today, more than 70 percent of U.S. companies have some form of variable-pay plan, up from only about 5 percent in 1970.[28] Unfortunately, recent survey data indicate that most employees still don't see a strong connection between pay and performance. Only 29 percent say that when they do a good job, their performances are rewarded.[29]

It is precisely the fluctuation in variable pay that has made these programs attractive to management. It turns part of an organization's fixed labor costs into a variable cost, thus reducing expenses when performance declines. So when the U.S. economy encountered a recession in 2001, companies with variable pay were able to reduce their labor costs much faster than companies that had maintained nonperformance–based compensation systems.[30] In addition, when pay is tied to performance, the employee's earnings recognize contribution rather than being a form of entitlement. Low performers find, over time, that their pay stagnates, while high performers enjoy pay increases commensurate with their contributions.

Let's examine the different types of variable-pay programs in more detail.

Piece-Rate Pay   Piece-rate wages have been popular for more than a century as a means of compensating production workers. In **piece-rate pay plans** workers are paid a fixed sum for each unit of production completed. When an employee gets no base salary and is paid only for what he or she produces, this is a *pure* piece-rate plan. People who work in ballparks selling peanuts and soda pop frequently are paid this way. If they sell only 40 bags, their take is only $40. The harder they work and the more peanuts they sell, the more they earn. Many organizations use a *modified* piece-rate plan, in which employees earn a base hourly wage plus a piece-rate differential. So, a medical transcriber might be paid $7 an hour plus 20 cents per page. Such modified plans provide a floor under an employee's earnings while still offering a productivity incentive.

Merit-Based Pay   Merit-based pay plans also pay for individual performance. However, unlike piece-rate plans, which pay based on objective output, **merit-based pay plans** are based on performance appraisal ratings. A main advantage of merit pay plans is that they allow employers to differentiate pay based on performance so that those people thought to be high performers are given bigger raises. The plans can be motivating because, if they are designed correctly, individuals perceive a strong relationship between what they do and the rewards they receive. The evidence supports the importance of this linkage.[31]

—*Merit pay plans allow organizations to compensate for external factors that may have reduced objective performance measures due to no fault of the employee.*

Moreover, unlike organization-based compensation (such as profit-sharing and gain-sharing plans, which we will discuss), merit pay plans pay for individual performance, which presumably is more directly under each individual's control. Thus, because most individuals desire control over their pay, employees tend to like merit pay plans. Finally, merit pay plans allow organizations to compensate for external factors that may have reduced objective performance measures due to no fault of the employee (such as sales being down nationwide).

Despite the intuitive appeal of pay for performance, merit pay plans have several limitations. One of them is that, typically, such plans are based on an annual performance appraisal. Thus, the merit pay is as valid or invalid as the performance ratings on which it is based. Another limitation of merit pay is that sometimes the pay raise pool fluctuates based on economic conditions or other factors that have little to do with an individual employee's performance. For example, a colleague at a top university who performed very well in teaching and research was given a pay raise of $300 one year. Why? Because the pay raise pool was very small. Yet that is hardly pay for performance.

Finally, unions typically resist merit pay plans. The vast majority of primary and secondary school teachers are paid on seniority rather than performance. Recently, California Governor Arnold Schwarzenegger proposed "that teacher pay be tied to merit, not tenure, and I propose that teacher employment be tied to performance, not to just showing up." This proposal drew a swift reaction. Terry Pesta, president of the

San Diego teacher's union, commented, "It's a crazy idea... just another blast at teachers."[32]

Bonuses   Annual bonuses in the tens of millions of dollars are not uncommon in U.S. corporations. Apple Computer's CEO Steve Jobs, for example, received a $90 million bonus in 2002 for his success in reenergizing the company.[33] Increasingly, bonus plans are casting a larger net within organizations to include lower-ranking employees. Many companies now routinely reward production employees with bonuses in the thousands of dollars when company profits improve. One advantage of bonuses over merit pay is that **bonuses** reward employees for recent performance rather than historical performance.

Profit-Sharing Plans   Organization-wide programs that distribute compensation based on some established formula designed around a company's profitability are **profit-sharing plans**. These can be direct cash outlays or, particularly in the case of top managers, allocations of stock options. When you read about executives such as Reuben Mark, the CEO at Colgate-Palmolive, earning $148 million in one year, almost all this comes from cashing in stock options previously granted based on company profit performance.

Gain Sharing   A variable-pay program that has gotten a great deal of attention in recent years is **gain sharing**.[34] This is a formula-based group incentive plan. Improvements in group productivity—from one period to another—determine the total amount of money that is to be allocated. The division of productivity savings can be split between the company and employees in any number of ways, but 50–50 is typical. How is gain sharing different from profit sharing? By focusing on productivity gains rather than on profits, gain sharing rewards specific behaviors that are less influenced by external factors. Employees in a gain sharing plan can receive incentive awards even when the organization isn't profitable.

Gain sharing's popularity seems to be narrowly focused among large manufacturing companies, such as American Safety Razor, Champion Spark Plug, Cincinnati Milacron, Hooker Chemical, and Mead Paper. For instance, approximately 45 percent of *Fortune* 1000 firms have implemented gain sharing plans.[35]

Employee Stock Ownership Plans   The term **employee stock ownership plan (ESOP)** can mean any number of things, from employees owning some stock in the company at which they work to their owning and personally operating the firm. ESOPs are company-established benefit plans in which employees acquire stock, often at below-market prices, as part of their benefits. Companies as varied as Publix Supermarkets, Graybar Electric, and W.L. Gore & Associates are now over 50 percent employee owned.[36] But most of the 10,000 or so ESOPs in the United States are in small, privately held companies.[37]

In the typical ESOP, an employee stock ownership trust is created. Companies contribute either stock or cash to buy stock for the trust and allocate the stock to employees. Employees usually cannot take physical possession of their shares or sell them as long as they're still employed at the company. The research on ESOPs indicates that they increase employee satisfaction.[38] But their impact on performance is less clear. For instance, one study compared 45 ESOPs against 238 conventional companies.[39] The ESOPs outperformed the conventional firms both in terms of employment and sales growth. Another study found that ESOPs had total shareholder returns that averaged 6.9 percentage points higher over the four years after the ESOP was set up than did market returns of similar companies without an ESOP.[40] Other studies have shown disappointing results.[41]

ESOPs have the potential to increase employee job satisfaction and work motivation, but employees need to psychologically experience ownership for this potential to be realized. That is, in addition to merely having a financial stake in the company, employees must be kept regularly informed of the status of the business and also have the opportunity to exercise influence over it. The evidence consistently indicates that it takes ownership and a participative style of management to achieve significant improvements in an organization's performance.[42]

Do variable-pay programs increase motivation and productivity? The answer is a qualified "Yes." Studies generally support the idea that organizations with profit-sharing plans have higher levels of profitability than those without them.[43] Similarly, gain sharing appears to improve productivity in a majority of cases and often has a positive impact on employee attitudes.[44] The downside of variable pay, from an employee's perspective, is its unpredictability. With a straight base salary, employees know what they'll be earning. They can finance cars and homes based on reasonably solid assumptions. That's more difficult to do with variable pay: Your group's performance might slip this year or a recession might undermine your company's profits. Depending on how your variable pay is determined, these can cut your income. Moreover, people begin to take repeated annual performance bonuses for granted. A 15 or 20 percent bonus, received three years in a row, begins to become expected in the fourth year. If it doesn't materialize, management will find itself with some disgruntled employees.

How to Pay: Rewarding Individual Employees Through Skill-Based Pay Plans

Organizations hire people for their skills, then typically put them in jobs and pay them based on their job title or rank. But if organizations hire people because of their competencies, why don't they pay them for those same competencies? Some organizations do. Employees at American Steel & Wire can boost their annual salaries by up to $12,480 by acquiring as many as 10 new skills. Frito-Lay Corporation ties its compensation for front-line operations managers to developing their skills in leadership, workforce development, and functional excellence. **Skill-based pay** is an alternative to job-based pay. Rather than having an individual's job title define his or her pay category, skill-based pay (also called *competency-based* or *knowledge-based pay*) sets pay levels on the basis of how many skills employees have or how many jobs they can do.

From management's perspective, the appeal of skill-based pay is flexibility. Filling staffing needs is easier when employee skills are interchangeable. This is particularly true today, as many organizations cut their workforces. Downsized organizations require more generalists and fewer specialists. Skill-based pay also facilitates communication across the organization because people gain a better understanding of each others' jobs. Where skill-based pay exists, you're less likely to hear the phrase "It's not my job!" In addition, skill-based pay helps meet the needs of ambitious employees who confront minimal advancement opportunities.

These people can increase their earnings and knowledge without a promotion in job title.

What about the downside of skill-based pay? People can *top out*—learning all the skills the program calls for them to learn. This can frustrate employees after they've become challenged by an environment of learning, growth, and continual pay raises. And skills can become obsolete. When this happens, what should management do? Cut employee pay or continue to pay for skills that are no longer relevant? Another problem is created by paying people for acquiring skills for which there may be no immediate need. Finally, skill-based plans don't address the level of performance. They deal only with the issue of whether or not someone can perform the skill.

Skill-Based Pay in Practice

A number of studies have investigated the use and effectiveness of skill-based pay. The overall conclusion, based on these studies, is that skill-based pay is expanding and that it generally leads to higher employee performance, satisfaction, and perceptions of fairness in pay systems.[45]

Research has also identified some interesting trends:

- The increased use of skills as a basis for pay appears particularly strong among organizations facing aggressive global competition and companies with shorter product life cycles and speed-to-market concerns.[46]

- Skill-based pay is moving from the shop floor to the white-collar workforce, and sometimes as far as the executive suite.[47]

Skilled-based pay appears to be an idea whose time has come. As one expert noted, "Slowly, but surely, we're becoming a skill-based society where your market value is tied to what you can do and what your skill set is. In this new world where skills and knowledge are what really counts, it doesn't make sense to treat people as jobholders. It makes sense to treat them as people with specific skills and to pay them for those skills."[48]

Flexible Benefits: Developing a Benefits Package

Flexible benefits allow each employee to put together a benefit package individually tailored to his or her own needs and situation. Consistent with expectancy theory's thesis that organizational rewards should be linked to each individual employee's goals, flexible benefits individualize rewards by allowing each employee to choose the compensation package that best satisfies his or her current needs.

—Flexible benefits individualize rewards by allowing each employee to choose the benefits package that best satisfies his or her current needs.

The three most popular types of benefit plans are modular plans, core-plus options, and flexible spending accounts:[49]

- *Modular plans* are predesigned packages of benefits, with each module put together to meet the needs of a specific group of employees. So a module designed for single employees with no dependents might include only essential benefits. Another, designed for single parents, might have additional life insurance, disability insurance, and expanded health coverage.

■ *Core-plus plans* consist of a core of essential benefits and a menulike selection of other benefit options from which employees can select and add to the core. Typically, each employee is given "benefit credits," which allow the "purchase" of additional benefits that uniquely meet his or her needs.

■ *Flexible spending plans* allow employees to set aside up to the dollar amount offered in the plan to pay for particular services. It's a convenient way, for example, for employees to pay for health-care and dental premiums. Flexible spending accounts can increase employee take-home pay because employees don't have to pay taxes on the dollars they spend out of these accounts.

Today, almost all major corporations in the United States offer flexible benefits, which have become the norm in other countries too. A recent survey of 307 firms in the United Kingdom found that while only 16 percent have flexible benefit programs in place, another 60 percent are either in the process of implementing them or are seriously considering doing so.[50]

Intrinsic Rewards: Employee Recognition Programs

Laura Schendell makes only $8.50 an hour working at her fast-food job in Pensacola, Florida, and the job isn't very challenging or interesting. Yet Laura talks enthusiastically about her job, her boss, and the company that employs her. "What I like is the fact that Guy [her supervisor] appreciates the effort I make. He compliments me regularly in front of the other people on my shift, and I've been chosen Employee of the Month twice in the past six months. Did you see my picture on that plaque on the wall?"

Organizations are increasingly recognizing what Laura Schendell knows: Important work rewards can be both intrinsic and extrinsic. Rewards are intrinsic in the form of employee recognition programs and extrinsic in the form of compensation systems.

Employee recognition programs range from a spontaneous and private thank you up to widely publicized formal programs in which specific types of behavior are encouraged and the procedures for attaining recognition are clearly identified.[51]

Nichols Foods Ltd., a British bottler of soft drinks and syrups, has a comprehensive recognition program.[52] The central hallway in its production area is lined with "bragging boards," where the accomplishments of various individuals and teams are regularly updated. Monthly awards are presented to people who have been nominated by peers for extraordinary effort on the job. And monthly award winners are eligible for further recognition at an annual off-site meeting for all employees. In contrast, most managers use a far more informal approach. Julia Stewart, president of Applebee's restaurants, frequently leaves sealed notes on the chairs of employees after everyone has gone home.[53] These notes explain how critical Stewart thinks the person's work is or how much she appreciates the completion of a recent project. Stewart also relies heavily on voice mail messages left after office hours to tell employees how appreciative she is for a job well done.

A few years ago, 1,500 employees were surveyed in a variety of work settings to find out what they considered to be the most powerful workplace motivator. Their response? Recognition, recognition, and more recognition.[54] Phoenix Inn, a West Coast chain of small hotels, encourages employees to smile by letting customers identify this desirable behavior and then recognizing with rewards and publicity those employees who are identified most often.

An obvious advantage of recognition programs is that they are inexpensive (praise, of course, is free!). It shouldn't be surprising, therefore, to find that employee recognition programs have grown in popularity. A 2002 survey of 391 companies found that 84 percent had some program to recognize worker achievements and that 4 in 10 said they were doing more to foster employee recognition than they were just a year earlier.[55]

Despite the increased popularity, critics argue that employee recognition programs are highly susceptible to political manipulation by management. When applied to jobs in which performance factors are relatively objective, such as sales, recognition programs are likely to be perceived by employees as fair. However, in most jobs, the criteria for good performance aren't self-evident, which allows managers to manipulate the system and recognize their favorite employees. When abused, this can undermine the value of recognition programs and lead to demoralizing employees.

IMPLICATIONS FOR MANAGERS

We've presented a number of motivation theories and applications in this and the previous chapter. Although it's always dangerous to synthesize a large number of complex ideas into a few simple guidelines, the following suggestions summarize the essence of what we know about motivating employees in organizations.

Recognize Individual Differences   Managers should be sensitive to individual differences and cultural contexts. For example, employees from Asian cultures prefer not to be singled out as special because it makes them uncomfortable. Employees have different needs. Don't treat them all alike. Spend the time necessary to understand what's important to each employee. This will allow you to individualize goals, level of involvement, and rewards to align with individual needs. Also, design jobs to align with individual needs and thereby maximize the motivation potential in jobs.

Use Goals and Feedback   Employees should have hard, specific goals, as well as feedback on how well they are faring in pursuit of those goals.

Allow Employees to Participate in Decisions That Affect Them   Employees can contribute to a number of decisions that affect them: setting work goals, choosing their own benefits packages, solving productivity and quality problems, and the like. This can increase employee productivity, commitment to work goals, motivation, and job satisfaction.

Link Rewards to Performance   Rewards should be contingent on performance. Importantly, employees must perceive a clear linkage. Regardless of how closely rewards are actually correlated to performance criteria, if individuals perceive this relationship to be low, the results will be low performance, a decrease in job satisfaction, and an increase in turnover and absenteeism.

Check the System for Equity   Rewards should also be perceived by employees as equating with the inputs they bring to their jobs. At a simplistic level, this should mean that experience, skills, abilities, effort, and other obvious inputs should explain differences in performance and, hence, pay, job assignments, and other obvious rewards.

CHAPTER 7

Emotions and Moods

After studying this chapter, you should be able to:

1. Differentiate emotions from moods.
2. Discuss the different aspects of emotions.
3. Identify the sources of emotions and moods.
4. Describe external constraints on emotions.
5. Discuss the impact emotional labor has on employees.
6. Discuss the case for and the case against emotional intelligence.
7. Apply concepts on emotions and moods to OB issues.

We've all been in "good" moods and "bad" moods at one time or another, and these moods most likely have affected our behavior. Perhaps feelings of anger have led you to snap at a friend or coworker, or, conversely, perhaps feelings of happiness have led you to help that same friend or coworker. Given the obvious role that emotions play in our work and everyday lives, it might surprise you to learn that, until recently, the field of OB has given the topic of emotions little or no attention.[1] How could this be? We can offer two possible explanations.

The first is the *myth of rationality*.[2] Since the late nineteenth century and the rise of scientific management, the protocol of the work world has been to keep a damper on emotions. A well-run organization was one that didn't allow employees to express frustration, fear, anger, love, hate, joy, grief, and similar feelings. The prevailing thought was that such emotions were the antithesis of rationality. Even though researchers and managers knew that emotions were an inseparable part of everyday life, they tried to create organizations that were free of emotion. That, of course, wasn't possible.

The second explanation was the belief that emotions of any kind are disruptive.[3] When researchers considered emotions, they looked at strong, negative emotions—especially anger—that interfered with an employee's ability to work effectively. They rarely viewed emotions as constructive or able to enhance performance.

Certainly some emotions, particularly when exhibited at the wrong time, can reduce employee performance. But this doesn't change the fact that employees bring their emotional sides with them to work every day and that no study of OB could be comprehensive without considering the role of emotions in workplace behavior.

WHAT ARE EMOTIONS AND MOODS?

Although we don't want to obsess over definitions, before we can proceed with our analysis, we need to clarify three terms that are closely intertwined: *affect*, *emotions*, and *moods*.

Affect is a generic term that covers a broad range of feelings that people experience. It's an umbrella concept that encompasses both emotions and moods.[4] **Emotions** are intense feelings that are directed at someone or something.[5] There are dozens of emotions, including anger, contempt, enthusiasm, envy, fear, frustration, disappointment, embarrassment, disgust, happiness, hate, hope, jealousy, joy, love, pride, surprise, and sadness. **Moods** are feelings that tend to be less intense than emotions and that often lack a contextual stimulus.[6] Exhibit 7-1 shows the relationships among affect, emotions, and mood.

As Exhibit 7-1 shows, emotions tend to be more fleeting than moods.[7] For example, if someone is rude to you, you'll feel angry. That intense feeling of anger probably comes and goes fairly quickly, maybe even in a matter of seconds. When you're in a bad mood, though, you can feel bad for several hours.

EXHIBIT 7-1   Affect, Emotions, and Moods

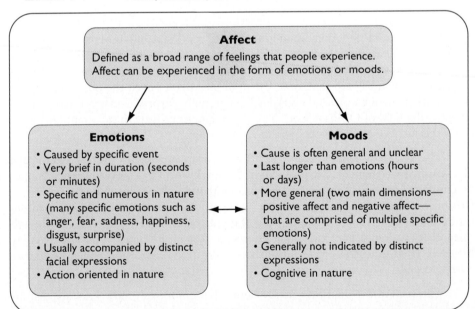

In addition, emotions are reactions to a person (seeing a friend at work may make you feel glad) or event (dealing with a rude client may make you feel angry). You show your emotions when you're "happy about something, angry at someone, afraid of something."[8] Moods, in contrast, aren't usually directed at a person or event. But emotions can turn into moods when you lose focus on the event or object that started the feeling. For example, when a colleague criticizes how you spoke to a client, you might become angry at him. That is, you show emotion (anger) toward a specific object (your colleague). But as the specific emotion dissipates, you might just feel generally dispirited. You can't attribute this feeling to any single event; you're just not your normal self. This affect state describes a mood.

Another difference between emotions and moods lies in the way we express each type of feeling. For example, unlike moods, emotions tend to be more clearly revealed with facial expressions (anger, disgust). Also, some researchers speculate that emotions may be more action oriented—they may lead us to some immediate action—whereas moods may be more cognitive, meaning they may cause us to think or brood for a while.[9]

Finally, the exhibit shows that emotions and moods can mutually influence each other. For example, an emotion, if it's strong and deep enough, can turn into a mood: Getting your dream job may generate the emotion of joy, but it also can put you in a good mood for several days. Similarly, if you're in a good or bad mood, it might make you experience a more intense positive or negative emotion than would otherwise be the case. For example, if you're in a bad mood, you might blow up in response to a coworker's comment when normally it would have just generated a mild reaction.

Although affect, emotions, and moods are separable in theory, in practice the distinction isn't always crystal clear. In fact, in some areas, researchers have studied mostly moods, and in other areas, mainly emotions. So, when we review the OB topics on emotions and moods, you may see more information on emotions in one area and moods in another. This is simply the state of the research.

Some Aspects of Emotions

We must consider some other fundamental aspects of emotions, such as the biology of emotions, the intensity of emotions, their frequency and duration, the relationship between rationality and emotions, and the functions of emotions. Let's deal with each of these aspects in turn.

The Biology of Emotions   All emotions originate in the brain's limbic system, which is about the size of a walnut and near our brain stem.[10] People tend to be happiest (report more positive than negative emotions) when their limbic systems are relatively inactive. When the limbic system becomes active, negative emotions such as anger and guilt dominate over positive ones such as joy and happiness. Overall, the limbic system provides a lens through which you interpret events. When it's active, you see things in a negative light. When it's inactive, you interpret information more positively.

Not everyone's limbic system is the same. Moderately depressed people have more active limbic systems, particularly when they encounter negative information.[11] And women tend to have more active limbic systems than men, which, some argue, explains why women are more susceptible to depression than men and are more likely to bond emotionally with children.[12] Of course, as always, these are average differences: Women are more likely to be depressed than men, but that doesn't mean that all depressed people are women or that men are incapable of bonding with their kids.

Intensity   People give different responses to identical emotion-provoking stimuli. In some cases, personality is responsible for the difference. Other times, it's a result of the job requirements.

People vary in their inherent ability to express emotional intensity. You may know people who almost never show their feelings. They rarely get angry. They never show rage. In contrast, you probably also know people who seem to be on an emotional roller coaster. When they're happy, they're ecstatic. When they're sad, they're deeply depressed. We'll explore the impact personality has on an individual's emotions in more detail later on in this chapter.

Jobs make different demands on our emotions. For instance, air traffic controllers, surgeons, and trial judges are expected to be calm and controlled, even in stressful situations. Conversely, the effectiveness of television evangelists, public-address announcers at sporting events, and lawyers can depend on their ability to alter their emotional intensity as the need arises.

Frequency and Duration   Some emotions occur more frequently than others (most people are amused more often than they are enraged). Emotions also differ in how long they last (one might feel sad for a minute, or for hours). Sean Wolfson is basically a quiet and reserved person. He loves his job as a financial planner. He doesn't enjoy, however, having to give speeches to increase his visibility and to promote his programs. But he still has to give speeches occasionally. "If I had to speak to large audiences every day, I'd quit this business," he says. "I think this works for me because I can fake excitement and enthusiasm for an hour, a couple of times a month."

Whether an employee can successfully meet the emotional demands of a given job depends not only on what emotions need to be displayed and their intensity but also on how frequently and for how long they need to make the effort.

Do Emotions Make Us Irrational?   How often have you heard someone say "Oh, you're just being emotional"? You might have been offended. The famous astronomer Carl Sagan once wrote, "Where we have strong emotions, we're liable to fool ourselves." These observations suggest that rationality and emotion are in conflict with one another and that if you exhibit emotion, you are likely to act irrationally. One team of authors argues that displaying emotions like sadness, to the point of crying, is so toxic to a career that we should leave the room rather than allow others to witness our emotional display.[13] The author Lois Frankel advises women to avoid being emotional at work because it will undermine how others rate their competence.[14] These perspectives suggest that the demonstration or even experience of emotions is likely to make us seem weak, brittle, or irrational. However, the research disagrees and is increasingly showing that emotions are actually critical to rational thinking.[15] In fact, there has been evidence of such a link for a long time.

Take the example of Phineas Gage. Gage was a railroad worker in Vermont. One September day in 1848, while setting an explosive charge at work, a three-foot, seven-inch iron bar flew into Gage's lower left jaw and out through the top of his skull. Remarkably, Gage survived his injury. He was still able to read and speak, and he performed well above average on cognitive ability tests. However, it became clear that Gage had lost his ability to experience emotion. He was emotionless at even the saddest misfortunes or happiest occasions. Gage's inability to express emotion eventually took away his ability to reason. He started making irrational choices about his life, often behaving erratically and against his self-interests. Despite being an intelligent man whose intellectual abilities were unharmed by the accident, Gage drifted from job to job, eventually taking up with a circus.

The example of Phineas Gage and many other brain injury studies show us that emotions are critical to rational thinking. We must have the ability to experience emotions to be rational because our emotions provide important information about how we understand the world around us. Although we might think of a computer as intellectually superior, a human so void of emotion would be unable to function. Think about a manager making a decision to fire an employee. Would you really want the manager to make the decision without regarding either his or the employee's emotions? The key to good decision making is to employ both thinking *and* feeling in one's decisions.

—*Our emotions provide important information about how we understand the world around us.*

What Functions Do Emotions Serve?   Why do we have emotions? What role do they serve? We just discussed one function: that we need them to think rationally. Charles Darwin, however, took a broader approach. In *The Expression of the Emotions in Man and Animals*, Darwin argued that emotions developed over time to help humans solve problems. Emotions are useful, he said, because they motivate people to engage in actions important for survival—actions such as foraging for food, seeking shelter, choosing mates, guarding against predators, and predicting others' behaviors. For example, disgust (an emotion) motivates us to avoid dangerous or harmful things (such as rotten foods). Excitement (also an emotion) motivates us to take on situations in which we require energy and initiative (for example, tackling a new career).

Drawing from Darwin are researchers who focus on **evolutionary psychology**. This field of study says we must experience emotions—whether they are positive or negative—because they serve a purpose.[16] For example, you would probably consider jealousy to be a negative emotion. Evolutionary psychologists would argue that it exists in people because it has a useful purpose. Mates may feel jealousy to increase the chance that their genes, rather than a rival's genes, are passed on to the next generation.[17] Although we tend to think of anger as being "bad," it actually can help us protect our rights when we feel they're being violated. For example, a person showing anger when she's double-crossed by a colleague is serving a warning to others not to repeat the same behavior. It's not that anger is always good. But as with all other emotions, it exists because it serves a useful purpose. Positive emotions also serve a purpose. For example, a service employee who feels empathy for a customer may provide better customer service.

Some researchers are not firm believers in evolutionary psychology. To understand why, consider fear (an emotion) and that it's just as easy to think of the harmful effects of fear as it is the beneficial effects. For example, running in fear from a predator increases the likelihood of survival. But what benefit does freezing in fear serve? Evolutionary psychology provides an interesting perspective on the functions of emotions, but it's hard to know whether or not this perspective is valid all the time.[18]

Sources of Emotions and Moods

Where do emotions and moods come from? Even though emotions are thought to be more influenced by events than moods, ironically, researchers have conducted more studies on the sources of moods than on the sources of particular emotions.

So, now we'll turn to the main sources of moods, though a lot of these sources also affect emotions.

Personality   Noel and Jose are coworkers. Noel has a tendency to get angry when a colleague criticizes her ideas during a brainstorming session. Jose, however, is quite calm and relaxed, viewing such criticism as an opportunity for improvement. Personality predisposes people to experience certain moods and emotions. For example, some people feel guilt and anger more readily than others do. Others may feel calm and relaxed no matter the situation. In other words, moods and emotions have a trait component to them: Most people have built-in tendencies to experience certain moods and emotions more frequently than others do. But, as we mentioned earlier, some people are predisposed to experience *any* emotion more intensely. Such people are high on **affect intensity**, or "individual differences in the strength with which individuals experience their emotions."[19] So, emotions differ in their intensity, but people also differ in how predisposed they are to experience emotions intensely. If a person gets really mad at a coworker, he would be experiencing an emotion intensely. But if that person gets mad, or excited, really easily, then he would be high on the personality trait of affect intensity.

Day of the Week and Time of the Day   Most people are at work or school Monday through Friday. For most of us, that means the weekend is a time of relaxation and leisure. Does that suggest that people are in their best moods on the weekends? Well, actually, yes. As Exhibit 7–2 shows, people tend to be in their worst moods (highest negative affect and lowest positive affect) early in the week and in their best moods (highest positive affect and lowest negative affect) late in the week.[20]

What about the time of day? When are you usually in your best mood? Your worst? We often think that people differ, depending on whether they are "morning"

EXHIBIT 7-2   Our Moods Are Affected by the Day of the Week

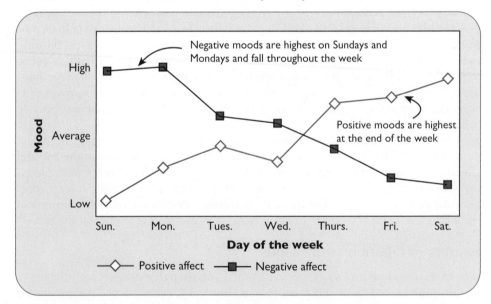

Source: D. Watson, Mood and Temperament, New York, Guilford Publications, 2006.

or "evening" people. However, the vast majority of us follow a similar pattern. People are generally in lower spirits early in the morning. During the course of the day, our moods tend to improve and then decline in the evening. Interestingly, regardless of what time people go to bed at night or get up in the morning, levels of positive affect tend to peak around the halfway point between waking and sleeping. Negative affect, however, shows little fluctuation throughout the day.[21]

What does this mean for organizational behavior? Asking someone for a favor or conveying bad news are probably not good ideas on Monday morning. Our workplace interactions will probably be more positive from mid-morning onward, as well as later in the week.

Weather   When do you think you would be in a better mood? When it's 70 degrees and sunny or when it's a gloomy, cold, rainy day? Many people believe their mood is tied to the weather. However, evidence suggests that weather has little effect on mood. One expert concluded, "Contrary to the prevailing cultural view, these data indicate that people do not report a better mood on bright and sunny days (or, conversely, a worse mood on dark and rainy days)."[22] *Illusory correlation* explains why people tend to *think* that nice weather improves their mood. **Illusory correlation** occurs when people associate two events that in reality have no connection.

Stress   As you might imagine, stress affects emotions and moods. At work, stressful daily events (a nasty e-mail, an impending deadline, the loss of a big sale, being reprimanded by your boss, and so on) negatively affect employees' moods. Also, the effects of stress build over time. As the authors of one study note, "a constant diet of even low-level stressful events has the potential to cause workers to experience gradually increasing levels of strain over time."[23] Such mounting levels of stress and strain at work can worsen our moods, and we experience more negative emotions.

Social Activities   For most people, social activities increase positive mood and have little effect on negative mood. But do people in positive moods seek out social interactions, or do social interactions cause people to be in good moods? It seems that both are true.[24] And, does the *type* of social activity matter? Indeed it does. Research suggests that physical (skiing or hiking with friends), informal (going to a party), or epicurean (taking pleasure in eating) activities are more strongly associated with increases in positive mood than formal (attending a meeting) or sedentary (watching TV with friends) events.[25]

Social interactions even have long-term health benefits. One study of longevity found that being in the company of others (as opposed to being socially isolated) was one of the *best* predictors of how long someone lives—more important than gender, or even blood pressure or cholesterol levels.[26] One of the reasons for this is positive affect.

Sleep   According to a recent poll, people are getting less and less sleep. On average, Americans sleep less than seven hours per weekday night—below the eight-hour recommendation. And the number of people who actually sleep eight or more hours a night has steadily decreased over the past few years to about one in four. Roughly 75 percent of those polled reported having at least one symptom of a sleep problem a few nights a week or more within the past year.[27]

As you might imagine, sleep quality affects mood. Undergraduates and adult workers who are sleep deprived report greater feelings of fatigue, anger, and hostility.[28] One of the reasons why less sleep, or poor sleep quality, puts people in a bad mood is that it impairs decision making and makes it difficult to control emotions.[29] A recent study suggests that poor sleep the previous night also impairs people's job satisfaction the next day, mostly because people feel fatigued, irritable, and less alert.[30]

Exercise   You often hear that people should exercise to improve their mood. But does "sweat therapy" really work? It appears so. Research consistently shows that exercise enhances people's positive mood.[31] It appears that the therapeutic effects of exercise are strongest for those who are depressed. Although the effects of exercise on moods are consistent, they are not terribly strong. So, exercise may help put you in a better mood, but don't expect miracles.

Age   Do you think that young people experience more extreme, positive emotions (so-called "youthful exuberance") than older people do? If you answered "Yes" you were wrong. One study of people aged 18 to 94 years revealed that negative emotions seem to occur less as people get older. Periods of highly positive moods lasted longer for older individuals and bad moods faded more quickly.[32] The study implies that emotional experience tends to improve with age, so that as we get older we experience fewer negative emotions.

Gender   The common belief is that women are more in touch with their feelings than men are—that they react more emotionally and are better able to read emotions in others. Is there any truth to these assumptions?

    The evidence does confirm differences between men and women when it comes to emotional reactions and the ability to read others. In contrasting the genders, women show greater emotional expression than men.[33] They experience emotions more intensely, and they display more frequent expressions of both positive and negative emotions, except anger.[34] In contrast to men, women also report more comfort in expressing emotions. Finally, women are better at reading nonverbal (e.g., facial expressions, body language) and paralinguistic cues, such as vocal quality, loudness, and tempo, than are men.[35]

    One explanation for these differences is the different ways men and women have been socialized.[36] Men are taught to be tough and brave, whereas women are socialized to be nurturing. A second explanation is that women may have more innate ability to read others and present their emotions than do men.[37] Third, women may have a greater need for social approval and, so, a higher propensity to show positive emotions, such as happiness.

External Constraints on Emotions

An emotion that is acceptable on the athletic playing field may be totally unacceptable when exhibited at the workplace. Similarly, what's appropriate in one country is often inappropriate in another. In this section, we look at organizational and cultural influences on emotions.

Organizational Influences   If you can't smile and appear happy, you're unlikely to have much of a career working at a Disney amusement park. Although there is no single emotional "set" that all organizations worldwide seek in their employees, in the United States the evidence indicates that there's a bias against the expression of negative and intense emotions.[38] Of course, such expressions are acceptable in some instances—for example, a brief grieving over the sudden death of a company's CEO or the celebration of a record year of profits. But for the most part, the climate in well-managed U.S. organizations is one that strives to be emotion free.

Cultural Influences   Does the degree to which people *experience* emotions vary across cultures? Do people's *interpretations* of emotions vary across cultures? Finally, do the norms for the *expression* of emotions differ across cultures? Let's tackle each of these questions one at a time.

   Does the degree to which people experience emotions vary across cultures? Yes. In China, for example, people report experiencing fewer positive and negative emotions than people in other cultures report, and whatever emotions the people in China do experience are less intense than what others report. Compared to Mainland Chinese, Taiwanese are more like Americans in their experience of emotions: On average, Taiwanese report more positive and fewer negative emotions than their Mainland Chinese counterparts.[39] In general, people in most cultures appear to experience certain positive and negative emotions, but the frequency of their experiences and their intensity do vary to some degree.

   Do people's interpretations of emotions vary across cultures? In general, people from all over the world interpret negative and positive emotions the same way. We all view negative emotions, such as hate, terror, and rage, as dangerous and destructive. And we all desire positive emotions—such as joy, love, and happiness. However, some cultures value certain emotions more than others. For example, Americans value enthusiasm whereas Chinese consider negative emotions to be more useful and constructive than do Americans. In general, pride is seen as a positive emotion in Western, individualistic cultures such as the United States, but Eastern cultures such as China and Japan tend to view pride as undesirable.[40]

   Do the norms for the expression of emotions differ across cultures? Absolutely. For example, Muslims see smiling as a sign of sexual attraction, so women have learned not to smile at men.[41] And research has shown that in collectivist countries people are more likely to believe that emotional displays have something to do with their own relationships with the people expressing the emotions, whereas people in individualistic cultures do not think that others' emotional expressions are directed at them.[42]

   Interestingly, some cultures lack words for standard American emotional terms such as *anxiety, depression,* and *guilt.* Tahitians, for example, don't have a word directly equivalent to *sadness.* When Tahitians are sad, their peers attribute their state to a physical illness.[43] Our discussion illustrates the need to consider cultural factors as influencing what managers consider emotionally appropriate. What's acceptable in one culture may seem extremely unusual or even dysfunctional in another. Managers need to know the emotional norms in each culture they do business in so they don't send unintended signals or misread the reactions of locals. For example, an American manager in Japan should know that whereas Americans tend to view smiling positively, Japanese are apt to attribute frequent smiling to a lack of intelligence.[44]

> —Managers need to know the emotional norms in each culture they do business in so they don't send unintended signals or misread the reactions of locals.

Emotional Labor

All employees expend physical and mental labor when they put their bodies and cognitive capabilities, respectively, into their jobs. But jobs also require **emotional labor**, which is an employee's expression of organizationally desired emotions during interpersonal transactions at work.[45]

The concept of emotional labor emerged from studies of service jobs, which makes sense given that these jobs demand employees to consistently display positive emotions. But really, emotional labor is relevant to almost every job. Managers expect employees to be courteous, not hostile, in interactions with coworkers. The true challenge is when employees have to project one emotion while simultaneously feeling another.[46] This disparity is **emotional dissonance**, and it can take a heavy toll on employees. Left untreated, bottled-up feelings of frustration, anger, and resentment can eventually lead to emotional exhaustion and burnout.[47]

Felt Versus Displayed Emotions

It can help you, on the job especially, if you separate emotions into *felt* or *displayed*.[48] **Felt emotions** are an individual's actual emotions. In contrast, **displayed emotions** are those that the organization requires workers to show and considers appropriate in a given job. They're not innate; they're learned. Thus, effective managers have learned to be serious when giving an employee a negative performance evaluation and to hide their anger when they've been passed over for promotion. And the salesperson who hasn't learned to smile and appear friendly, regardless of his true feelings at the moment, isn't typically going to last long on most sales jobs. How we *experience* an emotion isn't always the same as how we *show* it.[49]

Displaying fake emotions requires us to "act"—to suppress the emotions we really feel (not showing anger toward a customer, for example). **Surface acting** is hiding one's inner feelings and forgoing emotional expressions in response to display rules. For example, when a worker smiles at a customer even when he doesn't feel like it, he is surface acting. **Deep acting** is trying to modify one's true inner feelings based on display rules. A health-care provider trying to genuinely feel more empathy for her patients is deep acting.[50] Research shows that surface acting is more stressful to employees because it entails concealing one's true emotions.[51]

As we've noted, emotional norms vary across cultures. Cultural norms in the United States dictate that employees in service organizations should smile and act friendly when interacting with customers.[52] But this norm doesn't apply worldwide. In Israel, customers see smiling supermarket cashiers as inexperienced, so managers encourage cashiers to look somber.[53] And Wal-Mart has found that its emphasis on employee friendliness, which has won it a loyal following among U.S. shoppers, doesn't work in Germany. Accustomed to a culture in which the customer traditionally comes last, serious German shoppers have been turned off by Wal-Mart's friendly greeters and helpful personnel.[54]

EMOTIONAL INTELLIGENCE

—People who know their own emotions and are good at reading others' emotions may be more effective in their jobs.

People who know their own emotions and are good at reading others' emotions may be more effective in their jobs. That, in essence, is the theme underlying research on **emotional intelligence (EI)**—one's ability to detect and manage emotional cues and information.[55]

EI is composed of five dimensions:

- *Self-awareness:* being aware of what you're feeling
- *Self-management:* the ability to manage your own emotions and impulses

- *Self-motivation:* the ability to persist in the face of setbacks and failures
- *Empathy:* the ability to sense how others are feeling
- *Social skills:* the ability to handle the emotions of others

Several studies suggest that EI plays an important role in job performance. One illuminating study looked at the successes and failures of 11 U.S. presidents from Franklin Roosevelt to Bill Clinton. They were evaluated on six qualities: communication, organization, political skill, vision, cognitive style, and emotional intelligence. It was found that the key quality that differentiated the successful (like Roosevelt, Kennedy, and Reagan) from the unsuccessful (like Johnson, Carter, and Nixon) was emotional intelligence.[56]

The Case for EI

EI has been a controversial concept in OB. It has its supporters and detractors. Next, we'll review the arguments for, and against, the viability of EI in OB.

Intuitive Appeal   There's a lot of intuitive appeal to the EI concept. Most everyone would agree that it is good to possess street smarts and social intelligence. Those people who can detect emotions in others, control their own emotions, and handle social interactions well will have a powerful leg up in the business world, so the thinking goes. For example, partners in a multinational consulting firm who scored above the median on an EI measure delivered $1.2 million more in business than did the other partners.[57]

EI Predicts Criteria That Matter   Evidence is mounting that suggests a high level of EI means a person will perform well on the job. For example, a review of 59 studies indicated that, overall, EI correlated moderately with job performance.[58]

EI Is Biologically Based   One study has shown that people with damage (lesions) in the part of the brain that governs emotional processing (prefrontal cortex) score significantly lower on EI tests. Even though these brain-damaged people scored no lower on standard measures of intelligence than people without the same brain damage, they were still impaired in normal decision making. This study suggests that EI is neurologically based in a way that's unrelated to standard measures of intelligence, and that people who suffer neurological damage score lower on EI and make poorer decisions than people who are healthier in this regard.[59]

The Case Against EI

For all its supporters, EI has just as many critics.

EI Is Too Vague a Concept   To many researchers, it's not clear what EI is. Is it a form of intelligence? Most of us wouldn't think that being self-aware or self-motivated or having empathy is a matter of intellect. Moreover, many times different researchers focus on different skills, making it difficult to get a definition of EI. One researcher may study self-discipline, whereas another may study empathy. As one reviewer noted, "The concept of EI has now become so broad and the components so variegated that . . . it is no longer even an intelligible concept."[60]

EI Can't Be Measured   Many critics have raised questions about measuring EI. For instance, people argue that because EI is a form of intelligence there must be right and wrong answers about it on tests. However, many measures are self-reported, meaning there are no right or wrong answers. For example, an EI test question might ask you to respond to the statement "I'm good at 'reading' other people." In general, the measures of EI are diverse, and researchers have not subjected them to rigorous study as much as they have measures of personality and general intelligence.[61]

The Validity of EI Is Suspect   Some critics argue that because EI is so closely related to intelligence and personality, once you control for these factors, EI has nothing unique to offer. This argument has some merit. EI appears to be highly correlated with measures of personality, especially emotional stability.[62] But there hasn't been enough research on whether EI adds insight beyond measures of personality and general intelligence in predicting job performance. Still, among consulting firms and in the popular press, EI is wildly popular. For example, one company's promotional materials for an EI measure claimed, "EI accounts for more than 85 percent of star performance in top leaders."[63] To say the least, it's hard to validate this statement with the research literature.

Whatever your view of EI, one thing's for sure: The concept is here to stay.

APPLICATIONS OF EMOTIONS AND MOODS TO OB

Let's conclude our discussion of emotions and moods by considering their specific application to OB. We'll assess how an understanding of emotions and moods can improve our ability to explain and predict the selection process in organizations, decision making, creativity, motivation, leadership, interpersonal conflict, negotiation, customer service, job attitudes, and deviant workplace behaviors.

Selection

One implication from the evidence to date on EI is that employers should consider it a factor in hiring employees, especially in jobs that demand a high degree of social interaction. In fact, more and more employers are starting to use EI measures to hire people. A study of U.S. Air Force recruiters showed that top-performing recruiters exhibited high levels of EI. Using these findings, the Air Force revamped its selection criteria. A follow-up investigation found that future hires who had high EI scores were 2.6 times more successful than those who didn't. By using EI in selection, the Air Force was able to cut turnover rates among new recruiters in one year by more than 90 percent and save nearly $3 million in hiring and training costs. At L'Oreal, salespersons selected on EI scores outsold those hired using the company's old selection procedure. On an annual basis, salespeople selected on the basis of emotional competence sold $91,370 more than other salespeople did, for a net revenue increase of $2,558,360.[64]

Decision Making

OB researchers continue to debate the role of negative emotions and moods in decision making. One well-cited article suggested that depressed people (those who chronically experience bad moods or negative emotions such as sadness) make more accurate judgments than nondepressed people.[65] This suggestion led some researchers to argue that the saying "sadder but wiser" is true. However, more recent evidence has suggested that people who are depressed make poorer decisions than happy people because depressed people are slower at processing information and tend to weigh all possible options rather than the most likely ones.[66] Although it would seem that weighing all possible options is a good thing, the problem is that depressed people search for the perfect solution when rarely is any single solution perfect.

Positive people, in contrast, know when a solution is good enough. Indeed, positive emotions seem to help decision making. Positive emotions can increase problem-solving skills and help us understand and analyze new information. For example, someone in a positive mood may be better able to infer that a subordinate's performance problems were due to some nonwork problems.[67] People in good moods or those experiencing positive emotions are more likely to use heuristics, or rules of thumb to help them make good decisions quickly.[68] Sometimes, however, these heuristics can be wrong and can lead to stereotyping.

—*Positive emotions can increase problem-solving skills and help us understand and analyze new information.*

Creativity

People who are in good moods are more creative than people in bad moods, say some researchers.[69] They produce more ideas, others think their ideas are original, and they tend to identify more creative options to problems.[70] Supervisors should actively try to keep employees happy because this will create more good moods (employees like their leaders to encourage them and provide positive feedback on a job well done), which in turn leads people to be more creative.[71]

Some researchers, however, do not believe that a positive mood makes people more creative. They argue that when people are in positive moods, they may relax ("If I'm in a good mood, things must be going okay, and I must not need to think of new ideas") and not engage in the critical thinking necessary for some forms of creativity.[72] However, this view is controversial. Until there are more studies on the subject, we can safely conclude that for many tasks, positive moods increase our creativity.

Motivation

Two studies have highlighted the effects of mood and emotions on motivation and suggest that organizations that promote positive moods at work are likely to have a more motivated workforce. The first study had two groups of people solve a number of word puzzles. One group saw a funny video clip, which was intended to put the group in a good mood before having to solve the puzzles. The other group was not shown the clip and just started working on solving the word puzzles right away. The results? The positive-mood group reported higher expectations of being able to solve the puzzles, worked harder at them, and solved more puzzles as a result.[73]

The second study found that giving people feedback—whether real or fake—about their performance influenced their moods, which then influenced their motivation.[74] So, a cycle can exist in which positive moods cause people to be more creative, leading to positive feedback from those observing their work. This positive feedback then further reinforces their positive mood, which may then make them perform even better, and so on.

Leadership

Effective leaders rely on emotional appeals to help convey their messages.[75] In fact, the expression of emotions in speeches is often the critical element that makes us accept or reject a leader's message. "When leaders feel excited, enthusiastic, and active, they may be more likely to energize their subordinates and convey a sense of efficacy, competence, optimism, and enjoyment."[76] Politicians, as a case in point, have learned to show enthusiasm when talking about their chances of winning an election, even when polls suggest otherwise.

Corporate executives know that emotional content is critical if employees are to accept change and buy into their visions of their companies' futures. When higher-ups offer new visions, especially when the visions contain distant or vague goals, it is often difficult for employees to accept those visions and the changes they'll bring. So when effective leaders want to implement significant changes, they rely on "the evocation, framing, and mobilization of *emotions*."[77] By arousing emotions and linking them to an appealing vision, leaders increase the likelihood that managers and employees alike will accept change.

Interpersonal Conflict

—The manager who ignores the emotional elements in conflicts, focusing singularly on rational and task-focused concerns, is unlikely to resolve those conflicts.

Few issues are more intertwined with emotions than the topic of interpersonal conflict. Whenever conflicts arise among coworkers, you can be fairly certain that emotions are surfacing. A manager's success in trying to resolve conflicts, in fact, is often largely attributable to an ability to identify the emotional elements in the conflict and to get the parties to work through their emotions. The manager who ignores the emotional elements in conflicts, focusing singularly on rational and task-focused concerns, is unlikely to resolve those conflicts.

Negotiation

Negotiation is an emotional process; however, we often say a skilled negotiator has a "poker face." The founder of Britain's Poker Channel, Crispin Nieboer, stated, "It is a game of bluff and there is fantastic human emotion and tension, seeing who can bluff the longest."[78] Several studies have shown that negotiators who feign anger have an advantage over their opponents. Why? Because when a negotiator shows anger, the opponent concludes that the negotiator has conceded all that she can, and so the opponent gives in.[79]

Displaying a negative emotion (such as anger) can be effective, but feeling bad about your performance appears to impair future negotiations. Negotiators who do poorly experience negative emotions, develop negative perceptions of their counterparts, and are less willing to share information or be cooperative in future negotiations.[80] Interestingly, then, while moods and emotions have their benefits at work, unless we're putting up a false front (feigning anger) when negotiating, it seems that emotions may impair negotiator performance. In fact, one 2005 study found that people who suffered damage to the emotional centers of their brains (damage to the same part of the brain as Phineas Gage) may be the *best* negotiators, because they're not likely to overcorrect when faced with negative outcomes.[81] Consider another example: When Northwest Airlines faced a strike from the mechanics union, the company coolly prepared for the strike by hiring replacement workers in advance and, when the union struck, hired replacement workers and calmly asked for even more concessions.[82]

Customer Service

A worker's emotional state influences customer service, which influences levels of repeat business and levels of customer satisfaction.[83] Providing quality customer service makes demands on employees because it often puts them in a state of emotional dissonance. Over time, this state can lead to job burnout, declines in job performance, and lower job satisfaction.[84]

In addition, employees' emotions may also be transferred to the customer. Studies indicate a matching effect between employee and customer emotions, which OB practitioners call **emotional contagion**, the "catching" of emotions from others.[85] How does emotional contagion work? The primary explanation is that when someone experiences positive emotions and laughs and smiles at you, you begin to copy that person's behavior. So when employees express positive emotions, customers tend to respond positively. Emotional contagion is important because when customers catch the positive moods or emotions of employees, they shop longer.[86] But what about negative emotions and moods? Are they contagious too? Absolutely. When an employee is cranky or nasty, these negative emotions tend to have negative effects on customers.

Job Attitudes

Ever hear the advice "Never take your work home with you," meaning that people should forget about their work once they go home? As it turns out, that's easier said than done. Several studies have shown that people who had a good day at work tend to be in a better mood at home that evening. And people who had a bad day tend to be in a bad mood once they're at home.[87] Evidence also suggests that people who have a stressful day at work have trouble relaxing once they get off work.[88]

Even though people do emotionally take their work home with them, by the next day the effect is usually gone.[89] So, though it may be hard or even unnatural to "never take your work home with you," it doesn't appear that, for most people, a negative mood resulting from a bad day at work carries over to the next day.

Deviant Workplace Behaviors

Anyone who has spent much time in an organization realizes that people often behave in ways that violate established norms and that threaten the organization, its members, or both. Many of these deviant behaviors can be traced to negative emotions.

For instance, envy is an emotion that occurs when you resent someone for having something that you don't have but that you strongly desire, such as a better work assignment, larger office, or higher salary.[90] It can lead to malicious deviant behaviors. An envious employee, for example, could then act hostilely by backstabbing another employee, negatively distorting others' successes, and positively distorting his own accomplishments.[91] Evidence suggests that people who feel negative emotions, particularly those who feel angry or hostile, are more likely than people who don't feel negative emotions to engage in deviant behavior at work.[92]

IMPLICATIONS FOR MANAGERS

Emotions and moods are similar in that both are affective in nature, but moods are more general and less contextual than emotions. And, events do matter. The time of day and day of the week, stressful events, social activities, and sleep patterns are all factors that influence emotions and moods.

There are certainly limits, practically and ethically, to managers controlling their colleagues' and employees' emotions and moods. Emotions and moods are a natural part of an individual's makeup. Where managers err is if they ignore their coworkers' emotions and assess others' behavior as if it were completely rational. As one consultant aptly put it, "You can't divorce emotions from the workplace because you can't divorce emotions from people."[93] Managers who understand the role of emotions and moods will significantly improve their abilities to explain and predict their coworkers' behavior.

Emotions and moods do affect job performance. In fact, they can *hinder* performance, especially negative emotions. That's probably why organizations, for the most part, try to eliminate emotions from the workplace. But emotions and moods can also *enhance* performance in two ways:

1. Emotions and moods can increase arousal levels and can motivate employees to work better.
2. Emotional labor recognizes that certain feelings can be part of a job's requirements.

So, for instance, the ability to effectively manage emotions in leadership, sales, and customer service positions may be critical to success in those positions. At the same time, organizations that shun the display of positive emotions, or encourage employees to suppress negative emotions, may find that both take a toll on their workforces.

Although there is no precise answer to what differentiates functional from dysfunctional emotions and moods at work, some analysts have suggested that the critical moderating variable is the complexity of the individual's task.[94] The more complex a task, the less emotional a worker can be before emotions interfere with performance. While a minimal level of emotional arousal is probably necessary for good performance, high levels interfere with the ability to function, especially if the job requires calculative and detailed cognitive processes. Given that the trend is toward jobs becoming more complex, you can see why organizations are likely to become more concerned with the role of emotions—especially intense ones—in the workplace.

CHAPTER 8

Foundations of Group Behavior

After studying this chapter, you should be able to:

1. Differentiate between formal and informal groups.
2. Explain how role requirements change in different situations.
3. Describe how norms exert influence on an individual's behavior.
4. Explain what determines status in groups.
5. Define social loafing and its effect on group performance.
6. Identify the benefits and disadvantages of cohesive groups.
7. List the strengths and weaknesses of group decision making.
8. Contrast the effectiveness of interacting, brainstorming, nominal, and electronic meeting groups.

Our objectives in Chapters 8 and 9 are to introduce you to basic group concepts, to provide you with a foundation for understanding how groups work, and to show you how to create effective teams. Let's begin by defining groups and explaining why people join them.

DEFINING AND CLASSIFYING GROUPS

A **group** is defined as two or more individuals, interacting and interdependent, who have come together to achieve particular objectives. Groups can be either *formal* or *informal*. By **formal groups**, we mean those defined by the organization's structure, with designated work assignments establishing tasks, such as the six members making up an airline flight crew. In formal groups, the behaviors that one should engage in are stipulated by and directed toward organizational goals. In contrast, **informal groups** are alliances that are neither formally structured nor organizationally determined, such as three employees from different departments who regularly eat lunch together. These groups are natural formations in the work environment that appear in response to the need for social contact.

It's possible to further subclassify groups as *command, task, interest,* or *friendship groups.*[1] Command and task groups are dictated by the formal organization, whereas interest and friendship groups are informal alliances.

A **command group** is determined by the organization chart. It is composed of the individuals who report directly to a given manager. An elementary school principal and her 18 teachers form a command group, as do the director of postal audits and his five inspectors.

Task groups, also organizationally determined, represent those working together to complete a job task. However, a task group's boundaries are not limited to its immediate hierarchical superior. It can cross command relationships. For instance, if a college student is accused of a campus crime, it may require communication and coordination among the dean of academic affairs, the dean of students, the registrar, the director of security, and the student's advisor. Such a formation would constitute a task group.

People who may or may not be aligned into common command or task groups may affiliate to attain a specific objective of shared interest. This is an **interest group**. Employees who band together to have their vacation schedules altered, to support a peer who has been fired, or to seek improved working conditions represent the formation of a united body to further their common interest.

Groups often form because the individual members have one or more common characteristics. We call these formations **friendship groups**. Social alliances, which frequently extend outside the work situation, can be based on similar age or ethnic heritage, support for the same athletic team, interest in the same alternative rock band, or the holding of similar political views, for example.

No single reason explains why individuals join groups. Because most people belong to a number of groups, it's obvious that different groups provide different benefits to their members. Exhibit 8-1 summarizes the most popular reasons people have for joining groups.

GROUP PROPERTIES: ROLES, NORMS, STATUS, SIZE, AND COHESIVENESS

Work groups are not unorganized mobs. Work groups have properties that shape the behaviors of members and make it possible to explain and predict a large portion of individual behaviors within the group, as well as the performance of the group itself. Roles, norms, status, group size, and the degree of group cohesiveness are some of these properties.

Roles

All group members are actors, each playing a **role**. By this term, we mean a set of expected behavior patterns attributed to someone occupying a given position in a social unit. The understanding of role behavior would be dramatically simplified if each of us chose one role and played it out regularly and consistently. Unfortunately,

EXHIBIT 8-1   Why Do People Join Groups?

Security. By joining a group, individuals can reduce the insecurity of having to stand on their own. People feel stronger, have fewer self-doubts, and are more resistant to threats when they are part of a group.

Status. Inclusion in a group that is viewed as important by others provides recognition and status for its members.

Self-esteem. Groups can provide people with feelings of self-worth. That is, in addition to conveying status to those outside the group, membership can also give increased feelings of worth to the group members themselves.

Affiliation. Groups can fulfill social needs. People enjoy the regular interaction that comes with group membership. For many people, these on-the-job interactions are their primary source for fulfilling their needs for affiliation.

Power. What cannot be achieved individually often becomes possible through group action. There is power in numbers.

Goal Achievement. Sometimes it takes more than one person to accomplish a particular task, so people pool talents, knowledge, or power. In such instances, management will rely on the use of a formal group.

we are required to play a number of diverse roles, both on and off our jobs. As we'll see, one of the tasks in understanding behavior is grasping the role that a person is currently playing.

For example, Bill Patterson is a plant manager with EMM Industries, a large electrical equipment manufacturer in Phoenix. Bill has a number of roles that he fulfills on that job—for instance, EMM employee, member of middle management, electrical engineer, and primary community spokesperson for the company. Off the job, Bill Patterson finds himself in still more roles: husband, father, Catholic, Rotarian, tennis player, member of the Thunderbird Country Club, and president of his homeowners' association. Many of these roles are compatible; some create conflicts. For instance, how does Bill's religious involvement influence his managerial decisions regarding layoffs, expense account padding, and providing accurate information to government agencies? Say that a recent offer of promotion requires Bill to relocate, yet his family very much wants to stay in Phoenix. Can the role demands of his job be reconciled with the demands of Bill's roles as husband and father?

Like Bill Patterson, we all are required to play a number of roles, and our behaviors vary with the roles we are playing. So different groups impose different role requirements on individuals.

Role Identity   Certain attitudes and actual behaviors are consistent with a role, and they create the **role identity**. People have the ability to shift roles rapidly when they recognize that the situation and its demands clearly require major changes. For instance, when union stewards were promoted to supervisory positions, it was found that their attitudes changed from pro-union to pro-management within a few months of their promotion. When these promotions had to be rescinded later because of economic difficulties in the firm, it was found that the demoted supervisors had once again adopted their pro-union attitudes.[2]

Role Perception   Our view of how we're supposed to act in a given situation is a **role perception**. Based on an interpretation of how we believe we are supposed to behave, we engage in certain types of behavior.

We get these perceptions from stimuli all around us, such as friends, books, movies, television. For example, many current law enforcement officers might have learned their roles from reading Joseph Wambaugh novels; many of tomorrow's lawyers might be influenced by watching the actions of attorneys in *Law & Order;* and the role of crime investigators, as portrayed on the television program *CSI,* could direct people into careers in criminology. Of course, the primary reason that apprenticeship programs exist in many trades and professions is to allow beginners to watch an "expert" so that they can learn to act as they should.

Role Expectations   How others believe you should act in a given situation constitutes **role expectations**. How you behave is determined to a large extent by the role defined in the context in which you are acting. For instance, the role of a U.S. federal judge is viewed as having propriety and dignity, whereas a football coach is seen as aggressive, dynamic, and inspiring to his players.

In the workplace, it can be helpful to look at role expectations through the perspective of the **psychological contract**. An unwritten agreement exists between employees and their employers. This psychological contract sets out mutual expectations: what management expects from workers, and vice versa.[3] In effect, this contract defines the behavioral expectations that go with every role. Management is expected to treat employees justly, provide acceptable working conditions, clearly communicate what is a fair day's work, and give feedback on how well the employee is doing. Likewise, employees are expected to respond by demonstrating a good attitude, following directions, and showing loyalty to the organization.

If management is derelict in keeping up its part of the bargain by not fulfilling the role expectations defined in the psychological contract, we can expect negative repercussions on employee performance and satisfaction. When an employee fails to live up to expectations, the result is usually some form of disciplinary action up to and including firing.

Role Conflict   When an individual finds that compliance with one role requirement may make it more difficult to comply with another **role conflict** occurs.[4] In the extreme, it would include situations in which two or more role expectations contradict.

Bill Patterson had to deal with many roles that included several role conflicts—such as his attempt to reconcile the expectations placed on him as a husband and father with those placed on him as an executive with EMM Industries. The familial role emphasizes stability and concern for the desire of his wife and children to remain in Phoenix. The EMM role expects its employees to be responsive to the needs and requirements of the company. Although it might be in Bill's financial and career interests to accept a relocation, the conflict comes down to choosing between family and career role expectations.

Norms

—Norms tell members of a group what they ought and ought not to do under certain circumstances.

All groups have established **norms**, acceptable standards of behavior that are shared by the group's members. Norms tell members what they ought and ought not to do in specific circumstances. When agreed to and accepted by the group's members, norms act as a means of influencing the behavior of group members with a minimum of external controls. Norms differ among groups, communities, and societies, but they all have them.[5]

The Hawthorne Studies Behavioral scientists generally agree that, until the early 1930s, we did not fully appreciate the importance norms play in influencing worker behavior. This enlightenment grew out of a series of studies undertaken at the Western Electric Company's Hawthorne Works in Chicago between 1924 and 1932.[6] Originally initiated by Western Electric officials and later overseen by Harvard professor Elton Mayo, the Hawthorne studies concluded that:

- a worker's behavior and sentiments were closely related,
- group influences were significant in affecting individual behavior,
- group standards were highly effective in establishing individual worker output, and
- money was less a factor in determining worker output than were group standards, sentiments, and security.

Let's briefly discuss the Hawthorne investigations and examine the importance of these findings in explaining group behavior.

The Hawthorne researchers began by examining the relation between the physical environment and productivity. They began with illumination experiments with various groups of workers. The researchers manipulated the intensity of illumination upward and downward, while at the same time noting changes in group output. Results varied, but one thing was clear: In no case was the increase or decrease in output in proportion to the increase or decrease in illumination. These findings contradicted the researchers' anticipated results.

So, the researchers introduced a control group: An experimental group was presented with varying intensity of illumination, while the controlled unit worked under a constant illumination intensity. Again, the results bewildered the Hawthorne researchers. As the light level was increased in the experimental unit, output rose for both the control and the experimental group. But to the surprise of the researchers, as the light level was dropped in the experimental group, productivity continued to increase in both groups. In fact, a productivity decrease was observed in the experimental group only when the light intensity had been reduced to that of moonlight. The Hawthorne researchers concluded that illumination intensity was only a minor influence among the many influences that affected an employee's productivity, but they could not explain the behavior they had witnessed.

As a follow-up to the illumination experiments, the researchers began a second set of experiments in the relay assembly test room at Western Electric. A small group of women was isolated from the main work group so that the women's behavior could be more carefully observed. All went about their jobs of assembling small telephone relays in a room laid out similarly to their normal department. The only significant difference was the placement in the room of a research assistant who acted as an observer; kept records of output, rejects, and working conditions; and maintained a daily log sheet describing everything that happened. Observations covering a multi-year period showed that this small group's output increased steadily. The number of personal absences and those due to sickness was approximately one-third of those recorded by women in the regular production department. What became evident was that this group's performance was significantly influenced by its status of being a "special" group. The women in the test room thought that being in the experimental group was fun, that they were in an elite group, and that management showed concern for their interests by engaging in such experimentation. In essence, workers in both the illumination and assembly test-room experiments were reacting to the increased attention they were receiving.

A third study in the bank wiring observation room was introduced to ascertain the effect of a sophisticated wage incentive plan. The assumption was that individual workers would maximize their productivity when they saw that it was directly related to economic rewards. The most important finding coming out of this study was that employees did not individually maximize their outputs. Rather, their output became controlled by a group norm that determined what was a proper day's work. Output was not only restricted, but individual workers were giving erroneous reports. The total for a week would check with the total week's output, but the daily reports showed an implausibly steady level of output (when in reality actual daily production was much more variable). What was going on?

Through interviews it was determined that the group was operating well below its capability and was leveling output to protect itself. Members were afraid that if they significantly increased their output, the unit incentive rate would be cut, the expected daily output would be increased, layoffs might occur, or slower workers would be reprimanded. So the group established its idea of a fair output: neither too much nor too little. They helped each other out to ensure their reports were nearly level.

The norms the group established included a number of "don'ts." *Don't* be a rate-buster, turning out too much work. *Don't* be a chiseler, turning out too little work. *Don't* be a squealer on any of your peers. The group enforced these norms with methods that were neither gentle nor subtle and included sarcasm, name-calling, ridicule, and even physical punches to the upper arm of members who violated the group's norms. Members would also ostracize individuals who behaved against the group's interest.

The Hawthorne studies made an important contribution to our understanding of group behavior—particularly the significant place that norms have in determining individual work behavior.

Conformity   As a member of a group, you desire acceptance by the group. Because of your desire for acceptance, you are susceptible to conforming to the group's norms. Considerable evidence shows that groups can place strong pressures on individual members to change their attitudes and behaviors to conform to the group's standard.[7]

Do individuals conform to the pressures of all the groups to which they belong? Obviously not, because people belong to many groups and their norms vary. In some cases, they may even have contradictory norms. So they conform to the important groups to which they belong or hope to belong. The important groups have been called **reference groups**, and they're characterized as ones in which a person is aware of other members; defines himself or herself as a member, or would like to be a member; and feels that the group members are significant to him or her.[8] The implication, then, is that all groups do not impose equal conformity pressures on their members.

The impact that group pressures for **conformity** can have on an individual member's judgment and attitudes was demonstrated in the now-classic studies by Solomon Asch.[9] Asch made up groups of seven or eight people who sat around a table and were asked to compare two cards held by the experimenter. One card had one line, the other had three lines of varying length. As shown in Exhibit 8-2, one of the lines on the three-line card was identical to the line on the one-line card. Also as shown in Exhibit 8-2, the difference in line length was quite obvious; in fact, under ordinary conditions, subjects' errors were fewer than 1 percent. The object was to

EXHIBIT 8-2   Examples of Cards Used in Asch's Study

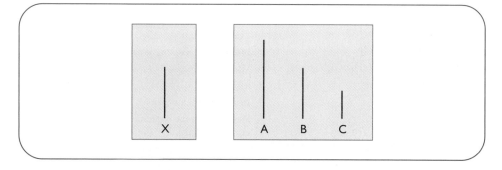

announce aloud which of the three lines matched the single line. But what happens if the members in the group begin to give incorrect answers? Will the pressures to con-form result in an unsuspecting subject (USS) altering an answer to align with the others? That was what Asch wanted to know. So he arranged the group so that only the USS was unaware that the experiment was "fixed." The seating was pre-arranged: The USS was placed so as to be one of the last to announce a decision.

The experiment began with several sets of matching exercises. All the subjects gave the right answers. On the third set, however, the first subject gave an obviously wrong answer—for example, saying "C" in Exhibit 8-2. The next subject gave the same wrong answer, and so did the others until the experiment got to the unknowing subject. He knew "B" was the same as "X," yet everyone had said "C." The decision confronting the USS was this: Do you publicly state a perception that differs from the preannounced position of the others in your group? Or do you give an answer that you strongly believe is incorrect in order to have your response agree with that of the other group members?

The results obtained by Asch demonstrated that over many experiments and many trials, 75 percent of the subjects gave at least one answer that conformed—that is, they gave an answer that they knew was wrong but that was consistent with the replies of other group members—and the average across all USSs was 37 percent. This suggests that there are group norms that press us toward conformity—that is, we desire to be one of the group and avoid being visibly different.

Asch's conclusions are based on research that was conducted 50 years ago. Has time altered their validity? And should we consider these findings generalizable across cultures? Evidence based on recent studies indicates that there have been changes in the level of conformity over time and that Asch's findings are culture bound.[10] Specifically, levels of conformity have steadily declined since Asch's studies in the early 1950s. In addition, conformity to social norms is higher in collectivist cultures than in individualistic cultures. Nevertheless, even in individualistic countries, you should consider conformity to norms to still be a powerful force in groups.

Deviant Workplace Behavior   Voluntary behavior that violates significant organi-zational norms and, in doing so, threatens the well-being of the organization or its members is **deviant workplace behavior** (also called *antisocial behavior* or *workplace incivility*).[11] Exhibit 8-3 provides a typology of deviant workplace behaviors, with examples of each.

EXHIBIT 8-3   Typology of Deviant Workplace Behavior

Category	Examples
Production	Leaving early
	Intentionally working slowly
	Wasting resources
Property	Sabotage
	Lying about hours worked
	Stealing from the organization
Political	Showing favoritism
	Gossiping and spreading rumors
	Blaming coworkers
Personal aggression	Sexual harassment
	Verbal abuse
	Stealing from coworkers

Source: Adapted from S. L. Robinson and R. J. Bennett, "A Typology of Deviant Workplace Behaviors: A Multidimensional Scaling Study," *Academy of Management Journal*, April 1995, p. 565.

As with norms in general, individual employees' antisocial actions are shaped by the group context within which they work. Evidence demonstrates that the antisocial behavior exhibited by a work group is a significant predictor of an individual's antisocial behavior at work.[12] In other words, deviant workplace behavior is likely to flourish where it's supported by group norms.

Additionally, just being part of a group can increase an individual's deviant behavior. In other words, someone who ordinarily wouldn't engage in deviant behavior might be more likely to do so when working in a group. In fact, a recent study suggests that, compared to individuals working alone, those working in a group were more likely to lie, cheat, and steal. As shown in Exhibit 8-4, in this study no individual working alone lied, but 22 percent of those working in groups did. Moreover, individuals working in groups also were more likely to cheat (55 percent of individuals working in a group cheated on a task versus 23 percent of individuals working alone) and steal (29 percent of individuals working in a group stole, compared to only 10 percent working alone).[13] Groups provide a shield of anonymity so that someone who ordinarily might be afraid of getting caught for stealing can rely on the fact that other group members had the same opportunity or reason to steal. This creates a false sense of confidence that may result in more aggressive behavior.

Status

Status—a socially defined position or rank given to groups or group members by others—permeates every society. Despite many attempts, we have made little progress toward a classless society. Even the smallest group will develop roles, rights, and rituals to differentiate its members. Status is an important factor in understanding human behavior because it is a significant motivator and has major behavioral consequences

EXHIBIT 8-4   Groups and Deviant Behavior

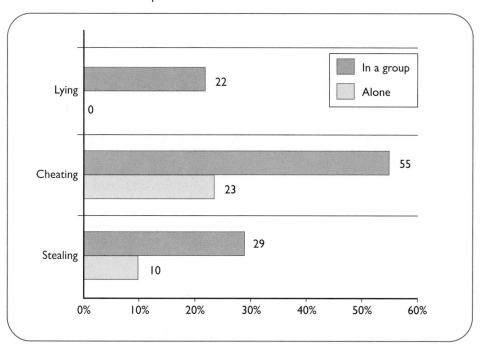

Source: A. Erez, H. Elms, and E. Fong, "Lying, Cheating, Stealing: Groups and the Ring of Gyges," paper presented at the Academy of Management Annual Meeting, Honolulu, HI, August 8, 2005.

when individuals perceive a disparity between what they believe their status to be and what others perceive it to be.

What Determines Status?   According to **status characteristics theory**, differences in status characteristics create status hierarchies within groups.[14] Moreover, status tends to be derived from one of three sources:

1. The power a person wields over others
2. A person's ability to contribute to a group's goals
3. An individual's personal characteristics[15]

People who control the outcomes of a group through their power tend to be perceived as high status. This is largely due to their ability to control the group's resources. So a group's formal leader or manager is likely to be perceived as high status when he or she can allocate resources such as preferred assignments, desirable schedules, and pay increases. People whose contributions are critical to the group's success also tend to have high status. The outstanding performers on sports teams, for example, typically have greater status on the team than do average players. Finally, someone who has personal characteristics that are positively valued by the group—such as good looks, intelligence, money, or a friendly personality—will typically have higher status than someone who has fewer valued attributes.

Status and Norms   Status has some interesting effects on the power of norms and

—High-status members of groups often are given more freedom to deviate from norms than are other group members.

pressures to conform. For instance, high-status members of groups often are given more freedom to deviate from norms than are other group members.[16] But this is true only as long as the high-status person's activities aren't severely detrimental to group goal achievement.[17] High-status people also are better able to resist conformity pressures than their lower-status peers. An individual who is highly valued by a group but who doesn't much need or care about the social rewards the group provides is particularly able to pay minimal attention to conformity norms.[18]

Status and Group Interaction   Interaction among members of groups is influenced by status. High-status people tend to be more assertive.[19] They speak out more often, criticize more, state more commands, and interrupt others more often. But status differences actually inhibit diversity of ideas and creativity in groups because lower-status members tend to be less active in group discussions. In situations in which lower-status members possess expertise and insights that could aid the group, their expertise and insights are not likely to be fully utilized, thus reducing the group's overall performance.

Status Inequity   It is important for group members to believe that the status hierarchy is equitable. When inequity (see Chapter 5) is perceived, it creates disequilibrium, which results in various types of corrective behavior.[20]

The trappings that go with formal positions are also important elements in maintaining equity. When we believe an inequity exists between the perceived ranking of an individual and the status accouterments that person is given by the organization, we are experiencing status incongruence. For example, incongruence may occur when a more desirable office location is held by a lower-ranking individual. In short, employees expect the things individuals have and receive to be congruent with their status.

Groups generally agree within themselves on status criteria and, hence, there is usually high concurrence in group rankings of individuals. However, individuals can find themselves in a conflict situation when they move among groups whose status criteria are different or when they join groups whose members have heterogeneous backgrounds. For instance, business executives may use personal income or the growth rate of their companies as determinants of status, whereas blue-collar workers may use years of seniority. In groups made up of heterogeneous individuals or when heterogeneous groups are forced to be interdependent, status differences may initiate conflict as the group attempts to reconcile and align the differing hierarchies.

Status and Culture   Do cultural differences affect status? The answer is a resounding "Yes."[21]

The importance of status does vary among cultures. The French, for example, are highly status conscious. Also, countries differ on the criteria that create status. Status for Latin Americans and Asians tends to be derived from family position and formal roles held in organizations. In contrast, although status is still important in some countries, such as the United States and Australia, it tends to be less "in your face." And it tends to be bestowed more on accomplishments than on titles and family trees.[22]

The message here is to make sure you understand who and what hold status when interacting with people from a culture different from your own. An American manager who doesn't understand that office size is not a measure of a Japanese executive's position or who fails to grasp the importance that the British place on family genealogy and social class is likely to unintentionally offend his Japanese or British counterpart and, in so doing, lessen his interpersonal effectiveness.

Size

Does the size of a group affect the group's overall behavior? The answer to this question is a definite "Yes," but the effect is contingent on what dependent variables you look at.[23] The evidence indicates that smaller groups are faster at completing tasks than are larger ones and that individuals perform better in smaller groups.[24] However, if the group is engaged in problem solving, large groups consistently get better marks than their smaller counterparts do.[25] Translating these results into specific numbers is a bit more hazardous, but we can offer some parameters. Large groups—with a dozen or more members—are good for gaining diverse input. So, if the goal of the group is fact-finding, larger groups should be more effective. On the other hand, smaller groups are better at doing something productive with that input. Groups of approximately seven members, therefore, tend to be more effective for taking action.

One of the most important findings related to the size of a group has been labeled **social loafing**. Social loafing is the tendency for individuals to expend less effort when working collectively than when working individually.[26] It directly challenges the logic that the productivity of the group as a whole should at least equal the sum of the productivity of each individual in that group.

A common stereotype about groups is that the sense of team spirit spurs individual effort and enhances the group's overall productivity. But that stereotype may be wrong. In the late 1920s, a German psychologist named Max Ringelmann compared the results of individual and group performance on a rope-pulling task.[27] He expected that the group's effort would be equal to the sum of the efforts of individuals within the group. That is, three people pulling together should exert three times as much pull on the rope as one person, and eight people should exert eight times as much pull. Ringelmann's results, however, didn't confirm his expectations. One person pulling on a rope alone exerted an average of 63 kilograms of force. In groups of three, the per-person force dropped to 53 kilograms. And in groups of eight, it fell to only 31 kilograms per person.

Replications of Ringelmann's research with similar tasks have generally supported his findings.[28] Group performance increases with group size, but the addition of new members to the group has diminishing returns on productivity. So more may be better in the sense that the total productivity of a group of four people is greater than that of three, but the individual productivity of each group member declines.

What causes this social loafing effect? It may be due to a belief that others in the group are not carrying their fair share. If you see others as lazy or inept, you can reestablish equity by reducing your effort. Another explanation is the dispersion of responsibility. Because the results of the group cannot be attributed to any single person, the relationship between an individual's input and the group's output is clouded. In such situations, individuals may be tempted to become "free riders" and coast on the group's efforts. In other words, efficiency declines when individuals think that their contributions cannot be measured.

Cohesiveness

Groups differ in their **cohesiveness**, the degree to which members are attracted to each other and are motivated to stay in the group.[29] Some work groups are cohesive because the members have spent a great deal of time together, or the group's small size facilitates high interaction, or the group has experienced external threats that have brought members close together. Cohesiveness is important because it has been found to be related to the group's productivity.[30]

Studies consistently show that the relationship between cohesiveness and productivity depends on the performance-related norms established by the group.[31] If performance-related norms are high (high output, quality work, cooperation with individuals outside the group), a cohesive group will be more productive than will a less cohesive group. But if a cohesive group has low performance norms, productivity will be low. When cohesiveness and performance-related norms are both low, productivity will tend to fall into the low-to-moderate range. These conclusions are summarized in Exhibit 8-5.

To encourage group cohesiveness you might try one or more of the following suggestions:

1. Make the group smaller.
2. Encourage agreement with group goals.
3. Increase the time members spend together.
4. Increase the status of the group and the perceived difficulty of attaining membership in the group.
5. Stimulate competition with other groups.
6. Give rewards to the group rather than to individual members.
7. Physically isolate the group.[32]

EXHIBIT 8-5   Relationship Among Group Cohesiveness, Performance Norms, and Productivity

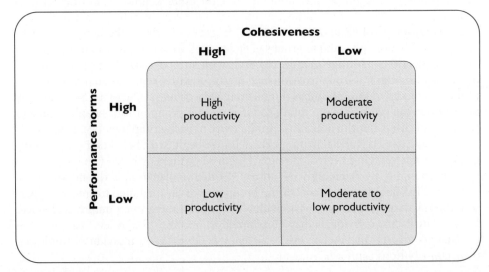

GROUP DECISION MAKING

The belief—characterized by juries—that two heads are better than one has long been accepted as a basic component of North American and many other countries' legal systems. This belief has expanded to the point that, today, many decisions in organizations are made by groups, teams, or committees.[33]

Groups Versus the Individual

Decision-making groups may be widely used in organizations, but does that imply that group decisions are preferable to those made by an individual alone? The answer to this question depends on a number of factors. Let's begin by looking at the strengths and weaknesses of group decision making.[34]

Strengths of Group Decision Making   Groups generate *more complete information and knowledge.* By aggregating the resources of several individuals, groups bring more input into the decision process. In addition to more input, groups can bring heterogeneity to the decision process. They offer *increased diversity of views.* This opens up the opportunity for more approaches and alternatives to be considered. In addition, groups lead to increased *acceptance of a solution.* Many decisions fail after the final choice is made because people don't accept the solution. Group members who participated in making a decision are likely to enthusiastically support the decision and encourage others to accept it.

Weaknesses of Group Decision Making   In spite of the advantages noted in the preceding paragraph, group decisions have their drawbacks. They're time-consuming because groups typically take more time to reach a solution than would an individual making the decision. There are *conformity pressures in groups.* The desire by group members to be accepted and considered an asset to the group can result in quashing any overt disagreement. Group discussion can be *dominated by one or a few members.* If this dominant coalition is composed of low- and medium-ability members, the group's overall effectiveness will suffer. Group decisions also suffer from *ambiguous responsibility.* In an individual decision, it's clear who is accountable for the final outcome. In a group decision, the responsibility of any single member is not as explicit.

Effectiveness and Efficiency   Whether groups are more effective than individuals depends on the criteria you use for defining effectiveness. In terms of *accuracy,* group decisions are generally more accurate than the decisions of the average individual in a group but less accurate than the judgments of the most accurate group member.[35] If decision effectiveness is defined in terms of *speed,* individuals are superior. If *creativity* is important, groups tend to be more effective than individuals. And if effectiveness means the degree of *acceptance* the final solution achieves, the nod again goes to the group.[36]

But effectiveness cannot be considered without also assessing efficiency. In terms of efficiency, groups almost always stack up as a poor second to the individual decision maker. With few exceptions, group decision making consumes more work hours than if an individual were to tackle the same problem alone. The exceptions tend to be the instances in which, to achieve comparable quantities of diverse input, the single decision maker must spend a great deal of time reviewing files and talking to people.

Because groups can include members from diverse areas, the time spent searching for information can be reduced. However, as we noted, these advantages in efficiency tend to be the exception. Groups are generally less efficient than individuals. In deciding whether to use groups, then, consideration should be given to assessing whether increases in effectiveness are more than enough to offset the losses in efficiency.

Groupthink and Groupshift

Two phenomena of group decision making—**groupthink** and **groupshift**—have the potential to affect a group's ability to appraise alternatives objectively and to arrive at quality decisions.

Groupthink   Have you ever felt like speaking up in a meeting, classroom, or informal group but decided against it? One reason may have been shyness. On the other hand, you may have been a victim of groupthink, the phenomenon that occurs when group members become so enamored of seeking concurrence that the norm for consensus overrides the realistic appraisal of alternative courses of action and the full expression of deviant, minority, or unpopular views. It describes a deterioration in an individual's mental efficiency, reality testing, and moral judgment as a result of group pressures.[37]

We have all seen the symptoms of the groupthink phenomenon:

1. Group members rationalize any resistance to the assumptions they have made. No matter how strongly the evidence may contradict their basic assumptions, members behave so as to reinforce those assumptions continually.
2. Members apply direct pressures on those who momentarily express doubts about any of the group's shared views or who question the validity of arguments supporting the alternative favored by the majority.
3. Members who have doubts or hold differing points of view seek to avoid deviating from what appears to be group consensus by keeping silent about misgivings and even minimizing to themselves the importance of their doubts.
4. An illusion of unanimity is present. If someone doesn't speak, it's assumed that he or she is in full accord. In other words, abstention becomes viewed as a "Yes" vote.[38]

In studies of historic U.S. foreign policy decisions, these symptoms were found to prevail when government policy-making groups failed—unpreparedness at Pearl Harbor in 1941, the U.S. invasion of North Korea, the Bay of Pigs fiasco, and the escalation of the Vietnam War.[39] More recently, the *Challenger* and *Columbia* space shuttle disasters and the failure of the main mirror on the *Hubble* telescope have been linked to decision processes at NASA in which groupthink symptoms were evident.[40]

Does groupthink attack all groups? No. It seems to occur most often when:

- a clear group identity exists,
- members hold a positive image of their group that they want to protect, and
- the group perceives a collective threat to this positive image.[41]

So groupthink is not a dissenter-suppression mechanism as much as it's a means for a group to protect its positive image.

To minimize groupthink, managers can monitor group size. Although no magic number will eliminate groupthink, individuals are likely to feel less personal responsibility when groups get larger than about 10 people. Managers should also encourage group leaders to actively seek input from all members and avoid expressing their own opinions, especially in the early stages of deliberation. Another tactic is to appoint one group member to play the role of devil's advocate to overtly challenge the majority position and offer divergent perspectives.

—Managers should encourage group leaders to actively seek input from all members and avoid expressing their own opinions, especially in the early stages of deliberation.

Groupshift   In comparing group decisions with the individual decisions of members within the group, evidence suggests that differences exist. In some cases, the group decisions are more conservative than the individual decisions. More often, the shift is toward greater risk.[42]

What appears to happen in groups is that the discussion leads to a significant shift in the positions of members toward a more extreme position in the direction in which they were already leaning before the discussion. So conservative types become more cautious and more aggressive types take on more risk. The group discussion tends to exaggerate the initial position of the group.

Groupshift can be viewed as actually a special case of groupthink. The decision of the group reflects the dominant decision-making norm that develops during the group's discussion. Whether the shift in the group's decision is toward greater caution or more risk depends on the dominant prediscussion norm. For instance, in cases where the initial group tendency is to be risk averse (risk seeking), the group will become even more risk averse.

The greater occurrence of the shift toward risk has generated several explanations for the phenomenon.[43] It's been argued that the discussion creates familiarization among the members. As they become more comfortable with each other, they also become more bold and daring. Another argument suggests that most First World societies value risk, that we admire individuals who are willing to take risks, and that group discussion motivates members to show that they are at least as willing as their peers to take risks. The most plausible explanation of the shift toward risk, however, seems to be that the group diffuses responsibility. Group decisions free any single member from accountability for the group's final choice. Greater risk can be taken in groups because no one member can be held wholly responsible, even if the decision fails.

To use the findings on groupshift, you should recognize that group decisions exaggerate the initial position of the individual members, that the shift has been shown more often to be toward greater risk, and that whether or not a group will shift toward greater risk or caution is a function of the members' prediscussion inclinations.

Group Decision-Making Techniques

The most common form of group decision making takes place in **interacting groups**. In these groups, members meet face to face and rely on both verbal and nonverbal interaction to communicate with each other. As our discussion of groupthink demonstrated, however, interacting groups often censor themselves and pressure individual members toward conformity of opinion. Brainstorming, the nominal group technique, and electronic meetings have been proposed as ways to reduce many of the problems inherent in the traditional interacting group.

Brainstorming is meant to overcome pressures for conformity in the interacting group that retard the development of creative alternatives.[44] It does this by utilizing an idea-generation process that specifically encourages any and all alternatives while with-holding any criticism of those alternatives.

In a typical brainstorming session, a half dozen to a dozen people sit around a table. The group leader states the problem in a clear manner so that it is understood by all participants. Members then free associate as many alternatives as they can in a given length of time. No criticism is allowed, and all the alternatives are recorded for later discussion and analysis.

Brainstorming may indeed generate ideas—but not in a very efficient manner. Research consistently shows that individuals working alone will generate more ideas than a group will in a brainstorming session. One of the primary reasons for that is *production blocking*. In other words, when people are generating ideas in a group, many people are talking at once, which blocks the thought process and eventually impedes the sharing of ideas.[45]

The **nominal group technique** restricts discussion or interpersonal communica-tion during the decision-making process, hence, the term *nominal*. Group members are all physically present, as in a traditional committee meeting, but members operate inde-pendently. Specifically, a problem is presented and then the following steps take place:

1. Members meet as a group, but before any discussion takes place each member inde-pendently writes down ideas about the problem.
2. After this silent period, each member presents one idea to the group. Each member takes a turn, presenting a single idea until all ideas have been presented and recorded. No discussion takes place until all ideas have been recorded.
3. The group then discusses the ideas for clarity and evaluates them.
4. Each group member silently and independently ranks the ideas in order of value or quality. The idea with the highest aggregate ranking determines the final decision.

The chief advantage of the nominal group technique is that it permits the group to meet formally but does not restrict independent thinking, as does the interacting group. Research generally shows that nominal groups outperform brainstorming groups.[46]

The most recent approach to group decision making blends the nominal group technique with sophisticated computer technology.[47] It's called the computer-assisted group or **electronic meeting**. Once the technology is in place, the concept is simple. Up to 50 people sit around a horseshoe-shaped table, empty except for a series of computer terminals. Issues are presented to participants, and they keyboard their responses into their computers. Individual comments, as well as aggregate votes, are displayed on a projection screen. The proposed advantages of electronic meetings are anonymity, honesty, and speed. Participants can anonymously type any message they want, and it flashes on the screen for all to see at the push of a participant's key. It also allows people to be brutally honest without penalty. And it's supposedly fast because chitchat is eliminated, discussions don't digress, and many participants can "talk" at once without stepping on one another's toes.

The early evidence, however, indicates that electronic meetings don't achieve most of their proposed benefits. Evaluations of numerous studies found that elec-tronic meetings actually led to *decreased* group effectiveness, required *more* time to complete tasks, and resulted in *reduced* member satisfaction when compared to face-to-face groups.[48] Nevertheless, current enthusiasm for computer-mediated communi-cations suggests that this technology is here to stay and is only likely to increase in popularity in the future.

IMPLICATIONS FOR MANAGERS

Performance   A number of group properties show a relationship to performance. Among the more prominent are role perception, norms, status differences, size of the group, and cohesiveness.

A positive relationship exists between role perception and an employee's performance evaluation.[49] The degree of congruence that exists between an employee and his or her boss in the perception of the employee's job influences the degree to which that employee will be judged as an effective performer by the boss. To the extent that the employee's role perception fulfills the boss's role expectations, the employee will receive a higher performance evaluation.

Norms control group-member behavior by establishing standards of right and wrong. The norms of a given group can help to explain the behaviors of its members for managers. When norms support high output, managers can expect individual performance to be markedly higher than when group norms aim to restrict output. Similarly, norms that support antisocial behavior increase the likelihood that individuals will engage in deviant workplace activities.

Status inequities create frustration and can adversely influence productivity and the willingness to remain with an organization. Among individuals who are equity sensitive, incongruence is likely to lead to reduced motivation and an increased search for ways to bring about fairness (e.g., taking another job). In addition, because lower-status people tend to participate less in group discussions, groups characterized by high status differences among members are likely to inhibit input from the lower-status members and to underperform their potential.

The impact of size on a group's performance depends on the type of task in which the group is engaged. Larger groups are more effective at fact-finding activities. Smaller groups are more effective at action-taking tasks. Our knowledge of social loafing suggests that if management uses larger groups, efforts should be made to provide measures of individual performance within the group.

Cohesiveness can play an important function in influencing a group's level of productivity. Whether or not it does depends on the group's performance-related norms.

Satisfaction   As with the role perception–performance relationship, high congruence between a boss and an employee as to the perception of the employee's job shows a significant association with high employee satisfaction.[50] Similarly, role conflict is associated with job-induced tension and job dissatisfaction.[51]

Most people prefer to communicate with others at their own status level or a higher one rather than with those below them.[52] As a result, we should expect satisfaction to be greater among employees whose jobs minimize interaction with individuals who are lower in status than themselves.

The group size–satisfaction relationship is what one would intuitively expect: Larger groups are associated with lower satisfaction.[53] As size increases, opportunities for participation and social interaction decrease, as does the ability of members to identify with the group's accomplishments. At the same time, having more members also prompts dissension, conflict, and the formation of subgroups, which all act to make the group less pleasant for individual participants.

CHAPTER 9

Understanding Work Teams

Having discussed groups in Chapter 8, now we'll turn our attention to a particular type of group, namely work teams. Decades ago, when companies like W. L. Gore, Volvo, and General Foods introduced teams into their production processes, it made news because no one else was doing it. Today, it's just the opposite. It's the organization that *doesn't* use teams that has become newsworthy. Approximately 80 percent of *Fortune* 500 companies now have half or more of their employees on teams. And 68 percent of small U.S. manufacturers are using teams in their production areas.[1] Thus, teams are increasingly becoming the primary means for organizing work in contemporary business firms.

WHY HAVE TEAMS BECOME SO POPULAR?

How do we explain the current popularity of teams? The evidence suggests that teams typically outperform individuals when the tasks being done require multiple skills, judgment, and experience.[2] As organizations have restructured themselves to compete more effectively and efficiently, they have turned to teams as a better way to use employee talents. Management has found that teams are more flexible and responsive to changing events than are traditional departments or other forms of permanent groupings. Teams have the capability to quickly assemble, deploy, refocus, and disband.

But don't overlook the motivational properties of teams. Consistent with our discussion in Chapter 6 of the role of employee involvement as a motivator, teams facilitate employee participation in operating decisions. For instance, some assembly-line workers at John Deere are part of sales teams that call on customers.[3] These workers know the products better than any traditional salesperson; and by traveling and speaking with farmers, these hourly workers develop new skills and become more involved in their jobs. So another explanation for the popularity of teams is that they are an effective means for management to democratize their organizations and increase employee motivation.

DIFFERENCES BETWEEN GROUPS AND TEAMS

Groups and teams are not the same, so we'll clarify the difference between a work group and a work team.

In Chapter 8, we defined a *group* as two or more individuals, interacting and interdependent, who have come together to achieve particular objectives. A **work group** is a group that interacts primarily to share information and to make decisions to help each member perform within his or her area of responsibility.

Work groups have no need or opportunity to engage in collective work that requires joint effort. So their performance is merely the summation of each group member's individual contribution. There is no positive synergy that would create an overall level of performance that is greater than the sum of the inputs.

In contrast, a **work team** generates positive synergy through coordinated effort. Their individual efforts result in a level of performance that is greater than the sum of those individual inputs. Exhibit 9-1 highlights the differences between work groups and work teams.

EXHIBIT 9-1   Comparing Work Groups and Work Teams

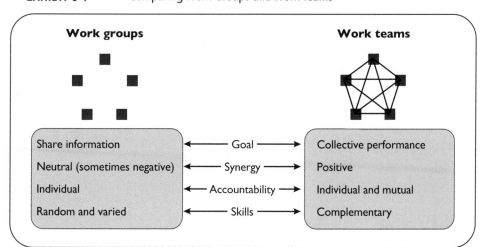

These definitions help clarify why so many organizations have recently restructured work processes around teams. Management is looking for that positive synergy that will allow their organizations to increase performance. The extensive use of teams creates the *potential* for an organization to generate greater outputs with no increase in inputs. Notice, however, we said "potential." There is nothing inherently magical in the creation of teams that ensures the achievement of this positive synergy. Merely calling a *group* a *team* doesn't automatically increase its performance. As we show later in this chapter, effective teams have certain common characteristics. If management hopes to gain increases in organizational performance through the use of teams, it must ensure that its teams possess these characteristics.

TYPES OF TEAMS

Teams can do a variety of things, including make products, provide services, negotiate deals, coordinate projects, offer advice, and make decisions. In this section we'll describe the four most common types of teams you're likely to find in an organization: *problem-solving teams*, *self-managed work teams*, *cross-functional teams*, and *virtual teams* (see Exhibit 9-2).

Problem-Solving Teams

If we look back 20 years or so, teams were just beginning to grow in popularity, and most of those teams took similar form. They were typically composed of 5 to 12 hourly employees from the same department who met for a few hours each week to discuss ways of improving quality, efficiency, and the work environment. We call these **problem-solving teams**.

In problem-solving teams, members share ideas or offer suggestions on how work processes and methods can be improved, although they rarely have the authority to unilaterally implement any of their suggested actions. For instance, Merrill Lynch created a problem-solving team to specifically figure out ways to reduce the number of days it took to open up a new cash management account.[4] By suggesting cuts in the number of steps in the process from 46 to 36, the team was able to reduce the average number of days from 15 to 8.

EXHIBIT 9-2   Four Types of Teams

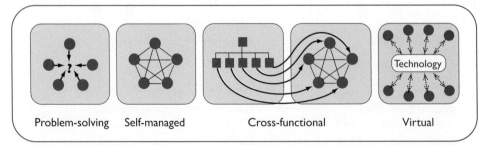

Problem-solving   Self-managed   Cross-functional   Virtual

Self-Managed Work Teams

Problem-solving teams were on the right track, but they didn't go far enough in getting employees involved in work-related decisions and processes. This led to experimentation with truly autonomous teams that could not only solve problems but could implement solutions and take full responsibility for outcomes.

Self-managed work teams are groups of employees (typically 10 to 15 in number) who perform highly related or interdependent jobs and take on many of the responsibilities of their former supervisors.[5] Typically, this includes planning and scheduling of work, assigning tasks to members, collective control over the pace of work, making operating decisions, taking action on problems, and working with suppliers and customers. Fully self-managed work teams even select their own members and have the members evaluate each other's performance. As a result, supervisory positions take on decreased importance and may even be eliminated.

A factory at Eaton Corp's Aeroquip Global Hose Division provides an example of how self-managed teams are being used in industry.[6] Located in the heart of Arkansas' Ozark Mountains, this factory makes a hydraulic hose that is used in trucks, tractors, and other heavy equipment. In 1994, to improve quality and productivity, Eaton-Aeroquip's management threw out the assembly line and organized the plant's 285 workers into more than 50 self-managed teams. Workers were suddenly free to participate in decisions that were previously reserved solely for management—the teams set their own schedules, selected new members, negotiated with suppliers, made calls on customers, and disciplined members who created problems. Between 1993 and 1999, this resulted in a 99 percent improvement in response time to customer concerns; productivity and manufacturing output both increased by more than 50 percent; and accident rates dropped by more than half.

Business periodicals have been chock-full of articles describing successful applications of self-managed teams, but a word of caution is merited. Some organizations have been disappointed with the results from self-managed teams. For instance, they don't seem to work well during organizational downsizing. Employees often view cooperating with the team concept as an exercise in assisting one's own executioner. The overall research on the effectiveness of self-managed work teams has not been uniformly positive.[7] Moreover, although individuals on these teams do tend to report higher levels of job satisfaction, they also sometimes have higher absenteeism and turnover rates. Inconsistency in findings suggests that the effectiveness of self-managed teams is situationally dependent.[8] In addition to downsizing, factors such as the strength and makeup of team norms, the type of tasks the team undertakes, and the reward structure can significantly influence how well the team performs. Finally, managers should take care when introducing self-managed teams globally. Evidence suggests that these types of teams have not fared well in Mexico, largely due to that culture's low tolerance of ambiguity and uncertainty and employees' strong respect for hierarchical authority.[9]

Cross-Functional Teams

The Boeing Company created a team made up of employees from production, planning, quality, tooling, design engineering, and information systems to automate shims on the company's C-17 program. The team's suggestions resulted in drastically reduced cycle time, cost, and improved quality on the C-17 program.[10]

This Boeing example illustrates the use of **cross-functional teams**. These teams are made up of employees from about the same hierarchical level, but from different work areas, who come together to accomplish a task.

Many organizations have used horizontal, boundary-spanning groups for decades. For example, IBM created a large task force in the 1960s—made up of employees from across departments in the company—to develop its highly successful System 360. And a *task force* is really nothing other than a temporary cross-functional team. Similarly, *committees* composed of members from across departmental lines are another example of cross-functional teams. But the popularity of cross-discipline work teams exploded in the late 1980s. For instance, all the major automobile manufacturers—including Toyota, Honda, Nissan, BMW, GM, Ford, and DaimlerChrysler—currently use this form of team to coordinate complex projects. And Harley-Davidson relies on specific cross-functional teams to manage each line of its motorcycles. These teams include Harley employees from design, manufacturing, and purchasing, as well as representatives from key outside suppliers.[11]

Cross-functional teams are an effective means for allowing people from diverse areas within an organization (or even between organizations) to exchange information, develop new ideas, solve problems, and coordinate complex projects. Of course, cross-functional teams are no picnic to manage. Their early stages of development are often very time-consuming as members learn to work with diversity and complexity. It takes time to build trust and teamwork, especially among people from different backgrounds with different experiences and perspectives.

Virtual Teams

The preceding types of teams do their work face to face. **Virtual teams** use computer technology to tie together physically dispersed members to achieve a common goal. They allow people to collaborate online—using communication links such as wide-area networks, video conferencing, or e-mail—whether they're only a room away or continents apart.

Virtual teams can do everything other teams do: share information, make decisions, complete tasks. And they can include members from the same organization or link an organization's members with employees from other organizations (such as suppliers and joint partners). They can convene for a few days to solve a problem, meet for a few months to complete a project, or exist permanently.

Three primary factors differentiate virtual teams from face-to-face teams:

1. The absence of paraverbal and nonverbal cues
2. Limited social context
3. The ability to overcome time and space constraints

In face-to-face conversation, people use paraverbal (tone of voice, inflection, and voice volume) and nonverbal (eye movement, facial expression, hand gestures, and other body language) cues. These help clarify communication by providing increased meaning, but they aren't available in online interactions. Virtual teams often suffer from less social rapport and less direct interaction among members. They aren't able to duplicate the normal give-and-take of face-to-face discussion. Especially when members haven't personally met, virtual teams tend to be more task oriented and exchange less social–emotional information. Not surprisingly, virtual team members report less satisfaction with the group interaction process than do face-to-face teams. Also, virtual teams are able to do their work even if members are thousands of miles apart and separated by a dozen or more time zones. It allows people to work together who might otherwise never be able to collaborate.

Some companies, such as Hewlett-Packard, Boeing, Ford, Motorola, GE, Lockheed Martin, VeriFone, and Royal Dutch/Shell, have become heavy users of virtual teams. Lockheed Martin, for instance, has put together a virtual team to build a new stealth fighter plane for the U.S. military. The team consists of engineers and designers from around the globe who will be working, simultaneously, on the $225 billion project. The company expects this team structure to save $250 million over the decade it will take to create the jet.[12]

CREATING EFFECTIVE TEAMS

There is no shortage of attempts to identify factors related to team effectiveness. However, recent studies have taken what was once a "veritable laundry list of characteristics"[13] and organized them into a relatively focused model.[14] Exhibit 9-3 summarizes what we currently know about what makes teams effective. As you'll see, it builds on many of the group concepts introduced in Chapter 8.

The following discussion is based on the model in Exhibit 9-3. Keep these two caveats in mind as we proceed:

- Teams differ in form and structure. Since the model we present attempts to generalize across all varieties of teams, you must be careful not to rigidly apply the model's predictions to all teams. The model should be used as a guide, not as an inflexible prescription.
- The model assumes that it's already been determined that teamwork is preferable over individual work. Creating "effective" teams in situations in which individuals can do the job better is equivalent to solving the wrong problem perfectly.

The key components making up effective teams can be separated into four general categories:

1. The resources and other *contextual* influences that make teams effective
2. The team's composition
3. *Work design*
4. *Process* variables that reflect what occurs in the team and influence effectiveness

What does *team effectiveness* mean in this model? Typically, this has included objective measures of the team's productivity, managers' ratings of the team's performance, and aggregate measures of member satisfaction.

Context

The four contextual factors that appear to be most significantly related to team performance are the presence of *adequate resources*, *effective leadership*, a *climate of trust*, and a *performance evaluation and reward system* that reflects team contributions.

EXHIBIT 9-3   Team Effectiveness Model

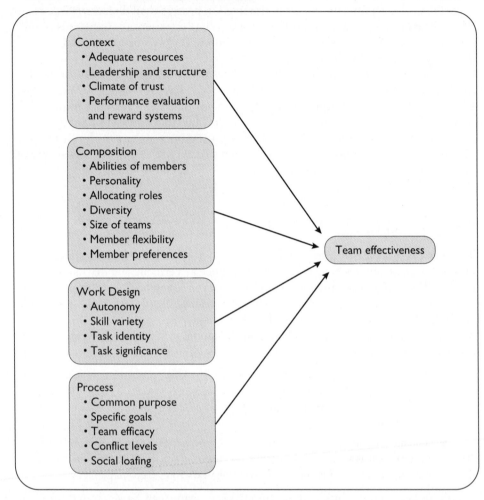

Adequate Resources   Teams are part of a larger organization system. A research team in Dow's plastic products division, for instance, must live within the budgets, policies, and practices set by Dow's corporate offices. As such, all work teams rely on resources outside the group to sustain it. A scarcity of resources directly reduces the ability of the team to perform its job effectively. As one set of researchers concluded, after looking at 13 factors potentially related to group performance, "Perhaps one of the most important characteristics of an effective work group is the support the group receives from the organization."[15] This support includes timely information, proper equipment, adequate staffing, encouragement, and administrative assistance. Teams must receive the necessary support from management and the larger organization if they are going to succeed in achieving their goals.

Leadership and Structure   Team members must agree on who is to do what and must ensure that all members contribute equally in sharing the workload. In addition, the team must determine how schedules will be set, what skills need to be developed, how the group will resolve conflicts, and how the group will make and modify decisions.[16] Agreeing on the specifics of work and how they fit together to integrate individual skills requires team leadership and structure. This can be provided directly by management or by the team members themselves. Leadership, of course, isn't always needed. For instance, the evidence indicates that self-managed work teams often perform better than teams with formally appointed leaders.[17] And leaders can obstruct high performance when they interfere with self-managing teams.[18] On self-managed teams, team members absorb many of the duties typically assumed by managers.

On traditionally managed teams, we find that two factors seem important in influencing team performance: the leader's expectations and his or her mood. Leaders who expect good things from their teams are more likely to get them. For instance, military platoons under leaders who held high expectations performed significantly better in training than did control platoons.[19] In addition, studies have found that leaders who exhibit a positive mood get better team performance and lower turnover.[20]

Climate of Trust   Members of effective teams trust each other and their leaders.[21] Interpersonal trust among team members facilitates cooperation, reduces the need to monitor each others' behavior, and bonds members around the belief that others on the team won't take advantage of them. Team members are more likely to take risks and expose vulnerabilities when they believe they can trust others on their team. Similarly, as we'll show in Chapter 11, trust is the foundation of leadership. Trust in leadership is important in that it allows team members to be willing to accept and commit to their leader's goals and decisions.

Performance Evaluation and Reward Systems   How do you get team members to be both individually and jointly accountable? The traditional, individually oriented evaluation and reward system must be modified to reflect team performance.[22]

Individual performance evaluations, fixed hourly wages, individual incentives, and the like are not consistent with the development of high-performance teams. So, in addition to evaluating and rewarding employees for their individual contributions, management should consider group-based appraisals, profit sharing, gain sharing, small-group incentives, and other system modifications that will reinforce team effort and commitment.

Composition

This category includes variables that relate to how teams should be staffed, including the abilities and personalities of team members, allocating roles and diversity, size of the team, member flexibility, and members' preference for teamwork.

Abilities of Members   Part of a team's performance depends on the knowledge, skills, and abilities of its individual members. It's true that we occasionally read about the athletic team composed of mediocre players who, because of excellent coaching, determination, and precision teamwork, beats a far more talented group of players. Such cases make the news precisely because they represent an aberration. As the old saying goes, "The race doesn't always go to the swiftest nor the battle to the strongest, but that's the way to bet." A team's performance is not merely the summation of its individual members' abilities. However, these abilities set parameters for what members can do and how effectively they will perform on a team.

To perform effectively, a team requires three different types of skills:

1. People with *technical expertise*
2. People with the *problem-solving and decision-making skills* who can identify problems, generate alternatives, evaluate those alternatives, and make competent choices
3. People with good listening, feedback, conflict resolution, and other *interpersonal skills*[23]

No team can achieve its performance potential without developing all three types of skills. The right mix is crucial. Too much of one at the expense of others will result in lower team performance. But teams don't need to have all the complementary skills in place at the beginning of their work. It's not uncommon for one or more members to take responsibility to learn the skills in which the group is deficient, thereby allowing the team to reach its full potential.

Research on the abilities of team members has revealed some interesting insights into team composition and performance. First, when the task entails considerable thought (for example, solving a complex problem like reengineering an assembly line), high-ability teams (teams composed of mostly intelligent members) do better, especially when the workload is distributed evenly. (That way, team performance does not depend on the weakest link.) High-ability teams are also more adaptable to changing situations in that they can more effectively adapt prior knowledge to suit a set of new problems.

Second, although high-ability teams generally have an advantage over lower-ability teams, this is not always the case. For example, when tasks are simple (tasks that individual team members might be able to solve on their own), high-ability teams do not perform as well, perhaps because in such tasks high-ability teams become bored and turn their attention to other activities that are more stimulating, whereas low-ability teams stay on task. High-ability teams should be used to tackle tough problems. So matching team ability to the task is important. Finally, the ability of the team's leader also matters. Research shows that smart team leaders help less intelligent team members when they struggle with a task. But a less intelligent leader can neutralize the effect of a high-ability team.[24]

Personality   We demonstrated in Chapter 4 that personality has a significant influence on individual employee behavior. This concept can also be extended to team behavior. Many of the dimensions identified in the Big Five personality model have been shown to be relevant to team effectiveness. Specifically, teams that rate higher in mean levels of extraversion, agreeableness, conscientiousness, openness to experience, and emotional stability tend to receive higher managerial ratings for team performance.[25]

Interestingly, the evidence indicates that the *variance* in personality characteristics may be more important than the mean.[26] So, for example, while higher mean levels of conscientiousness on a team are desirable, mixing both conscientious and not-so-conscientious members tends to lower performance. "This may be because, in such teams, members who are highly conscientious not only must perform their own tasks but also must perform or re-do the tasks of low-conscientious members. It may also be because such diversity leads to feelings of contribution inequity."[27] Another interesting finding related to personality is that "One bad apple can spoil the barrel." A single team member who lacks a minimal level of, say, agreeableness, can negatively affect the whole team's performance. So, including just one person who is low on agreeableness, conscientiousness, or extraversion can result in strained internal processes and decreased overall performance.[28]

Increasingly, we are learning why these traits are important to team performance.[29] For example, conscientious people are valuable because they're good at backing up fellow team members, and they're also good at sensing when that support is truly needed. Extraverts are better at training and motivating team members who are struggling. If a team is confronted with a poor fit between how the team is configured and the work environment (for example, a team is loosely structured but needs to closely coordinate on a project), emotionally stable team members are critical because they are better at adapting and helping others to adapt. Teams comprised of open people make better use of computer technology in making decisions. Open people communicate better with one another and throw out more ideas, which leads teams comprised of open people to be more creative and innovative. When an unforeseen change happens, teams comprised of conscientious, emotionally stable, and open members cope and adapt better. Personality also influences how teams respond to their surroundings. For example, extraverted teams and agreeable teams respond negatively to individual competitive rewards because such individualistic incentives tend to run counter to the social nature of extraverted and agreeable teams.

Personality composition is important to team success. It's best to staff teams with people who are extraverted, agreeable, conscientious, emotionally stable, and open. Management should also minimize the variability of these traits within teams.

Allocating Roles   Teams have different needs, and people should be selected for a team to ensure that all various roles are filled.

We can identify nine potential team roles (see Exhibit 9-4). Successful work teams have people to fill all these roles and have selected people to play these roles based on their skills and preferences.[30] (On many teams, individuals will play multiple roles.) Managers need to understand the individual strengths that each person can bring to a team, select members for their strengths, and allocate work assignments that fit with members' preferred styles. By matching individual preferences with team role demands, managers increase the likelihood that the team members will work well together.

—By matching individual preferences with team role demands, managers increase the likelihood that the team members will work well together.

Diversity   As previously noted, most team activities require a variety of skills and knowledge. Given this requirement, it would be reasonable to conclude that heterogeneous teams—those composed of dissimilar individuals—would be more likely to have diverse abilities and information and would be more effective. Research studies generally substantiate this conclusion, especially on cognitive, creativity-demanding tasks.[31]

When a team is diverse in terms of personality, gender, age, education, functional specialization, and experience, the probability is higher that the team will possess the needed characteristics to complete its tasks effectively. The team may be more conflict laden and less expedient as varied positions are introduced and assimilated, but the evidence generally supports the conclusion that heterogeneous teams perform more effectively than do those that are homogeneous. Essentially, diversity promotes conflict, which stimulates creativity, which leads to improved decision

EXHIBIT 9-4 Key Roles of Teams

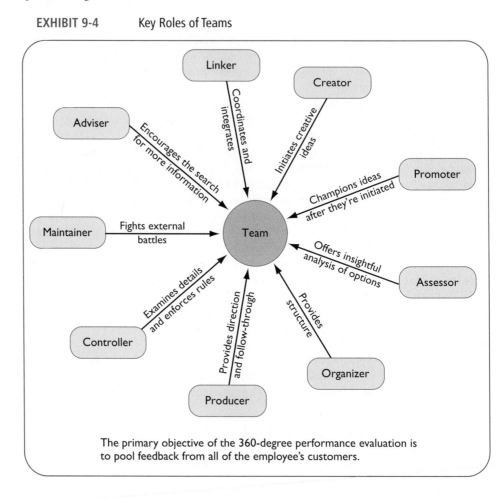

The primary objective of the 360-degree performance evaluation is to pool feedback from all of the employee's customers.

making. One study found that, on a cognitive task, homogenous groups of white males performed the worst relative to mixed race and gender teams or teams of only females. The authors (who were all men) concluded that this was true because male-only teams were overly aggressive and therefore prone to decision-making errors.[32]

But what about diversity created by racial or national differences? The evidence indicates that these elements of diversity interfere with team processes, at least in the short term.[33] Cultural diversity seems to be an asset for tasks that call for a variety of viewpoints, but culturally heterogeneous teams have more difficulty in learning to work with each other and in solving problems. The good news is that these difficulties seem to dissipate with time. Although newly formed, culturally diverse teams under-perform newly formed, culturally homogeneous teams, the differences disappear after about three months.[34] The reason is that it takes culturally diverse teams a while to learn how to work through disagreements and different approaches to solving problems.

An offshoot of the diversity issue has received a great deal of attention by group and team researchers. This is the degree to which members of a group share a common demographic attribute, such as age, sex, race, educational level, or length of service in the organization, and the impact of this attribute on turnover. We call this variable **group demography**.

We discussed individual demographic factors in Chapter 2. Here we consider the same type of factors but in a group context. That is, it's not whether a person is male or female or has been employed with the organization for a year rather than 10 years that concerns us now, but rather the individual's attributes in relationship to the attributes of others with whom he or she works. Let's work through the logic of group demography, review the evidence, and then consider the implications.

Groups, teams, and organizations are composed of **cohorts**, individuals who hold a common attribute. For instance, everyone born in 1960 is of the same age. This means they also have shared common experiences. People born in 1970 have experienced the information revolution but not the Korean conflict. People born in 1945 shared the Vietnam War but not the Great Depression. Women who were born before 1945 in the United States matured prior to the women's rights movement of the latter part of the twentieth century and have had experiences substantially different from those of women born after 1960. Group demography, therefore, suggests that attributes such as age or the date that someone joins a specific work team or organization should help us to predict turnover. Essentially, the logic goes like this: Turnover will be greater among those with dissimilar experiences because communication is more difficult. Conflict and power struggles are more likely and more severe when they occur. The increased conflict makes group membership less attractive, so employees are more likely to quit. Similarly, the losers in a power struggle are more apt to leave voluntarily or to be forced out.

A number of studies have sought to test this thesis, and the findings appear to be conclusive.[35] For example, in departments or separate work groups in which a large portion of members entered at the same time, considerably more turnover occurs among those outside this cohort. Also, when there are large gaps between cohorts, turnover is higher. People who enter a group or an organization together, or at approximately the same time, are more likely to associate with one another, have a similar perspective on the group or organization, and thus are more likely to stay. On the other hand, discontinuities or bulges in the group's date-of-entry distribution are likely to result in a higher turnover rate within that group.[36]

This line of inquiry implies that the composition of a team may be an important predictor of turnover. Differences per se may not predict turnover, but large differences within a single team will lead to turnover. If everyone is moderately dissimilar from everyone else in a team, the feelings of being an outsider are reduced. So, it's the degree of dispersion on an attribute, rather than the level, that matters most.

Size of Teams   The president of AOL Technologies says the secret to a great team is "Think small. Ideally, your team should have seven to nine people."[37] His advice is supported by evidence.[38] Generally speaking, the most effective teams have fewer than 10 members, and experts suggest using the smallest number of people who can do the task. Unfortunately, managers exhibit a pervasive tendency to err on the side of making teams too large. While a minimum of 4 or 5 members may be necessary to develop diversity of views and skills, managers seem to seriously underestimate how coordination problems can geometrically increase as team members are added. When teams have excess members, cohesiveness and mutual accountability decline, social loafing increases, and more and more people do less talking relative to others. Moreover, large teams have trouble coordinating with one another, especially when time pressure is present. So, in designing effective teams, managers should try to keep membership under 10. If a natural working unit is larger and you want a team effort, consider breaking the group into subteams.

—Teams made up of flexible individuals have members who can complete each other's tasks.

Member Flexibility   Teams made up of flexible individuals have members who can complete each other's tasks. This is an obvious plus to a team because it greatly improves its adaptability and makes it less reliant on any single member. So selecting members who themselves value flexibility, then cross-training them to be able to do each other's jobs, should lead to higher team performance over time.

Member Preferences   Not every employee is a team player. Given the option, many employees will select themselves *out* of team participation. When people who would prefer to work alone are required to team up, the team's morale and individual member satisfaction are directly threatened.[39] This suggests that, when selecting team members, individual preferences should be considered along with abilities, personalities, and skills. High-performing teams are likely to be composed of people who prefer working as part of a group.

Work Design

Effective teams must work together and take collective responsibility to complete significant tasks. They must be more than a team in name only.[40] Based on terminology we introduced in Chapter 6, the work-design category includes variables such as these:

- Freedom and autonomy
- The opportunity to use different skills and talents (skill variety)
- The ability to complete a whole and identifiable task or product (task identity)
- Working on a task or project that has a substantial impact on others (task significance)

The evidence indicates that these characteristics enhance member motivation and increase team effectiveness. These work-design characteristics motivate because they increase members' sense of responsibility and ownership over the work and because they make the work more interesting to perform.[41]

Process

The final category related to team effectiveness is process variables. These include member commitment to a common purpose, establishment of specific team goals, team efficacy, a managed level of conflict, and minimizing social loafing.

Why are processes important to team effectiveness? One way to answer this question is to return to the topic of social loafing. We found that 1 + 1 + 1 don't necessarily add up to 3. In team tasks for which each member's contribution is not clearly visible, individuals have a tendency to decrease their effort. Social loafing represents negative synergy; the whole is less than the sum of its parts, but team processes should produce positive results and create outputs greater than the sum of their inputs. Research teams are often used in research laboratories because they can draw on the diverse skills of various individuals to produce more meaningful research as a team than could be generated by all the researchers working independently. That is, they produce positive synergy. Their process gains exceed their process losses. Exhibit 9-5 illustrates how group processes can affect a group's actual effectiveness.[42]

Common Purpose   Effective teams have a common and meaningful purpose that provides direction, momentum, and commitment for members.[43] This purpose is a vision. It's broader than specific goals.

Members of successful teams put a tremendous amount of time and effort into discussing, shaping, and agreeing on a purpose that belongs to them both collectively and individually. This common purpose, when accepted by the team, becomes the equivalent of what celestial navigation is to a ship captain: It provides direction and guidance under any and all conditions.

Specific Goals   Successful teams translate their common purpose into specific, measurable, and realistic performance goals. Just as goals lead individuals to higher performance, as we demonstrated in Chapter 5, goals also energize teams. These specific goals facilitate clear communication. They also help teams maintain their focus on getting results.

Also, consistent with the research on individual goals, team goals should be challenging. Difficult goals have been found to raise team performance on those criteria for which they're set. So goals for quantity tend to raise quantity, goals for speed tend to raise speed, goals for accuracy raise accuracy, and so on.[44]

Team Efficacy   Effective teams have confidence in themselves. They believe they can succeed. We call this *team efficacy*.[45] Success breeds success. Teams that have been successful raise their beliefs about future success, which, in turn, motivates them to work harder. What, if anything, can management do to increase team efficacy? The following are two possible options:

1. *Helping the team to achieve small successes.* Small successes build team confidence. As a team develops an increasingly stronger performance record, it also increases the collective belief that future efforts will lead to success.
2. *Providing skill training.* Managers should consider providing training to improve members' technical and interpersonal skills. The greater the abilities of team members, the greater the likelihood that the team will develop confidence and the capability to deliver on that confidence.

EXHIBIT 9-5   Effects of Group Processes

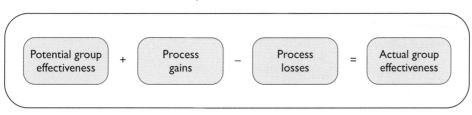

| Potential group effectiveness | + | Process gains | − | Process losses | = | Actual group effectiveness |

Conflict Levels Conflict on a team isn't necessarily bad. As we'll elaborate in Chapter 13, teams that are completely void of conflict are likely to become apathetic and stagnant. So, conflict can actually improve team effectiveness.[46] But not all types of conflict are helpful. Relationship conflicts—those based on interpersonal incompatibilities, tension, and animosity toward others—are almost always dysfunctional. However, on teams performing nonroutine activities, disagreement among members about task content (called *task conflicts*) is not detrimental. In fact, it is often beneficial because it lessens the likelihood of groupthink. Task conflicts stimulate discussion, promote critical assessment of problems and options, and can lead to better team decisions. So, effective teams will be characterized by an appropriate level of conflict.

—*Task conflicts stimulate discussion, promote critical assessment of problems and options, and can lead to better team decisions.*

Social Loafing We learned in the previous chapter that individuals can hide inside a group. They can engage in social loafing and coast on the group's effort because their individual contributions can't be identified. Effective teams undermine this tendency by holding themselves accountable at both the individual and team levels. A successful team makes members individually and jointly accountable for the team's purpose, goals, and approach. Therefore, members should clearly understand both their individual responsibilities and their joint responsibilities.

Turning Individuals into Team Players

Up to this point, we've made a strong case for the value and growing popularity of teams, but many people are not inherently team players. Also, many organizations have historically nurtured individual accomplishments, creating competitive work environments in which only the strong survive. If these organizations adopt teams, what do they do about the selfish, "I've-got-to-look-out-for-me" employees that they've created? Also, countries differ in terms of how they rate on individualism and collectivism. Teams fit well with countries that score high on collectivism.[47] But what if an organization wants to introduce teams into a work population that is made up largely of individuals born and raised in an individualistic society? One writer aptly described the role of teams in the United States: "Americans don't grow up learning how to function in teams. In school we never receive a team report card or learn the names of the team of sailors who traveled with Columbus to America."[48] This limitation would obviously be just as true of Canadians, British, Australians, and others from individualistic societies.

The Challenge

The previous points are meant to dramatize that one substantial barrier to using work teams is individual resistance. An employee's success is no longer defined in terms of individual performance. To perform well as team members, individuals must be able to communicate openly and honestly, to confront differences and resolve conflicts, and to sublimate personal goals for the good of the team. For many employees, this is a difficult—sometimes impossible—task. The challenge of creating team players will be greatest when:

- the national culture is highly individualistic and
- the teams are being introduced into an established organization that has historically valued individual achievement.

This describes, for instance, what faced managers at AT&T, Ford, Motorola, and other large U.S.-based companies. These firms prospered by hiring and rewarding corporate stars, and they bred a competitive climate that encouraged individual achievement and recognition. Employees in these types of firms can be jolted by this sudden shift to the importance of team play.[49] A veteran employee of a large company, who had done well working alone, described the experience of joining a team: "I'm learning my lesson. I just had my first negative performance appraisal in 20 years."[50]

On the other hand, the challenge for management is less demanding when teams are introduced where employees have strong collectivist values—such as in Japan or Mexico—or in new organizations that use teams as the initial form for structuring work. Saturn Corp., a U.S. organization owned by General Motors, was designed around teams from its inception. Everyone at Saturn was hired with the knowledge that they would be working in teams. The ability to be a good team player was a basic hiring qualification that had to be met by all new employees.

Shaping Team Players

Let's summarize the primary options managers have for trying to turn individuals into team players.

Selection Some people already possess the interpersonal skills to be effective team players. When hiring team members, managers should ensure that, in addition to the technical skills required to fill the job, candidates can fulfill both their team roles and technical requirements.

Many job candidates don't have team skills. This is especially true for those socialized around individual contributions. When faced with such candidates, managers basically have three options:

1. Have the candidates undergo training to make them into team players.
2. If this isn't possible or doesn't work, transfer the individual to another unit within the organization, without teams (if this possibility exists).
3. Don't hire the candidate.

In established organizations that decide to redesign jobs around teams, it should be expected that some employees will resist being team players and may be untrainable. Unfortunately, such people typically become casualties of the team approach.

Training On a more optimistic note, a large proportion of people raised on the importance of individual accomplishments can be trained to become team players. Training specialists conduct exercises that allow employees to experience the satisfaction that teamwork can provide. They typically offer workshops to help employees improve their problem-solving, communication, negotiation, conflict-management, and coaching skills.

Emerson Electric's Specialty Motor Division in Missouri, for instance, has achieved remarkable success in getting its 650-member workforce not only to accept but to welcome team training.[51] Outside consultants were brought in to give workers practical skills for working in teams. After less than a year, employees were enthusiastically accepting the value of teamwork.

Rewards   The reward system must be reworked to encourage cooperative efforts rather than competitive ones.[52] Hallmark Cards, Inc., added an annual bonus based on achievement of team goals to its basic individual-incentive system. Trigon Blue Cross Blue Shield changed its system to reward an even split between individual goals and teamlike behaviors.[53]

Promotions, pay raises, and other forms of recognition should be given to individuals for how effective they are as collaborative team members. This doesn't mean individual contributions are ignored; rather, they are balanced with selfless contributions to the team. Behaviors that should be rewarded include training new colleagues, sharing information with teammates, helping to resolve team conflicts, and mastering new skills that the team needs but in which it is deficient.

Lastly, don't forget the intrinsic rewards that employees can receive from teamwork. Teams provide camaraderie. It's exciting and satisfying to be an integral part of a successful team. The opportunity to engage in personal development and to help teammates grow can be a very satisfying and rewarding experience for employees.

TEAMS AND QUALITY MANAGEMENT

As we discussed in Chapter 1, the issue of *improving quality* has garnered increased attention from management in recent years. In this section, we want to demonstrate the important role that teams play in *quality management programs.*

The essence of **quality management (QM)** programs is process improvement, and employee involvement is the linchpin of process improvement. In other words, QM requires management to give employees the encouragement to share ideas and act on what they suggest. As one author put it, "None of the various [quality management] processes and techniques will catch on and be applied except in work teams. All such techniques and processes require high levels of communication and contact, response and adaptation, and coordination and sequencing. They require, in short, the environment that can be supplied only by superior work teams."[54]

Teams provide the natural vehicle for employees to share ideas and to implement improvements. Gil Mosard, a QM specialist at Boeing, put it this way: "When your measurement system tells you your process is out of control, you need teamwork for structured problem solving. Not everyone needs to know how to do all kinds of fancy control charts for performance tracking, but everybody does need to know where their process stands so they can judge if it is improving."[55]

Beware! Teams Aren't Always the Answer

Teamwork takes more time and often more resources than individual work. Teams have increased communication demands, conflicts to be managed, and meetings to be run. So the benefits of using teams have to exceed the costs—and that's not always the case.[56] In the excitement to enjoy the benefits of teams, some managers have introduced them into situations in which the work is better performed by individuals. So before you rush to implement teams, you should carefully assess whether the work requires or will benefit from a collective effort.

How do you know if the work of your group would be better done in teams? It's been suggested that three tests be applied to see if a team fits the situation:[57]

1. *Can the work be done better by more than one person?* A good indicator is the complexity of the work and the need for different perspectives. Simple tasks that don't require diverse input are probably better left to individuals.

2. *Does the work create a common purpose or set of goals for the people in the group that is more than the aggregate of individual goals?* For instance, many new-car dealer service departments have introduced teams that link customer service personnel, mechanics, parts specialists, and sales representatives. Such teams can better manage collective responsibility for ensuring that customer needs are properly met.

3. *Are the members of the group interdependent?* Teams make sense when tasks are interdependent—that is, when the success of the whole depends on the success of each one *and* the success of each one depends on the success of the others. Soccer is an obvious *team* sport. Success requires a great deal of coordination among interdependent players. Conversely, except for, possibly, relays, swim teams are not really teams. They're groups of individuals, performing individually, whose total performance is merely the aggregate summation of their individual performances.

IMPLICATIONS FOR MANAGERS

Few trends have influenced employee jobs as much as the massive movement to introduce teams into the workplace. The shift from working alone to working on teams requires employees to cooperate with others, share information, confront differences, and minimize personal interests for the greater good of the team. Effective teams have common characteristics:

- Adequate resources
- Effective leadership
- A climate of trust
- A performance evaluation and reward system that reflects team contributions

Effective teams have individuals with technical expertise, as well as problem-solving, decision-making, and interpersonal skills; team members also have high scores on the personality characteristics of extraversion, agreeableness, conscientiousness, and emotional stability. Effective teams also tend to be small—with fewer than 10 people—preferably made up of individuals with diverse backgrounds. They have members who fill role demands, are flexible, and prefer to be part of a group. The work that members do provides freedom and autonomy, the opportunity to use different skills and talents, the ability to complete a whole and identifiable task or product, and work that has a substantial impact on others. Also, effective teams have members committed to a common purpose, specific team goals, members who believe in the team's capabilities, a manageable level of conflict, and a minimal degree of social loafing.

Because individualistic organizations and societies attract and reward individual accomplishments, it is more difficult to create team players in these environments. To make the conversion, management should select individuals with the interpersonal skills to be effective team players, provide training to develop teamwork skills, and reward individuals for cooperative efforts.

CHAPTER 10

Communication

After studying this chapter, you should be able to:

1. Describe the communication process.
2. Contrast the advantages and disadvantages of oral versus written communication.
3. Compare the effectiveness of the chain, wheel, and all-channel networks.
4. Identify the factors affecting the use of the grapevine.
5. Discuss how computer-aided technology is changing organizational communication.
6. Identify common barriers to effective communication.
7. Describe the potential problems in cross-cultural communication.

No group or organization can exist without **communication**. It is only through transmitting meaning from one person to another that information and ideas can be conveyed. But communication is more than merely broadcasting a message. Communication must also be understood. In a group in which one member speaks only German and the others do not know German, the individual speaking German will not be fully understood. Therefore, communication must include both the *transference and the understanding of meaning*.

In this chapter, we'll show that good communication is essential to the effectiveness of any group or organization. Because individuals spend nearly 70 percent of their waking hours communicating—writing, reading, speaking, listening—it seems reasonable to conclude that one of the most inhibiting forces to successful group performance is a lack of effective communication. Indeed, research indicates that poor communication is probably the most frequently cited source of interpersonal conflict.[1]

FUNCTIONS OF COMMUNICATION

Communication serves four major functions within a group or organization: control, motivation, emotional expression, and information.[2]

1. *Control.* Communication acts to control member behavior in several ways. Organizations have authority hierarchies and formal guidelines that employees are required to follow. When employees are required to first communicate any job-related grievances to their immediate bosses, to follow their job descriptions, or to comply with company policies, communication is performing a control function. But informal communication also controls behavior. When work groups tease or harass a member who produces too much (and makes the rest of the group look bad), they are informally communicating with, and controlling, the member's behavior.

2. *Motivation.* Communication fosters motivation by clarifying to employees what is to be done, how well they are doing, and what can be done to improve performance if it's subpar. We saw this operating in our review of goal-setting and reinforcement theories in Chapter 5. The formation of specific goals, feedback on progress toward the goals, and reinforcement of desired behavior all stimulate motivation and require communication.

3. *Emotional expression.* For many employees, their work group is a primary source for social interaction. The communication that takes place within the group is a fundamental mechanism by which members show their frustrations and feelings of satisfaction. Communication, therefore, provides a release for the emotional expression of feelings and for fulfillment of social needs.

4. *Information.* Communication facilitates decision making. It provides the information that individuals and groups need to make decisions by transmitting the data to identify and evaluate alternative choices.

None of these four functions should be considered more important than the others. For groups to perform effectively, they need to maintain some form of control over members, stimulate members to perform, provide a means for emotional expression, and make decision choices. You can assume that almost every communication interaction that takes place in a group or organization performs one or more of these four functions.

THE COMMUNICATION PROCESS

Before communication can take place, it needs a purpose, expressed as a message to be conveyed. It passes between a sender and a receiver. The message is encoded (converted to a symbolic form) and passed by way of some medium (channel) to the receiver, who retranslates (decodes) the message initiated by the sender. The result is transference of meaning from one person to another.[3]

Exhibit 10-1 depicts this **communication process**. The key parts of this model are (1) the sender, (2) encoding, (3) the message, (4) the channel, (5) decoding, (6) the receiver, (7) noise, and (8) feedback.

The *sender* initiates a message by encoding a thought. The *message* is the actual physical product from the sender's *encoding*. When we speak, the speech is the message. When we write, the writing is the message. When we gesture, the movements of our arms and the expressions on our faces are the message. The *channel* is the medium through which the message travels. It is selected by the sender, who must determine whether to use a formal or informal channel. **Formal channels** are established by the organization and transmit messages that are related to the professional activities of members. They traditionally follow the authority chain within the organization.

EXHIBIT 10-1 The Communication Process

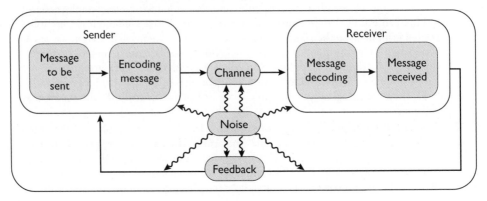

Other forms of messages, such as personal or social, follow the **informal channels** in the organization. These informal channels are spontaneous and emerge as a response to individual choices.[4] The *receiver* is the object to whom the message is directed. But before the message can be received, the symbols in it must be translated into a form that can be understood by the receiver. This step is the *decoding* of the message. *Noise* represents communication barriers that distort the clarity of the message. Examples of possible noise sources include perceptual problems, information overload, semantic difficulties, or cultural differences. The final link in the communication process is a feedback loop. *Feedback* is the check on how successful we have been in transferring our messages as originally intended. It determines whether understanding has been achieved.

Direction of Communication

Communication can flow vertically or laterally. The vertical dimension can be further divided into downward and upward directions.[5]

Downward Communication Communication that flows from one level of a group or organization to a lower level is downward communication. When we think of managers communicating with employees, we are usually thinking of the downward pattern. It's used by group leaders and managers to assign goals, provide job instructions, inform employees of policies and procedures, point out problems that need attention, and offer feedback about performance. But downward communication doesn't have to be oral or face-to-face contact. When a team leader sends an e-mail to the members of her team reminding them of an upcoming deadline, she's using downward communication.

Upward Communication Upward communication flows to a higher level in the group or organization. It's used to provide feedback to higher-ups, inform them of progress toward goals, and relay current problems. Upward communication keeps managers aware of how employees feel about their jobs, coworkers, and the organization in general. Managers also rely on upward communication for ideas on how things can be improved. Some organizational examples of upward communication are performance reports prepared by lower management for review by middle and top management, suggestion boxes, employee attitude surveys, grievance procedures, superior–subordinate discussions, and informal gripe sessions in which employees have the opportunity to identify and discuss problems with their bosses or representatives of higher management.

Lateral Communication When communication takes place among members of the same work group, among members of work groups at the same level, among managers at the same level, or among any horizontally equivalent personnel, we describe it as lateral communication.

Why would there be a need for horizontal communication if a group or organization's vertical communication is effective? The answer is that horizontal communication is often necessary to save time and facilitate coordination. In some cases, these lateral relationships are formally sanctioned. More often, they are informally created to short-circuit the vertical hierarchy and expedite action. So lateral communication can, from management's viewpoint, be good or bad. Because strict adherence to the formal vertical structure for all communication can impede the efficient and accurate transfer of information, lateral communication can be beneficial. In such cases, lateral communication occurs with the knowledge and support of superiors but can create dysfunctional conflicts when the formal vertical channels are breached, when members go above or around their superiors to get things done, or when bosses find out that actions have been taken or decisions made without their knowledge. For example, a manager may find it efficient for seasoned employees to communicate how things get done rather than having to communicate every expectation to each new employee individually. While this can be beneficial, if one or more of the seasoned employees also communicates ways of manipulating the system or covertly undermining the manager, this lateral communication can be detrimental to the manager.

INTERPERSONAL COMMUNICATION

How do group members transfer meaning between and among each other? People rely essentially on three basic communication methods: oral, written, and nonverbal.

Oral Communication

The chief means of conveying messages is oral communication. Speeches, formal one-on-one and group discussions, and the informal rumor mill or grapevine are popular forms of oral communication.

The advantages of oral communication are speed and feedback. A verbal message can be conveyed and a response received in a minimal amount of time. If the receiver is unsure of the message, rapid feedback allows for early detection by the sender and, hence, allows for early correction.

The major disadvantage of oral communication surfaces in organizations or whenever the message has to be passed through a number of people. The more people a message must pass through, the greater the potential for distortion. If you ever played the game telephone at a party, you know the problem. Each person interprets the message in his or her own way. The message's content, when it reaches its destination, is often very different from that of the original. In an organization in which decisions and other communiqués are verbally passed up and down the authority hierarchy, opportunities are considerable for messages to become distorted.

Written Communication

Written communication includes memos, letters, fax transmissions, electronic mail, instant messaging, organizational periodicals, notices placed on bulletin boards, or any other device that is transmitted via written words or symbols.

Why would a sender choose to use written communications? They're often tangible and verifiable. When printed, both the sender and receiver have a record of the communication; and the message can be stored for an indefinite period. If questions concerning the content of the message arise later, it is physically available for future reference. This feature is particularly important for complex and lengthy communications. The marketing plan for a new product is likely to contain a number of tasks spread out over several months. By putting it in writing, those who have to initiate the plan can readily refer to it over the life of the plan. A final benefit of all written communication comes from the process itself. You're usually more careful with the written word than the oral word. You're forced to think more thoroughly about what you want to convey in a written message than in a spoken one. Thus, written communications are more likely to be well thought out, logical, and clear.

Of course, written messages have their drawbacks. They're time-consuming. You could probably say the same thing in 10 to 15 minutes that it would take you an hour to write. The other major disadvantage is feedback, or lack of it. Oral communication allows the receiver to respond rapidly to what he thinks he hears. Written communication, however, does not have a built-in feedback mechanism. The result is that the mailing of a memo is no assurance it has been received, and, if received, there is no guarantee the recipient will interpret it as the sender intended.

Nonverbal Communication

No discussion of communication would be complete without consideration of *nonverbal communication*—which includes body movements, the intonations or emphasis we give to words, facial expressions, and the physical distance between the sender and receiver. For example, in a singles bar, a glance, a stare, a smile, a frown, and a provocative body movement all convey meaning.

It can be argued that every *body movement* has a meaning and that no movement is accidental. For example, through body language we say "Help me, I'm lonely"; "Take me, I'm available"; "Leave me alone, I'm depressed." And rarely do we send our messages consciously. We act out our state of being with nonverbal body language. We lift one eyebrow for disbelief. We clasp our arms to isolate ourselves or to protect ourselves. We shrug our shoulders for indifference, wink one eye for intimacy, tap our fingers for impatience, slap our forehead for forgetfulness.[6]

The two most important messages that body language conveys are these:

1. The extent to which an individual likes another and is interested in his or her views
2. The relative perceived status between a sender and receiver[7]

For instance, we're more likely to position ourselves closer to people we like and to touch them more often. Similarly, if you feel that you have higher status than another, you're more likely to display body movements—such as crossed legs or a slouched seating position—that reflect a casual and relaxed manner.[8]

EXHIBIT 10-2   Intonations: It's the Way You Say It!

Change your tone and you change your meaning:

Placement of the Emphasis	What It Means
Why don't I take **you** to dinner tonight?	I was going to take someone else.
Why don't **I** take you to dinner tonight?	Instead of the guy you were going with.
Why **don't** I take you to dinner tonight?	I'm trying to find a reason why I shouldn't take you.
Why don't I take you to dinner tonight?	Do you have a problem with me?
Why don't I **take** you to dinner tonight?	Instead of going on your own.
Why don't I take you to **dinner** tonight?	Instead of lunch tomorrow.
Why don't I take you to dinner **tonight**?	Not tomorrow night.

Source: Based on M. Kiely, "When 'No' Means 'Yes,'" *Marketing*, October 1993, pp. 7–9. Reproduced in A. Huczynski and D. Buchanan, *Organizational Behavior*, 4th ed. (Essex, England: Pearson Education, 2001), p. 194.

Body language adds to, and often complicates, verbal communication. A body position or movement does not by itself have a precise or universal meaning, but when it is linked with spoken language, it gives fuller meaning to a sender's message.

If you read the verbatim minutes of a meeting, you wouldn't grasp the impact of what was said in the same way you would if you had been there or saw the meeting on video because there is no tangible record of nonverbal communication. The emphasis given to words or phrases is missing. Exhibit 10-2 illustrates how *intonations* can change the meaning of a message. *Facial expressions* also convey meaning. Facial expressions, along with intonations, can show arrogance, aggressiveness, fear, shyness, and other characteristics that would never be communicated if you read a transcript of what had been said.

The way individuals space themselves in terms of *physical distance* also has meaning. What is considered proper spacing is largely dependent on cultural norms. For example, what is considered a businesslike distance in some European countries would be viewed as intimate in many parts of North America. If someone stands closer to you than is considered appropriate, it may indicate aggressiveness or sexual interest; if farther away than usual, it may mean disinterest or displeasure with what is being said.

It's important for the receiver to be alert to these nonverbal aspects of communication. You should look for nonverbal cues as well as listen to the literal meaning of a sender's words. You should particularly be aware of contradictions between the messages. Your boss may say she is free to talk to you about a pressing budget problem, but you may see nonverbal signals suggesting that this is not the time to discuss the subject. We misinform others when we express one message verbally, such as trust, but nonverbally communicate a contradictory message that communicates "I don't have confidence in you."

ORGANIZATIONAL COMMUNICATION

Now that we've covered interpersonal communication, let's move to organizational communication, including formal networks, the grapevine, computer-aided mechanisms used by organizations to facilitate communication, and the evolving topic of knowledge management.

EXHIBIT 10-3   Three Common Small-Group Networks

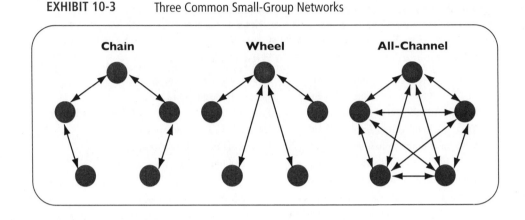

Formal Small-Group Networks

Formal organizational networks can be very complicated. They can include hundreds of people and a half dozen or more hierarchical levels. To simplify our discussion, we've condensed these networks into three common small groups—the chain, the wheel, and the all-channel—of five people each (see Exhibit 10-3). Although our examples may be oversimplified, we can still examine the unique qualities of each network:

- The *chain* rigidly follows the formal chain of command. This network approximates the communication channels you might find in a rigid three-level organization.
- The *wheel* relies on a central figure to act as the conduit for all the group's communication. It simulates the communication network you would find on a team with a strong leader.
- The *all-channel* network permits all group members to actively communicate with each other. The all-channel network is most often characterized in practice by self-managed teams, in which all group members are free to contribute and no one person takes on a leadership role.

As Exhibit 10-4 demonstrates, the effectiveness of each network depends on which dependent variable is emphasized. The chain is best if accuracy is most important, while the structure of the wheel facilitates the emergence of a leader, and the all-channel network is best for promoting high member satisfaction.

The Grapevine

Of course, the formal system is not the only communication network in a group or organization. An informal one, the **grapevine**, is no less important as a source of information. For instance, a survey found that 75 percent of employees hear about matters first through rumors on the grapevine.[9]

The grapevine has three main characteristics.[10] First, it is not controlled by management. Second, it is perceived by most employees as being more believable and reliable than formal communiqués issued by top management. Third, it is largely used to serve the self-interests of the people within it.

EXHIBIT 10-4   Small-Group Networks and Effective Criteria

	Networks		
Criteria	Chain	Wheel	All-Channel
Speed	Moderate	Fast	Fast
Accuracy	High	High	Moderate
Emergence of a leader	Moderate	High	None
Member satisfaction	Moderate	Low	High

Is the information that flows along the grapevine accurate? The evidence indicates that about 75 percent of what is carried is accurate.[11] But what conditions foster an active grapevine? What gets the rumor mill rolling?

It's frequently assumed that rumors start because they make titillating gossip. This is rarely the case. Rumors emerge as a response to situations that are *important* to us, when there is *ambiguity*, and under conditions that arouse *anxiety*.[12] Rumors flourish in organizations because work situations frequently contain these three elements. The secrecy and competition that typically prevail in large organizations—around issues such as the appointment of new bosses, downsizing decisions, and the realignment of work assignments—create conditions that encourage and sustain rumors on the grapevine.

Certainly the grapevine is an important part of any group or organization communication network and is well worth understanding. For employees, the grapevine is particularly valuable for translating formal communications into the jargon of their individual groups. It gives managers a feel for the morale of their organizations, identifies issues that employees consider important, and helps tap into employee anxieties. It acts, therefore, as both a filter and a feedback mechanism, picking up the issues that employees consider relevant. It is perhaps more important that managers can analyze grapevine information and predict its flow, given that only a small set of individuals (approximately 10 percent) actively pass on information to more than one other person. By assessing for which liaison individuals will consider a given piece of information to be relevant, managers can improve their abilities to explain and predict the pattern of the grapevine.

Can management entirely eliminate rumors? No. What management should do, however, is minimize the negative consequences of rumors by limiting their range and impact. Exhibit 10-5 offers a few suggestions for minimizing those negative consequences.

Computer-Aided Communication

Communication in today's organizations is enhanced and enriched by computer-aided technologies. These include electronic mail, instant messaging, intranet and extranet links, and videoconferencing.

E-mail   Electronic mail (or e-mail) uses the Internet to transmit and receive computer-generated text and documents. Its growth has been spectacular. In fact, over 100 million adults in the United States use e-mail regularly (at least once a day), and it's estimated that nearly 1 trillion e-mails are sent *daily* worldwide. A good percentage

EXHIBIT 10-5   Suggestions for Reducing the Negative Consequences of Rumors

1. Announce timetables for making important decisions.
2. Explain decisions and behaviors that may appear inconsistent or secretive.
3. Emphasize the downside, as well as the upside, of current decisions and future plans.
4. Openly discuss worst-case possibilities—it is almost never as anxiety provoking as the unspoken fantasy.

Source: Adapted from L. Hirschhorn, "Managing Rumors," in L. Hirschhorn (ed.), *Cutting Back* (San Francisco: Jossey-Bass, 1983), pp. 54–56. With permission.

(up to 70 percent—depending on the quality of one's spam filter) of this e-mail comes in the form of spam (unsolicited e-mail ads or other unwanted material) and phishing e-mails (Internet scams initiated with a spoof e-mail message). Nevertheless, the reason we put up with junk e-mail is because, for many of us, e-mail is an indispensable way of communicating.

As a communication tool, e-mail has a long list of benefits. E-mail messages can be quickly written, edited, and stored. They can be distributed to one person or thousands with a click of a mouse. They can be read, in their entirety, at the convenience of the recipient. And the cost of sending formal e-mail messages to employees is a fraction of what it would cost to print, duplicate, and distribute a comparable letter or brochure.

E-mail, of course, is not without its drawbacks. It can be a distraction from work activities when employees use it for personal purposes. And it can be impersonal, detracting from special attention to customers or coworkers. In fact, a recent study revealed that most e-mails from customers are ignored. In this study, the researchers posed as customers and used e-mail to inquire about purchasing a product or service from 147 retail companies in various industries. In 51 percent of the cases, a reply to the e-mail was never received.[13]

E-mail also lacks emotional content. The nonverbal cues in a face-to-face message or the tone of voice from a phone call convey important information that doesn't come across in e-mail. And given its impersonal nature, e-mail is not the ideal means to convey information about layoffs, plant closings, or other messages that might evoke emotional responses and require empathy or social support. Finally, the remote nature of e-mail fuels *conflict spirals* that have been found to escalate ill feelings at double the rate of face-to-face communiqués. Many people seem able to say things in e-mails that they would never say to someone face to face.

Instant Messaging   Instant messaging is essentially real-time e-mail. Employees create a list of colleagues and friends with whom they want to communicate. Then they click on a name displayed in a small box on the computer screen, type in a message in the designated space, click "Send," and watch as the message instantaneously pops up on both the sender's and the recipient's computer screens. The growth of IM has been spectacular. In 2001, for instance, just 8 percent of U.S. employees were using it. In 2003, it was up to 18 percent.

IM is a fast and inexpensive means for managers to stay in touch with employees and for employees to stay in touch with each other. However, IM isn't going to replace e-mail.

E-mail is still probably a better device for conveying long messages that need to be saved. IM is preferred for sending one- or two-line messages that would just clutter up an e-mail inbox. On the downside, some IM users find the technology intrusive and distracting. IM's continual online presence can make it hard for employees to concentrate and stay focused. Managers also indicate concern that IM will be used by employees to chat with friends and colleagues about nonwork issues. Finally, because instant messages are easily broken into, many organizations are concerned about IM security.

Intranet and Extranet Links   An *intranet* is an organization-wide information network that looks and functions like a Web site but is accessible only to people within an organization. Intranets are rapidly becoming a popular means for employees within companies to communicate with each other. IBM, as a case in point, recently brought together online 52,000 of its employees for what it called WorldJam.[14] Using the company's intranet, IBMers everywhere swapped ideas on everything from how to retain employees to how to work faster without undermining quality.

In addition, organizations are creating *extranet* links that connect internal employees with selected suppliers, customers, and strategic partners. For instance, an extranet allows GM employees to send electronic messages and documents to its steel and rubber suppliers and to communicate with its dealers. Similarly, all Wal-Mart vendors are linked into its extranet system, allowing Wal-Mart buyers to easily communicate with the company's suppliers and for suppliers to monitor the inventory status of its products at Wal-Mart stores.

Videoconferencing   *Videoconferencing* is an extension of intranet or extranet systems. It permits employees in an organization to have meetings with people at different locations. Live audio and video images of members allow them to see, hear, and talk with each other. Videoconferencing technology, in effect, allows employees to conduct interactive meetings without the necessity of all being physically in the same location.

In the late 1990s, videoconferencing was basically conducted from special rooms equipped with television cameras at company facilities. More recently, cameras and microphones are being attached to individual computers, allowing people to participate in videoconferences without leaving their desks. As the cost of this technology drops in price, videoconferencing is likely to be increasingly seen as an alternative to expensive and time-consuming travel.

Summary   Computer-aided communications are reshaping the way we communicate in organizations. It's no longer necessary for employees to be at their work stations or desks to be "available." Pagers, cellular phones, personal communicators, and phone messaging allow employees to be reached virtually anywhere, at any time. As a result, boundaries—between work and nonwork, within organizations and between organizations—are becoming blurred.

Knowledge Management

Knowledge management (KM) is a process of organizing and distributing an organization's collective wisdom so the right information gets to the right people at the right time.[15] When done properly, KM provides an organization with both a competitive edge and improved organizational performance because it makes its employees smarter.

Knowledge management is increasingly important today for at least three reasons:[16]

1. In many organizations, intellectual assets are now as important as physical or financial assets. Organizations that can quickly and efficiently tap into their employees' collective experience and wisdom are more likely to outsmart their competition.
2. As baby boomers begin to leave the workforce, awareness is increasing that they represent a wealth of knowledge that will be lost if no attempts are made to capture it.
3. A well-designed KM system will reduce redundancy and make the organization more efficient. A knowledge-management system can allow employees undertaking a new project to access what previous employees have learned and cut wasteful time retracing a path that has already been traveled.

KM begins by identifying what knowledge matters to the organization.[17] Management needs to review processes to identify those that provide the most value. Then it can develop computer networks and databases that can make that information readily available to the people who need it the most. But KM won't work unless the culture supports sharing of information.[18] Finally, KM must provide the mechanisms and the motivation for employees to share knowledge that employees find useful on the job and enables them to achieve better performance.[19] *More* knowledge isn't necessarily *better* knowledge. Information overload must be avoided by designing the system to capture only pertinent information and then organizing it so it can be quickly accessed by the people whom it can help.

BARRIERS TO EFFECTIVE COMMUNICATION

A number of barriers can retard or distort effective communication. Let's examine the more important of these barriers.

Filtering

Filtering refers to a sender's purposely manipulating information so it will be seen more favorably by the receiver. For example, when a manager tells his boss what he feels his boss wants to hear, he is filtering information.

The major determinant of filtering is the number of levels in an organization's structure. The more vertical levels in the organization's hierarchy, the more opportunities exist for filtering. But you can expect some filtering to occur wherever status differences occur. Factors such as fear of conveying bad news and the desire to please one's boss often lead employees to tell their superiors what they think those superiors want to hear, thus distorting upward communication.

Selective Perception

Chapter 4 introduced selective perception as one of the frequently used shortcuts people use when judging others. We broach the topic again here because the receivers in the communication process selectively see and hear based on their needs, motivations, experience, backgrounds, and other personal characteristics. Receivers also project their interests and expectations into communications as they decode them. The employment interviewer who expects a female job applicant to put her family ahead of her career is likely to see that in female applicants, regardless of whether the applicants feel that way or not. Human beings don't see reality; we interpret what we see and call it reality.

Information Overload

Individuals have a finite capacity for processing data. When the information we have to work with exceeds our processing capacity, the result is **information overload**. With e-mails, instant messaging, phone calls, faxes, meetings, and the need to keep current in one's field, the potential for today's managers and professionals to suffer from information overload is high.

When individuals have more information than they can sort out and use they tend to select out, ignore, pass over, or forget information, or they may put off further processing until the overload situation is over. Regardless, the result is lost information and less effective communication.

Emotions

How the receiver feels at the time of receipt of a communication will influence how he or she interprets it. The same message received when you're angry or distraught is often interpreted differently than when you're happy. Extreme emotions such as jubilation or depression are most likely to hinder effective communication. In such instances, we are most prone to disregard our rational and objective thinking processes and substitute emotional judgments.

> —How the receiver feels at the time of receipt of a communication will influence how he or she interprets it.

Language

Words mean different things to different people. Age, education, and cultural background are three of the more obvious variables that influence the language a person uses and the definitions he or she gives to words.

In an organization, employees usually come from diverse backgrounds. Further, the grouping of employees into departments creates specialists who develop their own buzzwords or technical jargon. In large organizations, members are also frequently widely dispersed geographically—even operating in different countries—and individuals in each locale will use terms and phrases that are unique to their specific areas. The existence of vertical levels can also cause language problems. Differences in meaning with regard to words such as *incentives* and *quotas* have been found at different levels in management. Top managers often speak about the need for incentives and quotas, yet these terms imply manipulation and create resentment among many lower managers.

The point is that although you and I probably speak a common language—English—our use of that language is far from uniform. If we knew how each of us modified the language, communication difficulties would be minimized. The problem is that members in an organization usually don't know how those with whom they interact have modified the language. Senders tend to assume that the words and terms they use mean the same to the receiver as they do to them. This assumption is often incorrect.

Communication Apprehension

Another major barrier to effective communication is that some people—an estimated 5 to 20 percent of the population[20]—suffer from debilitating **communication apprehension** or anxiety. Although lots of people dread speaking in front of a group, communication apprehension is a more serious problem because it affects a whole category of communication techniques. People who suffer from it experience undue tension and anxiety in oral communication, written communication, or both.[21] For example, oral apprehensives may find it extremely difficult to talk with others face to face or they may become extremely anxious when they have to use the telephone. As a result, they may rely on memos or faxes to convey messages when a phone call would be not only faster but more appropriate.

Studies demonstrate that oral-communication apprehensives avoid situations that require them to engage in oral communication.[22] We should expect to find some self-selection in jobs so that such individuals don't take positions, such as teacher, for which oral communication is a dominant requirement.[23] Almost all jobs, however, require some oral communication. Of greater concern is the evidence that high-oral-communication apprehensives distort the communication demands of their jobs to minimize the need for communication.[24] So managers need to be aware that some people in organizations severely limit their oral communication and rationalize this practice by telling themselves that more communication isn't necessary for them to do their jobs effectively.

CURRENT ISSUES IN COMMUNICATION

Three current issues related to communication in organizations bear closer examination:

1. Why do men and women often have difficulty communicating with each other?
2. What are the implications of the *politically correct* movement on communications in organizations?
3. How can individuals improve their cross-cultural communications?

Communication Barriers Between Women and Men

The classic studies by the sociolinguist Deborah Tannen provide us with some important insights into the differences between men and women in terms of their conversational styles.[25] In particular, Tannen has been able to explain why gender often creates oral communication barriers. The essence of Tannen's research is that men use talk to emphasize status, whereas women use it to create connection. Her conclusion, of course, doesn't apply to *every* man or *every* woman.

Tannen states that communication is a continual balancing act, juggling the conflicting needs for intimacy and independence. Intimacy emphasizes closeness and commonalities. Independence emphasizes separateness and differences. Here's the kick: Women speak and hear a language of connection and intimacy; men speak and hear a language of status, power, and independence. So, for many men, conversations are primarily a means to preserve independence and maintain status in a hierarchical social order. For many women, conversations are negotiations for closeness in which people try to seek and give confirmation and support.

Men are often more direct than women in conversation. A man might say "I think you're wrong on that point." A woman might say "Have you looked at the marketing department's research report on that point?" (the implication being that the report will show the error). Men frequently see female indirectness as "covert" or "sneaky," but women are not as concerned as men with the status and one-upmanship that directness often creates.

Women tend to be less boastful than men.[26] They often downplay their authority or accomplishments to avoid appearing as braggarts and to take the other person's feelings into account. However, men can frequently misinterpret this and incorrectly conclude that a woman is less confident and competent than she really is.

Finally, men often criticize women for seeming to apologize all the time. Women do apologize more than men.[27] Men tend to see the phrase "I'm sorry" as a weakness because they interpret the phrase to mean the woman is accepting blame when he knows she's not to blame. The woman also knows she's not to blame. The problem is that women frequently use "I'm sorry" to express regret and restore balance to a conversation: "I know you must feel bad about this; I do, too." For many women, "I'm sorry" is an expression of understanding and caring about the other person's feelings rather than an apology.

Politically Correct Communication

Most of us are acutely aware of how our vocabulary has been modified to reflect political correctness. Most of us have cleansed the words *handicapped, blind,* and *elderly* from our vocabulary—and replaced them with terms such as *physically challenged, visually impaired,* and *senior.* The *Los Angeles Times,* for instance, allows its journalists to use the term *old age* but cautions that the onset of old age varies from person to person, so a group of 75-year-olds aren't necessarily all old.[28]

We must be sensitive to others' feelings. Certain words can and do stereotype, intimidate, and insult individuals. In an increasingly diverse workforce, we must be sensitive to how words might offend others. But there's a downside to political correctness. It can complicate our vocabulary, making it more difficult for people to communicate. To illustrate, you probably know what these three terms mean: *garbage, quotas,* and *women.* But each of these words also has been found to offend one or more groups. They've been replaced with terms such as *postconsumer waste materials, educational equity,* and *people of gender.* The problem is that this latter group of terms is much less likely than the words replaced to convey a uniform message.

> High context cultures rely heavily on nonverbal and subtle situational cues when communicating with others; what is not said may be more significant than what is said.

Words are the primary means by which people communicate. When we eliminate words from use because they're politically incorrect, we reduce our options for conveying messages in the clearest and most accurate form. For the most part, the larger the vocabulary used by a sender and a receiver, the greater the opportunity to accurately transmit messages. By removing certain words from our vocabulary, we make it harder to communicate accurately. When we further replace these words with new terms whose meanings are less well understood, we have reduced the likelihood that our messages will be received as we had intended them.

We must be sensitive to how our word choices might offend others. But we also have to be careful not to sanitize our language to the point at which it clearly restricts clarity of communication. This dilemma has no simple solution. However, as a manager, you should be aware of the trade-offs and the need to find a proper balance.

Cross-Cultural Communication

Effective communication is difficult under the best of conditions. Cross-cultural factors clearly create the potential for increased communication problems. A gesture that is well understood and acceptable in one culture can be meaningless or lewd in another.[29]

Cultural Barriers   One author has identified four specific problems related to language difficulties in cross-cultural communications.[30]

1. *Barriers caused by semantics.* Words mean different things to different people. This is particularly true for people from different national cultures. Some words don't translate between cultures. Understanding the word *sisu* will help you when communicating with people from Finland, but this word is untranslatable into English. It means something akin to "guts" or "dogged persistence." Similarly, the new capitalists in Russia may have difficulty communicating with their British or Canadian counterparts because English terms such as *efficiency*, *free market*, and *regulation* are not directly translatable into Russian.

2. *Barriers caused by word connotations.* Words imply different things in different languages. Negotiations between Americans and Japanese executives are made more difficult because the Japanese word *hai* translates as "yes," but its connotation may be "Yes, I'm listening," rather than "Yes, I agree."

3. *Barriers caused by tone differences.* In some cultures, language is formal, in others it's informal. In some cultures, the tone changes depending on the context: People speak differently at home, in social situations, and at work. Using a personal, informal style in a situation in which a more formal style is expected can be embarrassing and off-putting.

4. *Barriers caused by differences among perceptions.* People who speak different languages actually view the world in different ways. The Inuit perceive snow differently because they have many words for it. Thais perceive "no" differently than do Americans because the former have no such word in their vocabulary.

Cultural Context   A better understanding of these cultural barriers and their implications for communicating across cultures can be achieved by considering the concepts of high- and low-context cultures.[31]

Cultures tend to differ in the importance to which context influences the meaning that individuals take from what is actually said or written in light of who the other person is. Countries like China, Korea, Japan, and Vietnam are **high-context cultures**. They rely heavily on nonverbal and subtle situational cues when communicating with others. What is *not* said may be more significant than what *is* said. A person's official status, place in society, and reputation carry considerable weight in communications. In contrast, people from Europe and North America reflect their **low-context cultures**. They rely essentially on words to convey meaning. Body language or formal titles are secondary to spoken and written words (see Exhibit 10-6).

These contextual differences actually mean quite a lot in terms of communication. Communication in high-context cultures implies considerably more trust by both parties. What may appear, to an outsider, as casual and insignificant conversation is important because it reflects the desire to build a relationship and create trust. Oral agreements imply strong commitments in high-context cultures. And who you are—your age, seniority, rank in the organization—is highly valued and heavily influences your credibility. But in low-context cultures, enforceable contracts will tend to be in writing, precisely worded, and highly legalistic. Similarly, low-context cultures value directness. Managers are expected to be explicit and precise in conveying intended

EXHIBIT 10-6   High-Context Versus Low-Context Cultures

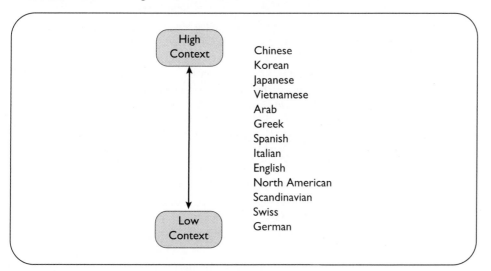

meaning. It's quite different in high-context cultures, in which managers tend to make suggestions rather than give orders.

A Cultural Guide   When communicating with people from a different culture, you can begin by assessing the cultural context in order to reduce misperceptions, misinterpretations, and misevaluations. You're likely to have fewer difficulties if people come from a cultural context similar to your own. In addition, the following four rules can be helpful.[32]

1. *Assume differences until similarity is proven.* Most of us assume that others are more similar to us than they actually are, and people from different countries often are very different from us. So you are far less likely to make an error if you assume others are different from you rather than assuming similarity until difference is proven.

2. *Emphasize description rather than interpretation or evaluation.* Interpreting or evaluating what someone has said or done, in contrast to description, is based more on the observer's culture and background than on the observed situation. As a result, delay judgment until you've had sufficient time to observe and interpret the situation from the differing perspectives of all the cultures involved.

3. *Practice empathy.* Before sending a message, put yourself in the recipient's shoes. What are his or her values, experiences, and frames of reference? What do you know about his or her education, upbringing, and background that can give you added insight? Try to see the other person as he or she really is.

4. *Treat your interpretation as a working hypothesis.* Once you've developed an explanation for a new situation or think you empathize with someone from a foreign culture, treat your interpretation as a hypothesis that needs further testing rather than as a certainty. Carefully assess the feedback provided by recipients to see if it confirms your hypothesis. For important decisions or communiqués, you can also check with other foreign and home-country colleagues to make sure that your interpretations are on target.

IMPLICATIONS FOR MANAGERS

A careful review of this chapter finds a common theme regarding the relationship between communication and employee satisfaction: the less the uncertainty, the greater the satisfaction. Distortions, ambiguities, and incongruities in communications all increase uncertainty and, hence, they have a negative impact on satisfaction.[33]

The less distortion that occurs in communication, the more management messages to employees will be received as they were intended.[34] This, in turn, should reduce ambiguities and clarify the group's task. Extensive use of vertical, lateral, and informal channels will increase communication flow, reduce uncertainty, and improve group performance and satisfaction. We should also expect incongruities between verbal and nonverbal communiqués to increase uncertainty and to reduce satisfaction.

Findings further suggest that the goal of perfect communication is unattainable. Yet, evidence demonstrates a positive relationship between effective communication (which includes factors such as perceived trust, perceived accuracy, desire for interaction, top-management receptiveness, and upward information requirements) and worker productivity.[35] Choosing the correct channel, being an effective listener, and using feedback may, therefore, make for more effective communication. But the human factor generates distortions that can never be fully eliminated. The communication process represents an exchange of messages, but the outcome is meanings that may or may not approximate those that the sender intended. Whatever the sender's expectations, the decoded message in the mind of the receiver represents his or her reality. And it is this "reality" that will determine performance, along with the individual's level of motivation and degree of satisfaction. The issue of motivation is critical, so we should briefly review how communication is central in determining an individual's degree of motivation.

You will remember from expectancy theory (see Chapter 5) that the degree of effort an individual exerts depends on his or her perception of the effort–performance, performance–reward, and reward–goal satisfaction links. If individuals are not given the data necessary to make the perceived probability of these links high, motivation will suffer. If rewards are not made clear, if the criteria for determining and measuring performance are ambiguous, or if individuals are not relatively certain that their efforts will lead to satisfactory performance, then effort will be reduced. So, communication plays a significant role in determining the level of employee motivation.

A final implication from the communication literature relates to predicting turnover. Employers may use programs to communicate realistic role expectations to new hires. Comparisons of turnover rates among organizations that use such realistic job previews versus either no preview or presentation of only positive job information show that those not using the realistic preview have, on average, almost 29 percent higher turnover.[36] This makes a strong case for managers to convey honest and accurate information about a job to applicants during the recruiting and selection process.

Leadership

1. Contrast leadership and management.
2. List the traits of effective leaders.
3. Define and give examples of the Ohio State leadership dimensions.
4. Compare and contrast trait and behavioral theories.
5. Describe Fiedler's contingency model.
6. Define the qualities of a charismatic leader.
7. Contrast transformational with transactional leadership.
8. Identify when leadership may not be necessary.
9. Explain how to find and create effective leaders.

Leaders can make the difference between success and failure. In this chapter, we'll look at the basic approaches to determining what makes an effective leader and what differentiates leaders from nonleaders. Here's what we'll discuss:

- Present trait theories, which dominated the study of leadership up to the late 1940s
- Behavioral theories, which were popular until the late 1960s
- Contingency theories, which followed on the heels of behavioral theories
- Charismatic and transformational leadership, which currently are the dominant approaches to the field of leadership

Before we review these approaches, let's first clarify what we mean by the term *leadership*.

WHAT IS LEADERSHIP?

Leadership and *management* are terms that are often confused. How do they differ?

John Kotter of the Harvard Business School argues that management is about coping with complexity.[1] Good management brings about order and consistency by generating formal plans, designing rigid organization structures, and monitoring results against the plans. Leadership, in contrast, is about coping with change. Leaders establish direction by developing a vision of the future; then they align people by communicating this vision and inspiring them to overcome hurdles.

Although Kotter provides separate definitions of the two terms, both researchers and practicing managers frequently make no such distinctions. So, we need to present leadership in a way that can capture how it is used in theory and practice.

We define **leadership** as the ability to influence a group toward the achievement of a vision or set of goals. The source of this influence may be formal, such as a person's managerial rank in an organization. Because management positions come with some degree of formally designated authority, a person may assume a leadership role simply because of the position he or she holds in the organization. However, not all leaders are managers, nor, for that matter, are all managers leaders. Just because managers are provided by their organizations with certain formal rights is no assurance that they will be able to lead effectively. We find that nonsanctioned leadership—the ability to influence that arises outside the formal structure of the organization—is often as important, or more important, than formal influence. In other words, leaders can emerge from within a group, as well as by formal appointment, to lead a group.

It is important to recognize that organizations need strong leadership *and* strong management for optimal effectiveness. In today's dynamic world, we need leaders to challenge the status quo, to create visions of the future, and to inspire organization members to want to achieve the visions. For instance, all Big Three auto makers (Ford, GM, Daimler Chrysler) had thought they were doing a good job managing their organizations, only to find out that they had not engaged in sufficient leadership to predict future trends (as had their competition, such as Toyota). We also need managers to formulate detailed plans, create efficient organizational structures, and oversee day-to-day operations.

—In today's dynamic world, leadership has the ability to influence a group toward the achievement of a vision or set of goals.

Trait Theories

Throughout history, strong leaders—Buddha, Napoleon, Mao, Churchill, Thatcher, Reagan—have all been described in terms of their traits. For instance, when Margaret Thatcher was prime minister of Great Britain, she was regularly described as confident, iron willed, determined, and decisive.

Trait theories of leadership differentiate leaders from nonleaders by focusing on personal qualities and characteristics. Individuals like Margaret Thatcher, South Africa's Nelson Mandela, Virgin Group CEO Richard Branson, Apple cofounder Steve Jobs, former New York City mayor Rudolph Giuliani, and American Express chairman Ken Chenault are recognized as leaders and described in terms such as *charismatic*, *enthusiastic*, and *courageous*. The search for personality, social, physical, or intellectual attributes that describe leaders and differentiate them from nonleaders goes back to the earliest stages of leadership research.

Research that was focused on isolating leadership traits resulted in a number of dead ends. For instance, a review conducted in the late 1960s of 20 different studies identified nearly 80 leadership traits, but only 5 of these traits were common to 4 or more of the investigations.[2] By the 1990s, after numerous studies and analyses, about the best thing that could be said was that most "leaders are not like other people," but the particular traits that were isolated varied a great deal from review to review.[3] It was a pretty confusing state of affairs.

A breakthrough, of sorts, came when researchers began organizing traits around the Big Five personality framework: extroversion, agreeableness, conscientiousness, emotional stability, and openness to experience (see Chapter 3). What became clear was that most of the myriad traits that emerged in various leadership reviews could be subsumed under one of the Big Five and that this approach resulted in consistent and strong support for traits as predictors of leadership. Ambition and energy—two common traits of leaders—are part of extroversion. Rather than focusing on these two specific traits, it is better to think of them in terms of the more general trait of extroversion.

A comprehensive review of the leadership literature, when organized around the Big Five, has found that extroversion is the most important trait of effective leaders.[4] But results show that extroversion is more strongly related to leader emergence than to leader effectiveness. This is not totally surprising since sociable and dominant people are more likely to assert themselves in group situations. Conscientiousness and openness to experience also showed strong and consistent relationships to leadership, though not quite as strong as extroversion. The traits of agreeableness and emotional stability weren't as strongly correlated with leadership. Overall, it does appear that the trait approach does have something to offer. Leaders who are extroverted (like being around people and are able to assert themselves), conscientious (are disciplined and keep commitments they make), and open (are creative and flexible) do seem to have an advantage when it comes to leadership, suggesting that good leaders do have key traits in common.

Recent studies indicate that another trait may indicate effective leadership: emotional intelligence (EI), which we discussed in Chapter 7. Advocates of EI argue that without it, a person can have outstanding training, a highly analytical mind, a compelling vision, and an endless supply of terrific ideas but still not make a great leader. This may be especially true as individuals move up in an organization. It appears that EI is critical to effective leadership because one of its core components is empathy. Empathetic leaders can sense others' needs, listen to what followers say (and don't say), and read the reactions of others. As one leader noted, "The caring part of empathy, especially for the people with whom you work, is what inspires people to stay with a leader when the going gets rough. The mere fact that someone cares is more often than not rewarded with loyalty."[5]

Despite these claims for its importance, the link between EI and leadership effectiveness is much less investigated compared to other traits. One reviewer noted, "Speculating about the practical utility of the EI construct might be premature. Despite such warnings, EI is being viewed as a panacea for many organizational malaises with recent suggestions that EI is essential for leadership effectiveness."[6] But until more rigorous evidence accumulates, we can't be confident about the connection.

Based on the latest findings, we offer two conclusions:

1. Traits can predict leadership. Twenty years ago, the evidence suggested otherwise, but this was probably due to the lack of a valid framework for classifying and organizing traits. The Big Five seems to have rectified that.
2. Traits do a better job of predicting the emergence of leaders and the appearance of leadership than in actually distinguishing between *effective* and *ineffective* leaders.[7]

The fact that an individual exhibits the traits and others consider that person to be a leader does not necessarily mean that the leader is successful at getting his or her group to achieve its goals.

Behavioral Theories

The presumed failures of early trait studies led researchers in the late 1940s through the 1960s to go in a different direction. They began looking at the behaviors exhibited by specific leaders. They wondered if something was unique in the way that effective leaders behave. To use contemporary examples, Siebel Systems Chairman Tom Siebel and Oracle CEO Larry Ellison have been very successful in leading their companies through difficult times.[8] And they both rely on a common leadership style—tough talking, intense, autocratic. Does this suggest that autocratic behavior is a preferred style for all leaders? In this section, we look at three different **behavioral theories of leadership** to answer that question. First, however, let's consider the practical implications of the behavioral approach.

If the behavioral approach to leadership were successful, it would have implications quite different from those of the trait approach. Trait research provides a basis for *selecting* the "right" persons to assume formal positions in groups and organizations requiring leadership. In contrast, if behavioral studies were to turn up critical behavioral determinants of leadership, we could *train* people to be leaders. The difference between trait and behavioral theories, in terms of application, lies in their underlying assumptions. Trait theories assume leaders are born rather than made. However, if specific behaviors characterize leaders, we could teach leadership—we could design programs that implanted these behavioral patterns in individuals who desired to be effective leaders. This is surely a more exciting avenue, for it means that the supply of leaders could be expanded. If training worked, we could have an infinite supply of effective leaders.

Ohio State Studies   The most comprehensive and replicated of the behavioral theories resulted from research that began at Ohio State University in the late 1940s. Researchers at Ohio State sought to identify independent dimensions of leader behavior. Beginning with over a thousand dimensions, they eventually narrowed the list to two categories that substantially accounted for most of the leadership behavior described by employees. They called these two dimensions *initiating structure* and *consideration*.

Initiating structure refers to the extent to which a leader is likely to define and structure his or her role and those of employees in the search for goal attainment. It includes behavior that attempts to organize work, work relationships, and goals. The leader characterized as high in initiating structure could be described as someone who assigns group members to particular tasks, expects workers to maintain definite standards of performance, and emphasizes the meeting of deadlines. Larry Ellison and Tom Siebel exhibit high initiating structure behavior.

Consideration is described as the extent to which a person is likely to have job relationships that are characterized by mutual trust, respect for employees' ideas, and regard for their feelings. Such a person shows concern for followers' comfort, well-being, status, and satisfaction. A leader high in consideration could be described as one who helps employees with personal problems, is friendly and approachable, and treats all employees as equals. AOL Time Warner's CEO Richard Parsons rates high on consideration behavior. His leadership style is very people oriented, emphasizing cooperation and consensus building.[9]

At one time, the results of the Ohio State studies were thought to be disappointing. However, a more recent review suggests that this two-factor conceptualization was given a premature burial. A review of 160 studies found that both initiating structure and consideration were associated with effective leadership. Specifically, consideration was more strongly related to the individual. In other words, the followers of leaders who were high in consideration were more satisfied with their jobs and more motivated and also had more respect for their leaders. Initiating structure, however, was more strongly related to higher levels of group and organization productivity and more positive performance evaluations.

University of Michigan Studies   Leadership studies undertaken at the University of Michigan's Survey Research Center, at about the same time as those being done at Ohio State, had similar research objectives: to locate behavioral characteristics of leaders that appeared to be related to measures of performance effectiveness.

The Michigan group also came up with two dimensions of leadership behavior that they labeled employee oriented and production oriented. **Employee-oriented leaders** were described as emphasizing interpersonal relations; they took a personal interest in the needs of their employees and accepted individual differences among members. The **production-oriented leaders**, in contrast, tended to emphasize the technical or task aspects of their jobs—their main concern was in accomplishing each group's tasks, and the group members were a means to that end. These dimensions—employee oriented and production oriented—are closely related to the Ohio State dimensions. Employee-oriented leadership is similar to consideration, and production-oriented leadership is similar to initiating structure. In fact, most leadership researchers use the terms synonymously.

The conclusions arrived at by the Michigan researchers strongly favored the leaders who were employee oriented in their behavior. Employee-oriented leaders were associated with higher group productivity and higher job satisfaction. Production-oriented leaders tended to be associated with low group productivity and lower job satisfaction. Although the Michigan studies emphasized employee-oriented leadership (or consideration) over production-oriented leadership (or initiating structure), the Ohio State studies garnered more research attention and suggested that *both* consideration and initiating structure are important to effective leadership.[10] Blake and Mouton used the Ohio State and Michigan studies in proposing a **managerial grid** (now sometimes called the *leadership grid*) based on the styles of *concern for people* and *concern for production*, which essentially represent the Ohio State dimensions of consideration and initiating structure or the Michigan dimensions of employee oriented and production oriented.

Summary of Trait Theories and Behavioral Theories

Judging from the evidence, the behavioral theories, like the trait theories, add to our understanding of leadership effectiveness. Leaders who have certain traits, and who display consideration and structuring behaviors, do appear to be more effective. Perhaps trait theories and behavioral theories should be integrated. For instance, you would think that conscientious leaders (conscientiousness is a trait) are more likely to be structuring (structuring is a behavior). And maybe extroverted leaders (extroversion is a trait) are more likely to be considerate (consideration is a behavior). Unfortunately, we can't be sure there is a connection. Future research is needed to integrate these approaches.

Contingency Theories

The rise and fall trajectory of many leaders, such as Enron executives Kenneth Lay and Jeffrey Skilling, illustrates that predicting leadership success is more complex than isolating a few traits or preferable behaviors. The supposed failure by researchers in the mid-twentieth century to obtain consistent results led to a focus on situational influences. The relationship between leadership style and effectiveness suggested that under condition *a*, style *x* would be appropriate, whereas style *y* would be more suitable for condition *b*, and style *z* for condition *c*. But what were the conditions *a*, *b*, *c*, and so forth? It was one thing to say that leadership effectiveness was dependent on the situation and another to be able to isolate those situational conditions. Several approaches to isolating key situational variables have proven more successful than others and, as a result, have gained wider recognition. We shall consider three of these: the *Fiedler model, leader–member exchange theory*, and *path–goal theory*.

Fiedler Model   The first comprehensive contingency model for leadership was developed by Fred Fiedler.[11] The **Fiedler contingency model** proposes that effective group performance depends on the proper match between the leader's style and the degree to which the situation gives control to the leader.

IDENTIFYING LEADERSHIP STYLE   Fiedler believes a key factor in leadership success is the individual's basic leadership style. So he begins by trying to find out what that basic style is. Fiedler created the **least preferred coworker (LPC) questionnaire** for this purpose; it purports to measure whether a person is task or relationship oriented. The LPC questionnaire contains sets of 16 contrasting adjectives (such as pleasant–unpleasant, efficient–inefficient, open–guarded, supportive–hostile). It asks respondents to think of all the coworkers they have ever had and to describe the one person they *least enjoyed* working with by rating that person on a scale of 1 to 8 for each of the 16 sets of contrasting adjectives. Fiedler believes that based on the respondents' answers to this LPC questionnaire, he can determine their basic leadership styles. If the least preferred coworker is described in relatively positive terms (a high LPC score), then the respondent is primarily interested in good personal relations with this coworker. That is, if you essentially describe the person you are least able to work with in favorable terms, Fiedler would label you *relationship oriented*. In contrast, if the least preferred coworker is seen in relatively unfavorable terms (a low LPC score), the respondent is primarily interested in productivity and thus would be labeled *task oriented*. About 16 percent of respondents score in the middle range. Such individuals cannot be classified as either relationship oriented or task oriented and thus fall outside the theory's predictions. The rest of our discussion, therefore, relates to the 84 percent who score in either the high or low range of the LPC.

Fiedler assumes that an individual's leadership style is fixed. If a situation requires a task-oriented leader and the person in that leadership position is relationship oriented, either the situation has to be modified or the leader replaced to achieve optimal effectiveness.

DEFINING THE SITUATION   After an individual's basic leadership style has been assessed through the LPC, management must match the leader with the situation. Fiedler has identified three contingency dimensions that, he argues, define the key situational factors that determine leadership effectiveness:

1. *Leader–member relations:* The degree of confidence, trust, and respect members have in a leader
2. *Task structure:* The degree to which job assignments are structured or unstructured
3. *Position power:* The degree of influence a leader has over power variables such as hiring, firing, discipline, promotions, and salary increases

The next step in the Fiedler model is to evaluate the situation in terms of these three contingency variables:

- Leader–member relations are either good or poor.
- Task structure is either high or low.
- Position power is either strong or weak.

Fiedler states that the better the leader–member relations, the more highly structured the job, and the stronger the position power, the more control the leader has. For instance, a very favorable situation (in which the leader would have a great deal of control) might involve a payroll manager who is well respected and whose employees have confidence in her (good leader–member relations), for which the activities to be done—such as wage computation, check writing, report filing—are specific and clear (high task structure), and for whom the job provides considerable freedom for the manager to reward and punish her employees (strong position power). However, an unfavorable situation might involve the disliked chairperson of a voluntary United Way fund-raising team with very little control in the job. Altogether, by compiling the three contingency dimensions, we find eight potential situations or categories in which leaders could find themselves (see Exhibit 11-1).

MATCHING LEADERS AND SITUATIONS   With knowledge of an individual's LPC and an assessment of the three contingency dimensions, the Fiedler model proposes matching them up to achieve maximum leadership effectiveness.[12] Based on his research, Fiedler concluded that task-oriented leaders tend to perform better in situations that were very favorable to them and in situations that were very unfavorable (see Exhibit 11-1). So Fiedler would predict that when faced with a category I, II, III, VII, or VIII situation, task-oriented leaders perform better. Relationship-oriented leaders, however, perform better in moderately favorable situations—categories IV through VI. In recent years, Fiedler has condensed these eight situations into three.[13] He now says that task-oriented leaders perform best in situations of high and low control, whereas relationship-oriented leaders perform best in situations of moderate control.

You would apply Fiedler's findings by matching leaders and situations. Individuals' LPC scores would determine the types of situations for which they were best suited. Such situations would be defined by evaluating the three contingency factors of leader–member relations, task structure, and position power. But remember

EXHIBIT 11-1   Findings from the Fiedler Model

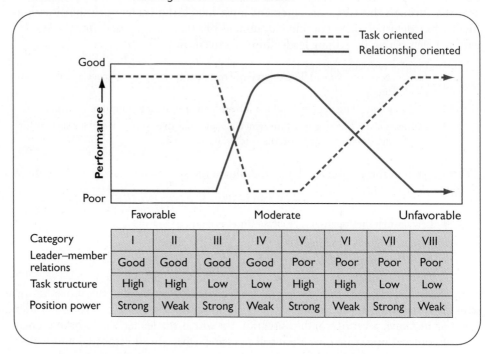

Category	I	II	III	IV	V	VI	VII	VIII
Leader–member relations	Good	Good	Good	Good	Poor	Poor	Poor	Poor
Task structure	High	High	Low	Low	High	High	Low	Low
Position power	Strong	Weak	Strong	Weak	Strong	Weak	Strong	Weak

that Fiedler views an individual's leadership style as being fixed. Therefore, leader effectiveness can be improved in only two ways:

1. *Change the leader to fit the situation:* As in a baseball game, a manager can put a right-handed pitcher or a left-handed pitcher into the game, depending on the situational characteristics of the hitter. So, for instance, if a group situation rates as highly unfavorable but is currently led by a relationship-oriented manager, the group's performance could be improved by replacing that manager with one who is task oriented.

2. *Change the situation to fit the leader:* That could be done by restructuring tasks or increasing or decreasing the power that the leader has to control factors such as salary increases, promotions, and disciplinary actions.

EVALUATION   As a whole, reviews of the major studies that tested the overall validity of the Fiedler model lead to a generally positive conclusion. Considerable evidence supports at least substantial parts of the model.[14] If predictions from the model use only three categories rather than the original eight, ample evidence supports Fiedler's conclusions. But problems with the LPC and the practical use of the model must be addressed. For instance, the logic underlying the LPC is not well understood, and studies have shown that respondents' LPC scores are not stable. Also, the contingency variables are complex and difficult for practitioners to assess. It's often difficult in practice to determine how good the leader–member relations are, how structured the task is, and how much position power the leader has.

Leader–Member Exchange Theory

For the most part, the leadership theories we've covered to this point have largely assumed that leaders treat all their followers in the same manner. They assume leaders use a fairly homogeneous style with all of the people in their work units. But think about your experiences in groups. Did you notice that leaders often act very differently toward different people? Did the leader tend to have favorites who made up his or her in-group? If you answered "Yes" to both these questions, you're acknowledging the foundation of leader–member exchange theory. The **leader–member exchange (LMX) theory** argues that because of time pressures, leaders establish a special relationship with a small group of their followers. These individuals make up the *in-group:* They are trusted, get a disproportionate amount of the leader's attention, and are more likely to receive special privileges. Other followers fall into the *out-group*: They get less of the leader's time, fewer of the preferred rewards that the leader controls, and have leader–follower relations based on formal authority interactions.

The theory proposes that early in the history of the interaction between a leader and a given follower, the leader implicitly categorizes the follower as an *in* or an *out* and that relationship is relatively stable over time. Leaders induce LMX by rewarding those employees with whom they want a closer linkage and punishing those with whom they do not. But for the LMX relationship to remain intact, the leader and the follower must invest in the relationship.

How the leader chooses who falls into each category is unclear, but evidence suggests that leaders tend to choose in-group members because they have attitude and personality characteristics that are similar to their own or a higher level of competence than do out-group members (see Exhibit 11-2).[15] For instance, followers who have a mastery orientation—who place high priority on learning what is required to perform the job well—develop closer leader–member exchanges because such employees turn to their supervisors for sources of valuable information and experience. As a result, employees are provided with prospects for skill development and self-improvement that can further benefit the organization.[16] However, communicating frequently with a supervisor appears to be helpful only for high LMX employees,

EXHIBIT 11-2   Leader–Member Exchange Theory

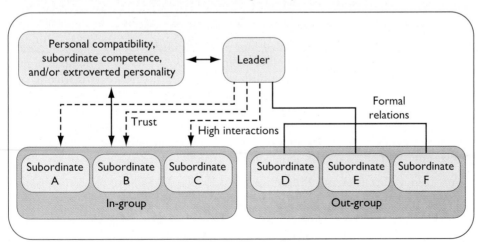

probably because supervisors perceive frequent communication from low LMX employees as annoying and a waste of their time.[17] The key point to note here is that even though it is the leader who is doing the choosing, it is the follower's characteristics that drive the leader's categorizing decision.

Few followers would want to be outside a leader's inner circle. There is a danger to being part of the inner circle, though, because your fortunes may rise and fall with your leader. When CEOs are ousted, for instance, their inner circle usually goes with them. When Tyco CEO Dennis Kozlowski was given the boot, eventually his closest associate, CFO Mark Swartz, was also forced to resign, although he was well regarded on Wall Street and was thought to be one of the executives who best understood the intricacies of Tyco's business.[18]

Research to test LMX theory has been generally supportive. More specifically, the theory and research surrounding it provide substantive evidence of the following:

- Leaders do differentiate among followers.
- These disparities are far from random.
- Followers with in-group status will have higher performance ratings, lower turnover intentions, greater satisfaction with their superiors, and higher overall satisfaction than will the out-group.[19]

These positive findings for in-group members shouldn't be totally surprising given our knowledge of the self-fulfilling prophecy. Leaders invest their resources with those they expect to perform best. And with the belief that in-group members are the most competent, leaders treat them as such and unwittingly fulfill their prophecies.[20]

Path–Goal Theory

Developed by Robert House, path–goal theory extracts elements from the Ohio State leadership research on initiating structure and consideration and the expectancy theory of motivation.

The Theory   The essence of **path–goal theory** is that it's the leader's job to provide followers with the information, support, or other resources necessary for them to achieve their goals. The term *path–goal* is derived from the belief that effective leaders clarify the path to help their followers get from where they are to the achievement of their work goals and to make the journey along the path easier by reducing roadblocks.

Leader Behaviors   House identified four leadership behaviors. The *directive leader* lets followers know what is expected of them, schedules work to be done, and gives specific guidance as to how to accomplish tasks. The *supportive leader* is friendly and shows concern for the needs of followers. The *participative leader* consults with followers and uses their suggestions before making a decision. The *achievement-oriented leader* sets challenging goals and expects followers to perform at their highest level. In contrast to Fiedler, House assumes leaders are flexible and that the same leader can display any or all of these behaviors, depending on the situation.

Contingency Variables and Predictions   As Exhibit 11-3 illustrates, path–goal theory proposes two classes of contingency variables that moderate leadership behavior:

1. Those *in the environment* that are outside the control of the employee (task structure, the formal authority system, and the work group)

EXHIBIT 11-3   The Path–Goal Theory

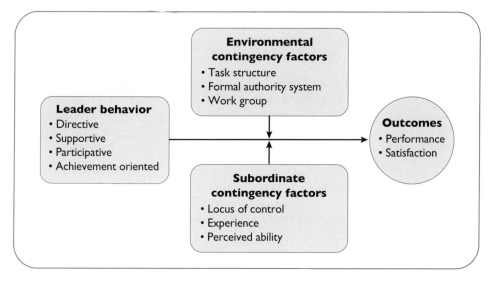

2. Those that are part of the *personal characteristics of the employee* (locus of control, expe-
    rience, and perceived ability)

Environmental factors determine the type of leader behavior required as a complement if follower outcomes are to be maximized, while personal characteristics of the
employee determine how the environment and leader behavior are interpreted. So,
the theory proposes that leader behavior will be ineffective when it is redundant with
sources of environmental structure or incongruent with employee characteristics. For
instance, path–goal theory would predict the following:

■ Directive leadership leads to greater satisfaction when tasks are ambiguous or stressful than when they are highly structured and well laid out.

■ Supportive leadership results in high employee performance and satisfaction when
   employees are performing structured tasks.

■ Directive leadership is likely to be perceived as redundant among employees with
   high perceived ability or with considerable experience.

■ Employees with an internal locus of control will be more satisfied with a participative
   style.

■ Achievement-oriented leadership will increase employees' expectancies that effort
   will lead to high performance when tasks are ambiguously structured.

Evaluation   Due to its complexity, testing path–goal theory has proven to be difficult. A review of the evidence suggests mixed support. As the authors of this review
commented, "These results suggest that either effective leadership does not rest in the
removal of roadblocks and pitfalls to employee path instrumentalities as path-goal
theories propose or that the nature of these hindrances is not in accord with the
proposition of the theories." Another review concluded that the lack of support was
"shocking and disappointing."[21] These conclusions have been challenged by others
who argue that adequate tests of the theory have yet to be conducted.[22] Thus, it is safe

to say that the jury is still out regarding the validity of path–goal theory. Because it is so complex to test, that may remain the case for some time to come.

INSPIRATIONAL APPROACHES TO LEADERSHIP

Now let's examine two contemporary leadership theories with a common theme. They view leaders as individuals who inspire followers through their words, ideas, and behaviors. These theories are charismatic leadership and transformational leadership.

Charismatic Leadership

John F. Kennedy, Martin Luther King Jr., Ronald Reagan, Bill Clinton, Mary Kay Ash (founder of Mary Kay Cosmetics), Steve Jobs (cofounder of Apple Computer), and former New York City mayor Rudy Giuliani are individuals frequently cited as being charismatic leaders. So, what do they have in common?

What Is Charismatic Leadership?   Max Weber, a sociologist, was the first scholar to discuss charismatic leadership. More than a century ago, he defined *charisma* (from the Greek for "gift") as "a certain quality of an individual personality, by virtue of which he or she is set apart from ordinary people and treated as endowed with supernatural, superhuman, or at least specifically exceptional powers or qualities. These are not accessible to the ordinary person, but are regarded as of divine origin or as exemplary, and on the basis of them the individual concerned is treated as a leader."[23] Weber argued that charismatic leadership was one of several ideal types of authority.

The first researcher to consider charismatic leadership in terms of OB was Robert House. According to House's **charismatic leadership theory**, followers make attributions of heroic or extraordinary leadership abilities when they observe certain behaviors. A number of studies have attempted to identify the characteristics of the charismatic leader. One of the best reviews of the literature has documented four such characteristics—*vision, willingness to take personal risks to achieve that vision, sensitivity to followers' needs*, and *exhibiting behaviors that are out of the ordinary*.[24] These characteristics are described in Exhibit 11-4.

How Charismatic Leaders Influence Followers   How do charismatic leaders actually influence followers? The evidence suggests a four-step process.[25]

1. It begins by the leader articulating an appealing *vision*. A **vision** is a long-term strategy on how to attain a goal or goals. This vision provides a sense of continuity for followers by linking the present with a better future for the organization. For instance, at Apple, Steve Jobs championed the iPod, noting, "It's as Apple as anything Apple has ever done." The creation of the iPod achieved Apple's goal of offering groundbreaking and easy-to-use technology. Apple's strategy was to create a product that had a user-friendly interface with which songs could be quickly uploaded and easily organized. It was the first major market device to link data storage capabilities with music downloading.

2. Once a vision is established, the leader then communicates high performance expectations and expresses confidence that followers can attain them. This enhances follower self-esteem and self-confidence. Centra Software CEO Paul Gudonis says that conveying confidence is a central tool in a manager's toolbox.[26]

EXHIBIT 11-4   Key Characteristics of Charismatic Leaders

1. *Vision and articulation.* Has a vision—expressed as an idealized goal—that proposes a future better than the status quo and is able to clarify the importance of the vision in terms that are understandable to others.
2. *Personal risk.* Willing to take on high personal risk, incur high costs, and engage in self-sacrifice to achieve the vision.
3. *Sensitivity to follower needs.* Perceptive of others' abilities and responsive to their needs and feelings.
4. *Unconventional behavior.* Engages in behaviors that are perceived as novel and counter to norms.

Source: Based on J. A. Conger and R. N. Kanungo, *Charismatic Leadership in Organizations* (Thousand Oaks, CA: Sage, 1998), p. 94.

3. Next, the leader conveys, through words and actions, a new set of values and, by his or her behavior, sets an example for followers to imitate. One study of Israeli bank employees showed, for instance, that charismatic leaders were more effective because their employees personally identified with their leaders.
4. Finally, the charismatic leader engages in emotion-inducing and often unconventional behavior to demonstrate courage and convictions about the vision. There is an emotional contagion in charismatic leadership in which followers unintentionally assume the emotions their leader is conveying.[27] The next time you see Martin Luther King Jr.'s "I Have a Dream" speech, focus on the reactions of the crowd, and it will bring to light how a charismatic leader can spread his emotion to his followers.

The key properties of a vision seem to be inspirational possibilities that are value centered, realizable, and imbued with superior imagery and articulation. Visions should generate possibilities that are inspirational and unique and that offer a new order that can produce organizational distinction. A vision is likely to fail if it doesn't offer a view of the future that is clearly and demonstrably better for the organization and its members. Desirable visions fit the times and circumstances and reflect the uniqueness of the organization. People in the organization must also believe that the vision is attainable. It should be perceived as challenging yet doable. Also, visions that have clear articulation and powerful imagery are more easily grasped and accepted.

The Dark Side of Charismatic Leadership   Many charismatic business leaders have become celebrities, not unlike Shaquille O'Neal or Madonna. Every company wants a charismatic CEO. To attract these people, companies have offered their leaders unprecedented autonomy and resources, such as private jets at their beck and call, use of $30 million penthouses, interest-free loans to buy beach homes and artwork, company-paid security staffs, and other luxurious benefits befitting royalty. And one study showed that charismatic CEOs were able to use their charisma to leverage higher salaries even when their performance was mediocre.[28]

Unfortunately, charismatic leaders who are larger than life don't necessarily act in the best interests of their organizations. At Enron, Tyco, WorldCom, and HealthSouth, such leaders recklessly used organizational resources for their personal benefit and executives broke laws and crossed ethical lines to generate financial numbers that temporarily inflated stock prices and allowed them to cash in millions of dollars in stock options for themselves. Many of these leaders used their power to remake their companies in their own image. These leaders often completely blurred the boundary separating their personal interests from their organizations' interests. At its worst, the perils of this ego-driven charisma are leaders who allow their self-interest and personal goals to override the goals of their organizations. Intolerant of criticism, they surround themselves with "yes people" who are rewarded for pleasing the leader and create a climate in which people are afraid to question or challenge the "king" or "queen" when they think he or she is making a mistake.

A study of 29 companies (e.g., GE, Wal-Mart, HP) that went from good to great (their cumulative stock returns were all at least three times better than the general stock market over 15 years) found an *absence* of ego-driven charismatic leaders. Although the leaders of these firms were fiercely ambitious and driven, their ambition was directed toward their company rather than themselves. They generated extraordinary results, but with little fanfare or hoopla. They took responsibility for mistakes and poor results and gave credit for successes to other people. They prided themselves on developing strong leaders inside the firm who could direct the company to greater heights after they were gone.[29]

We don't mean to suggest that charismatic leadership isn't effective. Overall, its effectiveness is well supported. The point is that a charismatic leader isn't always the answer. Yes, an organization with a charismatic leader at the helm is more likely to be successful, but that success depends, to some extent, on the situation and on the leader's vision. Some charismatic leaders, such as Adolf Hitler, are all too successful at convincing their followers to pursue a vision that can be disastrous.

Transformational Leadership

Another stream of research has focused on differentiating transformational leaders from transactional leaders.[30] Some of the leadership theories presented previously in this chapter—the Ohio State studies, Fiedler's model, and path–goal theory—have concerned **transactional leaders**. Such leaders guide or motivate their followers in the direction of established goals by clarifying role and task requirements. **Transformational leaders** inspire followers to transcend their own self-interests for the good of their organizations and are capable of having a profound and extraordinary effect on their followers. Contemporary examples include Andrea Jung at Avon, Richard Branson of the Virgin Group, and Boeing CEO Jim McNerney. Transformational leaders exhibit these characteristics:

- They pay attention to the concerns and developmental needs of individual followers.
- They change followers' awareness of issues by helping them to look at old problems in new ways.
- They are able to excite, arouse, and inspire followers to put out extra effort to achieve group goals.

Exhibit 11-5 briefly identifies and defines the characteristics that differentiate these two types of leaders.

Transactional and transformational leadership shouldn't be viewed as opposing approaches to getting things done. Transformational and transactional leadership complement each other, but that doesn't mean they're equally important. Transformational

EXHIBIT 11-5   Characteristics of Transactional and Transformational Leaders

Transactional Leader

Contingent Reward: Contracts exchange of rewards for effort, promises rewards for good performance, recognizes accomplishments.

Management by Exception (active): Watches and searches for deviations from rules and standards, takes correct action.

Management by Exception (passive): Intervenes only if standards are not met.

Laissez-Faire: Abdicates responsibilities, avoids making decisions.

Transformational Leader

Idealized Influence: Provides vision and sense of mission, instills pride, gains respect and trust.

Inspirational Motivation: Communicates high expectations, uses symbols to focus efforts, expresses important purposes in simple ways.

Intellectual Stimulation: Promotes intelligence, rationality, and careful problem solving.

Individualized Consideration: Gives personal attention, treats each employee individually, coaches, advises.

leadership builds *on top of* transactional leadership and produces levels of follower effort and performance that go beyond what would occur with a transactional approach alone. The reverse isn't true, so if you are a good transactional leader but do not have transformational qualities, you'll likely only be a mediocre leader. The best leaders are transactional *and* transformational.

Full Range of Leadership Model   Exhibit 11-6 shows the full range of leadership model. *Laissez-faire* is the most passive and therefore the least effective of the leader behaviors. Leaders using this style are rarely viewed as effective. *Management by exception*—regardless of whether it is active or passive—is slightly better than laissez-faire, but it's still considered ineffective leadership. Leaders who practice management-by-exception leadership tend to be available only when a problem occurs, which is often too late. *Contingent reward* leadership can be an effective style of leadership. However, leaders will not get their employees to go above and beyond the call of duty when practicing this style of leadership. Only the four remaining leadership styles—which are all aspects of transformational leadership—enable leaders to motivate followers to perform above expectations and transcend their own self-interest for the sake of the organization. *Individualized consideration, intellectual stimulation, inspirational motivation*, and *idealized influence* all result in extra effort from workers, higher productivity, higher morale and satisfaction, higher organizational effectiveness, lower turnover, lower absenteeism, and greater organizational adaptability. Based on this model, leaders are generally most effective when they regularly use each of the four transformational behaviors.

How Transformational Leadership Works   In the past few years, a great deal of research has been conducted to explain how transformational leadership works. Transformational leaders encourage their followers to be more innovative and creative.

EXHIBIT 11-6   Full Range of Leadership Model

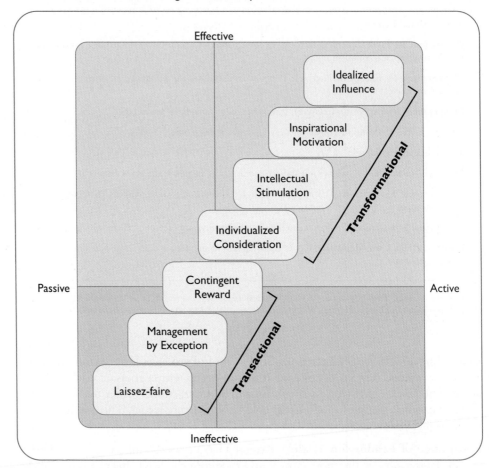

For instance, Col. Leonard Wong of the U.S. Army found that, in the Iraq war, the army was encouraging "reactive instead of proactive thought, compliance instead of creativity, and adherence instead of audacity." In response, Col. Wong is working to empower junior officers to be creative and to take more risks.[31] Transformational leaders are more effective because they themselves are more creative, but they're also more effective because they encourage those who follow them to be creative, too.

Goals are another key mechanism that explains how transformational leadership works. Followers of transformational leaders are more likely to pursue ambitious goals, be familiar with and agree on the strategic goals of the organization, and believe that the goals they are pursuing are personally important. VeriSign's CEO, Stratton Sclavos, says, "It comes down to charting a course—having the ability to articulate for your employees where you're headed and how you're going to get there. Even more important is choosing people to work with who have that same level of passion, commitment, fear, and competitiveness to drive toward those same goals."

Sclavos's remark about goals brings up vision. Just as research has shown that vision is important in explaining how charismatic leadership works, it has also shown that vision explains part of the effect of transformational leadership. Indeed, one study found that vision was even more important than a charismatic (effusive, dynamic, lively) communication style in explaining the success of entrepreneurial firms.[32] Transformational leadership also engenders commitment on the part of followers and instills in them a greater sense of trust in the leader.[33]

Evaluation of Transformational Leadership   The evidence supporting the superiority of transformational leadership over transactional leadership is impressive. Transformational leadership has been supported in different countries (Korea, Russia, Israel, India, Kenya, Norway, Taiwan), in disparate occupations (school principals, marine commanders, ministers, presidents of business associations, military cadets, union shop stewards, school teachers, sales reps), and at various job levels. A number of studies with U.S., Canadian, and German military officers found, at every level, that transformational leaders were evaluated as more effective than their transactional counterparts.[34] And a review of 87 studies testing transformational leadership found that it was related to the motivation and satisfaction of followers and to the higher performance and perceived effectiveness of leaders.[35]

Transformational leadership theory is not perfect. Concerns focus in part on whether contingent reward leadership is strictly a characteristic of transactional leaders only. Also, contrary to the full range of leadership model, contingent reward leadership is sometimes more effective than transformational leadership.

In summary, the overall evidence indicates that transformational leadership, more than transactional leadership, strongly correlates with lower turnover rates, higher productivity, and higher employee satisfaction. Like charisma, it appears that transformational leadership can be learned. One study of Canadian bank managers found that those managers who underwent transformational leadership training had bank branches that performed significantly better than branches with managers who did not undergo training. Other studies show similar results.[36]

Transformational Leadership Versus Charismatic Leadership   Some debate addresses the question of whether or not transformational leadership and charismatic leadership are the same. The researcher most responsible for introducing charismatic leadership to OB, Robert House, considers the terms synonymous, calling the differences "modest" and "minor." However, the individual who first researched transformational leadership, Bernard Bass, considers charisma to be part of transformational leadership but argues that transformational leadership is broader than charisma, suggesting that charisma is, by itself, insufficient to "account for the transformational process."[37] Another researcher commented, "The purely charismatic [leader] may want followers to adopt the charismatic's world view and go no further; the transformational leader will attempt to instill in followers the ability to question not only established views but eventually those established by the leader."[38] Although many researchers believe that transformational leadership is broader than charismatic leadership, studies show that in reality a leader who scores high on transformational leadership is also likely to score high on charisma. Therefore, in practice, measures of charisma and transformational leadership may be roughly equivalent.

Authentic Leadership   Although charismatic leadership theories and transformational leadership theories have added greatly to our understanding of effective leadership, they do not explicitly deal with the role of ethics and trust. Some scholars have argued that a consideration of ethics and trust is essential to complete the picture of effective leadership. Here we consider these two concepts under the rubric of authentic leadership.[39] **Authentic leaders** know who they are, know what they believe in and value, and act on those values and beliefs openly and candidly. Their followers would consider them to be ethical people. Authentic leadership adds to our understanding of transformational and charismatic leadership in arguing that leadership is not value free. Before we judge any leader to be effective, we should consider both the means used by the leader to achieve goals and the moral content of those goals. If we're looking for the best possible leader, it is not enough to be charismatic or visionary—one must also be ethical and create trust on the part of followers.

> —If we're looking for the best possible leader, it is not enough to be charismatic or visionary—one must also be ethical and create trust on the part of followers.

CHALLENGES TO THE LEADERSHIP CONSTRUCT

At the beginning of this chapter, we argued that leadership is important, and we believe it is. However, it's also true that sometimes leaders are given too much credit or blame. Leaders cannot do everything. Leadership has limits. Let's examine two perspectives that challenge the widely accepted belief in the importance of leadership. The first argument proposes that leadership is more about appearances than reality, that you don't have to be an effective leader as long as you look like one. The second argument directly attacks the notion that some leadership will always be effective regardless of the situation, because whatever actions leaders exhibit are irrelevant in many situations.

Leadership as an Attribution

We introduced attribution theory in Chapter 2. As you may remember, that theory deals with the ways in which people try to make sense out of cause-and-effect relationships. We said when something happens, we want to attribute it to something else. The **attribution theory of leadership** says that leadership is merely an attribution that people make about other individuals. The attribution theory has shown that people characterize leaders as having such traits as intelligence, outgoing personality, strong verbal skills, aggressiveness, understanding, and industriousness.[40] At the organizational level, the attribution framework accounts for the conditions under which people use leadership to explain organizational outcomes. Those conditions are extremes in organizational performance. When an organization has either extremely negative or extremely positive performance, people are prone to make leadership attributions to explain the performance. As noted previously, this tendency helps to account for the vulnerability of CEOs (and high-ranking state officials) when their organizations suffer a major financial setback, regardless of whether they had much to do with it, and also accounts for why CEOs tend to be given credit for extremely positive financial results—again, regardless of how much or how little they contributed.

One of the more interesting findings in the attribution theory of leadership literature is the perception that effective leaders are generally considered consistent or unwavering in their decisions.[41] One of the explanations for why Ronald Reagan (during his first term as U.S. president) was perceived as a leader was that he was fully committed, steadfast, and consistent in the decisions he made and the goals he set.

Former U.S. President George H. W. Bush, in contrast, undermined the public's perception of his leadership by increasing income taxes after stating categorically during his campaign "Read my lips. No new taxes."

Following the attribution theory of leadership, we'd say that what's important in being characterized as an effective leader is projecting the *appearance* of being a leader rather than focusing on *actual accomplishments*. Aspiring leaders can attempt to shape the perception that they're smart, personable, verbally adept, aggressive, hardworking, and consistent in their style. And by doing so, they increase the probability that their bosses, colleagues, and employees will *view* them *as* effective leaders.

Substitutes and Neutralizers to Leadership

Contrary to the arguments made throughout this and the previous chapter, leadership may not always be important. A theory of leadership suggests that, in many situations, whatever actions leaders exhibit are irrelevant. Certain individual, job, and organizational variables can act as *substitutes* for leadership or *neutralize* the leader's influence on his or her followers.

Neutralizers make it impossible for leader behavior to make any difference to follower outcomes. They negate the leader's influence. Substitutes, however, make a leader's influence not only impossible but also unnecessary. They act as replacements for the leader's influence. For instance, characteristics of employees—their experience, training, "professional" orientation, or indifference toward organizational rewards—can substitute for, or neutralize the effect of, leadership. Experience and training can replace the need for a leader's support or ability to create structure and reduce task ambiguity. Jobs that are inherently unambiguous and routine or that are intrinsically satisfying may place fewer demands on the leadership variable. Organizational characteristics such as explicit, formalized goals; rigid rules and procedures; and cohesive work groups can also replace formal leadership (see Exhibit 11-7).

EXHIBIT 11-7   Substitutes and Neutralizers for Leadership

Defining Characteristics	Relationship-Oriented Leadership	Task-Oriented Leadership
Individual		
Experience/training	No effect on	Substitutes for
Professionalism	Substitutes for	Substitutes for
Indifference to rewards	Neutralizes	Neutralizes
Job		
Highly structured task	No effect on	Substitutes for
Provides its own feedback	No effect on	Substitutes for
Intrinsically satisfying	Substitutes for	No effect on
Organization		
Explicit, formalized goals	No effect on	Substitutes for
Rigid rules and procedures	No effect on	Substitutes for
Cohesive work groups	Substitutes for	Substitutes for

Source: Based on S. Kerr and J. M. Jermier, "Substitutes for Leadership: Their Meaning and Measurement," *Organizational Behavior and Human Performance,* December 1978, p. 378.

This recognition that leaders don't always have an impact on follower outcomes should not be that surprising. After all, as we have discussed, a number of variables—attitudes, personality, ability, and group norms, to name but a few—have been documented as affecting employee performance and satisfaction. Yet supporters of the leadership concept place an undue burden on this variable for explaining and predicting behavior. It would be simplistic to consider employees as guided to goal accomplishments solely by the actions of their leaders. It's important, therefore, to recognize explicitly that leadership is merely another independent variable in our overall OB model. In some situations, it may contribute a lot to explaining employee productivity, absence, turnover, satisfaction, and citizenship behavior, but in other situations it may contribute little toward that end.

The validity of substitutes and neutralizers is controversial. One problem is that the theory is very complicated—with many possible substitutes for and neutralizers of many different types of leader behaviors across many different situations. Moreover, sometimes the difference between substitutes and neutralizers is fuzzy. For instance, if I'm working on a task that's intrinsically enjoyable, the theory predicts that leadership will be less important because the task itself provides enough motivation. But, does that mean that intrinsically enjoyable tasks neutralize leadership effects, that they substitute for them, or both? As this review points out, another problem is that substitutes for leadership (such as employee characteristics, the nature of the task, and so forth) matter, but they do not appear to substitute for or neutralize leadership.[42]

FINDING AND CREATING EFFECTIVE LEADERS

We have covered a lot of ground in this chapter. But the ultimate goal of our review is to answer this question: How can organizations find or create effective leaders? Let's try to answer that.

Selection

The entire process that organizations go through to fill management positions is essentially an exercise in trying to identify individuals who will be effective leaders. Your search might begin by reviewing the specific requirements for the position to be filled. What knowledge, skills, and abilities are needed to do the job effectively? You should try to analyze the situation to find candidates who will make a proper match.

—Personality tests can be used to look for traits associated with leadership: extroversion, conscientiousness, and openness to experience.

Testing is useful for identifying and selecting leaders. Personality tests can be used to look for traits associated with leadership: extroversion, conscientiousness, and openness to experience. Testing to find a leadership candidate's score on self-monitoring also makes sense. High self-monitors are likely to outperform their low-scoring counterparts because the former are better at reading situations and adjusting their actions accordingly. You can additionally assess candidates for emotional intelligence. Given the importance of social skills to managerial effectiveness, candidates with a high EI should have an advantage, especially in situations requiring transformational leadership.[43]

Interviews also provide an opportunity to evaluate leadership candidates. We know that experience is a poor predictor of leader effectiveness, but situation-specific experience is relevant. You can use the interview to determine if a candidate's prior experience fits with the situation you're trying to fill. Similarly, the interview is a reasonably good vehicle for identifying the degree to which a candidate has leadership traits, such as extroversion, self-confidence, a vision, the verbal skills to frame issues, or a charismatic physical presence.

We know the importance of situational factors in leadership success. And we should use this knowledge to match leaders to situations. Does the situation require a change-focused leader? If so, look for transformational qualities; if not, look for transactional qualities. You might also ask if leadership is actually important in this specific position. Situational factors may substitute for or neutralize leadership, in which case the leader essentially performs a figurehead or symbolic role, and the importance of selecting the "right" person is not particularly crucial.

Training

Organizations, in aggregate, spend billions of dollars, yen, and euros on leadership training and development.[44] These efforts take many forms—from $50,000 executive leadership programs offered by universities such as Harvard to sailing experiences at the Outward Bound School. Although much of the money spent on training may provide dubious benefits, our review suggests managers can do some things to get the maximum effect from their leadership-training budgets.[45]

First, let's recognize the obvious. People are not equally trainable. Leadership training of any kind is likely to be more successful with individuals who are high self-monitors than with low self-monitors. Such individuals have the flexibility to change their own behavior.

What kinds of things can individuals learn that might be related to higher leader effectiveness? It may be a bit optimistic to believe that we can teach "vision creation," but we can teach implementation skills. We can train people to develop "an understanding about content themes critical to effective visions."[46] We also can teach skills such as trust building and mentoring. And leaders can be taught situational-analysis skills. They can learn how to evaluate situations, how to modify situations to make them fit better with their styles, and how to assess which leader behaviors might be most effective in given situations. A number of companies have recently turned to executive coaches to help senior managers improve their leadership skills. For instance, Charles Schwab, eBay, Pfizer, Unilever, and American Express have hired executive coaches to provide specific one-on-one training for their companies' top executives to help them improve their interpersonal skills and to learn to act less autocratically.[47]

On an optimistic note, evidence suggests that behavioral training through modeling exercises can increase an individual's ability to exhibit charismatic leadership qualities. Researchers have had success training actual business leaders, and even in scripting undergraduate business students to "play" charismatic.[48] Finally, accumulating research shows that leaders can be trained in transformational leadership skills. Once learned, these skills have bottom-line results, whether it is in the financial performance of Canadian banks or the training effectiveness of soldiers in the Israeli Defense Forces.[49]

IMPLICATIONS FOR MANAGERS

Leadership plays a central part in understanding group behavior, for it's the leader who usually provides the direction toward goal attainment. Therefore, a more accurate predictive capability should be valuable in improving group performance.

To some degree, leadership success depends on having "the right stuff." Individuals who have the right traits (are extroverted, conscientious, and open) and exhibit the right behaviors (consideration, initiating structure) are more likely to be effective.

It's also true that leadership success depends on the situation. In particular, LPC theory and LMX theory suggest that aspects of the environment are critical in leadership.

Organizations are increasingly searching for managers who can exhibit transformational leadership qualities. They want leaders with visions and the charisma to carry those visions out. And although true leadership effectiveness may be a result of exhibiting the right behaviors at the right time, the evidence is quite strong that people have a relatively uniform perception of what a leader should look like.

For managers concerned with how to fill key positions in their organizations with effective leaders, they should select individuals with certain traits and behavioral tendencies, and they also should pay particular attention to charisma and inspirational qualities. We have also shown that we all can learn to become better leaders by showing these characteristics.

CHAPTER 12

Power and Politics

After studying this chapter, you should be able to:

1. Contrast leadership and power.
2. Define the five bases of power.
3. Explain which bases of power are most effective.
4. List and define nine influence tactics.
5. Distinguish between use and effectiveness of influence tactics.
6. List the individual and organizational factors that stimulate political behavior.
7. Explain how defensive behaviors can protect an individual's self-interest.
8. Identify seven techniques for managing the impression one makes on others.
9. List the three questions that can help determine if a political action is ethical.

*P*ower has been described as the last dirty word. It is easier for most of us to talk about sex or money than it is to talk about power. People who have power deny it, people who want it try not to appear to be seeking it, and those who are good at getting it are secretive about how they got it.

In this chapter, we show that power determines what goals a group will pursue and how the group's resources will be distributed among its members. Further, we show how group members with good political skills use their power to influence the distribution of resources in their favor.

A DEFINITION OF POWER

Power refers to a capacity that A has to influence the behavior of B so that B acts in accordance with A's wishes. This definition implies two facets of power:

1. Its *potential* need not be actualized to be effective.
2. It requires a dependency relationship.

Power may exist even when it's not used. It is, therefore, a capacity or potential. One can have power but not impose it, but probably the more important aspect of power is that power is a function of **dependency**. The greater *B*'s dependence on *A*, the greater *A*'s power in the relationship. Dependence, in turn, is based on alternatives that *B* perceives and the importance that *B* places on the alternative(s) that *A* controls. A person can have power over you only if he or she controls something you desire. If you want a college degree and have to pass a certain course to get it, and your current instructor is the only faculty member in the college who teaches that course, he or she has power over you. Your alternatives are highly limited, and you place a high degree of importance on obtaining a passing grade.

Contrasting Leadership and Power

A careful comparison of our description of power with our description of leadership in the previous two chapters reveals that the concepts are closely intertwined. Leaders use power as a means of attaining group goals. Leaders achieve goals, and power is a means of facilitating their achievement.

How do leadership and power differ?

- *Goal compatibility.* Power does not require goal compatibility, merely dependence. Leadership, on the other hand, requires some congruence between the goals of the leader and those being led.
- *Direction of influence.* Leadership focuses on the downward influence on one's followers. It minimizes the importance of lateral and upward influence patterns. Power does not.
- *Research emphasis.* Leadership research, for the most part, emphasizes style. It seeks answers to questions such as these: How supportive should a leader be? How much decision making should be shared with followers? In contrast, the research on power has tended to be broader and to focus on tactics for gaining compliance. It has gone beyond the individual as the exerciser of power because power can be used by groups as well as by individuals to control other individuals or groups.

BASES OF POWER

Where does power come from? What is it that gives an individual or a group influence over others? We can answer these questions by dividing the bases or sources of power into two general groupings—*formal* and *personal*—and then separating each of these into more specific categories.

Formal Power

—Formal power can come from the ability to coerce or reward, or it can come from formal authority.

Formal power is based on an individual's position in an organization. Formal power can come from the ability to coerce or reward, or from formal authority.

Coercive Power   The **coercive power** base is dependent on fear. One reacts to this power out of fear of the negative results that might occur if one failed to comply. It rests on the application, or the threat of application, of physical sanctions such as the infliction of pain, the generation of frustration through restriction of movement, or the controlling by force of basic physiological or safety needs. One example of coercive power is sexual harassment, when individuals use their power or position to coerce or intimidate others in unwanted ways. Research shows that sexual harassment is more likely to occur when large power differentials are present.[1]

Reward Power   The opposite of coercive power is **reward power**, which accrues when people comply with the wishes or directives of another because doing so produces positive benefits; therefore, one who can distribute rewards that others view as valuable will have power over those others. These rewards can be financial or nonfinancial:

- *Financial:* controlling pay rates, raises, and bonuses
- *Nonfinancial:* recognition, promotions, interesting work assignments, friendly colleagues, and preferred work shifts or sales territories.

Legitimate Power   In formal groups and organizations, probably the most frequent access to one or more of the power bases is one's structural position, called **legitimate power**. It represents the formal authority to control and use organizational resources. Positions of authority include coercive and reward powers. Legitimate power, however, is broader than the power to coerce and reward. Specifically, it includes acceptance by members in an organization of the authority of a position.

Personal Power

You don't have to have a formal position in an organization to have power. Many of the most competent and productive chip designers at Intel, for instance, have power, but they aren't managers and have no formal power. What they have is personal power—power that comes from an individual's unique characteristics. In this section, we look at two bases of personal power: *expert power* and the *respect and admiration of others*.

Expert Power   **Expert power** is influence wielded as a result of expertise, special skill, or knowledge. Expertise has become one of the most powerful sources of influence as the world has become more technologically oriented. As jobs become more specialized, we become increasingly dependent on experts to achieve goals. So, although it is generally acknowledged that physicians have expertise and hence expert power—most of us follow the advice that our doctors give us—you should also recognize that computer specialists, tax accountants, economists, industrial psychologists, and other specialists are able to wield power as a result of their expertise.

Referent Power   **Referent power** is based on identification with a person who has desirable resources or personal traits. If I like, respect, and admire you, you can exercise power over me because I want to please you. Referent power develops out of admiration of another and a desire to be like that person. It helps explain, for instance, why celebrities such as Tiger Woods or Catherine Zeta-Jones are paid millions of dollars to endorse products in commercials. One of the ways in which individuals acquire referent power is through charisma. Some people with referent power, while not in formal leadership positions, nevertheless are able to exert influence over others because of their charismatic dynamism, likeability, and emotional effects on others.

Which Bases of Power Are Most Effective?

Of the three bases of formal power (coercive, reward, legitimate) and two bases of personal power (expert, referent), research suggests pretty clearly that the personal sources of power are most effective. Both expert and referent power are positively related to employees' satisfaction with supervision, their organizational commitment, and their performance, whereas reward and legitimate power seem to be unrelated to these outcomes. Moreover, one source of formal power—coercive power—actually can backfire in that it is negatively related to employee satisfaction and commitment.[2]

POWER TACTICS

Bases of power are different from **power tactics**, which people can use. The former are pretty fixed—at least in the short term (one either has expertise or doesn't)—whereas the latter can, theoretically, be used by any person in any situation. So, what power tactics do people use to translate power bases into specific action? That is, what options do individuals have for influencing their bosses, coworkers, or employees? And are some of these options more effective than others?

Research has identified nine distinct influence tactics:[3]

- *Legitimacy:* Relying on one's authority position or stressing that a request is in accordance with organizational policies or rules.
- *Rational persuasion:* Presenting logical arguments and factual evidence to demonstrate that a request is reasonable.
- *Inspirational appeals:* Developing emotional commitment by appealing to a target's values, needs, hopes, and aspirations.
- *Consultation:* Increasing the target's motivation and support by involving him or her in deciding how the plan or change will be done.
- *Exchange:* Rewarding the target with benefits or favors in exchange for following a request.
- *Personal appeals:* Asking for compliance based on friendship or loyalty.
- *Ingratiation:* Using flattery, praise, or friendly behavior prior to making a request.
- *Pressure:* Using warnings, repeated demands, and threats.
- *Coalitions:* Enlisting the aid of other people to persuade the target or using the support of others as a reason for the target to agree.

Some tactics are usually more effective than others. Specifically, evidence indicates that rational persuasion, inspirational appeals, and consultation tend to be the most effective. On the other hand, pressure tends to frequently backfire and is typically the least effective of the nine tactics.[4] You can also increase your chance of success by using more than one type of tactic at the same time or sequentially, as long as your choices are compatible.[5] For instance, using both ingratiation and legitimacy can lessen the negative reactions that might come from the appearance of being dictated to by the boss.

Some influence tactics work better than others, depending on the direction of influence.[6] Studies have found that rational persuasion is the only tactic that is effective across organizational levels. Inspirational appeals work best as a downward-influencing tactic with subordinates. When pressure works, it's almost only to achieve downward influence. And the use of personal appeals and coalitions are most effective with lateral influence attempts. In addition to the direction of influence, a number of other factors have been found to affect which tactics work best. These include the sequencing of tactics, a person's skill in using the tactic, a person's relative power, the type of request and how it is perceived, the culture of the organization, and country-specific cultural factors.

You're more likely to be effective if you begin with "softer" tactics that rely on personal power such as personal and inspirational appeals, rational persuasion, and consultation. If these fail, you can move to "harder" tactics that emphasize formal power and involve greater costs and risks, such as exchange, coalitions, and pressure.[7] Interestingly, it's been found that using a single soft tactic is more effective than using a single hard tactic; and combining two soft tactics, or a soft tactic and rational persuasion, is more effective than using any single tactic or combination of hard tactics.[8]

Studies confirm that a tactic is "more likely to be successful if the target perceives it to be a socially acceptable form of influence behavior, if the agent has sufficient position and personal power to use the tactic, if the tactic can affect target attitudes about the desirability of the request, if it is used in a skillful way, if it is used for a request that is legitimate, and if it is consistent with the target person's values and needs."[9]

POWER IN GROUPS: COALITIONS

Those "out of power" and seeking to be "in" will first try to increase their power individually. Why share the spoils if one doesn't have to? But if this proves ineffective, the alternative is to form a **coalition**—an informal group bound together by the active pursuit of a single issue. The logic of a coalition is that there's strength in numbers.

The natural way to gain influence is to become a power holder. Therefore, those who want power will attempt to build a personal power base. In many instances, this may be difficult, risky, costly, or impossible. In such cases, efforts will be made to form a coalition of two or more "outs" who, by joining together, can combine their resources to increase rewards for themselves. Successful coalitions have been found to contain fluid membership and are able to form swiftly, achieve their target issue, and quickly disappear.[10]

—Successful coalitions have been found to contain fluid membership and are able to form swiftly, achieve their target issue, and quickly disappear.

We can make some predictions about coalition formation. First, coalitions in organizations often seek to maximize their size. In political science theory, coalitions move the other way: They try to minimize their size. They tend to be just large enough to exert the power necessary to achieve their objectives. But legislatures are different from organizations. Specifically, decision making in organizations does not end just with selection from among a set of alternatives. The decision must also be implemented. In organizations, the implementation of and commitment to the decision are at least as important as the decision itself. It's necessary, therefore, for any coalition to seek a broad constituency to support its objectives. This means expanding the coalition to encompass as many interests as possible.

Another prediction about coalitions relates to the degree of interdependence within the organization. More coalitions will likely be created when there is a great deal of task and resource interdependence. In contrast, there will be less interdependence among subunits and less coalition formation activity when subunits are largely self-contained or resources are abundant.

Coalition formation will be influenced by the actual tasks that workers do. The more routine the task of a group, the greater the likelihood that coalitions will form. The more routine the work that people do, the greater will be their substitutability for each other and, thus, the greater their dependence. To offset this dependence, they can be expected to resort to a coalition. This helps to explain the historical appeal of labor unions, especially among low-skilled workers. Such employees are better able to negotiate improved wages, benefits, and working conditions as a united coalition than if they acted individually. A one-person strike has little power over management. However, if a firm's entire workforce goes on strike, management has a serious problem.

POWER IN ACTION: POLITICS

When people get together in groups, they will exert power. People want to carve out niches from which to exert influence, to earn rewards, and to advance their careers. When employees in organizations convert their power into action, we describe them as being engaged in politics. Those with good political skills have the ability to use their bases of power effectively.

A Definition of Political Behavior

There has been no shortage of definitions for organizational politics. Essentially, however, definitions have focused on the use of power to affect decision making in the organization or on members' self-serving and organizationally nonsanctioned behaviors.[11] For our purposes, we shall define **political behavior** in organizations as activities that are not required as part of one's formal role in the organization but that influence, or attempt to influence, the distribution of advantages and disadvantages within the organization.[12]

This definition encompasses key elements from what most people mean when they talk about organizational politics. Political behavior is outside one's specified job requirements. The behavior requires some attempt to use one's power bases. In addition, our definition encompasses efforts to influence the goals, criteria, or processes used for *decision making* when we state that *politics is concerned with the distribution of advantages and disadvantages within the organization*. Our definition is broad enough to include varied power tactics, such as joining a coalition, exchanging favors with others in the organization for mutual benefit, and pressuring others on behalf of or against a particular individual or decision alternative.

Factors Contributing to Political Behavior

Not all groups or organizations are equally political. In some organizations, for instance, politicking is overt and rampant, while in others politics plays only a small role in influencing outcomes. Why does this variation occur? Recent research and observation have identified a number of factors that appear to encourage political behavior. Some are individual characteristics, derived from the unique qualities of the people the organization employs; others are a result of the organization's culture or internal environment.

Individual Factors   At the individual level, researchers have identified certain personality traits, needs, and other factors that are likely to be related to political behavior. In terms of traits, we find that employees who are high self-monitors, possess an internal locus of control, and have a high need for power are more likely to engage in political behavior.[13] The high self-monitor is more sensitive to social cues, exhibits higher levels of social conformity, and is more likely to be skilled in political behavior than the low self-monitor. Individuals with an internal locus of control, because they believe they can control their environments, are more prone to take a proactive stance and attempt to manipulate situations in their favor. Not surprisingly, the Machiavellian personality—characterized by the will to manipulate and the desire for power—is comfortable using politics as a means to further his or her self-interest.

In addition, an individual's investment in the organization, perceived alternatives, and expectations of success will influence the degree to which he or she will pursue illegitimate means of political action. The more a person has invested in the organization in terms of expectations of increased future benefits, the more that person has to lose if forced out. Such people are less likely to use illegitimate means. Individuals with more alternative job opportunities—due to a favorable job market or the possession of scarce skills or knowledge, a prominent reputation, or influential contacts outside the organization—are more likely to risk illegitimate political actions. Finally, if individuals have low expectations of success in using illegitimate means, they are unlikely to make such attempts. High expectations of success in the use of illegitimate means are most likely to be the province of both experienced and powerful individuals with polished political skills and inexperienced and naive employees who misjudge their chances.

Organizational Factors   Political activity is probably more a function of the organization's characteristics than of individual difference variables. This is so because many organizations have a large number of employees with the individual characteristics we listed, yet the extent of political behavior varies widely.

—Political activity is probably more a function of the organization's characteristics than of individual difference variables.

Although we acknowledge the role that individual differences can play in fostering politicking, the evidence more strongly supports that certain situations and cultures promote politics. More specifically, politicking is more likely to surface when an organization's resources are declining, when the existing pattern of resources is changing, and when opportunity for promotions is present. In addition, certain cultures create breeding grounds for politicking, including those characterized by unclear performance evaluation systems, low trust, role ambiguity, zero-sum reward allocation practices, democratic decision making, high pressures for performance, and self-serving senior managers.

When organizations downsize to improve efficiency, reductions in resources have to be made. Threatened with the loss of resources, people may engage in political actions to safeguard what they have. But any changes, especially those that imply significant reallocation of resources within the organization, are likely to stimulate conflict and increase politicking.

Research has consistently found that promotion decisions are one of the most political actions in organizations. The opportunity for promotions or advancement encourages people to compete for a limited resource and to try to positively influence the decision outcome.

The practice of performance evaluation is also far from a perfect science. The more that organizations use subjective criteria in the appraisal, emphasize a single outcome measure, or allow significant time to pass between the time of an action and its appraisal, the greater the likelihood that an employee can get away with politicking. Subjective performance criteria create ambiguity. The use of a single outcome measure encourages individuals to do whatever is necessary to look good on that measure, but that is often done at the expense of performing well on other important parts of the job that are not being appraised. The amount of time that elapses between an action and its appraisal is also a relevant factor. The longer the time, the more unlikely that the employee will be held accountable for his or her political behaviors.

The less the trust within the organization, the higher the level of political behavior will be and the greater the likelihood that the political behavior will be of the illegitimate kind. So high trust should suppress the level of political behavior in general and inhibit illegitimate actions in particular.

Role ambiguity means that the prescribed behaviors of the employee are not clear. There are fewer limits, therefore, to the scope and functions of the employee's political actions. Because political activities are defined as those not required as part of one's formal role, the greater the role ambiguity will be, and thus the more one can engage in political activity with little chance of it being visible.

The more that an organization's culture emphasizes the zero-sum or win–lose approach to reward allocations, the more employees will be motivated to engage in politicking. The zero-sum approach treats the reward as fixed in size so that any gain one person or group achieves has to come at the expense of another person or group. If I win, you must lose! If $15,000 in annual raises is to be distributed among five employees, then any employee who gets more than $3,000 takes money away from one or more of the others. Such a practice encourages making others look bad and increasing the visibility of what you do.

The more pressure that employees feel to perform well, the more likely they are to engage in politicking. When people are held strictly accountable for outcomes, this puts great pressure on them to make themselves look good. If a person perceives that his or her entire career is riding on next quarter's sales figures or next month's plant productivity report, that employee may be motivated to do whatever is necessary to make sure the numbers come out favorably.

Also, when employees see the people on top engaging in political behavior, especially when they do so successfully and are rewarded for it, a climate is created that supports politicking. In a sense, politicking by top management gives permission to those lower in the organization to play politics by implying that such behavior is acceptable.

The Human Response to Organizational Politics

Trish O'Donnell loves her job as a writer on a weekly television comedy series but hates the internal politics. "A couple of the writers here spend more time kissing up to the executive producer than doing any work. And our head writer clearly has his favorites. While they pay me a lot and I get to really use my creativity, I'm sick of having to be on alert for backstabbers and constantly having to self-promote my contributions. I'm tired of doing most of the work and getting little of the credit." Are Trish O'Donnell's comments typical of people who work in highly politicized workplaces? We all know of friends or relatives who regularly complain about the politics at their job. But how do people in general react to organizational politics? Let's look at the evidence.

Of factors that contribute to political behavior, our discussion has focused on the favorable outcomes for individuals who successfully engage in politicking. But for most people—who have modest political skills or are unwilling to play the politics game—outcomes tend to be predominantly negative. In fact, very strong evidence indicates that perceptions of organizational politics are negatively related to job satisfaction.[14] The perception of politics also tends to increase job anxiety and stress. Employees may perceive that, by not engaging in politics, they may be losing ground to others who are active politickers; or, conversely, they may feel additional pressures because of having entered into and competing in the political arena.[15] Not surprisingly, when politicking becomes too much to handle, it can lead to employees quitting.[16] Finally, preliminary evidence suggests that politics leads to self-reported declines in employee performance. This may occur because employees perceive political environments to be unfair, which demotivates them.[17]

In addition to these conclusions, researchers have noted several interesting qualifiers:

- The politics–performance relationship appears to be moderated by an individual's understanding of the "hows" and "whys" of organizational politics. "An individual who has a clear understanding of who is responsible for making decisions and why they were selected to be the decision makers would have a better understanding of how and why things happen the way they do than someone who does not understand the decision-making process in the organization."[18] When both politics and understanding are high, performance is likely to increase because the individual will see political actions as an opportunity. This is consistent with what one might expect among individuals with well-honed political skills. But when understanding is low, individuals are more likely to see politics as a threat, which would have a negative effect on job performance.[19]

- When politics is seen as a threat and consistently responded to with defensiveness, negative outcomes are almost certain to surface. When people perceive politics as a threat rather than as an opportunity, they often respond with **defensive behaviors**—reactive and protective behaviors to avoid action, blame, or change (Exhibit 12-1 provides some examples of these defensive behaviors).[20] And defensive behaviors are often associated with negative feelings toward the job and work environment.[21] In the short run, employees may find that defensiveness protects their self-interests. But in the long run, it wears them down. People who consistently rely on defensiveness find that, eventually, it is the only way they know how to behave. At that point, they lose the trust and support of their peers, bosses, employees, and clients.

Are our conclusions about responses to politics globally valid? Should we expect employees in Israel, for instance, to respond the same way to workplace politics that employees in the United States do? Almost all our conclusions on employee reactions to organizational politics are based on studies conducted in North America. The few studies that have included other countries suggest some minor modifications.[22] Israelis and Britons, for instance, seem to generally respond as do North Americans, viewing organizational politics as related to decreased job satisfaction and increased turnover.[23] But in countries that are more politically unstable, such as Israel, employees seem to demonstrate greater tolerance of intense political processes in the

EXHIBIT 12-1 Defensive Behaviors

Avoiding Action

Overconforming. Strictly interpreting your responsibility by saying things like "The rules clearly state . . . " or "This is the way we've always done it."

Buck passing. Transferring responsibility for the execution of a task or decision to someone else.

Playing dumb. Avoiding an unwanted task by falsely pleading ignorance or inability.

Stretching. Prolonging a task so that one person appears to be occupied—for example, turning a two-week task into a four-month job.

Stalling. Appearing to be more or less supportive publicly while doing little or nothing privately.

Avoiding Blame

Bluffing. This is a nice way to refer to "covering your rear." It describes the practice of rigorously documenting activity to project an image of competence and thoroughness.

Playing safe. Evading situations that may reflect unfavorably. It includes taking on only projects with a high probability of success, having risky decisions approved by superiors, qualifying expressions of judgment, and taking neutral positions in conflicts.

Justifying. Developing explanations that lessen one's responsibility for a negative outcome and/or apologizing to demonstrate remorse.

Scapegoating. Placing the blame for a negative outcome on external factors that are not entirely blameworthy.

Misrepresenting. Manipulation of information by distortion, embellishment, deception, selective presentation, or obfuscation.

Avoiding Change

Prevention. Trying to prevent a threatening change from occurring.

Self-protection. Acting in ways to protect one's self-interest during change by guarding information or other resources.

workplace. This is likely to be because people in these countries are used to power struggles and have more experienced in coping with them.[24] This suggests that people from politically turbulent countries in the Middle East or Latin America might be more accepting of organizational politics, and even more willing to use aggressive political tactics in the workplace, than are people from more orderly countries, such as Great Britain or Switzerland.

Impression Management

We know that people have an ongoing interest in how others perceive and evaluate them. For example, North Americans spend billions of dollars on diets, health club memberships, cosmetics, and plastic surgery—all intended to make them more attractive to others.[25] Being perceived positively by others should have benefits for people in organizations. It might, for instance, help them initially to get the jobs they want and, once hired, to get favorable evaluations, superior salary increases, and more rapid promotions. In a political context, it might help sway the distribution of advantages in their favor. The process by which individuals attempt to control the impression others form of them is called **impression management**. It's a subject that has gained the attention of OB researchers only recently.[26]

Is everyone concerned with impression management (IM)? No! Who, then, might we predict to engage in IM? No surprise here! It's our old friend: the high self-monitor.[27] Low self-monitors tend to present images of themselves that are consistent with their personalities, regardless of the beneficial or detrimental effects for them. In contrast, high self-monitors are good at reading situations and molding their appearances and behaviors to fit each situation. Given that you want to control the impression others form of you, what techniques could you use? Exhibit 12-2 summarizes some of the more popular IM techniques and provides an example of each.

EXHIBIT 12-2   Impression Management (IM) Techniques

Conformity

Agreeing with someone else's opinion in order to gain his or her approval.

Example: A manager tells his boss, "You're absolutely right on your reorganization plan for the western regional office. I couldn't agree with you more."

Excuses

Explanations of a predicament-creating event aimed at minimizing the apparent severity of the predicament.

Example: A sales manager says to her boss, "We failed to get the ad in the paper on time, but no one responds to those ads anyway."

Apologies

Admitting responsibility for an undesirable event and simultaneously seeking to get a pardon for the action.

Example: An employee says to his boss, "I'm sorry I made a mistake on the report. Please forgive me."

Self-Promotion

Highlighting one's best qualities, downplaying one's deficits, and calling attention to one's achievements.

Example: A salesperson tells her boss, "Matt worked unsuccessfully for three years to try to get that account. I sewed it up in six weeks. I'm the best closer this company has."

Flattery

Complimenting others about their virtues in an effort to make oneself appear perceptive and likeable.

Example: A new sales trainee says to his peer, "You handled that client's complaint so tactfully! I could never have handled that as well as you did."

Favors

Doing something nice for someone to gain that person's approval.

Example: A salesperson says to her prospective client, "I've got two tickets to the theater tonight that I can't use. Take them. Consider it a thank-you for taking the time to talk with me."

Association

Enhancing or protecting one's image by managing information about people and things with which one is associated.

Example: A job applicant says to an interviewer, "What a coincidence. Your boss and I were roommates in college."

Source: Based on B. R. Schlenker, *Impression Management* (Monterey, CA: Brooks/Cole, 1980); W. L. Gardner and M. J. Martinko, "Impression Management in Organizations," *Journal of Management*, June 1988, p. 332; and R. B. Cialdini, "Indirect Tactics of Image Management Beyond Basking," in R. A. Giacalone and P. Rosenfeld (eds.), *Impression Management in the Organization* (Hillsdale, NJ: Lawrence Erlbaum, 1989), pp. 45–71.

Keep in mind that IM does not imply that the impressions people convey are necessarily false (although, of course, they sometimes are). Excuses, for instance, may be offered with sincerity. Referring again to Exhibit 12–2, you can *actually* believe that ads contribute little to sales in your region. But misrepresentation can have a high cost. If the image claimed is false, you may be discredited. If you cry wolf once too often, no one is likely to believe you when the wolf really comes. So the impression manager must be cautious not to be perceived as insincere or manipulative.[28]

Are there *situations* in which individuals are more likely to misrepresent themselves or more likely to get away with it? Yes. Situations that are characterized by high uncertainty or ambiguity provide relatively little information for challenging a fraudulent claim and reduce the risks associated with misrepresentation.[29]

Most of the studies undertaken to test the effectiveness of IM techniques have related it to two criteria: (1) interview success and (2) performance evaluations. Let's consider each of these.

The evidence indicates that most job applicants use IM techniques in interviews[30] and that, when IM behavior is used, it works.[31] In one study, for instance, interviewers felt that applicants for a position as a customer service representative who used IM techniques performed better in the interview, and they seemed somewhat more inclined to hire these people.[32] Moreover, when the researchers considered applicants' credentials, they concluded that it was the IM techniques alone that influenced the interviewers. That is, it didn't seem to matter if applicants were well or poorly qualified; if they used IM techniques, they did better in the interview.

Research indicates that some IM techniques work better than others in interviews. Researchers have compared applicants who used IM techniques that focused on promoting one's accomplishments (called *self-promotion*) to applicants who used techniques that focused on complimenting the interviewer and finding areas of agreement (referred to as *ingratiation*). In general, applicants appear to use self-promotion more than ingratiation.[33] What's more, self-promotion tactics may be more important to interviewing success. Applicants who work to create an appearance of competence by enhancing their accomplishments, taking credit for successes, and explaining away failures do better in interviews. These effects reach beyond the interview—applicants who use more self-promotion tactics also seem to get more follow-up job-site visits, even after adjusting for grade-point average, gender, and job type. Ingratiation also works well in the interview, meaning that applicants who compliment the interviewer, agree with his or her opinions, and emphasize areas of fit do better than those who don't.[34]

In terms of performance ratings, the picture is quite different. Ingratiation is positively related to performance ratings, meaning that those who ingratiate with their supervisors get higher performance evaluations. However, self-promotion appears to backfire: Those who self-promote actually seem to receive *lower* performance evaluations.[35]

What explains these results? If you think about them, they make sense. Ingratiating always works because everyone likes to be treated nicely, whether it be the interviewer or the supervisor. However, self-promotion may work only in interviews and backfire on the job because whereas the interviewer has little idea whether you're bragging about your accomplishments, the supervisor knows because it's his or her job to observe you. Thus, if you're going to self-promote, remember that what works in the interview will not always work once you're on the job.

The Ethics of Behaving Politically

We conclude our discussion of politics by providing some ethical guidelines for political behavior. Although no clear-cut standards differentiate ethical from unethical politicking, you should consider asking some questions:

- *What is the utility of engaging in the behavior?* Sometimes we engage in political behaviors for little good reason. Major league baseball player Al Martin claimed he played football at the University of Southern California when in fact he never did. Because Martin was playing baseball, not football, there was little to be gained by his lie. Outright lies like this may be a rather extreme example of impression management, but many of us have distorted information to make a favorable impression. Before doing so, one should keep in mind whether it's really worth the risk.

- *How does the utility of engaging in the political behavior balance out any harm (or potential harm) it will do to others?* Complimenting a supervisor on his or her appearance to curry favor is probably much less harmful than grabbing credit that is deserved by others for a project.

- *Does the political activity conform to standards of equity and justice?* Sometimes it is hard to weigh the costs and benefits of a political action, but its ethicality is clear. The department head who inflates the performance evaluation of a favored employee and deflates the evaluation of a disfavored employee—and then uses these evaluations to justify giving the former a big raise and nothing to the latter—has treated the disfavored employee unfairly.

Unfortunately, the answers to these questions are often argued in ways to make unethical practices seem ethical. Powerful people, for example, can become very good at explaining self-serving behaviors in terms of the organization's best interests. Similarly, they can persuasively argue that unfair actions are really fair and just. In short, immoral people can justify almost any behavior. Those who are powerful, articulate, and persuasive are most susceptible because they are likely to be able to get away with unethical practices successfully. When faced with an ethical dilemma regarding organizational politics, consider the preceding issues (Is playing politics worth the risk and will others be harmed in the process?). If you have a strong power base, recognize the ability of power to corrupt. Remember, it's a lot easier for the powerless to act ethically, if for no other reason than that they typically have very little political discretion to exploit.

IMPLICATIONS FOR MANAGERS

If you want to get things done in a group or organization, it helps to have power. As a manager who wants to maximize your power, you will want to increase others' dependence on you. You can increase your power in relation to your boss by developing knowledge or a skill that she needs and for which she perceives no ready substitute. But power is a two-way street, and you will not be alone in attempting to build your power bases. Others, particularly employees and peers, will be seeking to make you dependent on them. The result is an unending battle. While you seek to maximize others' dependence on you, you will be seeking to minimize your dependence on others. And, of course, others you work with will be trying to do the same.

One way to increase your power in an organization is to, over time, acquire the bases of power that are most useful (expert, referent) and then to use the power tactics (consultation, inspirational appeal) that are most effective. Avoid tactics (like coercion) that tend to backfire (result in resistance and resentment).

The effective manager accepts the political nature of organizations. By assessing behavior in a political framework, you can better predict the actions of others and use this information to formulate political strategies that will gain advantages for you and your work unit.

CHAPTER 13

Conflict and Negotiation

After studying this chapter, you should be able to:

1. Define conflict.
2. Differentiate between the traditional, human relations, and interactionist views of conflict.
3. Contrast task, relationship, and process conflict.
4. Outline the conflict process.
5. Describe the five conflict-handling intentions.
6. Contrast distributive and integrative bargaining.
7. Identify the five steps in the negotiation process.
8. Describe whether there are individual differences in negotiator effectiveness.

It's been said that conflict is a theme that has occupied humans more than any other—with the exception of God and love. But what do we mean by the term *conflict?*

A DEFINITION OF CONFLICT

There's been no shortage of definitions of conflict. Despite the divergent meanings the term has acquired, several common themes underlie most definitions. Conflict must be perceived by the parties to it: If no one is aware of a conflict, it is generally agreed that no conflict exists. Two other commonalities the definitions share are opposition or incompatibility, as well as some form of interaction.[1]

We can define **conflict**, then, as a process that begins when one party perceives that another party has negatively affected, or is about to negatively affect, something that the first party cares about. This definition is purposely broad. It also employs the term *process* to denote that conflict should be viewed not as an isolated event but with causes, motivations, and resolutions. It describes that point in any ongoing activity when an interaction "crosses over" to become an interparty conflict. It encompasses the wide range of conflicts that people experience in organizations: incompatibility of goals, differences over interpretations of facts, disagreements based on behavioral expectations, and the like. Also, our definition is flexible enough to cover the full range of conflict levels—from overt and violent acts to subtle forms of disagreement.

TRANSITIONS IN CONFLICT THOUGHT

It is entirely appropriate to say that conflict has long existed over the role of conflict in groups and organizations. One school of thought has argued that conflict must be avoided—that it indicates a malfunctioning within the group. We call this the *traditional* view. Another school of thought, the *human relations* view, argues that conflict is a natural and inevitable outcome in any group and that it need not be evil, but rather it has the potential to be a positive force in determining group performance. The third, and most recent, perspective proposes not only that conflict can be a positive force in a group but explicitly argues that some conflict is *absolutely necessary* for a group to perform effectively. We label this third school the *interactionist* view. Let's take a closer look at each of these views.

The Traditional View

The early approach to conflict assumed that all conflict was bad. Conflict was viewed negatively, and it was used synonymously with such terms as *violence, destruction,* and *irrationality* to reinforce its negative connotation. Conflict, by definition, was harmful and was to be avoided. The **traditional view** was consistent with the attitudes that prevailed about group behavior in the 1930s and 1940s. Conflict was seen as a dysfunctional outcome resulting from poor communication, a lack of openness and trust among people, and the failure of managers to be responsive to the needs and aspirations of their employees.

The view that all conflict is bad certainly offers a simple approach to looking at the behavior of people who create conflict. Because all conflict is to be avoided, in that view we need merely direct our attention to the causes of conflict and correct those malfunctionings to improve group and organizational performance. Although research studies now provide strong evidence to dispute that this approach to conflict reduction results in high group performance, many of us still evaluate conflict situations using this outmoded standard.

The Human Relations View

The **human relations view** argued that conflict was a natural occurrence in all groups and organizations. Because conflict was inevitable, the human relations school advocated acceptance of it. Proponents rationalized its existence: It cannot be eliminated, and there are times when conflict may benefit a group's performance. The human relations view dominated conflict theory from the late 1940s through the mid-1970s.

The Interactionist View

While the human relations view accepted conflict, the **interactionist view** encourages conflict on the grounds that a harmonious, peaceful, tranquil, and cooperative group is prone to becoming static, apathetic, and nonresponsive to needs for change and innovation. The major contribution of the interactionist view, therefore, is encouraging group leaders to maintain an ongoing minimum level of conflict—enough to keep the group viable, self-critical, and creative.

> —The interactionist view encourages conflict on the grounds that a harmonious, peaceful, tranquil, and cooperative group is prone to becoming static, apathetic, and nonresponsive to needs for change and innovation.

The interactionist view does not propose that all conflicts are good. Rather, some conflicts support the goals of the group and improve its performance; these are **functional**, constructive forms of conflict. In contrast, conflicts that hinder group performance are **dysfunctional** or destructive forms of conflict. What differentiates functional from dysfunctional conflict? The evidence indicates that we should consider the *type* of conflict, and three types specifically:[2]

- *Task conflict* relates to the content and goals of the work. Intense arguments about who should do what become dysfunctional when they create uncertainty about task roles, increase the time to complete tasks, and lead to members working at cross-purposes. However, low to moderate levels of task conflict consistently demonstrate a positive effect on group performance because that stimulates discussion of ideas that helps groups perform better.
- *Relationship conflict* focuses on interpersonal relationships. Studies demonstrate that relationship conflicts are almost always dysfunctional.[3] It appears that the friction and interpersonal hostilities inherent in relationship conflicts increase personality clashes and decrease mutual understanding, which hinders the completion of organizational tasks.
- *Process conflict* relates to how the work gets done. However, low levels of process conflict and low to moderate levels of task conflict are functional. For process conflict to be productive, it must be kept low.

If David and Jennifer have a conflict over who should turn in a report, that is a task conflict. If Bart and Chris have an argument because each sees the other as domineering, that is a relationship conflict. If Mia and Jill have an argument over the best way to prepare a presentation, that is a process conflict. As you can see, many conflicts may involve a combination of these types.

THE CONFLICT PROCESS

The **conflict process** can be seen as comprising five stages: *potential opposition or incompatibility, cognition and personalization, intentions, behavior,* and *outcomes.* The process is diagrammed in Exhibit 13-1.

Stage I: Potential Opposition or Incompatibility

The first step in the conflict process is the presence of conditions that create opportunities for conflict to arise. They *need not* lead directly to conflict, but one of these conditions is necessary if conflict is to surface. For simplicity's sake, these conditions

EXHIBIT 13-1　　　The Conflict Process

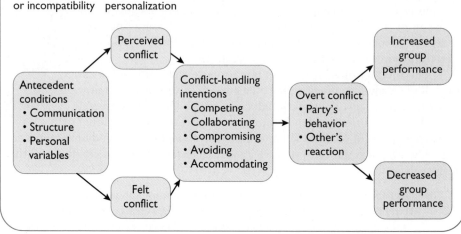

(which also may be looked at as causes or sources of conflict) have been condensed into three general categories: communication, structure, and personal variables.[4]

Communication　　The communication source represents the opposing forces that arise from semantic difficulties, misunderstandings, and *noise* in the communication channels. Much of this discussion can be related back to our comments on communication in Chapter 10.

　　A review of the research suggests that differing word connotations, jargon, insufficient exchange of information, and noise in the communication channel are all barriers to communication and potential antecedent conditions to conflict. Evidence demonstrates that semantic difficulties arise as a result of differences in training, selective perception, and inadequate information about others. Research has further demonstrated a surprising finding: The potential for conflict increases when either too little or too much communication takes place. Apparently, an increase in communication is functional up to a point, whereupon it is possible to overcommunicate, with a resultant increase in the potential for conflict. Too much information, as well as too little, can lay the foundation for conflict. Furthermore, the channel chosen for communicating can have an influence on stimulating opposition. The filtering process that occurs as information is passed between members and the divergence of communications from formal or previously established channels offer potential opportunities for conflict to arise.

Structure　　The term *structure* is used, in this context, to include variables such as size, degree of specialization in the tasks assigned to group members, jurisdictional clarity, member–goal compatibility, leadership styles, reward systems, and the degree of dependence among groups. Research indicates that size and specialization act as forces to stimulate conflict. The larger the group and the more specialized its activities, the greater the likelihood of conflict. Tenure and conflict appear inversely related, meaning the potential for conflict tends to be greatest when group members are younger and when turnover is high.

A close style of leadership—tight and continuous observation with general control of others' behaviors—increases conflict potential, but the evidence is not particularly strong. Too much reliance on participation may also stimulate conflict. Research tends to confirm that participation and conflict are highly correlated, apparently because participation encourages the promotion of differences. Reward systems, too, are found to create conflict when one member's gain is at another's expense. And if a group is dependent on another group (in contrast to the two being mutually independent) or if interdependence allows one group to gain at another's expense, opposing forces are stimulated.

Personal Variables   As practical experience has taught us, some people are conflict oriented and others are conflict aversive. Evidence indicates that certain personality types—for example, individuals who are highly authoritarian and dogmatic—lead to potential conflict. Emotions can also cause conflict. For example, an employee who shows up to work irate from her hectic morning commute may carry that anger to her 9:00 A.M. meeting. The problem? Her anger can annoy her colleagues, which may lead to a tension-filled meeting. In addition to personality traits, differing values can explain conflict. Value differences are the best explanation of diverse issues such as prejudice and disagreements over one's contribution to the group, as well as the rewards one deserves. Say that John dislikes African-Americans and Dana believes John's position indicates his ignorance. Say that an employee thinks he is worth $55,000 a year but his boss believes him to be worth $50,000. These are all value differences, which are important sources for creating the potential for conflict. It is also important to note that culture can be a source of differing values. For example, research indicates that individuals in Japan and in the United States view conflict differently. Compared to Japanese negotiators, Americans are more likely to see offers from their counterparts as unfair and to reject such offers.[5]

Stage II: Cognition and Personalization

If the conditions cited in stage I negatively affect something that one party cares about, then the potential for opposition or incompatibility becomes actualized in the second stage.

As our definition of conflict notes, perception is required. One or more of the parties must be aware of the existence of the antecedent conditions. However, because a conflict is **perceived** does not make it personalized. In other words, "*A* may be aware that *B* and *A* are in serious disagreement . . . but it may not make *A* tense or anxious, and it may have no effect whatsoever on *A*'s affection toward *B*."[6] It is at the **felt** level, when individuals become emotionally involved, that parties experience anxiety, tension, frustration, or hostility.

Stage III: Intentions

Intentions intervene among people's perceptions and emotions and overt behaviors. These intentions are decisions to act in a given way.

Intentions are separated out as a distinct stage because you have to infer the other's intent to know how to respond to that other's behavior. A lot of conflicts are escalated merely by one party attributing the wrong intentions to the other party. In addition, there is typically a great deal of slippage between intentions and behavior, so behavior does not always accurately reflect a person's intentions.

Exhibit 13-2 represents one author's effort to identify the primary conflict-handling intentions. Using two dimensions—*cooperativeness* (the degree to which one party attempts to satisfy the other party's concerns) and *assertiveness* (the degree to which one party attempts to satisfy his or her own concerns)—we can identify five conflict-handling intentions:

1. *Competing:* assertive and uncooperative, such as when you strive to achieve your goal at the expense of the other party achieving his.
2. *Collaborating:* assertive and cooperative—intending to find a win–win solution that makes both parties happy.
3. *Avoiding:* unassertive and uncooperative, such as when you avoid a conflict based on the hope it will just go away.
4. *Accommodating:* unassertive and cooperative, such as when you give in just to please someone else.
5. *Compromising:* mid-range on both assertiveness and cooperativeness, where the pie is sliced down the middle).[7]

People differ in the degree to which they generally rely on these strategies (e.g., some people are competitive in most situations), but the approach also will vary by the situation (e.g., a strategy one intends to use in a conflict with a loved one will often differ from a conflict with strangers).

Stage IV: Behavior

When most people think of conflict situations, they tend to focus on stage IV because this is where conflicts become visible. The behavior stage includes the statements, actions, and reactions made by the conflicting parties. These conflict behaviors are usually overt attempts to implement each party's intentions, but they have a stimulus

EXHIBIT 13-2   Dimensions of Conflict-Handling Intentions

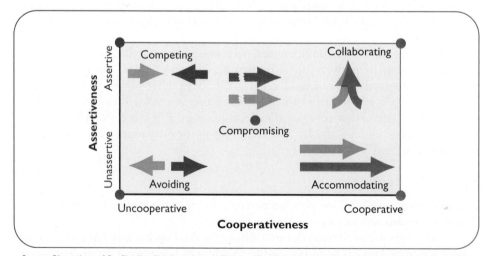

Source: Dimensions of Conflict-Handling Intentions, K. Thomas, "Conflict and Negotiation Processes in Organizations" M.D. Dunnette & L.M. Hough (eds), Handbook of Organizational Psychology, 2/e, Vol. 3, *Consulting Psychologists Press,* c 1992, p. 668

quality that is separate from intentions. As a result of miscalculations or unskilled enactments, overt behaviors sometimes deviate from original intentions.

It helps to think of stage IV as a dynamic process of interaction. For example, you make a demand on me; I respond by arguing; you threaten me; I threaten you back; and so on. All conflicts exist somewhere along this continuum. At the lower part of the continuum, we have conflicts characterized by subtle, indirect, and highly controlled forms of tension, such as a student questioning in class a point the instructor has just made. Conflict intensities escalate as they move upward along the continuum until they become highly destructive. Strikes, riots, and wars clearly fall in this upper range. For the most part, conflicts that reach the upper ranges of the continuum are almost always dysfunctional. Functional conflicts are typically confined to the lower range of the continuum.

Stage V: Outcomes

The action–reaction interplay among the conflicting parties results in consequences. As our model (see Exhibit 13-1) demonstrates, these outcomes may be functional in that the conflict results in an improvement in the group's performance, or it may be dysfunctional in that it hinders group performance.

Functional Outcomes   How might conflict act as a force to increase group performance? It is hard to visualize a situation in which open or violent aggression could be functional. Yet in a number of instances, it's possible to envision how low or moderate levels of conflict could improve the effectiveness of a group. Because people often find it difficult to think of instances in which conflict can be constructive, let's consider some examples and then review the research evidence. Note how all these examples focus on task and process conflicts and exclude the relationship variety.

Conflict is constructive when it:

- improves the quality of decisions,
- stimulates creativity and innovation,
- encourages interest and curiosity among group members,
- provides the medium through which problems can be aired and tensions released, and
- fosters an environment of self-evaluation and change.

The evidence suggests that conflict can improve the quality of decision making by allowing all points, particularly the ones that are unusual or held by a minority, to be weighed in important decisions.[8] Conflict is an antidote for groupthink. It doesn't allow the group to passively rubber-stamp decisions that may be based on weak assumptions, inadequate consideration of relevant alternatives, or other debilities. Conflict challenges the status quo and therefore furthers the creation of new ideas, promotes reassessment of group goals and activities, and increases the probability that the group will respond to change.

—Conflict challenges the status quo and therefore furthers the creation of new ideas, promotes reassessment of group goals and activities, and increases the probability that the group will respond to change.

You don't have to look further than automobile behemoth General Motors to see a company that suffered because it had too little functional conflict.[9] Many of GM's problems, from the late 1960s to the late 1990s, can be traced to a lack of functional conflict. It hired and promoted individuals who were yes-men, loyal to GM to the point of never questioning company actions. Managers were, for the most part, homogenous: conservative white males raised in the midwestern United States who resisted change: They preferred looking back to past successes rather than forward to new challenges. They were almost sanctimonious in their belief that what had worked in the past would continue to work in the future. Moreover, by sheltering executives in the company's Detroit offices and encouraging them to socialize with others inside the GM ranks, the company further insulated managers from conflicting perspectives.

Yahoo! provides a more recent example of a company that suffered because of too little functional conflict.[10] Begun in 1994, by 1999 Yahoo! had become one of the best-known brand names on the Internet. Then the implosion of dot.com stocks hit. By the spring of 2001, Yahoo!'s advertising sales were plunging and the company's stock was down 92 percent from its peak. It was at this point that Yahoo!'s most critical problem became exposed: The company was too insulated and void of functional conflict. It couldn't respond to change. Managers and staff were too comfortable with each other to challenge the status quo. This kept new ideas from percolating upward and held dissent to a minimum. The source of the problem was the company's CEO, Tim Koogle. He set the tone of nonconfrontation. Only when Koogle was replaced in 2001, with a new CEO who openly challenged the company's conflict-free climate, did Yahoo! begin to successfully solve its problems.

Research studies in diverse settings confirm the functionality of conflict, demonstrating that, among established groups, performance tended to improve more when conflict occurred among members than when fairly close agreement was prevalent. When groups analyzed decisions made by its individual members, investigators found the average improvement among the high-conflict groups was 73 percent greater than that of those groups characterized by low-conflict conditions.[11] Others have found similar results: Groups composed of members with different interests tend to produce higher-quality solutions to a variety of problems than do homogeneous groups.[12]

Dysfunctional Outcomes   The destructive consequences of conflict on a group's or organization's performance are generally well known. A reasonable summary might state that uncontrolled opposition breeds discontent, which acts to dissolve common ties, and eventually leads to the destruction of the group. And, of course, a substantial body of literature documents how conflict—the dysfunctional varieties—can reduce group effectiveness.[13] Among the more undesirable consequences are a retarding of communication, reductions in group cohesiveness, and subordination of group goals to the primacy of infighting among members. At the extreme, conflict can bring group functioning to a halt and potentially threaten the group's survival.

The demise of an organization as a result of too much conflict isn't as unusual as one might expect. For instance, one of New York's best-known law firms, Shea & Gould, closed down solely because the 80 partners couldn't get along.[14] As one legal consultant familiar with the organization said, "This was a firm that had basic and principled differences among the partners that were basically irreconcilable." That same consultant also addressed the partners at their last meeting: "You don't have an economic problem," he said. "You have a personality problem. You hate each other!"

Creating Functional Conflict   In this section we ask, if managers accept the interactionist view toward conflict, what can they do to encourage functional conflict in their organizations?[15]

Consultants generally agree that creating functional conflict is a tough job, particularly in large U.S. corporations. As one consultant put it, "A high proportion of people who get to the top are conflict avoiders. They don't like hearing negatives; they don't like saying or thinking negative things. They frequently make it up the ladder in part because they don't irritate people on the way up." Another suggests that at least 7 out of 10 people in U.S. business hush up when their opinions are at odds with those of their superiors, allowing bosses to make mistakes even when they know better.

Such anticonflict cultures may have been tolerable in the past but not in today's fiercely competitive global economy. Organizations that don't encourage and support dissent may find their survival threatened. Let's look at some approaches organizations are using to encourage their people to challenge the system and develop fresh ideas.

Hewlett-Packard rewards dissenters by recognizing go-against-the-grain types, or people who stay with the ideas they believe in even when those ideas are rejected by management. Herman Miller Inc., an office furniture manufacturer, has a formal system in which employees evaluate and criticize their bosses. IBM also has a formal system that encourages dissension. Employees can question their bosses with impunity. If the disagreement can't be resolved, the system provides a third party for counsel. Royal Dutch Shell Group, General Electric, and Anheuser-Busch build devil's advocates into the decision process. When the policy committee at Anheuser-Busch considers a major move, such as getting into or out of a business or making a major capital expenditure, it often assigns teams to make the case for each side of the question. This process frequently results in decisions and alternatives that hadn't been considered previously.

One common ingredient in organizations that successfully create functional conflict is that they reward dissent and punish conflict avoiders. The real challenge for managers, however, occurs when they hear news that they don't want to hear. The news may make their blood boil or their hopes collapse, but they can't show it. They have to learn to take the bad news without flinching. No tirades, no tight-lipped sarcasm, no eyes rolling upward, no gritting of teeth. Rather, managers should ask calm, even-tempered questions: "Can you tell me more about what happened?" "What do you think we ought to do?" A sincere "Thank you for bringing this to my attention" will probably reduce the likelihood that managers will be cut off from similar communications in the future.

Having considered conflict—its nature, causes, and consequences—now we turn to negotiation. Negotiation and conflict are closely related because negotiation often resolves conflict.

NEGOTIATION

Negotiation permeates the interactions of almost everyone in groups and organizations. There's the obvious: Labor bargains with management. There's the not so obvious: Managers negotiate with employees, peers, and bosses; salespeople negotiate with customers; purchasing agents negotiate with suppliers. And there's the subtle: An employee agrees to answer a colleague's phone for a few minutes in exchange for some past or future benefit. In today's loosely structured organizations, in which members are increasingly finding themselves having to work with colleagues over whom they have no direct authority and with whom they may not even share a common boss, negotiation skills become critical.

We define **negotiation** as a process in which two or more parties exchange goods or services and attempt to agree on the exchange rate for them.[16] Note that we'll use the terms *negotiation* and *bargaining* interchangeably.

Bargaining Strategies

There are two general approaches to negotiation: *distributive bargaining* and *integrative bargaining*. As Exhibit 13-3 shows, distributive and integrative bargaining differ in goal and motivation, focus, interests, information sharing, and duration of relationship. Let's examine the differences between these two approaches.

Distributive Bargaining   Let's say you see a used car advertised for sale in the newspaper. It appears to be just what you've been looking for. You go out to see the car. It's great and you want it. The owner tells you the asking price. You don't want to pay that much. The two of you then negotiate over the price. The negotiating strategy you're engaging in is called **distributive bargaining**. Its most identifying feature is that it operates under zero-sum conditions. That is, any gain I make is at your expense, and vice versa. Referring back to the used-car example, every dollar you can get the seller to cut from the car's price is a dollar you save. Conversely, every dollar more the seller can get from you comes at your expense. So the essence of distributive bargaining is negotiating over who gets what share of a **fixed pie**. The fixed pie concept means the bargaining parties believe there only a finite amount of goods or services are available to be divvied up. Therefore, fixed pies are zero-sum games. When parties believe the pie is fixed, they tend to bargain distributively.

Probably the most widely cited example of distributive bargaining is in labor–management negotiations over wages. Typically, labor's representatives come to the bargaining table determined to get as much money as possible out of management. Because every cent more that labor negotiates increases management's costs,

EXHIBIT 13-3   Distributive Versus Integrative Bargaining

Bargaining Characteristic	Distributive Bargaining	Integrative Bargaining
Goal	Get as much of the pie as possible	Expand the pie so that both parties are satisfied
Motivation	Win–lose	Win–win
Focus	Positions ("I can't go beyond this point on this issue.")	Interests ("Can you explain why this issue is so important to you?")
Interests	Opposed	Congruent
Information sharing	Low (sharing information will only allow other party to take advantage)	High (sharing information will allow each party to find ways to satisfy interests of each party)
Duration of relationship	Short term	Long term

each party bargains aggressively and treats the other as an opponent who must be defeated.

The essence of distributive bargaining is depicted in Exhibit 13-4. Parties *A* and *B* represent two negotiators. Each has a *target point* that defines what he or she would like to achieve. Each also has a *resistance point*, which marks the lowest acceptable outcome—the point below which they would break off negotiations rather than accept a less-favorable settlement. The area between these two points makes up each one's aspiration range. As long as *A*'s and *B*'s aspiration ranges have some overlap, there is a settlement range in which each one's aspirations can be met.

When engaged in distributive bargaining, one's tactics focus on trying to get one's opponent to agree to a specific target point or to get as close to it as possible. Examples of such tactics are persuading your opponent of the impossibility of getting to his or her target point and the advisability of accepting a settlement near yours; arguing that your target is fair, while your opponent's isn't; and attempting to get your opponent to feel emotionally generous toward you and thus accept an outcome close to your target point.

Integrative Bargaining   Let's say a sales representative for a women's sportswear manufacturer has just closed a $15,000 order from a small clothing retailer. The sales rep calls in the order to her firm's credit department. She is told that the firm can't approve credit to this customer because of a past slow-payment record. The next day, the sales rep and the firm's credit manager meet to discuss the problem. The sales rep doesn't want to lose the business. Neither does the credit manager, but he also doesn't want to get stuck with an uncollectible debt. The two openly review their options. After considerable discussion, they agree on a solution that meets both of their needs: The credit manager will approve the sale, but the clothing store's owner will provide a bank guarantee that will ensure payment if the bill isn't paid within 60 days. This sales-credit negotiation is an example of **integrative bargaining**. In contrast to distributive bargaining, integrative bargaining operates under the assumption that one or more settlements can create a win–win solution.

In terms of intraorganizational behavior, all things being equal, integrative bargaining is preferable to distributive bargaining because the former builds long-term

EXHIBIT 13-4   Staking Out the Bargaining Zone

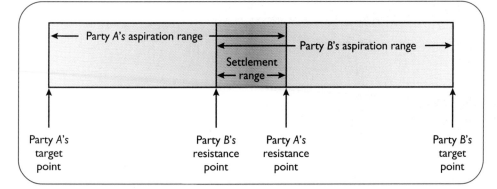

relationships and bonds negotiators, allowing them to leave the bargaining table feeling that they have achieved a victory. Distributive bargaining, however, leaves one party a loser. It tends to build animosities and deepen divisions when people have to work together on an ongoing basis.

Why, then, don't we see more integrative bargaining in organizations? The answer lies in the conditions necessary for this type of negotiation to succeed. To bargain integratively, you need to disclose your true interests to the other party, and this requires a certain amount of trust. Also, you often need to inquire about the other party's interests and to be sensitive to their needs. Because these conditions often don't exist in organizations, it isn't surprising that negotiations often take on a win-at-any-cost dynamic.

The Negotiation Process

Exhibit 13-5 provides a simplified model of the negotiation process. It views negotiation as made up of five steps:

1. Preparation and planning
2. Definition of ground rules
3. Clarification and justification
4. Bargaining and problem solving
5. Closure and implementation[17]

Preparation and Planning   Before you start negotiating, you need to do your homework. What's the nature of the conflict? What's the history leading up to this negotiation? Who's involved, and what are their perceptions of the conflict?

EXHIBIT 13-5   The Negotiation Process

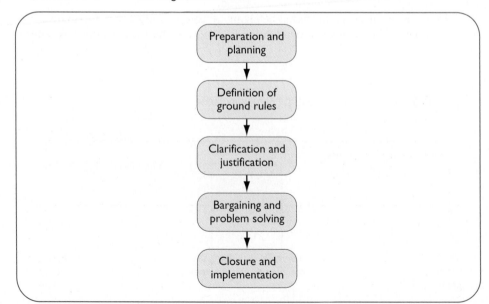

What do you want from the negotiation? What are *your* goals? If you're a supply manager at Dell Computer, for instance, and your goal is to get a significant cost reduction from your supplier of keyboards, make sure that this goal stays paramount in your discussions and doesn't get overshadowed by other issues. It often helps to put your goals in writing and develop a range of outcomes—from "most hopeful" to "minimally acceptable"—to keep your attention focused.

You also want to prepare an assessment of what you think the other party's goals are. What are they likely to request? How entrenched are they likely to be in their position? What intangible or hidden interests may be important to them? What might they be willing to settle on? When you can anticipate your opponent's position, you are better equipped to counter arguments with the facts and figures that support your position.

The importance of sizing up the other party is illustrated by the experience of Keith Rosenbaum, a partner in a major Los Angeles law firm. "Once when we were negotiating to buy a business, we found that the owner was going through a nasty divorce. We were on good terms with the wife's attorney and we learned the seller's net worth. California is a community-property-law state, so we knew he had to pay her half of everything. We knew his time frame. We knew what he was willing to part with and what he was not. We knew a lot more about him than he would have wanted us to know. We were able to twist him a little bit, and get a better price."[18]

Once you've gathered your information, use it to develop a strategy. For example, expert chess players have a strategy. They know ahead of time how they will respond to any given situation. As part of your strategy, you should determine yours and the other side's *B*est *A*lternative *T*o a *N*egotiated *A*greement (**BATNA**). Your BATNA determines the lowest value acceptable to you for a negotiated agreement. For example, an airline may find that at a certain level of settlement, the cost of hiring replacement workers is the same. Thus, in negotiating, hiring replacement workers would be its BATNA. Any offer you receive that is higher than your BATNA is better than an impasse. Conversely, you shouldn't expect success in your negotiation effort unless you're able to make the other side an offer it finds more attractive than its BATNA. If you go into your negotiation having a good idea of what the other party's BATNA is, even if you're not able to meet it, you might be able to get it changed.

Definition of Ground Rules   Once you've done your planning and developed a strategy, you're ready to begin defining the ground rules and procedures with the other party for the negotiation itself. Who will do the negotiating? Where will it take place? What time constraints, if any, will apply? To what issues will negotiation be limited? Will there be a specific procedure to follow if an impasse is reached? During this phase, the parties will also exchange their initial proposals or demands.

Clarification and Justification   When initial positions have been exchanged, both you and the other party will explain, amplify, clarify, bolster, and justify your original demands. This needn't be confrontational. Rather, it's an opportunity for educating and informing each other on the issues, why they are important, and how each of you arrived at their initial demands. This is the point at which you might want to provide the other party with any documentation that helps support your position.

Bargaining and Problem Solving   The essence of the negotiation process is the actual give-and-take involved in hashing out an agreement. It is here where concessions will undoubtedly need to be made by both parties.

Closure and Implementation   The final step in the negotiation process is formalizing the agreement that has been negotiated and developing any procedures that are necessary for implementation and monitoring. Major negotiations—labor–management negotiations, bargaining over lease terms, buying a piece of real estate, negotiating a job offer for a senior management position—will require hammering out the specifics in a formal contract. For most cases, however, closure of the negotiation process is nothing more formal than a handshake.

Individual Differences in Negotiation

We conclude our discussion of negotiation by reviewing whether some individuals are better negotiators than others. We focus on three characteristics: *personality*, *gender*, and *cultural differences*.

Personality   Can you predict an opponent's negotiating tactics if you know something about his or her personality? It's tempting to answer "Yes" to this question. You might assume that high-risk takers would be more aggressive bargainers who make fewer concessions. Surprisingly, the evidence hasn't always supported this intuition.

Assessments of the personality–negotiation relationship have held that personality traits have no significant direct effect on either the bargaining process or the negotiation outcomes. However, recent research has started to question this conclusion. In fact, it appears that several of the Big Five traits are related to negotiation outcomes. For example, negotiators who are agreeable or extraverted are not very successful when it comes to distributive bargaining. This is so because extraverts are outgoing and friendly, so they tend to share more information than they should. And, agreeable people are more interested in finding ways to cooperate rather than butt heads. These traits, while slightly helpful in integrative negotiations, are liabilities when interests are opposed.[19] So, the best distributive bargainer appears to be a disagreeable introvert—that is, someone who is interested in his own outcomes rather than pleasing the other party and having a pleasant social exchange.

A big ego can also affect negotiations. For example, Samantha is an executive with a major clothing manufacturer. She is convinced that everything she touches turns to gold, and she cannot stand to look bad. An important contract with one of her company's suppliers just came up for negotiation. Excited, Samantha thinks she will take the reins during the negotiation process, but her boss tells her she is off the negotiating team. Is her boss smart to keep such a hardliner off the case? Absolutely. A study found that individuals who are concerned with appearing competent and successful in negotiations (that is, saving face)—can have a negative effect on the outcome of the negotiation process. Such individuals were less likely to reach agreements than those who were less concerned with coming out on top. This is because those who are overly competitive in negotiating negotiate to look good personally rather than to attain the best agreement for all concerned.[20] So those who are able to check their egos at the door are able to negotiate better agreements—for themselves and for others, whether the bargaining situation is distributive or integrative.

Gender   Do men and women negotiate differently? And does gender affect negotiation outcomes? The answer to the first question appears to be "No."[21] The answer to the second is a qualified "Yes."[22]

A popular stereotype held by many is that women are more cooperative and pleasant in negotiations than are men. The evidence doesn't support this belief. However, men have been found to negotiate better outcomes than women, although the difference is relatively small. Researchers have postulated that this difference might be due to men and women placing divergent values on outcomes. "It is possible that a few hundred dollars more in salary or the corner office is less important to women than forming and maintaining an interpersonal relationship."[23]

The belief that women are "nicer" than men in negotiations is probably due to confusing gender and the lower power traditionally held by women in most large organizations. The research indicates that low-power managers, regardless of gender, attempt to placate their opponents and use softly persuasive tactics rather than direct confrontation and threats. In situations in which women and men have similar power bases, there shouldn't be any significant differences in their negotiation styles. It's interesting to note that when typical stereotypes are activated—that is, women are "nicer" and men are "tougher"—it becomes a self-fulfilling prophecy, reinforcing the stereotypical gender differences between male and female negotiators.[24] For example, Maria may set lower aspirations and give in more readily when negotiating because she thinks, even subconsciously, that's how women are expected to bargain. Similarly, Sunil may think he has to bargain aggressively because he believes that's how men are expected to negotiate.

The evidence suggests that women's attitudes toward negotiation and toward themselves as negotiators appear to be quite different from men's. Managerial women demonstrate less confidence in anticipation of negotiating and are less satisfied with their performance after the process is complete, even when their performance and the outcomes they achieve are similar to those for men.[25] This latter conclusion suggests that women may penalize themselves unduly by failing to engage in negotiations when such action would be in their best interests.

Cultural Differences   Negotiating styles clearly vary across national cultures.[26] The French like conflict. They frequently gain recognition and develop their reputations by thinking and acting against others. As a result, the French tend to take a long time in negotiating agreements and they aren't overly concerned about whether their opponents like or dislike them.[27] The Chinese also draw out negotiations, but that's because they believe negotiations never end. Just when you think you've pinned down every detail and reached a final solution with a Chinese executive, that executive might smile and start the process all over again. The Chinese—and the Japanese, too—negotiate to develop a relationship and a commitment to work together rather than to tie up every loose end.[28] Compared to American negotiators, the Japanese communicate indirectly and adapt their behaviors to the situation.[29] Americans are known around the world for their impatience and their desire to be liked.[30] Astute negotiators from other countries often turn these characteristics to their advantage by dragging out negotiations and making friendship conditional on the final settlement.

—Negotiating styles clearly vary across national cultures.

The cultural context of the negotiation significantly influences the following:

- The amount and type of preparation for bargaining
- The relative emphasis on task versus interpersonal relationships

- The tactics used
- Where the negotiation should be conducted

To further illustrate some of these differences, let's look at two studies that compare the influence of culture on business negotiations.

The first study compared North Americans, Arabs, and Russians.[31] Among the factors researchers examined were the negotiating style, how negotiators responded to an opponent's arguments, their approach to making concessions, and how they handled negotiating deadlines. North Americans tried to persuade by relying on facts and appealing to logic. They countered opponents' arguments with objective facts. They made small concessions early in the negotiation to establish a relationship and usually reciprocated their opponents' concessions. North Americans treated deadlines as very important. The Arabs tried to persuade by appealing to emotion. They countered opponent's arguments with subjective feelings. They made concessions throughout the bargaining process and almost always reciprocated their opponents' concessions. Arabs approached deadlines very casually. The Russians based their arguments on asserted ideals. They made few, if any, concessions. Any concession offered by an opponent was viewed as a weakness and almost never reciprocated. Finally, the Russians tended to ignore deadlines.

The second study looked at verbal and nonverbal negotiation tactics exhibited by North Americans, Japanese, and Brazilians during half-hour bargaining sessions.[32] Some of the differences were particularly interesting. For instance, the Brazilians on average said "No" 83 times, compared to 5 times for the Japanese and 9 times for the North Americans. The Japanese displayed more than 5 periods of silence lasting longer than 10 seconds during the 30-minute sessions. North Americans averaged 3.5 such periods; the Brazilians had none. The Japanese and North Americans interrupted their opponents about the same number of times, but the Brazilians interrupted 2.5 to 3 times more often than the North Americans and the Japanese. And, the Japanese and the North Americans had no physical contact with their opponents during negotiations except for handshaking, but the Brazilians touched each other almost 5 times every half hour.

IMPLICATIONS FOR MANAGERS

Managing Conflict

Many people assume that conflict is related to lower group and organizational performance. This chapter has demonstrated that this assumption is often false. Conflict can be either constructive or destructive to the functioning of a group or unit. When it's too high or too low, conflict hinders performance. At an optimal level, there is enough conflict to prevent stagnation, stimulate creativity, allow tensions to be released, and initiate the seeds for change, yet not so much as to be disruptive.

What advice can we give to managers faced with excessive conflict and the need to reduce it? Don't assume that one conflict-handling approach will always be best! Select the resolution technique appropriate for each situation. Here are some guidelines:[33]

- Use *competition* when quick, decisive action is vital (in emergencies); on important issues, for which unpopular actions need implementing (in cost cutting, enforcing unpopular rules, discipline); on issues vital to the organization's welfare when you know you're right; and against people who take advantage of noncompetitive behavior.

- Use *collaboration* to find an integrative solution when both sets of concerns are too important to be compromised; when your objective is to learn; to merge insights from people with different perspectives; to gain commitment by incorporating concerns into a consensus; and to work through feelings that have interfered with a relationship.

- Use *avoidance* when an issue is trivial or when more important issues are pressing; when you perceive no chance of satisfying your concerns; when potential disruption outweighs the benefits of resolution; to let people cool down and regain perspective; when gathering information supersedes an immediate decision; when others can resolve the conflict more effectively; and when issues seem tangential or symptomatic of other issues.

- Use *accommodation* when you find you are wrong and to allow a better position to be heard, to learn, and to show your reasonableness; when issues are more important to others than to yourself and to satisfy others and maintain cooperation; to build social credits for later issues; to minimize loss when you are outmatched and losing; when harmony and stability are especially important; and to allow subordinates to develop by learning from mistakes.

- Use *compromise* when goals are important but not worth the effort of potential disruption of more assertive approaches; when opponents with equal power are committed to mutually exclusive goals; to achieve temporary settlements of complex issues; to arrive at expedient solutions under time pressure; and as a backup when collaboration or competition is unsuccessful.

Improving Negotiation Skills

The following recommendations should help improve your effectiveness at negotiating:[34]

- *Set ambitious goals.* Research shows that the best agreements are negotiated by people who set goals and make aggressive initial offers. So, set ambitious goals and take the lead by making an aggressive first offer.

- *Pay little attention to initial offers.* Because initial offers often "anchor" negotiations, resist being anchored by the other party's offer. Particularly in distributive negotiations, stick to your goals.

- *Research your opponent.* Acquire as much information as you can about your opponent's interests and goals. What constituencies must he or she appease? What is his or her strategy? This knowledge will help you to better understand your opponent's behavior, predict responses to your offers, and help you to frame solutions in terms of his or her interests.

- *Address the problem, not personalities.* Concentrate on the negotiation issues, not on the personal characteristics of your opponent. When negotiations get tough, avoid the tendency to attack your opponent. It's your opponent's ideas or position that you disagree with, not him or her personally. Separate the people from the problem, and don't personalize differences.

■ *Be creative and emphasize win–win solutions.* If conditions are supportive, look for an integrative solution. Frame options in terms of your opponent's interests, and look for solutions that can allow both you and your opponent to declare a victory. Try to create options that may make both parties happy. Remember, no danger lies in putting forward possible solutions as long as all of them are intended to meet your goals.

CHAPTER 14

Foundations of Organization Structure

After studying this chapter, you should be able to:

1. Identify the six key elements that define an organization's structure.
2. Explain the characteristics of a bureaucracy.
3. Describe a matrix organization.
4. Explain the characteristics of a virtual organization.
5. Summarize why managers want to create boundaryless organizations.
6. Contrast mechanistic and organic structural models.
7. List the factors that favor different organizational structures.
8. Explain the behavioral implications of different organizational designs.

The theme of this chapter is that organizations have different structures and that these structures have a bearing on employee attitudes and behavior. More specifically, in the following pages, we'll define the key components that make up an organization's structure, present half a dozen or so structural design options, identify the contingency factors that make certain structural designs preferable in different situations, and conclude by considering the different effects that various organization structures have on employee behavior.

WHAT IS ORGANIZATIONAL STRUCTURE?

An **organizational structure** defines how job tasks are formally divided, grouped, and coordinated. Managers need to address six key elements when they design an organization's structure: *work specialization, departmentalization, chain of command, span of control, centralization and decentralization*, and *formalization*.[1] Exhibit 14-1 presents each of these elements as answers to an important structural question.

Work Specialization

Early in the twentieth century, Henry Ford became rich and famous by building automobiles on an assembly line. Every Ford worker was assigned a specific, repetitive task. One person would put on the right-front wheel and someone else would install the right-front door. By breaking up jobs into small standardized tasks, which could be performed over and over again, Ford was able to produce cars at the rate of one every 10 seconds, while using employees who had relatively limited skills.

Ford demonstrated that work can be performed more efficiently if employees are allowed to specialize. Today we use the term **work specialization**, or *division of labor*, to describe the degree to which activities in the organization are subdivided into separate jobs. The essence of work specialization is that an entire job is divided into a number of steps, with each step being completed by a separate individual—rather than one individual completing the entire job.

By the late 1940s, most manufacturing jobs in industrialized countries were being done with high work specialization. Management saw this as a means to make the most efficient use of its employees' skills. In most organizations, some tasks require highly developed skills and others can be performed by untrained workers. If all workers were engaged in each step of, say, an organization's manufacturing process, all would have to have the skills necessary to perform both the most demanding and the least demanding jobs. The result would be that, except when performing the most skilled or highly complex tasks, employees would be working below their skill levels. And, because skilled workers are paid more than unskilled workers and their wages tend to reflect their highest level of skill, it represents an inefficient use of organizational resources to pay highly skilled workers to do easy tasks.

EXHIBIT 14-1   Key Design Questions and Answers for Designing the Proper Organizational Structure

The Key Question	The Answer Is Provided By
1. To what degree are activities subdivided into separate jobs?	Work specialization
2. On what basis will jobs be grouped together?	Departmentalization
3. To whom do individuals and groups report?	Chain of command
4. How many individuals can a manager efficiently and effectively direct?	Span of control
5. Where does decision-making authority lie?	Centralization and decentralization
6. To what degree will rules and regulations be used to direct employees and managers?	Formalization

Managers also saw other efficiencies that could be achieved through work specialization. Employee skills at performing a task successfully increase through repetition. Less time is spent in changing tasks, in putting away one's tools and equipment from a prior step in the work process, and in getting ready for another. Equally important, training for specialization is more efficient from the organization's perspective. It's easier and less costly to find and train workers to do specific and repetitive tasks. This is especially true of highly sophisticated and complex operations. For example, how many Citation jets could Cessna produce a year if one person had to build each entire plane alone? Not many! Finally, work specialization increases efficiency and productivity by encouraging the creation of special inventions and machinery.

For much of the first half of the twentieth century, managers viewed work specialization as an unending source of increased productivity. And they were probably right. Because specialization was not widely practiced, its introduction almost always generated higher productivity. But by the 1960s, increasing evidence demonstrated that a good thing can be carried too far. The point had been reached in some jobs at which the human costs from specialization—which surfaced as boredom, fatigue, stress, low productivity, poor quality, increased absenteeism, and high turnover—more than offset the economic advantages (see Exhibit 14-2). In such cases, productivity could be increased by enlarging, rather than narrowing, the scope of job activities. In addition, a number of companies found that by giving employees a variety of activities to do, allowing them to do a whole and complete job, and putting them into teams with interchangeable skills, they often achieved significantly higher output, with increased employee satisfaction.

Today, most managers see work specialization as neither obsolete nor an unending source of increased productivity. Rather, managers recognize the economies it provides in certain types of jobs and the problems it creates when it's carried too far. You'll find, for example, high work specialization being used by McDonald's to

EXHIBIT 14-2   Economies and Diseconomies of Work Specialization

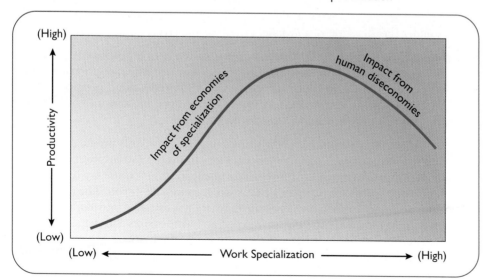

efficiently make and sell hamburgers and fries. You'll also find it being used by medical specialists in most health maintenance organizations. On the other hand, some companies, such as Saturn Corporation, have achieved success by broadening the scope of jobs and reducing specialization.

Departmentalization

Once you've divided up jobs through work specialization, you need to group these jobs together so that common tasks can be coordinated. The basis by which jobs are grouped together is called **departmentalization**.

Functional   One of the most popular ways to group activities is by *functions* performed. A manufacturing manager might organize a plant by separating engineering, accounting, manufacturing, personnel, and supply specialists into common departments. Of course, departmentalization by function can be used in all types of organizations. Only the functions change to reflect the organization's objectives and activities. A hospital might have departments devoted to research, patient care, accounting, and so forth. A professional football franchise might have departments entitled Player Personnel, Ticket Sales, and Travel and Accommodations. The major advantage to this type of grouping is obtaining efficiencies from putting like specialists together. Functional departmentalization seeks to achieve economies of scale by placing people with common skills and orientations into common units.

Product   Jobs can also be departmentalized by the type of *product* the organization produces. Procter & Gamble, for instance, is organized along these lines. Each major product—such as Tide, Pampers, Charmin, and Pringles—is placed under the authority of an executive who has complete global responsibility for that product. This type of grouping provides the major advantage of increased accountability for product performance, since all activities related to a specific product are under the direction of a single manager. If an organization's activities are service related rather than product related, each service would be autonomously grouped. For instance, Automatic Data Processing has departments for each of its employer-provided services—payroll, retirement, expense management, taxes, and the like. Each offers a common array of services under the direction of a product or service manager.

Geography   Another way to departmentalize is on the basis of *geography* or territory. The sales function may have western, southern, midwestern, and eastern regions. Each of these regions is, in effect, a department organized around geography. If an organization's customers are scattered over a large geographic area and have similar needs, this form of departmentalization can be valuable.

Process   At an Alcoa aluminum tubing plant in upstate New York, production is organized into five departments: casting; press; tubing; finishing; and inspecting, packing, and shipping. This is an example of *process* departmentalization because each department specializes in one specific phase in the production of aluminum tubing. The metal is cast in huge furnaces; sent to the press department, where it is extruded into aluminum pipe; transferred to the tube mill, where it is stretched into various sizes and shapes of tubing; moved to finishing, where it is cut and cleaned; and finally it arrives in the inspecting, packing, and shipping department. Since each process requires different skills, this method offers a basis for the homogeneous categorizing of activities.

Process departmentalization can be used for processing customers as well as products. If you've ever been to a state motor vehicle office to get a driver's license, you probably went through several departments before receiving your license. In one state, applicants must go through three steps, each handled by a separate department: (1) validation by motor vehicle division, (2) processing by the licensing department, and (3) payment collection by the treasury department.

Customer   Microsoft is organized around four customer markets: consumers, large corporations, software developers, and small businesses. This an example of departmentalization according to the type of *customer* the organization seeks to reach. The assumption underlying customer departmentalization is that customers have common sets of problems and needs and can best be served by departments specializing in those problems.

Large organizations may use all the forms of departmentalization we've described. A major Japanese electronics firm organizes each of its divisions along functional lines and its manufacturing units around processes; it departmentalizes sales around seven geographic regions and divides each sales region into four customer groupings. Also, across organizations of all sizes, one strong trend has emerged over the past decade: Rigid, functional departmentalization is being increasingly complemented by teams that cross over traditional departmental lines. As tasks have become more complex and more diverse skills have been needed to accomplish those tasks, management has turned to cross-functional teams, which we described in Chapter 9.

—As tasks have become more complex and more diverse skills have been needed to accomplish those tasks, management has turned to cross-functional teams.

Chain of Command

Thirty-five years ago, the *chain-of-command* concept was a basic cornerstone in the design of organizations. As you'll see, it has far less importance today, but contemporary managers should still consider its implications when they decide how best to structure their organizations. The **chain of command** is an unbroken line of authority that extends from the top of the organization to its lowest echelon and clarifies who reports to whom. It answers questions for employees such as "To whom do I go if I have a problem?" and "To whom am I responsible?"

You can't discuss the chain of command without discussing two complementary concepts: *authority* and *unity of command*. **Authority** refers to the rights inherent in a managerial position to give orders and expect the orders to be obeyed. To facilitate coordination, each managerial position is given a place in the chain of command, and each manager is given a degree of authority with which to meet his or her responsibilities. The **unity-of-command** principle helps preserve the concept of an unbroken line of authority. It states that a person should have one and only one superior to whom that person is directly responsible. If the unity of command is broken, an employee might have to cope with conflicting demands or priorities from several superiors.

Times change and so do the basic tenets of organizational design. The concepts of chain of command, authority, and unity of command have substantially less relevance today because of advancements in information technology and the trend toward empowering employees. Today, a low-level employee can access information in seconds that 35 years ago was available only to top managers. Similarly, networked computers increasingly allow employees anywhere in an organization to communicate with anyone else without going through formal channels. Moreover, the concepts of authority and maintaining the chain of command are increasingly less relevant as operating employees are being empowered to make decisions that previously were reserved for management. Add to this the popularity of self-managed and cross-functional teams and the creation of new structural designs that include multiple bosses, and the unity-of-command concept is less relevant. Of course, many organizations still find that they can be most productive by enforcing the chain of command—it just seems fewer of them are around nowadays.

Span of Control

How many employees can a manager efficiently and effectively direct? This question of **span of control** is important because, to a large degree, it determines the number of levels and managers an organization has. All things being equal, the wider or larger the span, the more efficient the organization. For instance, assume that we have two organizations, both of which have approximately 4,100 operative-level employees. As Exhibit 14-3 illustrates, if one has a uniform span of four and the other a span of eight, the wider span would have two fewer levels and approximately 800 fewer managers. If the average manager made $50,000 a year, the wider span would save $40 million a year in management salaries! Obviously, wider spans are more efficient in terms of cost. However, at some point wider spans reduce effectiveness. When the span becomes too large, employee performance suffers because supervisors no longer have the time to provide the necessary leadership and support.

Narrow or small spans have their advocates. By keeping the span of control to five or six employees, a manager can maintain close control. But narrow spans have

EXHIBIT 14-3   Contrasting Spans of Control

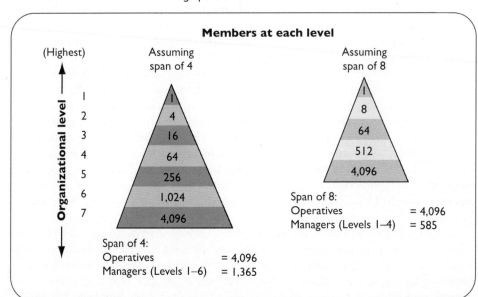

three major drawbacks. First, as already described, they're expensive because they add levels of management. Second, they make vertical communication in the organization more complex. The added levels of hierarchy slow down decision making and tend to isolate upper management. Third, narrow spans of control encourage overly tight supervision and discourage employee autonomy.

The trend in recent years has been toward wider spans of control. They're consistent with recent efforts by companies to reduce costs, cut overhead, speed up decision making, increase flexibility, get closer to customers, and empower employees. However, to ensure that performance doesn't suffer because of these wider spans, organizations have been investing heavily in employee training. Managers recognize that they can handle a wider span when employees know their jobs inside and out or can turn to their coworkers when they have questions.

Centralization and Decentralization

In highly centralized organizations, top managers make all the decisions. Lower-level managers merely carry out top management's directives. At the other extreme are decentralized organizations in which decision making is pushed down to the managers who are closest to the action.

The term **centralization** refers to the degree to which decision making is concentrated at a single point in the organization. The concept includes only formal authority: the rights inherent in one's position. Typically, if top management makes the organization's key decisions with little or no input from lower-level personnel, the organization is centralized. In contrast, the more that lower-level personnel provide input or are actually given the discretion to make decisions, the more decentralization there is. An organization characterized by centralization is an inherently different structural animal from one that is decentralized. In a decentralized organization, action can be taken more quickly to solve problems, more people provide input into decisions, and employees are less likely to feel alienated from those who make the decisions that affect their work lives.

The marked trend toward decentralizing decision making that has been observed is consistent with recent management efforts to make organizations more flexible and responsive. In large companies, lower-level managers are closer to actual operations and typically have more detailed knowledge about problems than do top managers. Big retailers, such as Kohl's and JCPenney, have given their store managers considerably more discretion in choosing what merchandise to stock.

Formalization

Formalization refers to the degree to which jobs within the organization are standardized. If a job is highly formalized, the job incumbent has a minimum amount of discretion over what is to be done, when it is to be done, and how it is to be done. Employees can be expected always to handle the same input in exactly the same way, resulting in a consistent and uniform output. Explicit job descriptions, lots of organizational rules, and clearly defined procedures characterize work processes in organizations in which there is high formalization. Where formalization is low, job behaviors are relatively nonprogrammed and employees have a great deal of freedom to exercise discretion in their work. The greater the standardization, the less input the employee has into how the work is to be done, because an individual's discretion on the job is inversely related to the degree of formalization. Standardization not only eliminates the possibility of employees engaging in alternative behaviors, but it also removes the need for employees to consider alternatives.

The degree of formalization can vary widely between organizations and within organizations. Certain jobs are well-known to have little formalization. College book travelers—the representatives of publishers who call on professors to inform them of their companies' new publications—have a great deal of freedom in their jobs. They have no standard sales spiel, and the extent of rules and procedures governing their behavior may be little more than the requirement that they submit a weekly sales report and some suggestions on what to emphasize for the various new titles. At the other extreme, some clerical and editorial positions in the same publishing houses require employees to be at their desks by 8:00 A.M. or be docked a half hour's pay and, once at that desk, to follow a set of precise procedures dictated by management.

COMMON ORGANIZATIONAL DESIGNS

Now that we've covered some fundamental aspects of organizational structure, let's examine three of the more common organizational designs found in use: the *simple structure*, the *bureaucracy*, and the *matrix structure*.

The Simple Structure

What do a small retail store, an electronics firm run by a hard-driving entrepreneur, and an airline in the midst of a company-wide pilot's strike have in common? They probably all use the simple structure.

The simple structure is said to be characterized most by what it is not rather than by what it is. The **simple structure** has a low degree of departmentalization, wide spans of control, authority centralized in a single person, and little formalization. The simple structure is a "flat" organization; it usually has only two or three vertical levels, a loose body of employees, and one individual in whom the decision-making authority is centralized. It's most widely practiced in small businesses in which the manager and the owner are one and the same. But it is also the preferred structure in a time of temporary crisis because it centralizes control.

—The simple structure has a low degree of departmentalization, wide spans of control, authority centralized in a single person, and little formalization.

The strength of the simple structure lies in its simplicity. It's fast, flexible, and inexpensive to maintain, and accountability is clear. One major weakness is that it's difficult to maintain in anything other than small organizations. It becomes increasingly inadequate as an organization grows because its low formalization and high centralization tend to create information overload at the top. As size increases, decision making typically becomes slower and can eventually come to a standstill as the single executive tries to continue making all the decisions. This often proves to be the undoing of many small businesses. When an organization begins to employ 50 or 100 people, it's very difficult for the owner-manager to make all the choices. If the structure isn't changed and made more elaborate, the firm often loses momentum and can eventually fail. The simple structure's other weakness is that it's risky: Everything depends on one person. One heart attack can literally destroy the organization's information and decision-making center.

The Bureaucracy

Standardization! That's the key concept that underlies all bureaucracies. Take a look at the bank where you keep your checking account, the department store where you buy your clothes, or the government offices that collect your taxes, enforce health regulations, or provide local fire protection. They all rely on standardized work processes for coordination and control.

The **bureaucracy** is characterized by highly routine operating tasks achieved through specialization, very formalized rules and regulations, tasks that are grouped into functional departments, centralized authority, narrow spans of control, and decision making that follows the chain of command.

The primary strength of the bureaucracy lies in its ability to perform standardized activities in a highly efficient manner. Putting like specialties together in functional departments results in economies of scale, minimum duplication of personnel and equipment, and employees who have the opportunity to speak in a common language among their peers. Furthermore, bureaucracies can get by nicely with less talented—and, hence, less costly—middle- and lower-level managers. The pervasiveness of rules and regulations substitutes for managerial discretion. Standardized operations, coupled with high formalization, allow decision making to be centralized. There is little need, therefore, for innovative and experienced decision makers below the level of senior executives.

One of the major weaknesses of bureaucracy is that specialization creates subunit conflicts. Functional unit goals can override the overall goals of the organization. The other major weakness of bureaucracy is something we've all experienced at one time or another when having to deal with people who work in these organizations: obsessive concern with following the rules. When cases arise that don't precisely fit the rules, modification is impossible. The bureaucracy is efficient only as long as employees confront problems that they have previously encountered and for which programmed decision rules have already been established.

The peak of bureaucracy's popularity was probably in the 1950s and 1960s. At that time, just about every major corporation in the world—including IBM, General Electric, Volkswagen, Matsushita, and Royal Dutch Shell—was organized as a bureaucracy. Although the bureaucracy is out of fashion today—largely because it has difficulty responding rapidly to change—the majority of large organizations still take on basic bureaucratic characteristics, particularly specialization and high formalization. However, spans of control have generally been widened, authority has become more decentralized, and functional departments have been supplemented with an increased use of teams.

The Matrix Structure

The matrix structure is another popular organizational design option. You'll find it being used in advertising agencies, aerospace firms, research and development laboratories, construction companies, hospitals, government agencies, universities, management consulting firms, and entertainment companies. Essentially, the **matrix structure** combines two forms of departmentalization: functional and product.

The strength of functional departmentalization lies in putting like specialists together, which minimizes the number necessary while allowing the pooling and sharing of specialized resources across products. Its major disadvantage is the difficulty of coordinating the tasks of diverse functional specialists so that their activities are completed on time and within budget. Product departmentalization, on the other hand, has exactly the opposite benefits and disadvantages. It facilitates coordination among specialties to achieve on-time completion and to meet budget targets. Furthermore, it provides clear responsibility for all activities related to a product, but with duplication of activities and costs. The matrix attempts to gain the strengths of each, while avoiding their weaknesses.

The most obvious structural characteristic of the matrix is that it breaks the unity-of-command concept. Employees in the matrix have two bosses—their functional department managers and their product managers. Therefore, the matrix has a dual chain of command.

Exhibit 14-4 shows the matrix form as used in a college of business administration. The academic departments of accounting, decision and information systems, marketing, and so forth are functional units. In addition, specific programs (that is, products) are overlaid on the functions. In this way, members in a matrix structure have a dual assignment—to their functional department and to their product groups. For instance, a professor of accounting who is teaching an undergraduate course may report to the director of undergraduate programs as well as to the chairperson of the accounting department.

The strength of the matrix lies in its ability to facilitate coordination when the organization has a multiplicity of complex and interdependent activities. As an organization gets larger, its information-processing capacity can become overloaded. In a bureaucracy, complexity results in increased formalization. The direct and frequent contact between different specialties in the matrix can make for better communication and more flexibility. Information permeates the organization and more quickly

EXHIBIT 14-4   Matrix Structure for a College of Business Administration

Programs / Academic departments	Undergraduate	Master's	Ph.D.	Research	Executive development	Community service
Accounting						
Finance						
Decision and information systems						
Management						
Marketing						

reaches the people who need to take account of it. Furthermore, the matrix reduces *bureaupathologies* because the dual lines of authority reduce the tendencies of departmental members to become so busy protecting their little worlds that the organization's overall goals become secondary.

The matrix has another advantage. It facilitates the efficient allocation of specialists. When individuals with highly specialized skills are lodged in one functional department or product group, their talents are monopolized and underused. The matrix achieves the advantages of economies of scale by providing the organization with both the best resources and an effective way of ensuring their efficient deployment.

The major disadvantages of the matrix lie in the confusion it creates, its propensity to foster power struggles, and the stress it places on individuals.[2] When you dispense with the unity-of-command concept, ambiguity is significantly increased, and ambiguity often leads to conflict. For example, it's frequently unclear who reports to whom, and it is not unusual for product managers to fight over getting the best specialists assigned to their products. Confusion and ambiguity also create the seeds of power struggles. Bureaucracy reduces the potential for power grabs by defining the rules of the game. When those rules are available for anyone to define, power struggles between functional and product managers result. For individuals who desire security and absence from ambiguity, this work climate can produce stress. Reporting to more than one boss introduces role conflict, and unclear expectations introduce role ambiguity. The comfort of bureaucracy's predictability is absent in the matrix structure, replaced by insecurity and stress.

NEW STRUCTURAL OPTIONS

In recent years, senior managers in a number of organizations have been working to develop new structural options that can better help their firms to compete effectively. In this section, we describe three such structural designs: the *team structure*, the *virtual organization*, and the *boundaryless organization*.

The Team Structure

As described in Chapter 9, teams have become an extremely popular structure for organizing work activities. The primary characteristics of the team structure are that it breaks down departmental barriers and decentralizes decision making to the level of the work team.

In smaller companies, the team structure can define the entire organization. Radius, an upscale restaurant in Boston that employs 30 people, is organized completely around teams. Teams staff every station in the kitchen—meat, fish, pastry— and each has full responsibility for its part of the meal. Even a few large companies, such as Gore-Tex maker W.L. Gore & Associates, are using teams throughout. Although W.L. Gore employs 6,200 people, the company's plants are kept to 200 employees or fewer, and everyone is part of a self-managed team.

More often, particularly among larger organizations, the team structure complements what is typically a bureaucracy. The organization is thus able to achieve the efficiency of bureaucracy's standardization while gaining the flexibility that teams provide.

The Virtual Organization

Why own when you can rent? That question captures the essence of the **virtual organization** (also sometimes called the *network* or *modular organization*), typically a small, core organization that outsources major business functions.[3] In structural terms, the virtual organization is highly centralized, with little or no departmentalization.

The prototype of the virtual structure is today's movie-making organization. In Hollywood's golden era, movies were made by huge, vertically integrated corporations. Studios such as MGM, Warner Brothers, and 20th Century Fox owned large movie lots and employed thousands of full-time specialists: set designers, camera people, film editors, directors, and even actors. Today, most movies are made by a collection of individuals and small companies who come together and make films project by project.[4] This structural form allows each project to be staffed with the talent most suited to its demands, rather than having to choose just from the people employed by the studio. It minimizes bureaucratic overhead because no lasting organization has to be maintained. And it lessens long-term risks and their costs because there is no long term—a team is assembled for a finite period and then disbanded.

Ancle Hsu and David Ji run a virtual organization. Their firm, California-based Apex Digital, is one of the world's largest producers of DVD players, yet the company neither owns a factory nor employs an engineer. They contract everything out to firms in China. With minimal investment, Apex has grown from nothing to annual sales of over $500 million in just three years. Similarly, Paul Newman's food products company, Newman's Own, sells about $190 million in food every year, yet it employs only 18 people. This is because it outsources almost everything: manufacturing, procurement, shipping, and quality control.

When large organizations use the virtual structure, they frequently use it to outsource manufacturing. Cisco, for instance, is essentially a research and development company that uses outside suppliers and independent manufacturers to assemble the Internet routers that its engineers design. National Steel Corp. contracts out its mailroom operations, and Procter & Gamble outsources its information-technology operation to Hewlett-Packard.

This is all going on in a quest for maximum flexibility. These virtual organizations have created networks of relationships that allow them to contract out manufacturing, distribution, marketing, or any other business function that management feels others can do better or more cheaply. The virtual organization stands in sharp contrast to the typical bureaucracy that has many vertical levels of management and where control is sought through ownership. In such organizations, research and development are done in-house, production occurs in company-owned plants, and sales and marketing are performed by the company's own employees. To support all this, management has to employ extra staff, including accountants, human resource specialists, and lawyers. The virtual organization, however, outsources many of these functions and concentrates on what it does best. For most U.S. firms, that means focusing on design or marketing.

Exhibit 14-5 shows a virtual organization in which management outsources all of the primary functions of the business. The core of the organization is a small group of executives whose job is to oversee directly any activities that are done in-house and to coordinate relationships with the other organizations that manufacture, distribute, and perform other crucial functions for the virtual organization. The dotted lines in

EXHIBIT 14-5   A Virtual Organization

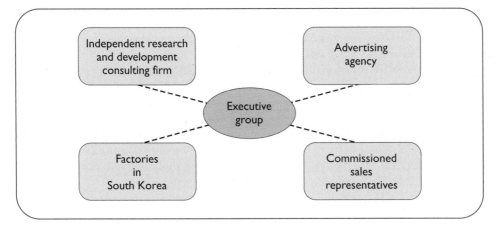

Exhibit 14-5 represent the relationships typically maintained under contracts. In essence, managers in virtual structures spend most of their time coordinating and controlling external relations, typically by way of computer-network links.

The major advantage to the virtual organization is its flexibility. It allows individuals with an innovative idea and little money, such as Ancle Hsu and David Ji, to successfully compete against the likes of Sony, Hitachi, and Sharp Electronics. The primary drawback to this structure is that it reduces management's control over key parts of its business.

The Boundaryless Organization

General Electric's former chairman, Jack Welch, coined the term **boundaryless organization** to describe his idea of what he wanted GE to become. Welch wanted to turn his company into a "family grocery store."[5] That is, in spite of its monstrous size (2005 revenues were in excess of $150 billion, making it, as it long has been, one of the 10 largest U.S. companies), he wanted to eliminate *vertical* and *horizontal* boundaries within GE and break down *external* barriers between the company and its customers and suppliers. The boundaryless organization seeks to eliminate the chain of command, have limitless spans of control, and replace departments with empowered teams. Because it relies so heavily on information technology, some have turned to calling this structure the *T-form* (or technology-based) organization.[6] Although GE has not yet achieved this boundaryless state—and probably never will—it has made significant progress toward that end. So have other companies, such as Hewlett-Packard, AT&T, Motorola, and Oticon A/S. Let's take a look at what a boundaryless organization would look like and what some firms are doing to try to make it a reality.

By removing vertical boundaries, management flattens the hierarchy. Status and rank are minimized. Cross-hierarchical teams (which include top executives, middle managers, supervisors, and operative employees), participative decision-making practices, and the use of 360-degree performance appraisals (in which peers and others above and below the employee evaluate performance) are examples of what GE is doing to break down vertical boundaries. At Oticon A/S, a $160-million-a-year

Danish hearing aid manufacturer, all traces of hierarchy have disappeared. Everyone works at uniform mobile workstations. And project teams, not functions or departments, are used to coordinate work.

Functional departments create horizontal boundaries. And these boundaries stifle interaction among functions, product lines, and units. The way to reduce these barriers is to replace functional departments with cross-functional teams and to organize activities around processes. For instance, Xerox now develops new products through multidisciplinary teams that work in a single process instead of around narrow functional tasks. Similarly, some AT&T units are now doing annual budgets based not on functions or departments but on processes such as the maintenance of a worldwide telecommunications network. Another way management can cut through horizontal barriers is to use lateral transfers, rotating people into and out of different functional areas. This approach turns specialists into generalists.

—Globalization, strategic alliances, customer-organization links, and telecommuting are all examples of practices that reduce external boundaries.

When fully operational, the boundaryless organization also breaks down barriers to external constituencies (suppliers, customers, regulators, and so on) and barriers created by geography. Globalization, strategic alliances, customer–organization links, and telecommuting are all examples of practices that reduce external boundaries. Coca-Cola sees itself as a global corporation, not as a U.S. or Atlanta company. Firms such as NEC Corp., Boeing, and Apple Computer each have strategic alliances or joint partnerships with dozens of companies. These alliances blur the distinction between one organization and another as employees work on joint projects. And some companies are allowing customers to perform functions that previously were done by management. For instance, some AT&T units are receiving bonuses based on customer evaluations of the teams that serve them. In addition, telecommuting is blurring organizational boundaries. The security analyst with Merrill Lynch who does his job from his ranch in Montana or the software designer who works for a San Francisco company but does her job in Boulder, Colorado, are just two examples of the millions of workers who are now doing their jobs outside the physical boundaries of their employers' premises.

Increasingly, boundaryless organizations are using technology to permeate their boundaries. Most large companies have developed private nets or *intranets*. Interorganizational networks now make it possible for Wal-Mart suppliers to monitor inventory levels because their computer systems are networked to Wal-Mart's system. For instance, Procter & Gamble and Levi Strauss are able to monitor inventory levels of their laundry products and their jeans, respectively.

WHY DO STRUCTURES DIFFER?

We've described a variety of organizational designs, ranging from the highly structured and standardized bureaucracy to the loose and amorphous boundaryless organization, as well as designs that tend to exist somewhere between these two extremes. Let's reconceptualize this discussion by considering it in the context of two extreme models of organizational design, as presented in Exhibit 14-6. One extreme we'll call the *mechanistic model*. It's generally synonymous with the bureaucracy in that it has extensive departmentalization, high formalization, a limited information network (mostly downward communication), and little participation by low-level members in decision making. At the other extreme is the *organic model*. This model looks a lot like the boundaryless

EXHIBIT 14-6 Mechanistic Versus Organic Models

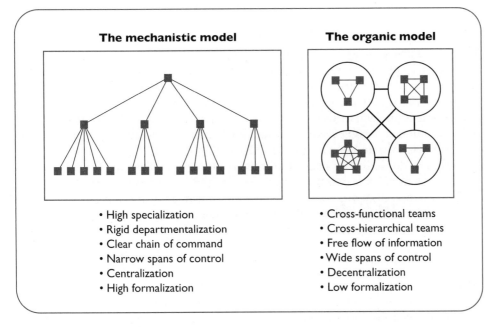

The mechanistic model

• High specialization
• Rigid departmentalization
• Clear chain of command
• Narrow spans of control
• Centralization
• High formalization

The organic model

• Cross-functional teams
• Cross-hierarchical teams
• Free flow of information
• Wide spans of control
• Decentralization
• Low formalization

organization. It's flat, uses cross-hierarchical and cross-functional teams, has low formalization, possesses a comprehensive information network (using lateral and upward communication as well as downward), and involves high participation in decision making.

With these two models in mind, we're now prepared to address these questions: Why are some organizations structured along more mechanistic lines, whereas others follow organic characteristics? What are the forces that influence the design that is chosen? In the following pages, we present the major forces that have been identified as causes or determinants of an organization's structure.[7]

Strategy

An organization's structure is a means to help management achieve its objectives. Because objectives are derived from the organization's overall strategy, it's only logical that strategy and structure should be closely linked. More specifically, structure should follow strategy. If management makes a significant change in its organization's strategy, the structure must be modified to accommodate and support this change. Most current strategy frameworks focus on three strategy dimensions: *innovation, cost minimization*, and *imitation*—and the structural design that works best with each.[8]

To what degree does an organization introduce major new products or services? An **innovation strategy** does not mean a strategy merely for simple or cosmetic changes from previous offerings but rather one for meaningful and unique innovations. Obviously, not all firms pursue innovation. This strategy may appropriately characterize 3M Co. and Apple Computer, but it's not a strategy pursued by conservative retailer Marks & Spencer.

An organization that is pursuing a **cost-minimization strategy** tightly controls costs, refrains from incurring unnecessary innovation or marketing expenses, and cuts prices in selling a basic product. This would describe the strategy pursued by Wal-Mart or the makers of generic grocery products.

Organizations following an **imitation strategy** try to capitalize on the best of both of the previous strategies. They seek to minimize risk and maximize opportunity for profit. Their strategy is to move into new products or new markets only after viability has been proven by innovators. They take the successful ideas of innovators and copy them. Manufacturers of mass-marketed fashion goods that are rip-offs of designer styles follow the imitation strategy. This label probably also characterizes well-known firms such as IBM and Caterpillar. They essentially follow their smaller and more innovative competitors with superior products, but only after their competitors have demonstrated that the market exists.

So how do we link strategy and structure? Innovators need the flexibility of the organic structure, while cost minimizers seek the efficiency and stability of the mechanistic structure. Imitators combine the two structures. They use a mechanistic structure in order to maintain tight controls and low costs in their current activities, while at the same time they create organic subunits in which to pursue new undertakings.

Organization Size

Considerable evidence supports the idea that an organization's size significantly affects its structure.[9] For instance, large organizations—those that typically employ 2,000 or more people—tend to have more specialization, more departmentalization, more vertical levels, and more rules and regulations than do small organizations. However, the relationship isn't linear. Rather, size affects structure at a decreasing rate. The impact of size becomes less important as an organization expands. Essentially, once an organization has around 2,000 employees, it's already fairly mechanistic. An additional 500 employees will not have much impact. On the other hand, adding 500 employees to an organization that has only 300 members is likely to result in a significant shift toward a more mechanistic structure.

Technology

The term **technology** refers to how an organization transfers its inputs into outputs. Every organization has at least one technology for converting financial, human, and physical resources into products or services. The Ford Motor Co., for instance, predominantly uses an assembly-line process to make its products. On the other hand, colleges may use a number of instruction technologies: the ever-popular formal lecture method, the case-analysis method, the experiential exercise method, the programmed learning method, and so forth. In this section we want to show that organizational structures adapt to their technology.

Numerous studies have been carried out on the technology-structure relationship.[10] The details of those studies are quite complex, so we'll go straight to the point and attempt to summarize what we know. The common theme that differentiates technologies is their *degree of routineness*. By this we mean that technologies tend toward either routine or nonroutine activities. The former are characterized by automated and standardized operations. Nonroutine activities are customized, including such varied operations as furniture restoring, custom shoemaking, and genetic research.

Although the relationship between technology and structure is not overwhelmingly strong, we find that routine tasks are associated with taller and more departmentalized structures. The relationship between technology and formalization, however, is stronger. Studies consistently show routineness to be associated with the presence of rule manuals, job descriptions, and other formalized documentation.

Environmental Uncertainty

An organization's environment is composed of the institutions or forces that are outside the organization and potentially affect the organization's performance. The environment has acquired a large following of researchers as a key determinant of structure.

An organization's structure is affected by its environment because of environmental uncertainty. Some organizations face relatively static environments: no new competitors, no new technological breakthroughs by current competitors, or little activity by public pressure groups to influence the organization. Other organizations face very dynamic environments: rapidly changing government regulations affecting their business, new competitors, difficulties in acquiring raw materials, continually changing product preferences by customers, and so on. Static environments create significantly less uncertainty for managers than do dynamic ones. And because uncertainty is a threat to an organization's effectiveness, management will try to minimize it. One way to reduce environmental uncertainty is through adjustments in the organization's structure.[11]

Substantial evidence shows the degree of environmental uncertainty relates to different structural arrangements. Essentially, the more dynamic and uncertain the environment, the greater the need for flexibility. Hence, the organic structure will lead to higher organizational effectiveness. Conversely, in stable and predictable environments, the mechanistic form will be the structure of choice.

ORGANIZATIONAL DESIGNS AND EMPLOYEE BEHAVIOR

We opened this chapter by stating that an organization's structure can have significant effects on its members. In this section, we assess directly just what those effects might be.

A review of the evidence linking organizational structures to employee performance and satisfaction leads to a pretty clear conclusion: You can't generalize! Not everyone prefers the freedom and flexibility of organic structures. Some people are most productive and satisfied when work tasks are standardized and ambiguity is minimized—that is, in mechanistic structures. So any discussion of the effect of organizational design on employee behavior has to address individual differences. To illustrate this point, let's consider employee preferences for work specialization, span of control, and centralization.[12]

The evidence generally indicates that *work specialization* contributes to higher employee productivity—but at the price of reduced job satisfaction. However, this statement ignores individual differences and the type of job tasks people do. As we noted, work specialization is not an unending source of higher productivity. Problems start to surface, and productivity begins to suffer, when the human costs of doing repetitive and narrow tasks overtake the economies of specialization. As the workforce has become more highly educated and desirous of jobs that are intrinsically rewarding, the point at which productivity begins to decline seems to be reached more quickly than in decades past.

While more people today are turned off by overly specialized jobs than were their parents or grandparents, it would be naive to ignore the reality that a segment of the workforce prefers the routine and repetitiveness of highly specialized jobs. Some individuals want work that makes minimal intellectual demands and provides the security of routine. For these people, high work specialization is a source of job satisfaction. The empirical question, of course, is whether this represents 2 percent of the workforce or 52 percent. Given that some self-selection is operating in the choice of careers, we might conclude that negative behavioral outcomes from high specialization are most likely to surface in professional jobs occupied by individuals with high needs for personal growth and diversity.

A review of the research turns up no evidence to support a relationship between *span of control* and *employee performance*. It is intuitively attractive to argue that large spans lead to higher employee performance because they provide more distant supervision and more opportunity for personal initiative, but the research fails to support this notion. At this time, it is impossible to state that any particular span of control is best for producing high performance or high satisfaction among subordinates. Again, the reason is probably individual differences. Some people like to be left alone, whereas others prefer the security of a boss who is quickly available at all times. People also differ in how they respond to monitoring. Several of the contingency theories of leadership discussed in Chapter 11 would lead us to expect factors such as employees' experience and abilities and the degree of structure in their tasks to explain when wide or narrow spans of control are likely to contribute to their performance and job satisfaction.

We find fairly strong evidence linking *centralization* and *job satisfaction*. In general, organizations that are less centralized have a greater amount of participative decision making. And, the evidence suggests that participative decision making is positively related to job satisfaction. But, again, individual differences surface. The decentralization–satisfaction relationship is strongest with employees who have low self-esteem. Because individuals with low self-esteem have less confidence in their abilities, they place a higher value on shared decision making, which means that they're not held solely responsible for decision outcomes.

Our overall conclusion: To maximize employee performance and satisfaction, managers should consider individual differences—such as experience, personality, and the work task.

IMPLICATIONS FOR MANAGERS

An organization's internal structure contributes to explaining and predicting employee behavior. That is, in addition to individual and group factors, the structural relationships in which people work have an important bearing on their attitudes and behavior.

What's the basis for the argument that structure has an effect on both attitudes and behavior? Because an organization's structure reduces ambiguity and clarifies relationships, it shapes employees' attitudes and facilitates and motivates them to higher levels of performance.

Of course, structure also constrains employees, to the extent that it limits and controls what they do. For example, an organization gives employees little autonomy when it is structured around high levels of formalization and specialization, strict adherence to the chain of command, limited delegation of authority, and narrow spans of control. Controls in such organizations are tight, and behavior will tend to vary within a narrow range. In contrast, an organization structured around limited specialization, low formalization, wide spans of control, and the like provides employees greater freedom and, thus, will be characterized by greater behavioral diversity.

Organizational Culture

Just as individuals have personalities, so, too, do organizations. In Chapter 3, we found that individuals have relatively enduring and stable traits that help us predict their attitudes and behaviors. In this chapter, we propose that organizations, like people, can be characterized as, for example, rigid, friendly, warm, innovative, or conservative. These traits, in turn, can then be used to predict attitudes and behaviors of the people within these organizations.

The culture of any organization, although it may be hard to measure precisely, nevertheless exists and is generally recognized by its employees. We call this variable *organizational culture*. Just as tribal cultures have totems and taboos that dictate how each member will act toward fellow members and outsiders, organizations have cultures that govern how members behave. In this chapter, we'll discuss just what organizational culture is, how it affects employee attitudes and behavior, where it comes from, and whether it can be managed.

WHAT IS ORGANIZATIONAL CULTURE?

A number of years back, an executive was asked what he thought *organizational culture* meant. He gave essentially the same answer that a Supreme Court justice once gave in attempting to define pornography: "I can't define it, but I know it when I see it." This executive's approach to defining organizational culture isn't acceptable for our purposes. We need a basic definition to provide a point of departure for our quest to better understand the phenomenon. In this section, we propose a specific definition and review several peripheral issues that revolve around this definition.

Organizational Culture: A Definition

There seems to be wide agreement that **organizational culture** refers to a system of shared meaning held by members that distinguishes the organization from other organizations. This system of shared meaning is, on closer examination, a set of key characteristics that the organization values. The research suggests that seven primary characteristics, in aggregate, capture the essence of an organization's culture:[1]

1. *Innovation and risk taking:* The degree to which employees are encouraged to be innovative and take risks.
2. *Attention to detail:* The degree to which employees are expected to exhibit precision, analysis, and attention to detail.
3. *Outcome orientation:* The degree to which management focuses on results or outcomes rather than on the techniques and processes used to achieve those outcomes.
4. *People orientation:* The degree to which management decisions take into consideration the effect of outcomes on people within the organization.
5. *Team orientation:* The degree to which work activities are organized around teams rather than individuals.
6. *Aggressiveness:* The degree to which people are aggressive and competitive rather than easygoing.
7. *Stability:* The degree to which organizational activities emphasize maintaining the status quo in contrast to growth.

Each of these characteristics exists on a continuum from low to high. Appraising the organization on these seven characteristics, then, can give us a composite picture of the organization's culture. This picture becomes the basis for feelings of shared understanding that members have about the organization, how things are done in it, and the way members are supposed to behave.

Culture Is a Descriptive Term

—Organizational culture is concerned with how employees perceive the characteristics of an organization's culture, not with whether or not they like them.

Organizational culture is concerned with how employees perceive the characteristics of an organization's culture, not with whether or not they like them. That is, it's a descriptive term. This is important because it differentiates this concept from that of job satisfaction.

Research on organizational culture has sought to measure how employees see their organizations: Does it encourage teamwork? Does it reward innovation? Does it stifle initiative? In contrast, job satisfaction seeks to measure affective responses to the work environment. It's concerned with how employees feel about the organization's expectations, reward practices, and the like. Although the two terms undoubtedly have overlapping characteristics, keep in mind that the term *organizational culture* is descriptive, whereas *job satisfaction* is evaluative.

Do Organizations Have Uniform Cultures?

Organizational culture represents a common perception held by the organization's members. Remember, culture is a system of *shared* meaning. We should expect, therefore, that individuals with different backgrounds or at different levels in the organization will tend to describe the organization's culture in similar terms.

Acknowledgment that organizational culture has common properties does not, however, preclude subcultures within any given culture. Most large organizations have a *dominant culture* and numerous sets of subcultures. A **dominant culture** expresses the core values that are shared by a majority of the organization's members. When we talk about an organization's culture, we are referring to its dominant culture. It is this macro view of culture that gives an organization its distinct personality. **Subcultures** tend to develop in large organizations to reflect common problems, situations, or experiences that members face. These subcultures are likely to be defined by department designations and geographical separation. The purchasing department, for example, can have a subculture that is uniquely shared by members of that department. It will include the **core values** of the dominant culture, plus additional values unique to members of the purchasing department. Similarly, an office or unit of the organization that is physically separated from the organization's main operations may take on a different personality. Again, the core values are essentially retained, but they are modified to reflect the separated unit's distinct situation.

If organizations had no dominant culture and were composed only of numerous subcultures, the value of organizational culture as an explanatory concept would be significantly lessened because there would be no uniform interpretation of what represented appropriate and inappropriate behavior. It is the *shared meaning* aspect of culture that makes it such a potent device for guiding and shaping behavior. That's what allows us to say, for example, that Microsoft's culture values aggressiveness and risk taking and then to use that information to better understand the behavior of Microsoft executives and employees.[2] But we cannot ignore the reality that many organizations also have subcultures that can influence the behavior of members.

Strong Versus Weak Cultures

It has become increasingly popular to differentiate between strong and weak cultures. The argument here is that strong cultures have a greater impact on employee behavior and are more directly related to reduced turnover.

In a **strong culture**, the organization's core values are both intensely held and widely shared. The more the number of members who accept the core values and the greater their commitment to those values, the stronger the culture is. Consistent with this definition, a strong culture will have a great influence on the behavior of its members because the high degree of sharing and intensity creates an internal climate of high behavioral control. For example, Seattle-based Nordstrom has developed one of the strongest service cultures in the retailing industry. Nordstrom employees know in no uncertain terms what is expected of them, and those expectations go a long way in shaping the way they behave.

One specific result of a strong culture should be lower employee turnover. A strong culture demonstrates high agreement among members about what the organization stands for. Such unanimity of purpose builds cohesiveness, loyalty, and organizational commitment. These qualities, in turn, lessen employees' propensity to leave the organization.[3]

Organizational Culture Versus National Culture

Throughout this book we've argued that national differences—that is, national cultures—must be taken into account if accurate predictions are to be made about organizational behavior in different countries. But does national culture override an organization's culture? Is an IBM facility in Germany, for example, more likely to reflect German ethnic culture or IBM's corporate culture?

The research indicates that national culture has a greater impact on employees than does their organization's culture.[4] German employees at an IBM facility in Munich, therefore, will be influenced more by German culture than by IBM's culture. This means that as influential as organizational culture is in shaping employee behavior, national culture is even more influential. We need to qualify this conclusion to reflect the candidate self-selection that goes on at the hiring stage. A British multinational corporation, for example, is likely to be less concerned with hiring Italians for its Italian operations than in hiring Italians who fit with the corporation's way of doing things. We should expect, therefore, that the employee selection process will be used by multinationals to find and hire job applicants who fit in well with the organizations' dominant cultures, even if such applicants are atypical inhabitants of the countries where they reside.

WHAT DO CULTURES DO?

So far, we've asserted that organizational culture affects behavior and that a strong culture should be associated with reduced turnover. Now, let's carefully review the functions that culture performs and assess whether culture can be a liability for an organization.

Culture's Functions

Culture performs a number of functions within an organization:

- Culture has a boundary-defining role, creating distinctions between one organization and others.
- Culture conveys a sense of identity for organization members.
- Culture facilitates the generation of commitment to something larger than one's individual self-interest.
- Culture enhances the stability of the social system. It is the social glue that helps hold the organization together by providing appropriate standards for what employees should say and do.

■ Culture serves as a sense-making and control mechanism that guides and shapes the attitudes and behavior of employees.

It is this last function that is of particular interest to us. As the following quote makes clear, culture defines the rules of the game:

> Every organization develops a core set of assumptions, understandings, and implicit rules that govern day-to-day behavior in the workplace. . . . Until newcomers learn the rules, they are not accepted as full-fledged members of the organization. Transgressions of the rules on the part of high-level executives or front-line employees result in universal disapproval and powerful penalties. Conformity to the rules becomes the primary basis for reward and upward mobility.[5]

The role of culture in influencing employee behavior appears to be increasingly important in today's workplace.[6] As organizations have widened spans of control, flattened structures, introduced teams, reduced formalization, and empowered employees, the shared meaning provided by a strong culture ensures that everyone is pointed in the same direction.

As we show later in this chapter, the individual–organization *fit*—whether the applicant or employee's attitudes and behavior are compatible with the culture–strongly influences who receives a job offer to join the organization, who is appraised as a high performer, and who gets the promotion. It's not a coincidence that employees at Disney theme parks appear to be almost universally attractive, clean, and wholesome looking, with bright smiles. That's the image Disney seeks. The company selects employees who will maintain that image. And once on the job, a strong culture, supported by formal rules and regulations, ensures that Disney theme-park employees will act in a relatively uniform and predictable way.

Culture as a Liability

We are treating culture in a nonjudgmental manner. We haven't said that it's good or bad, only that it exists. Many of its functions, as outlined, are valuable for both the organization and the employee. Culture enhances organizational commitment and increases the consistency of employee behavior. These are clearly benefits to an organization. From an employee's standpoint, culture is valuable because it reduces ambiguity. It tells employees how things are done and what's important. But we shouldn't ignore the potentially dysfunctional aspects of culture, especially a strong one, on an organization's effectiveness.

—Culture enhances organizational commitment and increases the consistency of employee behavior.

Barriers to Change Culture is a liability when the shared values are not in agreement with those that will further the organization's effectiveness. This is most likely to occur when an organization's environment is dynamic.[7] When an environment is undergoing rapid change, an organization's entrenched culture may no longer be appropriate. If consistency of behavior is an asset to an organization when it faces a stable environment, it may burden the organization and make it difficult to respond to changes in the environment. This helps to explain the challenges that executives at organizations such as Mitsubishi, Eastman Kodak, Boeing, and the U.S. Federal Bureau of Investigation have faced in recent years in adapting to upheavals in their environments.[8] These organizations have strong cultures that worked well for them in the past. These strong cultures become barriers to change, however, when "business as usual" is no longer effective.

Barriers to Diversity   Hiring new employees who, because of race, age, gender, disability, or other differences, are not like the majority of the organization's members creates a paradox. Management wants new employees to accept the organization's core cultural values. Otherwise, these employees are unlikely to fit in or be accepted. But, at the same time, management wants to openly acknowledge and demonstrate support for the differences that these employees bring to the workplace. Obviously, this creates a dilemma. Organizations hire diverse individuals because of the alternative strengths these people bring to the workplace, yet these diverse behaviors and strengths are likely to diminish in strong cultures as people attempt to fit in.

Management's challenge in this paradox of diversity is to balance two conflicting goals: get employees to accept the organization's dominant values and encourage the acceptance of differences. Too much attention to investiture rites is likely to create employees who are misfits. On the other hand, too much emphasis on divestiture rites may eliminate the unique strengths that people of different backgrounds bring to the organization.

Barriers to Acquisitions and Mergers   Historically, the key factors that management looked at in making acquisition or merger decisions were related to financial advantages or product synergy. In recent years, cultural compatibility has become the primary concern.[9] While a favorable financial statement or product line may be the initial attraction of an acquisition candidate, whether the acquisition actually works seems to have more to do with how well the two organizations' cultures match up.

Many acquisitions fail shortly after their consummation. A survey by consultants A.T. Kearney revealed that 58 percent of mergers failed to reach the value goals set by top managers.[10] The primary cause of failure is conflicting organizational cultures. As one expert commented, "Mergers have an unusually high failure rate, and it's always because of people issues." For instance, the 2001 $183 billion merger between America Online (AOL) and Time Warner was the largest in corporate history. The merger has been a disaster: Only two years later, the stock fell an astounding 90 percent. Culture clash is commonly argued to be one of the causes of AOL Time Warner's problems. As one expert noted, "In some ways the merger of AOL and Time Warner was like the marriage of a teenager to a middle-aged banker. The cultures were vastly different. There were open collars and jeans at AOL. Time Warner was more buttoned-down."[11]

CREATING AND SUSTAINING CULTURE

An organization's culture doesn't pop out of thin air. And once established, it rarely fades away. What forces influence the creation of a culture? What reinforces and sustains these forces once they're in place? Let's examine both of these questions.

How a Culture Begins

An organization's current customs, traditions, and general way of doing things are largely due to what it has done before and the degree of success it has had with those endeavors. This leads us to the ultimate source of an organization's culture: its founders.

The founders of an organization traditionally have a major influence on that organization's early culture. They have a vision of what the organization should be. They are unconstrained by previous customs or ideologies. The small size that typically characterizes new organizations further facilitates the founders' imposition of their vision on all organizational members. Culture creation occurs in three ways.[12] First, founders hire and keep only employees who think and feel the same way they do. Second, they indoctrinate and socialize these employees to their way of thinking and feeling. And finally, the founders' own behavior acts as a role model that encourages employees to identify with them and thereby internalize their beliefs, values, and assumptions. When the organization succeeds, the founders' vision becomes seen as a primary determinant of that success. At this point, the founders' entire personality becomes embedded in the culture of the organization.

The culture at Hyundai, the giant Korean conglomerate, is largely a reflection of its founder Chung Ju Yung. Hyundai's fierce, competitive style and its disciplined, authoritarian nature are the same characteristics often used to describe Chung. Other contemporary examples of founders who have had an immeasurable impact on their organizations' cultures include Bill Gates at Microsoft, Ingvar Kamprad at IKEA, Herb Kelleher at Southwest Airlines, Fred Smith at Federal Express, and Richard Branson at the Virgin Group.

Keeping a Culture Alive

Once a culture is in place, practices within the organization serve to maintain it by giving employees a set of similar experiences. For example, many human resource practices reinforce the organization's culture. The selection process, performance evaluation criteria, training and development activities, and promotion procedures ensure that those hired fit in with the culture, reward those who support it, and penalize (and even expel) those who challenge it. Three forces play a particularly important part in sustaining a culture: *selection practices*, the *actions of top management*, and *socialization methods*. Let's take a closer look at each.

Selection The explicit goal of the selection process is to identify and hire individuals who have the knowledge, skills, and abilities to perform the jobs within the organization successfully. However, once that goal is assured, the recruiter's attention turns to hiring people who have values essentially consistent with those of the organization, or at least a good portion of those values. In addition, the selection process provides information to applicants about the organization. Candidates learn about the organization and, if they perceive a conflict between their values and those of the organization, they can self-select themselves out of the applicant pool. Selection, therefore, becomes a two-way street, allowing employer or applicant to pass on the opportunity if there appears to be a mismatch. In this way, the selection process sustains an organization's culture by selecting out those individuals who might attack or undermine its core values.

For instance, W.L. Gore & Associates, the maker of Gore-Tex fabric used in outerwear, prides itself on its democratic culture and teamwork. There are no job titles at Gore, nor bosses, nor chains of command. All work is done in teams. In Gore's selection process, teams of employees put job applicants through extensive interviews to ensure that candidates are selected out who can't deal with the level of uncertainty, flexibility, and teamwork that employees have to manage in Gore plants.[13]

Top Management   The actions of top management also have a major effect on the organization's culture. Through what they say and how they behave, senior executives establish norms that filter down through the organization, such as these:

- Whether risk taking is desirable
- How much freedom managers should give their employees
- What is appropriate dress
- What actions will pay off in terms of pay raises, promotions, and other rewards
- And the like

For example, Robert A. Keirlin has been called "the cheapest CEO in America."[14] Keirlin is chairman and CEO of Fastenal Co., the largest specialty retailer of nuts and bolts in the United States, with 6,500 employees. He takes a salary of only $60,000 a year. He owns only three suits, each of which he bought used. He clips grocery coupons, drives a Toyota, and stays in low-priced motels when he travels on business. Does Keirlin need to pinch pennies? No. The market value of his stock in Fastenal is worth about $300 million. But the man prefers a modest personal lifestyle. And he prefers the same for his company. Keirlin argues that his behavior should send a message to all his employees: *We don't waste things in this company.* Keirlin sees himself as a role model for frugality, and employees at Fastenal have learned to follow his example.

Socialization   No matter how good a job the organization does in recruiting and selection, new employees are not fully indoctrinated in the organization's culture. Because they are unfamiliar with the organization's culture, new employees are potentially likely to disturb the beliefs and customs that are in place. The organization will, therefore, want to help new employees adapt to its culture. This adaptation process is called **socialization**.

All Marines must go through boot camp, where they "prove" their commitment. Of course, at the same time, the Marine trainers are indoctrinating new recruits in the "Marine way." At Limited Brands, newly hired vice presidents and regional directors go through an intensive one-month program, called onboarding, designed to immerse these executives in the culture of Limited Brands.[15] During this month they have no direct responsibilities for tasks associated with their new positions. Instead, they spend all their work time meeting with other senior leaders and mentors, working the floors of retail stores, evaluating employee and customer habits, investigating the competition, and studying the past and current operations of Limited Brands.

The most critical socialization stage is at the time of entry into the organization. This is when the organization seeks to mold the outsider into an employee "in good standing." Employees who fail to learn the essential or pivotal role behaviors risk being labeled "nonconformists" or "rebels," which often leads to expulsion. And the organization will continue to socialize every employee, though maybe not as explicitly, throughout his or her entire career in the organization. This further contributes to sustaining the culture.

Socialization can be conceptualized as a process in three stages: *prearrival*, *encounter*, and *metamorphosis*.[16] The first stage encompasses all the learning that occurs before a new member joins the organization. In the second stage, the new employee sees what the organization is really like and confronts the possibility that expectations and reality may diverge. In the third stage, the relatively long-lasting changes take place. The new employee masters the skills required for the job, successfully performs the new role, and adjusts to the work group's values and norms. This three-stage process affects the new employee's work productivity, commitment to the organization's objectives, and eventual decision to stay with the organization. Exhibit 15-1 depicts this process.

The **prearrival stage** explicitly recognizes that each individual arrives with a set of values, attitudes, and expectations. These cover both the work to be done and the organization. For instance, in many jobs, particularly professional work, new members will have undergone a considerable degree of prior socialization in training and in school. One major purpose of a business school, for example, is to socialize business students to the attitudes and behaviors that business firms want. If business executives believe that successful employees value the profit ethic, are loyal, will work hard, and desire to achieve, they can hire individuals out of business schools who have been pre-molded in this pattern. Moreover, most people in business realize that no matter how well they think they can socialize newcomers, the most important predictor of new-comers' future behavior is their past behavior. Research shows that what people know before they join organizations, and how proactive their personalities are (as described in Chapter 3), are critical predictors of how well they adjust to a new culture.[17]

On entry into the organization, the new member enters the **encounter stage**. Here the individual confronts the possible dichotomy between expectations—about the job, the coworkers, the boss, and the organization in general—and reality. If expectations prove to have been more or less accurate, the encounter stage merely provides a reaffirmation of the perceptions gained earlier. However, this is often not the case. Where expectations and reality differ, the new employee must undergo socialization that will detach her from her previous assumptions and replace them with another set that the organization deems desirable. At the extreme, a new member may become totally disillusioned with the actualities of the job and resign. Proper selection should significantly reduce the probability of the latter occurrence. Also, an employee's network of friends and coworkers can play a critical role in helping him or her learn the culture and the work. Newcomers are more committed to the organization when their friendship networks are large and diverse. So, organizations can help newcomers socialize by encouraging friendship ties in organizations.

—Newcomers are more committed to the organization when their friendship networks are large and diverse.

EXHIBIT 15-1 A Socialization Model

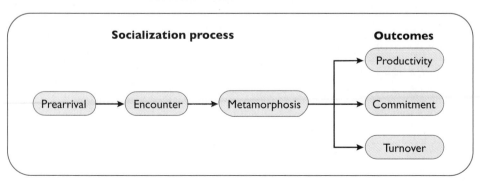

Finally, the new member must work out any problems discovered during the encounter stage. This may mean going through changes—hence, we call this the **metamorphosis stage**. The options presented in Exhibit 15-2 are alternatives designed to bring about the desired metamorphosis. Note, for example, that the more management relies on socialization programs that are formal, collective, fixed, and serial and that emphasize divestiture, the greater the likelihood that newcomers' differences and perspectives will be stripped away and replaced by standardized and predictable behaviors. Careful selection by management of newcomers' socialization experiences can—at the extreme—create conformists who maintain traditions and customs, or inventive and creative individualists who consider no organizational practice sacred.

We can say that metamorphosis and the entry socialization process are complete when new members have become comfortable with the organization and their job. They have internalized the norms of the organization and their work groups and understand and accept those norms. They feel accepted by their peers as trusted and valued individuals. They are self-confident that they have the competence to complete the job successfully. They understand the system—not only their own tasks but also the rules, procedures, and informally accepted practices. Finally, they know how they will be evaluated—that is, what criteria will be used to measure and appraise their work. They know what is expected of them and what constitutes a job "well done." As Exhibit 15-2 shows, successful metamorphosis should have a positive effect on new employees' productivity and their commitment to the organization and should reduce their propensity to leave the organization.

EXHIBIT 15-2   Entry Socialization Options

Formal Versus Informal. The more a new employee is segregated from the ongoing work setting and differentiated in some way to make explicit his or her newcomer's role, the more formal socialization is. Specific orientation and training programs are examples. Informal socialization puts the new employee directly into the job, with little or no special attention.

Individual Versus Collective. New members can be socialized individually. This describes how it's done in many professional offices. They also can be grouped together and processed through an identical set of experiences, as in military boot camp.

Fixed Versus Variable. This refers to the time schedule in which newcomers make the transition from outsider to insider. A fixed schedule establishes standardized stages of transition. This characterizes rotational training programs. It also includes probationary periods, such as the 8- to 10-year *associate* status used by accounting and law firms before deciding on whether or not a candidate is made a partner. Variable schedules give no advance notice of their transition timetables. Variable schedules describe the typical promotion system, in which one is not advanced to the next stage until one is "ready."

Serial Versus Random. Serial socialization is characterized by the use of role models who train and encourage newcomers. Apprenticeship and mentoring programs are examples. In random socialization, role models are deliberately withheld. New employees are left on their own to figure things out.

Investiture Versus Divestiture. Investiture socialization assumes that the newcomer's qualities and qualifications are the necessary ingredients for job success, so these qualities and qualifications are confirmed and supported. Divestiture socialization tries to strip away certain characteristics of the recruit. Fraternity and sorority pledges go through divestiture socialization to shape them into proper roles.

Source: Based on J. Van Maanen, "People Processing: Strategies of Organizational Socialization," *Organizational Dynamics,* Summer 1978, pp. 19-36; and E. H. Schein, "Organizational Culture, "*American Psychologist,* February 1990, p. 116.

EXHIBIT 15-3   How Organizational Cultures Form

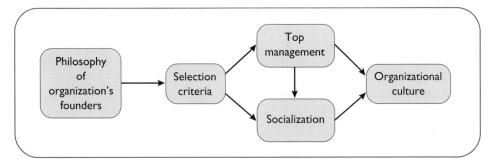

Summary: How Cultures Form

Exhibit 15-3 summarizes how an organization's culture is established and sustained. The original culture is derived from the founder's philosophy. This, in turn, strongly influences the criteria used in hiring. The actions of the current top management set the general climate of what is acceptable behavior and what is not. How employees are socialized will depend both on the degree of success achieved in matching new employees' values to those of the organization's in the selection process and on top management's preference for socialization methods.

HOW EMPLOYEES LEARN CULTURE

Culture is transmitted to employees in a number of forms, the most potent being stories, rituals, material symbols, and language.

Stories

During the days when Henry Ford II was chairman of the Ford Motor Co., one would have been hard-pressed to find a manager who hadn't heard the story about Mr. Ford reminding his executives, when they got too arrogant, that "It's my name that's on the building." The message was clear: Henry Ford II ran the company.

Nike has a number of senior executives who spend much of their time serving as corporate storytellers, and the stories they tell are meant to convey what Nike is about.[18] When they tell the story of how cofounder (and Oregon track coach) Bill Bowerman went to his workshop and poured rubber into his wife's waffle iron to create a better running shoe, they're talking about Nike's spirit of innovation. When new hires hear tales of Oregon running star Steve Prefontaine's battles to make running a professional sport and to attain better-performance equipment, they learn of Nike's commitment to helping athletes.

Stories such as these circulate through many organizations. They typically contain a narrative of events about the organization's founders, rule breaking, rags-to-riches successes, reductions in the workforce, relocation of employees, reactions to past mistakes, and organizational coping. These stories anchor the present in the past and provide explanations and legitimacy for current practices.

Rituals

Rituals are repetitive sequences of activities that express and reinforce the key values of the organization: what goals are most important, which people are important, and which people are expendable.[19] One of the better-known corporate rituals is Wal-Mart's company chant. Begun by the company's founder, Sam Walton, as a way to motivate and unite his workforce, "Gimme a W, gimme an A, gimme an L, gimme a squiggle, give me an M, A, R, T!" has become a company ritual that bonds Wal-Mart workers and reinforces Sam Walton's belief in the importance of his employees to the company's success. Similar corporate chants are used by IBM, Ericsson, Novell, Deutsche Bank, and Pricewaterhouse-Coopers.[20]

Material Symbols

The headquarters of Alcoa doesn't look like your typical head-office operation. There are few individual offices, even for senior executives. It is essentially made up of cubicles, common areas, and meeting rooms. This informal corporate headquarters conveys to employees that Alcoa values openness, equality, creativity, and flexibility. Some corporations provide their top executives with chauffeur-driven limousines and, when they travel by air, unlimited use of the corporate jet. Others may not get to ride in limousines or private jets, but they might still get a car and air transportation paid for by the company—only the car is a Chevrolet (with no driver) and the jet seat is in the economy section of a commercial airliner.

The layout of corporate headquarters, the types of automobiles top executives are given, and the presence or absence of corporate aircraft are a few examples of material symbols. Others include the size of offices, the elegance of furnishings, executive perks, and attire. These material symbols convey to employees who is important, the degree of egalitarianism desired by top management, and the kinds of behavior (for instance, risk taking, conservative, authoritarian, participative, individualistic, social) that are appropriate.

Language

Many organizations and units within organizations use language as a way to identify members of a culture or subculture. By learning this language, members attest to their acceptance of the culture and, in so doing, help to preserve it. The following are examples of terminology used by employees at Knight-Ridder Information, a California-based data redistributor: *accession number* (a number assigned to each individual record in a database); *KWIC* (a set of key-words-in-context); and *relational operator* (searching a database for names or key terms in some order). If you're a new employee at Boeing, you'll find yourself learning a whole unique vocabulary of acronyms, including BOLD (Boeing online data), CATIA (computer-graphics-aided three-dimensional interactive application), MAIDS (manufacturing assembly and installation data system), POP (purchased outside production), and SLO (service level objectives).[21]

Organizations, over time, often develop unique terms to describe equipment, offices, key personnel, suppliers, customers, or products that relate to its business. New employees are frequently overwhelmed with acronyms and jargon that, after six months on the job, have become fully part of their language. Once assimilated, this terminology acts as a common denominator that unites members of a given culture or subculture.

MANAGING CULTURAL CHANGE

Because an organization's culture is made up of relatively stable characteristics, it's difficult to change. An organization's culture develops over many years and is rooted in deeply held values to which employees are strongly committed. In addition, a number of forces continually operate to maintain a given culture. These include written statements about the organization's mission and philosophy, the design of physical spaces and buildings, the dominant leadership style, historical selection criteria, past promotion practices, entrenched rituals, popular stories about key people and events, the organization's past performance evaluation criteria, and the organization's formal structure.

—An organization's culture develops over many years and is rooted in deeply held values to which employees are strongly committed.

Although changing an organization's culture is difficult, it isn't impossible. For cultural change to be effective, it helps if certain conditions are prevalent. The evidence suggests cultural change is most likely to take when most or all of the following four conditions exist:[22]

1. *A dramatic crisis exists or is created:* This is the shock that undermines the status quo and calls into question the relevance of the current culture. Such crises might be a surprising financial setback, the loss of a major customer, or a dramatic technological breakthrough by a competitor. It is not unheard of for some executives to purposely create a crisis to stimulate cultural change.

2. *Turnover in leadership:* New top leaders, who can provide an alternative set of key values, are usually needed to make cultural change work. They are more likely to be perceived as capable of responding to the crisis. Bringing in a new CEO from outside the organization is likely to increase the chances that new cultural values will be introduced.

3. *Young and small organization:* Cultural change is more likely to take if the organization is both young and small. Cultures in younger organizations are less entrenched. And it's easier for management to communicate its new values when the organization is small. This, incidentally, helps explain the difficulty that multibillion-dollar corporations often experience when trying to change their cultures.

4. *Weak culture:* The more widely held a culture is and the higher the agreement among members on its values, the more difficult it will be to change. Conversely, weak cultures are more amenable to change than strong ones.

Even when these conditions are favorable, managers shouldn't look for immediate or dramatic shifts in their organizations' culture. Cultural change is a lengthy process—and should be measured in years rather than months.

CREATING AN ETHICAL ORGANIZATIONAL CULTURE

The content and strength of a culture influence an organization's ethical climate and the ethical behavior of its members.[23] An organizational culture most likely to shape high ethical standards is one that's high in risk tolerance, low to moderate in aggressiveness, and focused on means as well as outcomes. Managers in such a culture are supported for taking risks and innovating, are discouraged from engaging in unbridled competition, and will pay attention to *how* goals are achieved as well as to *what* goals are achieved.

A strong organizational culture will exert more influence on employees than will a weak one. If the culture is strong and supports high ethical standards, it should have a very powerful and positive influence on employee behavior. Johnson & Johnson, for example, has a strong culture that has long stressed corporate obligations to customers, employees, the community, and shareholders, in that order. When Tylenol (a Johnson & Johnson product) was found poisoned on store shelves, employees at Johnson & Johnson across the United States independently pulled the product from these stores before management had even issued a statement concerning the tamperings. No one had to tell these individuals what was morally right; they knew what Johnson & Johnson leadership would expect them to do. On the other hand, a strong culture that encourages pushing the limits can be a powerful force in shaping unethical behavior. For instance, Enron's aggressive culture, with unrelenting pressure on executives to rapidly expand earnings, encouraged ethical corner cutting and eventually contributed to the company's collapse and the ultimate conviction of leaders Ken Lay and Jeff Skilling.[24]

What can management do to create a more ethical culture? We suggest a combination of the following practices:

- *Be a visible role model.* Employees will look to top-management behavior as a benchmark for defining appropriate behavior. When senior management is seen as taking the ethical high road, it provides a positive message for all employees.

- *Communicate ethical expectations.* Ethical ambiguities can be minimized by creating and disseminating an organizational code of ethics. It should state the organization's primary values and the ethical rules that employees are expected to follow.

- *Provide ethical training.* Set up seminars, workshops, and similar ethical training programs. Use these training sessions to reinforce the organization's standards of conduct, to clarify what practices are and are not permissible, and to address possible ethical dilemmas.

- *Visibly reward ethical acts and punish unethical ones.* Performance appraisals of managers should include a point-by-point evaluation of how his or her decisions measure up against the organization's code of ethics. Appraisals must include the means taken to achieve goals as well as the ends themselves. People who act ethically should be visibly rewarded for their behavior. Just as important, unethical acts should be conspicuously punished.

- *Provide protective mechanisms.* The organization needs to provide formal mechanisms so that employees can discuss ethical dilemmas and report unethical behavior without fear of reprimand. This might include creation of ethical counselors, ombudsmen, or ethical officers.

CREATING A CUSTOMER-RESPONSIVE CULTURE

French retailers have a well-established reputation for indifference to customers.[25] Salespeople, for instance, routinely make it clear to customers that their phone conversations should not be interrupted. Just getting any help at all from a salesperson can be a challenge. And no one in France finds it particularly surprising that the owner of a Paris store should complain that he was unable to work on his books all morning because he kept being bothered *by customers!*

Most organizations today are trying very hard to be un-French-like. They are attempting to create a customer-responsive culture because they recognize that this is the path to customer loyalty and long-term profitability. Companies that have created such cultures—like Southwest Airlines, FedEx, Johnson & Johnson, Nordstrom, Olive Garden, Walt Disney theme parks, Enterprise Rent-A-Car, Whole Foods, and L.L. Bean—have built a strong and loyal customer base and have generally outperformed their competitors in revenue growth and financial performance.

Key Variables Shaping Customer-Responsive Cultures

Let's identify the variables that shape customer-responsive cultures and consider ways in which management can create such cultures. A review of the evidence finds that half a dozen variables are routinely evident in responsive cultures:[26]

1. The *type of employees* themselves. Successful, service-oriented organizations hire employees who are outgoing and friendly.
2. *Low formalization*. Service employees need to have the freedom to meet changing customer-service requirements. Rigid rules, procedures, and regulations make this difficult.
3. *Widespread use of empowerment*, an extension of low formalization. Empowered employees have the decision discretion to do what's necessary to please the customer.
4. *Good listening skills*. Employees in customer-responsive cultures have the ability to listen to and understand messages sent by the customer.
5. *Role clarity*. Service employees act as "boundary spanners" between the organization and its customers. They have to acquiesce to the demands of both the employer and the customer. This can create considerable role ambiguity and conflict, which reduces employees' job satisfaction and can hinder employee service performance. Successful customer-responsive cultures reduce employee uncertainty about the best way to perform their jobs and the importance of job activities.
6. *Organizational citizenship behavior*. Employees are conscientious in their desire to please the customer. Also, they're willing to take the initiative, even when it's outside their normal job requirements, to satisfy a customer's needs.

In summary, customer-responsive cultures hire service-oriented employees with good listening skills and the willingness to go beyond the constraints of their job descriptions to do what's necessary to please customers. It then clarifies their roles, frees them up to meet changing customer needs by minimizing rules and regulations, and provides them with a wide range of decision discretion to do their jobs as they see fit.

—Customer-responsive cultures hire service-oriented employees with good listening skills and the willingness to go beyond the constraints of their job description to do what's necessary to please the customer.

Managerial Action

Based on these characteristics, we can suggest a number of actions that management can take if it wants to make its culture more customer responsive. These actions are designed to create employees with the competence, ability, and willingness to solve customer problems as they arise.

Selection   The place to start in building a customer-responsive culture is hiring service-contact people with the personality and attitudes consistent with a high service orientation. Southwest Air lines is a shining example of a company that has focused its hiring process on selecting out job candidates whose personalities aren't people friendly. Job applicants go through an extensive interview process at Southwest in which company employees and executives carefully assess whether candidates have the outgoing and fun-loving personality that they want in all employees.

Training   Organizations that are trying to become more customer responsive don't always have the option of hiring all new employees. In such cases, the emphasis will be on training rather than hiring. This describes the dilemma that senior executives at companies such as General Motors, Shell, and J.P. Morgan Chase have faced in the past decade as they have attempted to move away from their product focus. The content of these training programs will vary widely but should focus on improving product knowledge, active listening, showing patience, and displaying emotions.

Structural Design   To become more customer responsive, organization structures must give employees more control. This can be achieved by reducing rules and regulations. Employees are better able to satisfy customers when they have some control over the service encounter. So, management must allow employees to adjust their behaviors to the changing needs and requests of customers.

Empowerment   Consistent with low formalization is empowering employees with the discretion to make day-to-day decisions about job-related activities. It's a necessary component of a customer-responsive culture because it allows service employees to make on-the-spot decisions to satisfy customers completely.[27] Enterprise Rent-A-Car has found that high customer satisfaction doesn't require a problem-free experience. The "completely satisfied" customer was one who, when he or she had a problem, found that it was quickly and courteously resolved by an employee. By empowering its employees to make decisions on the spot, Enterprise improved its customer satisfaction ratings.[28]

Leadership   Leaders convey the organization's culture through both what they say and what they do. Effective leaders in customer-responsive cultures deliver by conveying a customer-focused vision and demonstrating by their continual behavior that they are committed to customers. In almost every organization that has successfully created and maintained a strong customer-responsive culture, the chief executive officer has played a major role in championing the message. Taiwan microchip manufacturer United Microelectronics Corp. recently hired Jackson Hu as its new CEO, specifically for his prior successes at changing a company's culture to focus employees on better understanding customer needs and improving customer service.[29]

Performance Evaluation   An impressive amount of evidence demonstrates that behavior-based performance evaluations are consistent with improved customer service.[30] Behavior-based evaluations appraise employees on the basis of how they behave or act—on criteria such as effort, commitment, teamwork, friendliness, and the ability to solve customer problems—rather than on the measurable outcomes they achieve. Behaviors are superior to outcomes for improving service because they provide incentives to employees to engage in behaviors that are conducive to improved service quality and give them more control over the conditions that affect their performance evaluations.

Reward Systems If management wants employees to give good service, it has to reward good service. It must provide ongoing recognition to employees who have demonstrated extraordinary effort to please customers and have been singled out by customers for "going the extra mile." It also must make pay and promotions contingent on outstanding customer service.

IMPLICATIONS FOR MANAGERS

With little doubt, culture has a strong influence on employee behavior. But what can management do to design a culture that molds employees in the way management wants?

When an organization is just being established, management has a great deal of influence. No traditions have been established. The organization is small. Subcultures, if any, are few. Everyone knows the founder and is directly touched by his or her vision of the organization. Not surprisingly, under these conditions management has the opportunity to create a culture that will best facilitate the achievement of the organization's goals. However, when the organization is well established, so too is its dominant culture. Given that this culture is made up of relatively stable and permanent characteristics, it becomes very resistant to change. The culture took time to form, and once established it tends to become entrenched. Strong cultures are particularly resistant to change because employees become so committed to them. So, if a given culture, over time, becomes a handicap to management and inappropriate to an organization, management may be able to do little to change it, especially in the short run. Under the most favorable conditions, cultural changes must be measured in years, not weeks or months. The favorable conditions that increase the probability that cultural change can be successfully implemented are the existence of a dramatic crisis, a turnover in the organization's top leadership, an organization that is both young and small, and a dominant culture that is weak.

CHAPTER 16

Organizational Change and Development

After studying this chapter, you should be able to:

1. Describe forces that act as stimulants to change.
2. Contrast two views of change.
3. Summarize Lewin's three-step change model.
4. Describe factors that lead to resistance to change and how resistance can be reduced.
5. Explain the values underlying most organizational development (OD) efforts.
6. Contrast continuous improvement processes and process reengineering.
7. Describe potential sources of, and ways of managing, work stress.
8. List characteristics of a learning organization.
9. Explain how organizational change may be culture bound.

In this chapter, we describe environmental forces that require managers to implement comprehensive change programs. We consider why people and organizations often resist change, discuss how this resistance can be overcome, and review various processes for managing organizational change. We also examine work stress, as well as contemporary change issues for today's managers.

FORCES FOR CHANGE

More and more organizations today face a dynamic and changing environment. This, in turn, requires these organizations to adapt. "Change or die!" is the rallying cry among today's managers worldwide. Exhibit 16-1 summarizes six specific forces that act as stimulants for change.

Throughout this book, we've discussed the *changing nature of the workforce*. Almost every organization is having to adjust to a multicultural environment. Human resource policies and practices have to change to reflect the needs of an aging labor force. And many companies are having to spend large amounts of money on training to upgrade reading, math, computer, and other employee skills.

Technology is changing jobs and organizations. Computers are now foundational to almost every organization; and cell phones and handheld PDAs are seen as indispensable by many. Computer networks are also reshaping entire industries—nearly all businesses now have to balance technology access with privacy issues. For the longer term, recent breakthroughs in deciphering the human genetic code offer the potential for pharmaceutical companies to produce drugs designed for specific individuals and create serious ethical dilemmas for insurance companies as to who is insurable and who isn't.

We live in an age of discontinuity. In the 1950s and 1960s, the past was a pretty good prologue to the future. Tomorrow was essentially an extended trend line from yesterday. That's no longer true. Beginning in the gas shortages in the early 1970s, and recurring with the explosive growth of energy prices in recent years, *economic shocks* have continued to impose changes on organizations. In recent years, new dot-com businesses were created, turning tens of thousands of investors into overnight millionaires, and then crashed. The stock market decline from 2000 to 2002 eroded approximately 40 percent of the average employee's retirement account. Although the

EXHIBIT 16-1   Forces for Change

Force	Examples
Nature of the workforce	More cultural diversity Aging population Many new entrants with inadequate skills
Technology	Faster, cheaper, and more mobile computers Online music sharing Deciphering of the human genetic code
Economic shocks	Volatility of stock market Immigration in high- and low-skill jobs Skyrocketing energy costs
Competition	Global competitors Mergers and consolidations Growth of e-commerce
Social trends	Internet chat rooms Retirement of baby boomers Rise in discount and "big box" retailers
World politics	Iraq–U.S. war Opening of markets in Pacific Rim War on terrorism

stock market recovered, many retirement funds did not, which has forced many employees to postpone their anticipated retirement dates. And the volatility of the housing market has led to a financial roller coaster ride for home builders and remodelers, furniture retailers, mortgage bankers, and other home-related businesses.

Competition is changing. The global economy means that competitors are as likely to come from across the ocean as from across town. Heightened competition also makes it necessary for established organizations to defend themselves against both traditional competitors who develop new products and services and small, entrepreneurial firms with innovative offerings. Successful organizations will be the ones that can change in response to the competition. They'll be fast on their feet, capable of developing new products rapidly and getting them to market quickly. They'll rely on short production runs, short product cycles, and an ongoing stream of new products. In other words, they'll be flexible. They will require an equally flexible and responsive workforce that can adapt to rapidly and even radically changing conditions.

Social trends don't remain static. In contrast to just 15 years ago, people are meeting and sharing information in Internet chat rooms and web logs *(blogs)*; baby boomers have begun to retire; and consumers are increasingly doing their shopping at discount warehouses and "big box" retailers such as Home Depot and Circuit City.

Throughout this book we have promoted the importance of seeing OB in a global context. Business schools have been preaching a global perspective since the early 1980s, but no one—not even the strongest proponents of globalization—could have imagined how *world politics* would change in recent years. We've seen the opening up of South Africa and China; almost daily suicide bombings in the Middle East; and, of course, the rise of Muslim fundamentalism. The unilateral invasion of Iraq by the United States has led to an expensive postwar rebuilding and an increase in anti-American attitudes in much of the world. The terrorist attacks on New York, Washington, London, and Madrid have led to changes in business practices related to the creation of backup systems, employee security, employee stereotyping and profiling, and post–terrorist-attack anxiety.

Change Agents

—Change agents can be managers or nonmanagers, current employees of the organization, newly hired employees, or outside consultants.

Who in organizations is responsible for managing change activities? The answer is *change agents*.[1] Change agents can be managers or nonmanagers, current employees of the organization, newly hired employees, or outside consultants.

For major change efforts, internal management will hire the services of outside consultants to provide advice and assistance with major change efforts. Because they are from the outside, these individuals can offer an objective perspective often unavailable to insiders. Outside consultants, however, are disadvantaged because they usually have an inadequate understanding of the organization's history, culture, operating procedures, and personnel. Outside consultants also may be prone to initiating more drastic changes—which can be a benefit or a disadvantage—because they don't have to live with the repercussions after the change is implemented. In contrast, internal staff specialists or managers, when acting as change agents, may be more thoughtful (and possibly more cautious) because they have to live with the consequences of their actions.

Two Views of Change

Simile 1   The organization is like a large ship traveling across the calm Mediterranean Sea to a specific port. The ship's captain has made this exact trip hundreds of times before with the same crew. Every once in a while, however, a storm will appear, and the crew has to respond. The captain will make the appropriate adjustment—that is, implement changes—and, having maneuvered through the storm, will return to calm waters. Implementing change in organizations is seen as a response to a break in the status quo and is needed only in occasional situations.

Simile 2   The organization is more akin to a 40-foot raft than to a large ship. Rather than sailing a calm sea, this raft must traverse a raging river made up of an uninterrupted flow of permanent white-water rapids. To make things worse, the raft is handled by 10 people who have never worked together, and none of them have traveled the river before. Much of the trip is in the dark, the river is dotted by unexpected turns and obstacles, and the exact destination is unclear. At irregular intervals the raft is hauled ashore, where new crew members are added and others leave. Change is a natural state and managing change is a continual process.

These two similes present very different approaches to understanding and responding to change. Let's take a closer look at each one.[2]

The "Calm Waters" Simile   Until very recently, the "calm waters" simile dominated the thinking of practicing managers and academics. It's best illustrated in Kurt Lewin's three-step description of the change process.[3] (See Exhibit 16-2.) According to Lewin, successful change requires *unfreezing* the status quo, *changing* to a new state, and *refreezing* the new change to make it permanent. The status quo can be considered an equilibrium state. Moving from this equilibrium requires unfreezing, which can be achieved in one of three ways:

1. The *driving forces*, which direct behavior away from the status quo, can be increased.
2. The *restraining forces*, which hinder movement from the existing equilibrium, can be decreased.
3. The two approaches can be *combined*.

Once unfreezing has been accomplished, the change itself can be implemented. However, the mere introduction of change does not ensure that it will take hold. The new situation, therefore, needs to be *refrozen* so it can be sustained over time. Unless this last step is attended to, it is very likely that the change will be short-lived and that employees will revert to the previous equilibrium state. The objective of refreezing, then, is to stabilize the new situation by balancing the driving and restraining forces.

Note how Lewin's three-step process treats change as a break in the organization's equilibrium state. The status quo has been disturbed, and change is necessary to establish a new equilibrium state. This view might have been appropriate to the relatively calm

EXHIBIT 16-2   Lewin's Three-Step Change Model

Unfreezing → Changing → Refreezing

environment that most organizations faced 30 or 40 years ago, but one can argue that "calm waters" no longer describe the kind of seas that current managers have to negotiate.

The "White Water Rapids" Simile   The "white-water rapids" simile is consistent with the discussion in Chapter 14 of uncertain and dynamic environments. It is also consistent with the dynamics associated with going from an industrial society to a world dominated by information and ideas.

To get a feeling for what managing change might be like when you have to continuously maneuver in uninterrupted rapids, consider attending a university that has the following curriculum: Courses vary in length. Unfortunately, when you sign up, you don't know how long a course will last. Classes may meet for 2 weeks or 30. Furthermore, the instructor can end a course any time he or she wants, with no prior warning. If that isn't bad enough, the length of the class changes each time it meets—sometimes it lasts 20 minutes, other times it runs for three hours—and determination of the next class's meeting time is set by the instructor during this class. Oh yes, there's one more thing. The exams are all unannounced, so you have to be ready for a test at any time.

To succeed in this university, you'd have to be incredibly flexible and able to respond quickly to every changing condition. Students who were overstructured, rigid, or slow on their feet wouldn't survive.

A growing number of managers are coming to accept that their job is much like what a student would face in such a university. Stability and predictability don't exist. Nor are disruptions in the status quo only occasional and temporary, followed by a return to calm waters. Many of today's managers never get out of the rapids. They face constant change, bordering on chaos. These managers are forced to play a game they've never played before, governed by rules that are created as the game progresses.

Putting the Two Views in Perspective

Does *every* manager face a world of constant and chaotic change? No, but the set of managers who don't is dwindling rapidly.

Managers in businesses such as women's high-fashion clothing have long confronted a world that looks like white-water rapids. They used to look with envy at their counterparts in industries such as auto manufacturing, oil exploration, banking, fast-food restaurants, office equipment, publishing, telecommunications, and air transportation because those managers historically faced a stable and predictable environment. But that's no longer true.

Few organizations today can treat change as the occasional disturbance in an otherwise peaceful world. Even the few do so at great risk. Too much is changing too fast for any organization or its managers to be complacent. As Tom Peters aptly noted, the old saw "If it ain't broke, don't fix it" no longer applies. In its place, he suggests "If it ain't broke, you just haven't looked hard enough. Fix it anyway."[4]

RESISTANCE TO CHANGE

One of the most well-documented findings from studies of individual and organizational behavior is that organizations and their members resist change. In a sense, this is positive: It provides a degree of stability and predictability to behavior. Without any resistance, organizational behavior would take on the characteristics of chaotic randomness. Resistance to change can also be a source of functional conflict. For example, resistance to a reorganization plan or a change in a product line can stimulate a healthy debate over the merits of the idea and result in a better decision. But there is a definite downside to resistance to change. It hinders adaptation and progress.

> —*One of the most well-documented findings from studies of individual and organizational behavior is that organizations and their members resist change.*

People often resist change due to individual reasons, where resistance to change resides in basic human characteristics such as perceptions, personalities, and needs. Perhaps the most obvious individual sources of resistance is *habit*. Every day, when you go to work or school, do you continually use the same route and streets? Probably. If you're like most people, you find a single route and use it regularly. As human beings, we're creatures of habit. Life is complex enough; we don't need to consider the full range of options for the hundreds of decisions we have to make every day. To cope with this complexity, we all rely on habits, or programmed responses. When we are confronted with change, this tendency to respond in our accustomed ways becomes a source of resistance. So when your department is moved to a new office building across town, it means you're likely to have to change many habits: waking up 10 minutes earlier, taking a new set of streets to work, finding a new parking place, adjusting to the new office layout, developing a new lunchtime routine, and so on.

Another individual factor that often leads to resistance to change is *security*. By its very nature, change leads people into the unknown. So, change often threatens our security. When GM announces another major layoff or when Davis Controls, an Ontario-based manufacturer of process-control instrumentation, introduces a new software system, many employees feel insecure—that they may lose their jobs or be unable to learn new skills.

Organizational factors also lead to resistance to change. One major organizational source of resistance is *structural inertia*. Organizations have built-in mechanisms to produce stability:

- The selection process systematically selects certain people in and certain people out.
- Training and other socialization techniques reinforce specific role requirements and skills.
- Formalization provides job descriptions, rules, and procedures for employees to follow.

In short, the people who are hired into an organization are chosen for fit; they are then shaped and directed to behave in certain ways. When an organization is confronted with change, this structural inertia acts as a counterbalance to sustain stability.

Another organizational factor that leads to resistance to change is the *limited focus of change*. Organizations are made up of interdependent subsystems. One can't change without affecting the others. For example, if management changes the technological processes without simultaneously modifying the organization's structure to match, the change in technology is not likely to be accepted. So, limited changes in subsystems tend to get nullified by the larger system.

Overcoming Resistance to Change

While numerous forces act to resist change, change agents can take actions to lessen this resistance. Let's briefly examine five of them:

1. *Education and Communication:* Resistance can be reduced by communicating with employees to help them see the logic of a change. Communication can reduce

resistance on two levels. First, it fights the effects of misinformation and poor communication. If employees receive the full facts and get any misunderstandings cleared up, resistance should subside. Second, communication can be helpful in promoting the need for change. Indeed, research shows that the way the need for change is sold matters: Change is more likely when the necessity of changing is packaged properly.[5]

2. *Participation:* It's difficult for individuals to resist a change decision in which they participated. Prior to making a change, those opposed can be brought into the decision process. Assuming that the participants have the expertise to make meaningful contributions, their involvement can reduce resistance, obtain commitment, and increase the quality of the change decision. However, the disadvantages of this approach include the potential for a poor solution and great consumption of time.

3. *Building Support and Commitment:* Change agents can offer a range of supportive efforts to reduce resistance. When employees' fear and anxiety are high, employee counseling and therapy, new-skills training, or a short paid leave of absence may facilitate adjustment. Research on middle managers has shown that when managers or employees have low emotional commitment to change, they favor the status quo and resist it.[6] So, energizing employees can also help them emotionally commit to the change rather than embrace the status quo.

4. *Selecting People Who Accept Change:* Research suggests that the ability to easily accept and adapt to change is related to personality. It appears that people who adjust best to change are those who are open to experience, take a positive attitude toward change, are willing to take risks, and are flexible in their behavior. One study of managers in the United States, Europe, and Asia found that those with a positive self-concept and high risk tolerance coped better with organizational change. The study authors suggested that organizations could facilitate the change process by selecting people who score high on these characteristics. Another study found that selecting people based on a resistance-to-change scale worked well in winnowing out those who tended to react emotionally to change or to be rigid.[7]

5. *Coercion:* Last on the list of tactics is coercion—that is, the application of direct threats or force on the resisters. If the corporate management really is determined to close a manufacturing plant if employees don't acquiesce to a pay cut, coercion would be the label attached to its change tactic. Other examples of coercion are threats of transfer, loss of promotions, negative performance evaluations, and a poor letter of recommendation. As we learned in Chapter 12, coercion has its limits—used alone, it's likely to harden resistance to change or lead to "hidden revolts."

MANAGING CHANGE THROUGH ORGANIZATIONAL DEVELOPMENT

No discussion of managing change would be complete without including organizational development. **Organizational development (OD)** is not an easily defined or singular concept. Rather, it's a term used to encompass a collection of planned-change interventions built on humanistic–democratic values that seek to improve organizational effectiveness and employee well-being.[8]

The OD paradigm values human and organizational growth, collaborative and participative processes, and a spirit of inquiry.[9] The change agent may be directive in

OD; however, collaboration is strongly emphasized. The following list briefly identifies the underlying values in most OD efforts:

1. *Respect for People:* Individuals are perceived as being responsible, conscientious, and caring. They should be treated with dignity and respect.
2. *Trust and Support:* The effective and healthy organization is characterized by trust, authenticity, openness, and a supportive climate.
3. *Power Equalization:* Effective organizations de-emphasize hierarchical authority and control.
4. *Confrontation:* Problems shouldn't be swept under the rug. They should be openly confronted.
5. *Participation:* The more that people who will be affected by a change are involved in the decisions surrounding that change, the more they will be committed to implementing those decisions.

What are some of the OD techniques or interventions for bringing about change? In the following pages, we present five interventions that change agents might consider using.

Sensitivity Training

It can go by a variety of names—**sensitivity training**, laboratory training, encounter groups, or T-groups (training groups)—but all refer to a method of changing behavior through unstructured group interaction.[10] Members are brought together in a free and open environment in which participants discuss themselves and their interactive processes, loosely directed by a professional behavioral scientist. The group is process oriented, which means that individuals learn through observing and participating rather than from being told. The professional creates the opportunity for participants to express their ideas, beliefs, and attitudes and does not accept—in fact, overtly rejects—any leadership role.

The objectives of T-groups are to provide the subjects with increased awareness of their own behaviors and how others perceive them, greater sensitivity to the behaviors of others, and increased understanding of group processes. Specific results sought include increased ability to empathize with others, improved listening skills, greater openness, increased tolerance of individual differences, and improved conflict-resolution skills.

Survey Feedback

One tool for assessing attitudes held by organizational members, identifying discrepancies among member perceptions, and solving these differences is the **survey feedback** approach.[11]

Everyone in an organization can participate in survey feedback, but of key importance is the organizational family: the manager of any given unit and the employees who report directly to him or her. A questionnaire is usually completed by all members in the organization or unit. Organization members may be asked to suggest questions or may be interviewed to determine what issues are relevant. The questionnaire typically asks members for their perceptions and attitudes on a broad range of topics, including decision-making practices; communication effectiveness;

coordination among units; and satisfaction with the organization, job, peers, and immediate supervisor.

The data from this questionnaire are tabulated with data pertaining to an individual's specific "family" and to the entire organization and then distributed to employees. These data then become the springboard for identifying problems and clarifying issues that may be creating difficulties for people. Particular attention is given to the importance of encouraging discussion and ensuring that discussions focus on issues and ideas and not on attacking individuals.

Finally, group discussion in the survey feedback approach should result in members identifying possible implications of the questionnaire's findings. Are people listening? Are new ideas being generated? Can decision making, interpersonal relations, or job assignments be improved? Answers to questions along these lines, it is hoped, will result in the group agreeing on commitments to various actions that will remedy the problems that are identified.

Process Consultation

No organization operates perfectly. Managers often sense that a unit's performance can be improved, but they're unable to identify what can be improved and how it can be improved. The purpose of **process consultation (PC)** is for an outside consultant to assist a client, usually a manager, "to perceive, understand, and act upon process events" with which the manager must deal.[12] These might include work flow, informal relationships among unit members, and formal communication channels.

PC is similar to sensitivity training in its assumption that organizational effectiveness can be improved by dealing with interpersonal problems and in its emphasis on involvement. But PC is more task directed than is sensitivity training. Consultants in PC are there to "give the client 'insight' into what is going on around him, within him, and between him and other people" and do not solve the organization's problems.[13] Rather, the consultant is a guide or coach who advises on the process to help the client solve his or her own problems. The consultant works with the client in *jointly* diagnosing what processes need improvement. The emphasis is on "jointly" because the client develops a skill at analyzing processes within his or her unit that can be continually called on long after the consultant is gone. In addition, by having clients actively participate in both the diagnosis and the development of alternatives, they will have a greater understanding of the process and the remedy and less resistance to the action plan chosen.

Intergroup Development

A major area of concern in OD is the dysfunctional conflict that exists among groups. As a result, this has been a subject to which change efforts have been directed.

Intergroup development seeks to change the attitudes, stereotypes, and perceptions that groups have of each other. For example, in one company, the engineers saw the accounting department as composed of shy and conservative types and the human resources department as consisting of ultra-liberals more concerned that some protected group of employees might feel hurt than with the company making a profit. Such stereotypes can have an obvious negative impact on the coordination efforts among departments.

Several approaches may improve intergroup relations.[14] A particularly popular method emphasizes problem solving.[15] In this method, each group meets independently to develop lists of its perception of itself, the other group, and how it believes the other group perceives it. The groups then share their lists, after which similarities and differences are discussed. Differences are clearly articulated, and the groups look for the causes of the disparities.

Are the groups' goals at odds? Were perceptions distorted? On what basis were stereotypes formulated? Have some differences been caused by misunderstandings of intentions? Have words and concepts been defined differently by each group? Answers to these questions help clarify the exact nature of the conflict. Once the causes of the difficulty have been identified, the groups can move to the integration phase, beginning with working to develop solutions that will improve relations among the groups. Subgroups, with members from each of the conflicting groups, can now be created for further diagnosis and to begin to formulate possible alternative actions that will improve relations.

Appreciative Inquiry

Most OD approaches are problem centered: They identify a problem or set of problems, then look for a solution. **Appreciative inquiry (AI)** accentuates the positive.[16] Rather than looking for problems to fix, this approach seeks to identify the unique qualities and special strengths of an organization, which can then be built upon to improve performance. That is, it focuses on an organization's successes rather than on its problems.

Advocates of AI argue that problem-solving approaches always ask people to look backward at yesterday's failures, to focus on shortcomings, and rarely result in new visions. Instead of creating a climate for positive change, action research and OD techniques, such as survey feedback and process consultation, end up placing blame and generating defensiveness. AI proponents claim it makes more sense to refine and enhance what the organization is already doing well. This allows the organization to change by playing to its strengths and competitive advantages.

The AI process essentially consists of four steps, often played out in a large-group meeting over a two- or three-day time period, and overseen by a trained change agent. The first step is one of *discovery*. The idea is to find out what people think are the strengths of the organization. Employees are asked to recount times they felt the organization worked best or when they specifically felt most satisfied with their jobs. The second step is *dreaming*. The information from the discovery phase is used to speculate on possible futures for the organization. People are asked to envision the organization in five years and to describe what's different. The third step is *design*. Based on the dream articulation, participants focus on finding a common vision of how the organization will look and then agree on its unique qualities. The fourth stage seeks to define the organization's *destiny*. In this final step, participants discuss how the organization is going to fulfill its dream. This typically includes the writing of action plans and development of implementation strategies.

AI has proven to be an effective change strategy in organizations such as GTE, Roadway Express, and the U.S. Navy. During a recent three-day AI seminar with Roadway employees in North Carolina, workers were asked to recall ideal work experiences—when they were treated with respect, when trucks were loaded to capacity or arrived on time. Assembled into nine groups, the workers were then encouraged to devise money-saving ideas. A team of short-haul drivers came up with 12 cost-cutting and revenue-generating ideas, one alone that could generate $1 million in additional profits.[17]

CONTEMPORARY ISSUES IN ORGANIZATIONAL CHANGE

Next, let's address four contemporary change issues:

1. *How are changes in technology affecting the work lives of employees?*
2. Since change is stressful to most, *how do I reduce stress among my work staff?*
3. *How do managers create organizations that continually learn and adapt?*
4. *Is managing change culture bound?*

Technology in the Workplace

Recent advances in technology are changing the workplace and affecting the work lives of employees. Two specific issues related to process technology and work are *continuous improvement processes* and *process reengineering*.

Continuous Improvement Processes   In Chapter 1, we described quality management as seeking the constant attainment of customer satisfaction through the continuous improvement of all organizational processes. This search for continuous improvement recognizes that *good isn't good enough* and that even excellent performance can, and should, be improved upon. For instance, a 99.9 percent error-free performance sounds like a high standard of excellence. However, it doesn't sound so great when you realize that this standard would result in the United States Postal Service losing 2,000 pieces of mail an hour or two plane crashes a day at O'Hare Airport in Chicago![18] Quality management programs seek to achieve continuous process improvements so that variability is constantly reduced. When you eliminate variations, you increase the uniformity of the product or service. Increasing uniformity, in turn, results in lower costs and higher quality.

—Quality management programs seek to achieve continuous process improvements so that variability is constantly reduced.

As tens of thousands of organizations introduce continuous process improvement, how will employees be affected? They will no longer be able to rest on their previous accomplishments and successes. So, some people may experience increased stress from a work climate that no longer accepts complacency with the status quo. A race with no finish line can never be won—and that's a situation that creates constant tension. This tension may be positive for the organization (remember *functional conflict* from Chapter 13?), but the pressures from an unrelenting search for process improvements can create stress in some employees.

Process Reengineering   We also introduced process reengineering—how you would do things if you could start all over from scratch—in Chapter 1. The term *reengineering* comes from the process of taking apart an electronic product and designing a better version. As applied to organizations, process reengineering means that management should start with a clean sheet of paper—rethinking and redesigning those processes by which the organization creates value and does work, ridding itself of operations that have become antiquated.[19] The three key elements of process reengineering are these:

- Identifying an organization's distinctive competencies
- Assessing core processes
- Reorganizing horizontally by process

An organization's distinctive competencies define what it is that the organization does better than its competition. And, identifying distinctive competencies is so important because it guides decisions regarding what activities are crucial to the organization's success. Dell, for instance, differentiates itself from its competitors by emphasizing high-quality hardware, comprehensive service and technical support, and low prices.

Management also needs to assess the core processes that clearly add value to the organization's distinctive competencies—the processes that transform materials, capital, information, and labor into products and services that the customer values. When the organization is viewed as a series of processes, ranging from strategic planning to after-sales customer support, management can determine to what degree each adds value. This process–value analysis typically uncovers a whole lot of activities that add little or nothing of value and whose only justification is "We've always done it this way."

Process reengineering requires management to reorganize around horizontal processes. This means using cross-functional and self-managed teams. It means focusing on processes rather than functions. It also means cutting out unnecessary levels of middle management.

Process reengineering has been popular since the early 1990s. One of the main consequences has been that many people—especially support staff and middle managers—have lost their jobs. Those employees who keep their jobs after process reengineering have typically found that their jobs are no longer the same. These new jobs typically require a wider range of skills, including more interaction with customers and suppliers, greater challenge, increased responsibilities, and higher pay. However, the three- to five-year period it takes to implement process reengineering is usually tough on employees. They suffer from uncertainty and anxiety associated with taking on new tasks and having to discard long-established work practices and formal social networks.

Work Stress

Most of us are aware that employee stress is an increasing problem in organizations. Friends tell us they're stressed out from greater workloads and having to work longer hours because of downsizing at their company (see Exhibit 16-3). Parents of college students talk about the lack of job stability in today's world and reminisce about a time when a job with a large company implied lifetime security. We read surveys in which employees complain about the *stress* created in trying to balance work and family responsibilities.[20] **Stress** is a dynamic condition in which an individual is confronted with an opportunity, demand, or resource related to what the individual desires and for which the outcome is perceived to be both uncertain and important.[21] This is a complicated definition. Let's look at its components more closely.

EXHIBIT 16-3   Too Much Work, Too Little Time

With companies downsizing workers, those who remain find their jobs are demanding increasing amounts of time and energy. A national sample of U.S. employees finds that they:

Feel overworked	54%
Are overwhelmed by workload	55%
Lack time for reflection	59%
Don't have time to complete tasks	56%
Must multitask too much	45%

Source: Business Week, July 16, 2001, p. 12.

Stress is not necessarily bad in and of itself. Although stress is typically discussed in a negative context, it also has a positive value.[22] It's an opportunity when it offers potential gain. Consider, for example, the superior performance that an athlete or stage performer gives in crucial situations. Such individuals often use stress positively to rise to the occasion and perform at or near their maximum. Similarly, many professionals see the pressures of heavy workloads and deadlines as positive challenges that enhance the quality of their work and the satisfaction they get from their jobs.

In short, some stress can be good, and some can be bad. Recently, researchers have argued that *challenge stress*, or stress associated with challenges in the work environment (such as having lots of projects, assignments, and responsibilities), operates quite differently from *hindrance stress*, or stress that keeps you from reaching your goals (red tape, office politics, confusion over job responsibilities). Although research on challenge and hindrance stress is just starting to accumulate, early evidence suggests that challenge stress has many fewer negative implications than hindrance stress.[23]

More typically, stress is associated with **demands** and **resources**. Demands are responsibilities, pressures, obligations, and even uncertainties that individuals face in the workplace. Resources are matters within an individual's control that can be used to resolve demands. This demands–resources model has received increasing support in the literature.[24]

For example, when you take a test at school or you undergo your annual performance review at work, you feel stress because you confront opportunities and performance pressures. A good performance review may lead to a promotion, greater responsibilities, and a higher salary, but a poor review may prevent you from getting the promotion. An extremely poor review might even result in your being fired. In such a situation, to the extent you can apply resources to the demands—such as being prepared, placing the exam or review in perspective, or obtaining social support—you will feel less stress.

Managing Stress   Not all stress is dysfunctional. Moreover, realistically, stress can never be totally eliminated from a person's life, either off the job or on. As we review stress-reduction techniques, keep in mind that our concern is with reducing the part of stress that is dysfunctional.

In terms of organizational factors, any attempt to lower stress levels has to begin with employee *selection*. Management needs to make sure that an employee's abilities match the requirements of the job. When employees are in over their heads, their stress levels will typically be high. An objective job preview during the selection process will also lessen stress by reducing ambiguity. Improved *organizational communications* will keep ambiguity-induced stress to a minimum. Similarly, a *goal-setting* program will clarify job responsibilities and provide clear performance objectives. *Job redesign* is another way to reduce stress. If stress can be traced directly to boredom or work overload, jobs should be redesigned to increase challenge or reduce the workload. Redesigns that increase opportunities for employees to participate in decisions and to gain social support have also been found to lessen stress.

Stress that arises from an employee's personal life creates two problems. First, it's difficult for the manager to control directly. Second, there are ethical considerations. Specifically, does the manager have any right to intrude—even in the most subtle ways—in the employee's personal life? If a manager believes it is ethical to do so and the employee is receptive, the manager can consider a few approaches. Employee *counseling* can provide stress relief. Employees often want to talk to someone about their problems; and the organization—through its managers, in-house personnel counselors, or free or low-cost outside professional help—can meet that need. For employees whose personal lives suffer from a lack of planning and organization that, in turn, creates stress, the offering of a *time management program* may prove beneficial in helping them sort their priorities. Still another approach is organizationally sponsored *physical activity programs*. Some large corporations employ physical fitness specialists who provide employees with exercise advice, teach relaxation techniques, and show individual employees physical activities they can use to keep their stress levels down.

Creating a Learning Organization

The *learning organization* has recently developed a groundswell of interest from managers and organization theorists looking for new ways to successfully respond to a world of interdependence and change.[25]

What's a Learning Organization?   A **learning organization** is an organization that has developed the continuous capacity to adapt and change. Just as individuals learn, so too do organizations. "All organizations learn, whether they consciously choose to or not—it is a fundamental requirement for their sustained existence."[26] However, some organizations just do it better than others.

Most organizations engage in what has been called **single-loop learning**.[27] When errors are detected, the correction process relies on past routines and present policies. In contrast, learning organizations use **double-loop learning**. When an error is detected, it's corrected in ways that involve the modification of the organization's objectives, policies, and standard routines. Double-loop learning challenges deeply rooted assumptions and norms within an organization. In this way, it provides opportunities for radically different solutions to problems and dramatic jumps in improvement.

Exhibit 16-4 summarizes the five basic characteristics of a learning organization, in which people put aside their old ways of thinking, learn to be open with each other, understand how their organizations really work, form a plan or vision that everyone can agree on, and then work together to achieve that vision.[28]

Proponents of the learning organization envision it as a remedy for three fundamental problems inherent in traditional organizations: fragmentation, competition, and reactiveness.[29]

EXHIBIT 16-4   Characteristics of a Learning Organization

1. There exists a shared vision which everyone agrees on.
2. People discard their old ways of thinking and the standard routines they use for solving problems or doing their jobs.
3. Members think of all organizational processes, activities, functions, and interactions with the environment as part of a system of interrelationships.
4. People openly communicate with each other (across vertical and horizontal boundaries) without fear of criticism or punishment.
5. People sublimate their personal self-interests and fragmented departmental interests to work together to achieve the organization's shared vision.

Source: Based on P. M. Senge, *The Fifth Discipline* (New York: Doubleday, 1990).

1. *Fragmentation* based on specialization creates "walls" and "chimneys" that separate different functions into independent and often warring fiefdoms.

2. An overemphasis on *competition* often undermines collaboration. Members of the management team compete with one another to show who is right, who knows more, or who is more persuasive. Divisions compete with one another when they ought to cooperate and share knowledge. Team project leaders compete to show who is the best manager.

3. *Reactiveness* misdirects management's attention to problem solving rather than creation. The problem solver tries to make something go away, whereas a creator tries to bring something new into being. An emphasis on reactiveness pushes out innovation and continuous improvement and, in its place, encourages people to run around "putting out fires."

It may help to better understand what a learning organization is if you think of it as an *ideal* model that builds on a number of previous OB concepts. No company has successfully achieved all the characteristics described in Exhibit 16-4. As such, you should think of a learning organization as an ideal to strive toward rather than a realistic description of structured activity. Note, too, how learning organizations draw on previously described OB concepts, such as quality management, organizational culture, the boundaryless organization, functional conflict, and transformational leadership. For instance, the learning organization adopts quality management's commitment to continuous improvement. Learning organizations are also characterized by a specific culture that values risk taking, openness, and growth. It seeks boundarylessness through breaking down barriers created by hierarchical levels and fragmented departmentation. A learning organization supports the importance of disagreements, constructive criticism, and other forms of functional conflict. And, transformational leadership is needed in a learning organization to implement the shared vision.

Managing Learning   How do you change an organization to make it into a continual learner? What can managers do to make their firms learning organizations?

- *Establish a strategy.* Management needs to make explicit its commitment to change, innovation, and continuous improvement.
- *Redesign the organization's structure.* The formal structure can be a serious impediment to learning. By flattening the structure, eliminating or combining departments, and

increasing the use of cross-functional teams, interdependence is reinforced and inter-personal boundaries are reduced.

- *Reshape the organization's culture.* As we noted previously, learning organizations are characterized by risk taking, openness, and growth. Management sets the tone for the organization's culture both by what it says (strategy) and what it does (behavior). Managers need to demonstrate by their actions that taking risks and admitting failures are desirable traits. That means rewarding people who take chances and make mistakes. And, management needs to encourage functional conflict. "The key to unlocking real openness at work," says one expert on learning organizations, "is to teach people to give up having to be in agreement. We think agreement is so important. Who cares? You have to bring paradoxes, conflicts, and dilemmas out in the open, so collectively we can be more intelligent than we can be individually."[30]

> —Managers need to demonstrate by their actions that taking risks and admitting failures are desirable traits.

Managing Change: It's Culture Bound

A number of change issues we've discussed in this chapter are culture bound. Consider these five questions:

1. Do people believe change is possible?
2. If it's possible, how long will it take to bring it about?
3. Is resistance to change greater in some cultures than in others?
4. Does culture influence how change efforts will be implemented?
5. Do successful idea champions do things differently in different cultures?

Do people believe change is possible? Remember that cultures vary in terms of beliefs about their ability to control their environments. In cultures in which people believe that they can dominate their environments, individuals will take a proactive view of change. This, for example, would describe the United States and Canada. In many other countries, such as Iran and Saudi Arabia, people see themselves as subjugated to their environments and thus will tend to take a passive approach toward change.

If change is possible, how long will it take to bring it about? A culture's time orientation can help us answer this question. Societies that focus on the long term, such as Japan, will demonstrate considerable patience while waiting for positive outcomes from change efforts. In societies with a short-term focus, such as the United States and Canada, people expect quick improvements and will seek change programs that promise fast results.

Is resistance to change greater in some cultures than in others? Resistance to change will be influenced by a society's reliance on tradition. Italians, for example, focus on the past, whereas Americans emphasize the present. Italians, therefore, should generally be more resistant to change efforts than their American counterparts are.

Does culture influence how change efforts will be implemented? Power distance can help with this issue. In high-power-distance cultures, such as Spain or Thailand, change efforts will tend to be autocratically implemented by top management. In contrast, low-power-distance cultures value democratic methods. We'd predict, therefore, a greater use of participation in countries such as Denmark and the Netherlands.

Do successful idea champions do things differently in different cultures? The evidence indicates that the answer is "Yes."[31] People in collectivist cultures, in contrast to individualistic cultures, prefer appeals for cross-functional support for innovation efforts; people in high-power-distance cultures prefer champions to work closely with those in authority to approve innovative activities before work is conducted on them. The higher the uncertainty avoidance of a society, the more champions should work within the organization's rules and procedures to develop the innovation. These findings suggest that effective managers will alter their organizations' championing strategies to reflect cultural values. So, although idea champions in Russia might succeed by ignoring budgetary limitations and working around confining procedures, champions in Austria, Denmark, Germany, or other cultures high in uncertainty avoidance will be more effective by closely following budgets and procedures.

IMPLICATIONS FOR MANAGERS

The need for change encompasses almost all the concepts within organizational behavior. Think about attitudes, perceptions, teams, leadership, motivation, organizational design, and the like. It's impossible to think about these concepts without inquiring about change.

If environments were perfectly static, if employees' skills and abilities were always up to date and incapable of deteriorating, and if tomorrow were always exactly the same as today, organizational change would have little or no relevance to managers. But, the real world is turbulent, requiring organizations and their members to undergo dynamic change if they are to perform at competitive levels.

In the past, managers could treat change as an occasional disturbance in their otherwise peaceful and predictable world. Such a world no longer exists for most managers. Today's managers are increasingly finding that the world is one of constant and chaotic change. In this world, managers must continually act as change agents.

Epilogue

The end of a book typically has the same meaning to an author that it has to the reader: It generates feelings of both accomplishment and relief. As both of us rejoice at having completed our tour of the essential concepts in organizational behavior, this is a good time to examine where we've been and what it all means.

The underlying theme of this book has been that the behavior of people at work is not a random phenomenon. Employees are complex entities, but their attitudes and behaviors can nevertheless be explained and predicted with a reasonable degree of accuracy. Our approach has been to look at organizational behavior at three levels: the individual, the group, and the organization system.

We started with the individual and reviewed the major psychological contributions to understanding why individuals act as they do. We found that many of the individual differences among employees can be systematically labeled and categorized, and therefore generalizations can be made. For example, we know that individuals with a conventional type of personality are better matched to certain jobs in corporate management than are people with investigative personalities. So placing people into jobs that are compatible with their personality types should result in higher-performing and more satisfied employees.

Next, our analysis moved to the group level. We argued that the understanding of group behavior is more complex than merely multiplying what we know about individuals by the number of members in the group, because people act differently when in a group than when alone. We demonstrated how roles, norms, leadership styles, power relationships, and other similar group factors affect employee behavior.

Finally, we overlaid systemwide variables on our knowledge of individual and group behavior to further improve our understanding of organizational behavior. Major emphasis was given to showing how an organization's structure, design, and culture affect both the attitudes and behaviors of employees.

It may be tempting to criticize the stress this book placed on theoretical concepts. But, as noted psychologist Kurt Lewin is purported to have said, "There is nothing so practical as a good theory." Of course, it's also true that there is nothing so impractical as a good theory that leads nowhere. To avoid presenting theories that led nowhere, this book included a wealth of examples and illustrations. And, we regularly stopped to inquire about the implications of theory for the practice of management. The result has been the presentation of numerous concepts that, individually, offer some insights into behavior, but which, when taken together, provide a complex system to help you explain, predict, and control organizational behavior.

Endnotes

CHAPTER 1

1. Cited in R. Alsop, "Playing Well with Others."

2. *The 2002 National Study of the Changing Workforce* (New York: Families and Work Institute, 2002).

3. I. S. Fulmer, B. Gerhart, and K. S. Scott, "Are the 100 Best Better? An Empirical Investigation of the Relationship Between Being a 'Great Place to Work' and Firm Performance," *Personnel Psychology*, Winter 2003, pp. 965–93.

4. See, for instance, J. E. Garcia and K. S. Keleman, "What Is Organizational Behavior Anyhow?" paper presented at the 16th Annual Organizational Behavior Teaching Conference, Columbia, Missouri, June 1989; and C. Heath and S. B. Sitkin, "Big-B Versus Big-O: What Is *Organizational* About Organizational Behavior?" *Journal of Organizational Behavior*, February 2001, pp. 43–58. For a review of what one eminent researcher believes *should* be included in organizational behavior, based on survey data, see J. B. Miner, "The Rated Importance, Scientific Validity, and Practical Usefulness of Organizational Behavior Theories: A Quantitative Review," *Academy of Management Learning & Education*, September 2003, pp. 250–68.

5. Chris Woodyard, "War, Terrorism Scare Off Business Travelers," *USA Today*, March 25, 2003.

6. See M. E. A. Jayne and R. L. Dipboye, "Leveraging Diversity to Improve Business Performance: Research Findings and Recommendations for Organizations," *Human Resource Management*, Winter 2004, pp. 409–24; S. E. Jackson and A. Joshi, "Research on Domestic and International Diversity in Organizations: A Merger That Works?" in N. Anderson, et al. (eds.), *Handbook of Industrial, Work & Organizational Psychology*, vol. 2 (Thousand Oaks, CA: Sage, 2001), pp. 206–31; and L. Smith, "The Business Case for Diversity," *Fortune*, October 13, 2003, pp. S8–S12.

7. See, for instance, E. Naumann and D. W. Jackson Jr., "One More Time: How Do You Satisfy Customers?" *Business Horizons*, 1999, 42(3), pp. 71–76; W-C. Tsai, "Determinants and Consequences of Employee Displayed Positive Emotions," *Journal of Management*, 27(4), 2001, pp. 497–512; S. D. Pugh, "Service with a Smile: Emotional Contagion in the Service Encounter," *Academy of Management Journal*, October 2001, pp. 1,018–27; M. K. Brady and J. J. Cronin Jr., "Customer Orientation: Effects on Customer Service Perceptions and Outcome Behaviors," *Journal of Service Research*, February 2001, pp. 241–51; and M. Workman and W. Bommer, "Redesigning Computer Call Center Work: A Longitudinal Field Experiment," *Journal of Organizational Behavior*, May 2004, pp. 317–37.

8. See, for instance, S. Armour, "Workers Put Family First Despite Slow Economy, Jobless Fears," *USA Today*, June 6, 2002, p. 3B; V. S. Major, K. J. Klein, and M. G. Ehrhart, "Work Time, Work Interference with Family, and Psychological Distress," *Journal of Applied Psychology*, June 2002, pp. 427–36; D. Brady, "Rethinking the Rat Race," *BusinessWeek*, August 26, 2002, pp. 142–43; J. M. Brett and L. K. Stroh, "Working 61 Plus Hours a Week: Why Do Managers Do It?" *Journal of Applied Psychology*, February 2003, pp. 67–78; and T. A. Judge and J. A. Colquitt, "Organizational Justice and Stress: The Mediating Role of Work–Family Conflict," *Journal of Applied Psychology*, June 2004, pp. 395–404.

9. J. Merritt, "For MBAs, Soul-Searching 101," *BusinessWeek*, September 16, 2002, pp. 64–66; and S. Greenhouse, "The Mood at Work: Anger and Anxiety," *New York Times*, October 29, 2002, p. E1.

CHAPTER 2

1. See, for instance, J. E. Hunter and R. F. Hunter, "Validity and Utility of Alternative Predictors of Job Performance," *Psychological Bulletin*, January 1984, pp. 72–98; and M. J. Ree, T. R. Carretta, and J. R. Steindl, "Cognitive Ability," in N. Anderson, D. S. Ones, H. K. Sinangil, and C. Viswesvaran (eds.), *Handbook of Industrial, Work & Organizational Psychology*, vol. 1 (Thousand Oaks, CA: Sage, 2001), pp. 219–32.

2. J. F. Salgado, N. Anderson, S. Moscoso, C. Bertua, F. de Fruyt, and J. P. Rolland, "A Meta-Analytic Study of General Mental Ability Validity for Different Occupations in the European Community," *Journal of Applied Psychology*, December 2003, pp. 1,068–81; and F. L. Schmidt and J. E. Hunter, "Select on Intelligence," in E. A. Locke (ed.), *Handbook of Principles of Organizational Behavior* (Malden, MA: Blackwell, 2004).

3. J. A. LePine, J. A. Colquitt, and A. Erez, "Adaptability to Changing Task Contexts: Effects of General Cognitive Ability, Conscientiousness, and Openness to Experience," *Personnel Psychology*, 53(3), 2000, pp. 563–593; and J. A. Harris, "Measured Intelligence, Achievement, Openness to Experience, and Creativity," *Personality and Individual Differences*, 36(4), 2004, pp. 913–929.

4. Y. Ganzach, "Intelligence and Job Satisfaction," *Academy of Management Journal*, 41(5), 1998, pp. 526–539; and Y. Ganzach, "Intelligence, Education, and Facets of Job Satisfaction," *Work and Occupations*, 30(1), 2003, pp. 97–122.

5. S. J. Breckler, "Empirical Validation of Affect, Behavior, and Cognition as Distinct Components of Attitude," *Journal of Personality and Social Psychology*, May 1984, pp. 1,191–1,205; and

S. L. Crites Jr., L. R. Fabrigar, and R. E. Petty, "Measuring the Affective and Cognitive Properties of Attitudes: Conceptual and Methodological Issues," *Personality and Social Psychology Bulletin*, December 1994, pp. 619–34.

6. See, for instance, D. J. Schleicher, J. D. Watt, and G. J. Greguras, "Reexamining the Job Satisfaction–Performance Relationship: The Complexity of Attitudes," *Journal of Applied Psychology*, 89(1), 2004, pp. 165–77.

7. See, for instance, M. Geyelin, "Tobacco Executive Has Doubts About Health Risks of Cigarettes," *Wall Street Journal*, March 3, 1998, p. B10; and J. A. Byrne, "Philip Morris: Inside America's Most Reviled Company," *U.S. News & World Report*, November 29, 1999, pp. 176–92.

8. L. Festinger, *A Theory of Cognitive Dissonance* (Stanford, CA: Stanford University Press, 1957).

9. A. W. Wicker, "Attitude Versus Action: The Relationship of Verbal and Overt Behavioral Responses to Attitude Objects," *Journal of Social Issues*, Autumn 1969, pp. 41–78.

10. See S. Sutton, "Predicting and Explaining Intentions and Behavior: How Well Are We Doing?" *Journal of Applied Social Psychology*, August 1998, pp. 1,317–38; and I. Ajzen, "Nature and Operation of Attitudes," in S. T. Fiske, D. L. Schacter, and C. Zahn-Waxler (eds.), *Annual Review of Psychology*, vol. 52 (Palo Alto, CA: Annual Reviews, Inc., 2001), pp. 27–58.

11. D. J. Bem, "Self-Perception Theory," in L. Berkowitz (ed.), *Advances in Experimental Social Psychology*, vol. 6 (New York: Academic Press, 1972), pp. 1–62.

12. See S. E. Taylor, "On Inferring One's Attitudes from One's Behavior: Some Delimiting Conditions," *Journal of Personality and Social Psychology*, January 1975, pp. 126–31; and A. M. Tybout and C. A. Scott, "Availability of Well-Defined Internal Knowledge and the Attitude Formation Process: Information Aggregation Versus Self-Perception," *Journal of Personality and Social Psychology*, March 1983, pp. 474–91.

13. See, for example, S. Rabinowitz and D. T. Hall, "Organizational Research in Job Involvement," *Psychological Bulletin*, March 1977, pp. 265–88; I. M. Paullay, G. M. Alliger, and E. F. Stone-Romero, "Construct Validation of Two Instruments Designed to Measure Job Involvement and Work Centrality," *Journal of Applied Psychology*, 79(2), 1994, pp. 224–28.

14. See, for example, K. W. Thomas and B. A. Velthouse, "Cognitive Elements of Empowerment: An 'Interpretive' Model of Intrinsic Task Motivation," *Academy of Management Review*, 15(4), 1990, pp. 666–81; and S. E. Seibert, S. R. Silver, and W. A. Randolph, "Taking Empowerment to the Next Level: A Multiple-Level Model of Empowerment, Performance, and Satisfaction," *Academy of Management Journal*, 47(3), 2004, pp. 332–49.

15. B. J. Avolio, W. Zhu, W. Koh, and P. Bhatia, "Transformational Leadership and Organizational Commitment: Mediating Role of Psychological Empowerment and Moderating Role of Structural Distance," *Journal of Organizational Behavior*, 25(8), 2004, pp. 951–968.

16. J. M. Diefendorff, D. J. Brown, A. M. Kamin, and R. G. Lord, "Examining the Roles of Job Involvement and Work Centrality in Predicting Organizational Citizenship Behaviors and Job Performance," *Journal of Organizational Behavior*, February 2002, pp. 93–108.

17. G. J. Blau, "Job Involvement and Organizational Commitment as Interactive Predictors of Tardiness and Absenteeism," *Journal of Management*, Winter 1986, pp. 577–84; and M. R. Barrick, M. K. Mount, and J. P. Strauss, "Antecedents of Involuntary Turnover Due to a Reduction in Force," *Personnel Psychology* 47(3), 1994, pp. 515–35.

18. G. J. Blau and K. R. Boal, "Conceptualizing How Job Involvement and Organizational Commitment Affect Turnover and Absenteeism," *Academy of Management Review*, April 1987, p. 290.

19. J. P. Meyer, N. J. Allen, and C. A. Smith, "Commitment to Organizations and Occupations: Extension and Test of a Three-Component Conceptualization," *Journal of Applied Psychology*, 78(4), 1993, pp. 538–51.

20. M. Riketta, "Attitudinal Organizational Commitment and Job Performance: A Meta-Analysis," *Journal of Organizational Behavior*, March 2002, pp. 257–66.

21. See, for instance, J. L. Pierce and R. B. Dunham, "Organizational Commitment: Pre-Employment Propensity and Initial Work Experiences," *Journal of Management*, Spring 1987, pp. 163–78; and T. Simons and Q. Roberson, "Why Managers Should Care About Fairness: The Effects of Aggregate Justice Perceptions on Organizational Outcomes," *Journal of Applied Psychology*, 88(3), 2003, pp. 432–43.

22. R. B. Dunham, J. A. Grube, and M. B. Castañeda, "Organizational Commitment: The Utility of an Integrative Definition," *Journal of Applied Psychology*, 79(3), 1994, pp. 370–80.

23. D. M. Rousseau, "Organizational Behavior in the New Organizational Era," in J. T. Spence, J. M. Darley, and D. J. Foss (eds.), *Annual Review of Psychology*, vol. 48 (Palo Alto, CA: Annual Reviews, 1997), p. 523.

24. See, for example, E. Snape and T. Redman, "An Evaluation of a Three-Component Model of Occupational Commitment: Dimensionality and Consequences Among United Kingdom Human Resource Management Specialists," *Journal of Applied Psychology*, 88(1), 2003, pp. 152–59.

25. L. Rhoades, R. Eisenberger, and S. Armeli, "Affective Commitment to the Organization: The Contribution of Perceived Organizational Support," *Journal of Applied Psychology*, 86(5), 2001, pp. 825–36.

26. D. R. May, R. L. Gilson, and L. M. Harter, "The Psychological Conditions of Meaningfulness, Safety and Availability and the Engagement of the Human Spirit at Work," *Journal of Occupational and Organizational Psychology*, 77(1), 2004, pp. 11–37.

27. J. K. Harter, F. L. Schmidt, and T. L. Hayes, "Business-Unit-Level Relationship Between Employee Satisfaction, Employee Engagement, and Business Outcomes: A Meta-Analysis," *Journal of Applied Psychology*, 87(2), 2002, pp. 268–79.

28. L. Rhoades and R. Eisenberger, "Perceived Organizational Support: A Review of the Literature," *Journal of Applied Psychology*, 87(4), 2002, pp. 698–714.

29. E. Graham, "Work May Be a Rat Race, but It's Not a Daily Grind," *Wall Street Journal*, September 19, 1997, p. R1; and

K. Bowman, "Attitudes About Work, Chores, and Leisure in America," *AEI Opinion Studies*; released August 25, 2003.

30. L. Grant, "Unhappy in Japan," *Fortune*, January 13, 1997, p. 142; "Survey Finds Satisfied Workers in Canada," *Manpower Argus*, January 1997, p. 6; and T. Mudd, "Europeans Generally Happy in the Workplace," *Industry Week*, October 4, 1999, pp. 11–12.

31. W. K. Balzer, J. A. Kihm, P. C. Smith, et al., *Users' Manual for the Job Descriptive Index* (JDI), 1997 Revision, and *The Job in General Scales* (Bowling Green, OH: Bowling Green State University, 1997).

32. T. A. Judge, C. J. Thoresen, J. E. Bono, and G. K. Patton, "The Job Satisfaction–Job Performance Relationship: A Qualitative and Quantitative Review," *Psychological Bulletin*, May 2001, pp. 376–407.

33. J. K. Harter, F. L. Schmidt, and T. L. Hayes, "Business-Unit Level Relationship," Between Employee Satisfaction, Employee Engagement, and Business Outcomes: A Meta-Analysis," *Journal of Applied Psychology*, April 2002, pp. 268–79.

34. See T. S. Bateman and D. W. Organ, "Job Satisfaction and the Good Soldier: The Relationship Between Affect and Employee 'Citizenship,'" *Academy of Management Journal*, December 1983, pp. 587–95.

35. J. A. LePine, A. Erez, and D. E. Johnson, "The Nature and Dimensionality of Organizational Citizenship Behavior: A Critical Review and Meta-Analysis," *Journal of Applied Psychology*, February 2002, pp. 52–65.

36. M. A. Konovsky and D. W. Organ, "Dispositional and Contextual Determinants of Organizational Citizenship Behavior," *Journal of Organizational Behavior*, May 1996, pp. 253–66.

37. See, for instance, J. Griffith, "Do Satisfied Employees Satisfy Customers? Support-Services Staff Morale and Satisfaction Among Public School Administrators, Students, and Parents," *Journal of Applied Social Psychology*, August 2001, pp. 1,627–58.

38. M. J. Bitner, B. H. Booms, and L. A. Mohr, "Critical Service Encounters: The Employee's Viewpoint," *Journal of Marketing*, October 1994, pp. 95–106.

39. See, for instance, R. Steel and J. R. Rentsch, "Influence of Cumulation Strategies on the Long-Range Prediction of Absenteeism," *Academy of Management Journal*, vol. 2: Organizational psychology. Anderson, Neil; Ones, Deniz S.; Sinangil, Handan Kepir; Viswesvaran, Chockalingam; (Thousand Oaks, CA, US: Sage Publications, Inc. 2002), pp. 232–252.

40. F. J. Smith, "Work Attitudes as Predictors of Attendance on a Specific Day," *Journal of Applied Psychology*, February 1977, pp. 16–19.

41. R. W. Griffeth, P. W. Hom, and S. Gaertner, "A Meta-Analysis of Antecedents and Correlates of Employee Turnover: Update, Moderator Tests, and Research Implications for the Next Millennium," *Journal of Management*, 26(3), 2000, p. 479.

42. See, for example, C. L. Hulin, M. Roznowski, and D. Hachiya, "Alternative Opportunities and Withdrawal Decisions: Empirical and Theoretical Discrepancies and an Integration," *Psychological Bulletin*, July 1985, pp. 233–50; and J. M. Carsten and P. E. Spector, "Unemployment, Job Satisfaction, and

Employee Turnover: A Meta-Analytic Test of the Muchinsky Model," *Journal of Applied Psychology*, August 1987, pp. 374–81.

43. D. G. Spencer and R. M. Steers, "Performance as a Moderator of the Job Satisfaction–Turnover Relationship," *Journal of Applied Psychology*, August 1981, pp. 511–14.

44. K. A. Hanisch, C. L. Hulin, and M. Roznowski, "The Importance of Individuals' Repertoires of Behaviors: The Scientific Appropriateness of Studying Multiple Behaviors and General Attitudes," *Journal of Organizational Behavior*, 19(5), 1998.

45. See, for instance, H. M. Weiss, "Learning Theory and Industrial and Organizational Psychology," in M. D. Dunnette and L. M. Hough (eds.), *Handbook of Industrial & Organizational Psychology*, 2nd ed., vol. 1 (Palo Alto: Consulting Psychologists Press, 1990), pp. 172–73.

46. B. F. Skinner, *Contingencies of Reinforcement* (East Norwalk, CT: Appleton-Century-Crofts, 1971).

47. J. A. Mills, *Control: A History of Behavioral Psychology* (New York: New York University Press, 2000).

48. A. Bandura, *Social Learning Theory* (Upper Saddle River, NJ: Prentice Hall, 1977).

49. A. D. Stajkovic and F. Luthans, "A Meta-Analysis of the Effects of Organizational Behavior Modification on Task Performance, 1975–95," *Academy of Management Journal*, October 1997, pp. 1,122–49.

50. E. A. Locke, "Beyond Determinism and Materialism, or Isn't It Time We Took Consciousness Seriously?" *Journal of Behavior Therapy & Experimental Psychiatry*, 26(3), 1995, pp. 265–273.

CHAPTER 3

1. See R. R. McCrae and T. Costa Jr., "Reinterpreting the Myers–Briggs Type Indicator from the Perspective of the Five Factor Model of Personality," *Journal of Personality*, March 1989, pp. 17–40; and N. L. Quenk, *Essentials of Myers–Briggs Type Indicator Assessment* (New York: Wiley, 2000).

2. See, for instance, R. M. Capraro and M. M. Caprano, "Myers–Briggs Type Indicator Score Reliability Across Studies: A Meta-Analytic Reliability Generalization Study," *Educational & Psychological Measurement*, August 2002, pp. 590–602; and R. C. Arnau, B. A. Green, D. H. Rosen, D. H. Gleaves, and J. G. Melancon, "Are Jungian Preferences Really Categorical? An Empirical Investigation Using Taxometric Analysis," *Personality & Individual Differences*, January 2003, pp. 233–51.

3. See, for example, J. M. Digman, "Personality Structure: Emergence of the Five-Factor Model," in M. R. Rosenzweig and L. W. Porter (eds.), *Annual Review of Psychology*, vol. 41 (Palo Alto, CA: Annual Reviews, 1990), pp. 417–40; and T. A. Judge, D. Heller, and M. K. Mount, "Five-Factor Model of Personality and Job Satisfaction: A Meta-Analysis," *Journal of Applied Psychology*, June 2002, pp. 530–41.

4. See, for instance, J. Hogan and B. Holland, "Using Theory to Evaluate Personality and Job-Performance Relations: A Socioanalytic Perspective," *Journal of Applied Psychology*, February 2003, pp. 100–12; and M. R. Barrick and M. K. Mount, "Select on Conscientiousness and Emotional Stability," in E. A. Locke (ed.), *Handbook of Principles of Organizational Behavior* (Malden, MA: Blackwell, 2004), pp. 15–28.

5. P. M. Podsakoff, S. B. MacKenzie, J. B. Paine, and D. G. Bachrach, "Organizational Citizenship Behaviors: A Critical Review of the Theoretical and Empirical Literature and Suggestions for Future Research," *Journal of Management*, 6(3), 2000, pp. 513–63.

6. L. I. Spirling and R. Persaud, "Extraversion as a Risk Factor," *Journal of the American Academy of Child & Adolescent Psychiatry*, 42(2), 2003, p. 130.

7. B. Laursen, L. Pulkkinen, and R. Adams, "The Antecedents and Correlates of Agreeableness in Adulthood," *Developmental Psychology*, 38(4), 2002, pp. 591–603.

8. T. Bogg and B. W. Roberts, "Conscientiousness and Health-Related Behaviors: A Meta-Analysis of the Leading Behavioral Contributors to Mortality," *Psychological Bulletin*, 130(6), 2004, pp. 887–919.

9. M. Tamir and M. D. Robinson, "Knowing Good from Bad: The Paradox of Neuroticism, Negative Affect, and Evaluative Processing," *Journal of Personality & Social Psychology*, 87(6), 2004, pp. 913–25.

10. T. A. Judge and J. E. Bono, "A Rose by Any Other Name. . . Are Self-Esteem, Generalized Self-Efficacy, Neuroticism, and Locus of Control Indicators of a Common Construct?" In B. W. Roberts and R. Hogan (eds.), *Personality Psychology in the Workplace* (Washington, DC: American Psychological Association), pp. 93–118.

11. P. A. Creed, T. D. Bloxsome, and K. Johnston, "Self-Esteem and Self-Efficacy Outcomes for Unemployed Individuals Attending Occupational Skills Training Programs," *Community, Work and Family*, 4(3), 2001, pp. 285–303.

12. J. B. Rotter, "Generalized Expectancies for Internal Versus External Control of Reinforcement," *Psychological Monographs*, 80(609), 1966.

13. T. A. Judge, J. E. Bono, and E. A. Locke, "Personality and Job Satisfaction: The Mediating Role of Job Characteristics," *Journal of Applied Psychology*, 85(2), 2000, pp. 237–49.

14. A. Erez and T. A. Judge, "Relationship of Core Self-Evaluations to Goal Setting, Motivation, and Performance," *Journal of Applied Psychology*, 86(6), 2001, pp. 1,270–79.

15. U. Malmendier and G. Tate, "CEO Overconfidence and Corporate Investment," Research Paper #1799, Stanford Graduate School of Business, http://gobi.stanford.edu/ResearchPapers/detail1.asp?Document_ID=2528, June 2004.

16. R. G. Vleeming, "Machiavellianism: A Preliminary Review," *Psychological Reports*, February 1979, pp. 295–310.

17. R. Christie and F. L. Geis, *Studies in Machiavellianism* (New York: Academic Press, 1970), p. 312; and N. V. Ramanaiah, A. Byravan, and F. R. J. Detwiler, "Revised Neo Personality Inventory Profiles of Machiavellian and Non-Machiavellian People," *Psychological Reports*, October 1994, pp. 937–38.

18. Christie and Geis, *Studies in Machiavellianism*.

19. M. Maccoby, "Narcissistic Leaders: The Incredible Pros, the Inevitable Cons," *Harvard Business Review*, www.maccoby.com/Articles/NarLeaders.html, January–February 2000.

20. W. K. Campbell and C. A. Foster, "Narcissism and Commitment in Romantic Relationships: An Investment Model Analysis," *Personality and Social Psychology Bulletin*, 28(4), 2002, pp. 484–95.

21. T. A. Judge, J. A. LePine, and B. L. Rich, "Loving Yourself Abundantly: Relationship of the Narcissistic Personality to Self and Other Perceptions of Workplace Deviance, Leadership, and Task and Contextual Performance," *Journal of Applied Psychology*, in press.

22. M. Snyder, *Public Appearances/Private Realities: The Psychology of Self-Monitoring* (New York: W. H. Freeman, 1987).

23. D. V. Day, D. J. Schleicher, A. L. Unckless, and N. J. Hiller, "Self-Monitoring Personality at Work: A Meta-Analytic Investigation of Construct Validity," *Journal of Applied Psychology*, April 2002, pp. 390–401.

24. M. Kilduff and D. V. Day, "Do Chameleons Get Ahead? The Effects of Self-Monitoring on Managerial Careers," *Academy of Management Journal*, August 1994, pp. 1,047–60; and A. Mehra, M. Kilduff, and D. J. Brass, "The Social Networks of High and Low Self-Monitors: Implications for Workplace Performance," *Administrative Science Quarterly*, March 2001, pp. 121–46.

25. R. N. Taylor and M. D. Dunnette, "Influence of Dogmatism, Risk-Taking Propensity, and Intelligence on Decision-Making Strategies for a Sample of Industrial Managers," *Journal of Applied Psychology*, August 1974, pp. 420–23.

26. See, for example, W. H. Stewart Jr. and L. Roth, "Risk Propensity Differences Between Entrepreneurs and Managers: A Meta-Analytic Review," *Journal of Applied Psychology*, February 2001, pp. 145–53; and W. H. Stewart Jr. and P. L. Roth, "Data Quality Affects Meta-Analytic Conclusions: A Response to Miner and Raju (2004) Concerning Entrepreneurial Risk Propensity," *Journal of Applied Psychology*, 89(1), 2004, pp. 14–21.

27. N. Kogan and M. A. Wallach, "Group Risk Taking as a Function of Members' Anxiety and Defensiveness," *Journal of Personality*, March 1967, pp. 50–63.

28. M. Friedman and R. H. Rosenman, *Type A Behavior and Your Heart* (New York: Alfred A. Knopf, 1974), p. 84.

29. Ibid., pp. 84–85.

30. K. W. Cook, C. A. Vance, and E. Spector, "The Relation of Candidate Personality with Selection-Interview Outcomes," *Journal of Applied Social Psychology*, 30, 2000, pp. 867–85.

31. S. E. Seibert, M. L. Kraimer, and J. M. Crant, "What Do Proactive People Do? A Longitudinal Model Linking Proactive Personality and Career Success," *Personnel Psychology*, Winter 2001, p. 850.

32. J. M. Crant and T. S. Bateman, "Charismatic Leadership Viewed from Above: The Impact of Proactive Personality," *Journal of Organizational Behavior*, February 2000, pp. 63–75.

33. J. M. Crant, "Proactive Behavior in Organizations," *Journal of Management*, 26(3), 2000, p. 436.

34. J. D. Kammeyer-Mueller and C. R. Wanberg, "Unwrapping the Organizational Entry Process: Disentangling Multiple Antecedents and Their Pathways to Adjustment," *Journal of Applied Psychology*, 88(5), 2003, pp. 779–94.

35. See, for instance, R. R. McCrae, P. T. Costa Jr., T. A. Martin, et al., "Consensual Validation of Personality Traits Across

Cultures," *Journal of Research in Personality*, 38(2), 2004, pp. 179–201.

36. A. T. Church and M. S. Katigbak, "Trait Psychology in the Philippines," *American Behavioral Scientist*, September 2000, pp. 73–94.

37. J. F. Salgado, "The Five Factor Model of Personality and Job Performance in the European Community," *Journal of Applied Psychology*, February 1997, pp. 30–43.

38. P. B. Smith, F. Trompenaars, and S. Dugan, "The Rotter Locus of Control Scale in 43 Countries: A Test of Cultural Relativity," *International Journal of Psychology*, June 1995, pp. 377–400.

39. M. Friedman and R. H. Rosenman, *Type A Behavior and Your Heart*, p. 84.

40. M. Rokeach, *The Nature of Human Values* (New York: Free Press, 1973), p. 5.

41. Ibid., p. 6.

42. For example, see W. C. Frederick and J. Weber, "The Values of Corporate Managers and Their Critics: An Empirical Description and Normative Implications," in W. C. Frederick and L. E. Preston (eds.), *Business Ethics: Research Issues and Empirical Studies* (Greenwich, CT: JAI Press, 1990), pp. 123–44.

43. Ibid.

44. See, for example L. C. Lancaster and D. Stillman, *When Generations Collide* (San Francisco: Jossey-Bass, 2002); and N. Watson, "Generation Wrecked," *Fortune*, October 14, 2002, pp. 183–90.

45. R. E. Hattwick, Y. Kathawala, M. Monipullil, and L. Wall, "On the Alleged Decline in Business Ethics," *Journal of Behavioral Economics*, 18, 1989, pp. 129–43.

46. B. Z. Posner and W. H. Schmidt, "Values and the American Manager: An Update Updated," *California Management Review*, 34(3), 1992, p. 86.

47. See, for instance, G. Hofstede, *Culture's Consequences: Comparing Values, Behaviors, Institutions, and Organizations Across Nations*, 2nd ed. (Thousand Oaks, CA: Sage, 2001). For criticism of this research, see B. McSweeney, "Hofstede's Model of National Cultural Differences and Their Consequences: A Triumph of Faith—a Failure of Analysis," *Human Relations*, 55(1), 2002, pp. 89–118.

48. T. Fang, "A Critique of Hofstede's Fifth National Culture Dimension," *International Journal of Cross-Cultural Management*, 3(3), 2003, pp. 347–68.

49. R. J. House, P. J. Hanges, M. Javidan, and P. W. Dorfman (eds.), *Leadership, Culture, and Organizations: The GLOBE Study of 62 Societies* (Thousand Oaks, CA: Sage, 2004).

50. J. L. Holland, *Making Vocational Choices: A Theory of Vocational Personalities and Work Environments* (Odessa, FL: Psychological Assessment Resources, 1997).

51. See, for example, J. L. Holland, "Exploring Careers with a Typology: What We Have Learned and Some New Directions," *American Psychologist*, April 1996, pp. 397–406; and S. X. Day and J. Rounds, "Universality of Vocational Interest Structure Among Racial and Ethnic Minorities," *American Psychologist*, July 1998, pp. 728–36.

52. See A. L. Kristof-Brown, K. J. Jansen, and A. E. Colbert, "A Policy-Capturing Study of the Simultaneous Effects of Fit with Jobs, Groups, and Organizations," *Journal of Applied Psychology*, October 2002, pp. 985–93; and J. W. Westerman and L. A. Cyr, "An Integrative Analysis of Person–Organization Fit Theories" *International Journal of Selection & Assessment*, 12(4), 2004, pp. 252–61.

53. Based on T. A. Judge and D. M. Cable, "Applicant Personality, Organizational Culture, and Organization Attraction," *Personnel Psychology*, Summer 1997, pp. 359–94.

54. M. L. Verquer, T. A. Beehr, and S. E. Wagner, "A Meta-Analysis of Relations Between Person–Organization Fit and Work Attitudes," *Journal of Vocational Behavior*, 63(3), 2003, pp. 473–89.

55. T. A. Judge and R. Ilies, "Relationship of Personality to Performance Motivation: A Meta-Analytic Review," *Journal of Applied Psychology*, August 2002, pp. 797–807.

CHAPTER 4

1. H. H. Kelley, "Attribution in Social Interaction," in E. Jones et al. (eds.), *Attribution: Perceiving the Causes of Behavior* (Morristown, NJ: General Learning Press, 1972).

2. See A. G. Miller and T. Lawson, "The Effect of an Informational Option on the Fundamental Attribution Error," *Personality and Social Psychology Bulletin*, June 1989, pp. 194–204.

3. See, for instance, M. Goerke, J. Moller, S. Schulz-Hardt, U. Napiersky, and D. Frey, "'It's not My Fault—but Only I Can Change It': Counterfactual and Prefactual Thoughts of Managers," *Journal of Applied Psychology*, April 2004, pp. 279–92.

4. See K. R. Murphy, R. A. Jako, and R. L. Anhalt, "Nature and Consequences of Halo Error: A Critical Analysis," *Journal of Applied Psychology*, April 1993, pp. 218–25; and C. E. Naquin and R. O. Tynan, "The Team Halo Effect: Why Teams Are Not Blamed for Their Failures," *Journal of Applied Psychology*, April 2003, pp. 332–340.

5. J. S. Bruner and R. Tagiuri, "The Perception of People," in E. Lindzey (ed.), *Handbook of Social Psychology* (Reading, MA: Addison-Wesley, 1954), p. 641.

6. J. L. Hilton and W. von Hippel, "Stereotypes," in J. T. Spence, J. M. Darley, and D. J. Foss (eds.), *Annual Review of Psychology*, vol. 47 (Palo Alto, CA: Annual Reviews Inc., 1996), pp. 237–71.

7. See, for example, G. N. Powell, "The Good Manager: Business Students' Stereotypes of Japanese Managers Versus Stereotypes of American Managers," *Group & Organizational Management*, March 1992, pp. 44–56; W. C. K. Chiu, A. W. Chan, E. Snape, and T. Redman, "Age Stereotypes and Discriminatory Attitudes Towards Older Workers: An East–West Comparison," *Human Relations*, May 2001, pp. 629–61; C. Ostroff and L. E. Atwater, "Does Whom You Work with Matter? Effects of Referent Group Gender and Age Composition on Managers' Compensation," *Journal of Applied Psychology*, August 2003, pp. 725–40; and M. E. Heilman, A. S. Wallen, D. Fuchs, and M. M. Tamkins, "Penalties for Success: Reactions to Women Who Succeed at Male Gender-Typed Tasks," *Journal of Applied Psychology*, June 2004, pp. 416–27.

8. See H. A. Simon, "Rationality in Psychology and Economics," *Journal of Business*, October 1986, pp. 209–24; and E. Shafir and R. A. LeBoeuf, "Rationality," in S. T. Fiske, D. L. Schacter, and C. Zahn-Waxler (eds.), *Annual Review of Psychology*, vol. 53 (Palo Alto, CA: Annual Reviews, 2002), pp. 491–517.

9. For a review of the rational model, see E. F. Harrison, *The Managerial Decision-Making Process*, 5th ed. (Boston: Houghton Mifflin, 1999), pp. 75–102.

10. J. G. March, *A Primer on Decision Making* (New York: Free Press, 1994), pp. 2–7; and D. Hardman and C. Harries, "How Rational Are We?" *Psychologist*, February 2002, pp. 76–79.

11. J. E. Perry-Smith and C. E. Shalley, "The Social Side of Creativity: A Static and Dynamic Social Network Perspective" *Academy of Management Review*, January 2003, pp. 89–106.

12. G. J. Feist and F. X. Barron, "Predicting Creativity from Early to Late Adulthood: Intellect, Potential, and Personality," *Journal of Research in Personality*, 37(2), April 2003, pp. 62–88.

13. R. W. Woodman, J. E. Sawyer, and R. W. Griffin, "Toward a Theory of Organizational Creativity," *Academy of Management Review*, April 1993, p. 298; and J. M. George and J. Zhou, "When Openness to Experience and Conscientiousness Are Related to Creative Behavior: An Interactional Approach," *Journal of Applied Psychology*, June 2001, pp. 513–24.

14. This section is based on T. M. Amabile, "Motivating Creativity in Organizations," *California Management Review*, Fall 1997, pp. 42–52.

15. See N. Madjar, G. R. Oldham, and M. G. Pratt, "There's No Place Like Home? The Contributions of Work and Nonwork Creativity Support to Employees' Creative Performance," *Academy of Management Journal*, August 2002, pp. 757–67; and C. E. Shalley, J. Zhou, and G. R. Oldham, "The Effects of Personal and Contextual Characteristics on Creativity: Where Should We Go from Here?" *Journal of Management*, November 2004, pp. 933–58.

16. D. L. Rados, "Selection and Evaluation of Alternatives in Repetitive Decision Making," *Administrative Science Quarterly*, June 1972, pp. 196–206; and G. Klein, *Sources of Power: How People Make Decisions* (Cambridge, MA: MIT Press, 1998).

17. D. Kahneman, "Maps of Bounded Rationality: Psychology for Behavioral Economics," *The American Economic Review*, 93(5), 2003, pp. 1,449–75.

18. See H. A. Simon, *Administrative Behavior*, 4th ed. (New York: Free Press, 1997); and M. Augier, "Simon Says: Bounded Rationality Matters," *Journal of Management Inquiry*, September 2001, pp. 268–75.

19. S. P. Robbins, *Decide & Conquer: Making Winning Decisions and Taking Control of Your Life* (Upper Saddle River, NJ: Financial Times/Prentice Hall, 2004), p. 13.

20. S. Plous, *The Psychology of Judgment and Decision Making* (New York: McGraw-Hill, 1993), p. 217.

21. S. Lichtenstein and B. Fischhoff, "Do Those Who Know More Also Know More About How Much They Know?" *Organizational Behavior and Human Performance*, December 1977, pp. 159–83.

22. B. Fischhoff, P. Slovic, and S. Lichtenstein, "Knowing with Certainty: The Appropriateness of Extreme Confidence,"

Journal of Experimental Psychology: Human Perception and Performance, November 1977, pp. 552–64.

23. J. Kruger and D. Dunning, "Unskilled and Unaware of It: How Difficulties in Recognizing One's Own Incompetence Lead to Inflated Self-Assessments," *Journal of Personality and Social Psychology*, November 1999, pp. 1,121–34.

24. Fischhoff, Slovic, and Lichtenstein, "Knowing with Certainty."

25. Kruger and Dunning, "Unskilled and Unaware of It."

26. See, for instance, A. Tversky and D. Kahneman, "Judgment Under Uncertainty: Heuristics and Biases," *Science*, September 1974, pp. 1,124–31.

27. See E. Jonas, S. Schultz-Hardt, D. Frey, and N. Thelen, "Confirmation Bias in Sequential Information Search After Preliminary Decisions," *Journal of Personality and Social Psychology*, April 2001, pp. 557–71.

28. See B. J. Bushman and G. L. Wells, "Narrative Impressions of Literature: The Availability Bias and the Corrective Properties of Meta-Analytic Approaches," *Personality and Social Psychology Bulletin*, September 2001, pp. 1,123–30.

29. M. Hutton, "Black Youths All but Ignore Tennis, Golf and Swimming as They Eye NBA," *The Post-Tribune*, February 18, 2002.

30. See, for instance, B. M. Staw, "The Escalation of Commitment to a Course of Action," *Academy of Management Review*, October 1981, pp. 577–87; and A. Zardkoohi, "Do Real Options Lead to Escalation of Commitment? Comment," *Academy of Management Review*, January 2004, pp. 111–19.

31. B. M. Staw, "Knee-Deep in the Big Muddy: A Study of Escalating Commitment to a Chosen Course of Action," *Organizational Behavior and Human Performance*, vol. 16, 1976, pp. 27–44.

32. See, for instance, A. James and A. Wells, "Death Beliefs, Superstitious Beliefs and Health Anxiety," *British Journal of Clinical Psychology*, March 2002, pp. 43–53.

33. R. L. Guilbault, F. B. Bryant, J. H. Brockway, and E. J. Posavac, "A Meta-Analysis of Research on Hindsight Bias," *Basic and Applied Social Psychology*, September 2004, pp. 103–17; and L. Werth, F. Strack, and J. Foerster, "Certainty and Uncertainty: The Two Faces of the Hindsight Bias," *Organizational Behavior and Human Decision Processes*, March 2002, pp. 323–41.

34. J. M. Bonds-Raacke, L. S. Fryer, S. D. Nicks, and R. T. Durr, "Hindsight Biases Demonstrated in the Prediction of a Sporting Event," *Journal of Social Psychology*, June 2001, pp. 349–52.

35. As described in H. A. Simon, "Making Management Decisions: The Role of Intuition and Emotion," *Academy of Management Executive*, February 1987, pp. 59–60.

36. See, for instance, W. H. Agor (ed.), *Intuition in Organizations* (Newbury Park, CA: Sage Publications, 1989); D. Myers, *Intuition: Its Powers and Perils;* and L. Simpson, "Basic Instincts," *Training*, January 2003, pp. 56–59.

37. H. Moon, "The Two Faces of Conscientiousness: Duty and Achievement Striving in Escalation of Commitment Dilemmas," *Journal of Applied Psychology*, vol. 86 (2001), pp. 535–40.

38. This section is based on S. Nolen-Hoeksema, J. Larson, and C. Grayson, "Explaining the Gender Difference in Depressive Symptoms," *Journal of Personality & Social Psychology*, November 1999, pp. 1,061–72; S. Nolen-Hoeksema and S. Jackson, "Mediators of the Gender Difference in Rumination," *Psychology of Women Quarterly*, March 2001, pp. 37–47; S. Nolen-Hoeksema, "Gender Differences in Depression," *Current Directions in Psychological Science*, October 2001, pp. 173–76; and S. Nolen-Hoeksema, *Women Who Think Too Much* (New York: Henry Holt, 2003).

39. H. Connery and K. M. Davidson, "A Survey of Attitudes to Depression in the General Public: A Comparison of Age and Gender Differences," *Journal of Mental Health*, 15(2), April 2006, pp. 179–89.

40. M. Elias, "Thinking It Over, and Over, and Over," *USA Today*, February 6, 2003, p. 10D.

41. A. Wildavsky, *The Politics of the Budgetary Process* (Boston: Little, Brown, 1964).

42. N. J. Adler, *International Dimensions of Organizational Behavior*, 4th ed. (Cincinnati, OH: Southwestern, 2002), pp. 182–89.

43. G. F. Cavanagh, D. J. Moberg, and M. Valasquez, "The Ethics of Organizational Politics," *Academy of Management Journal*, June 1981, pp. 363–74.

CHAPTER 5

1. Cited in D. Jones, "Firms Spend Billions to Fire Up Workers—with Little Luck," *USA Today*, May 10, 2001, p. 1A.

2. See, for instance, T. R. Mitchell, "Matching Motivational Strategies with Organizational Contexts," in L. L. Cummings and B. M. Staw (eds.), *Research in Organizational Behavior*, vol. 19 (Greenwich, CT: JAI Press, 1997), pp. 60–62.

3. A. Maslow, *Motivation and Personality* (New York: Harper & Row, 1954).

4. See, for example, E. E. Lawler III and J. L. Suttle, "A Causal Correlation Test of the Need Hierarchy Concept," *Organizational Behavior and Human Performance*, April 1972, pp. 265–87; and J. Rauschenberger, N. Schmitt, and J. E. Hunter, "A Test of the Need Hierarchy Concept by a Markov Model of Change in Need Strength," *Administrative Science Quarterly*, December 1980, pp. 654–70.

5. D. McGregor, *The Human Side of Enterprise* (New York: McGraw-Hill, 1960).

6. F. Herzberg, B. Mausner, and B. Snyderman, *The Motivation to Work* (New York: Wiley, 1959).

7. R. J. House and L. A. Wigdor, "Herzberg's Dual-Factor Theory of Job Satisfaction and Motivations: A Review of the Evidence and Criticism," *Personnel Psychology*, Winter 1967, pp. 369–89; and J. Phillipchuk and J. Whittaker, "An Inquiry into the Continuing Relevance of Herzberg's Motivation Theory," *Engineering Management Journal*, vol. 8, 1996, pp. 15–20.

8. D. C. McClelland, *The Achieving Society* (New York: Van Nostrand Reinhold, 1961); and M. J. Stahl, *Managerial and Technical Motivation: Assessing Needs for Achievement, Power, and Affiliation* (New York: Praeger, 1986).

9. Ibid.

10. J. B. Miner, N. R. Smith, and J. S. Bracker, "Role of Entrepreneurial Task Motivation in the Growth of Technologically Innovative Firms: Interpretations from Follow-up Data," *Journal of Applied Psychology*, October 1994, pp. 627–30.

11. R. E. Boyatzis, "The Need for Close Relationships and the Manager's Job," in D. A. Kolb, I. M. Rubin, and J. M. McIntyre, *Organizational Psychology: Readings on Human Behavior in Organizations*, 4th ed. (Upper Saddle River, NJ: Prentice Hall, 1984), pp. 81–86.

12. D. G. Winter, "The Motivational Dimensions of Leadership: Power, Achievement, and Affiliation," in R. E. Riggio, S. E. Murphy, and F. J. Pirozzolo (eds.), *Multiple Intelligences and Leadership* (Mahwah, NJ: Lawrence Erlbaum, 2002), pp. 119–38.

13. D. McClelland, "Toward a Theory of Motive Acquisition," *American Psychologist*, May 1965, pp. 321–33; and D. Miron and D. C. McClelland, "The Impact of Achievement Motivation Training on Small Businesses," *California Management Review*, Summer 1979, pp. 13–28.

14. See, for example, E. L. Deci, R. Koestner, and R. M. Ryan, "A Meta-Analytic Review of Experiments Examining the Effects of Extrinsic Rewards on Intrinsic Motivation," *Psychological Bulletin*, 125(6), 1999, pp. 627–68; and N. Houlfort, R. Koestner, M. Joussemet, A. Nantel-Vivier, and N. Lekes, "The Impact of Performance-Contingent Rewards on Perceived Autonomy and Competence," *Motivation & Emotion*, 26(4), 2002, pp. 279–95.

15. E. A. Locke and G. P. Latham, "Building a Practically Useful Theory of Goal Setting and Task Motivation: A 35-Year Odyssey," *American Psychologist*, 57(9), 2002, pp. 705–17.

16. J. M. Ivancevich and J. T. McMahon, "The Effects of Goal Setting, External Feedback, and Self-Generated Feedback on Outcome Variables: A Field Experiment," *Academy of Management Journal*, June 1982, pp. 359–72.

17. See, for example, T. D. Ludwig and E. S. Geller, "Assigned Versus Participative Goal Setting and Response Generalization: Managing Injury Control Among Professional Pizza Deliverers," *Journal of Applied Psychology*, April 1997, pp. 253–61; and S. G. Harkins and M. D. Lowe, "The Effects of Self-Set Goals on Task Performance," *Journal of Applied Social Psychology*, January 2000, pp. 1–40.

18. M. Erez, P. C. Earley, and C. L. Hulin, "The Impact of Participation on Goal Acceptance and Performance: A Two-Step Model," *Academy of Management Journal*, March 1985, pp. 50–66.

19. E. A. Locke, "The Motivation to Work: What We Know," *Advances in Motivation and Achievement*, vol. 10, 1997, pp. 375–412; G. P. Latham, M. Erez, and E. A. Locke, "Resolving Scientific Disputes by the Joint Design of Crucial Experiments by the Antagonists," *Journal of Applied Psychology*, 73(4), 1988, pp. 753–72.

20. R. Hollenbeck, C. R. Williams, and H. J. Klein, "An Empirical Examination of the Antecedents of Commitment to Difficult Goals," *Journal of Applied Psychology*, February 1989, pp. 18–23. See also J. E. Bono and A. E. Colbert, "Understanding Responses to Multi-Source Feedback: The Role of Core Self-Evaluations," *Personnel Psychology*, Spring 2005, pp. 171–203.

21. R. E. Wood, A. J. Mento, and E. A. Locke, "Task Complexity as a Moderator of Goal Effects: A Meta Analysis," *Journal of Applied Psychology*, August 1987, pp. 416–25; and A. M. O'Leary-Kelly, J. J. Martocchio, and D. D. Frink, "A Review of the Influence of Group Goals on Group Performance," *Academy of Management Journal*, October 1994, pp. 1,285–301.

22. See, for instance, S. J. Carroll and H. L. Tosi, *Management by Objectives: Applications and Research* (New York, Macmillan, 1973); and R. Rodgers and J. E. Hunter, "Impact of Management by Objectives on Organizational Productivity," *Journal of Applied Psychology*, April 1991, pp. 322–36.

23. See, for instance, R. Rodgers, J. E. Hunter, and D. L. Rogers, "Influence of Top Management Commitment on Management Program Success," *Journal of Applied Psychology*, February 1993, pp. 151–55; and M. Tanikawa, "Fujitsu Decides to Backtrack on Performance-Based Pay," *New York Times*, March 22, 2001, p. W1.

24. A. Bandura, "Cultivate Self-Efficacy for Personal and Organizational Effectiveness," in E. Locke (ed.), *Handbook of Principles of Organizational Behavior* (Malden, MA: Blackwell, 2004), pp. 120–36.

25. A. Bandura and D. Cervone, "Differential Engagement in Self-Reactive Influences in Cognitively-Based Motivation," *Organizational Behavior and Human Decision Processes*, August 1986, pp. 92–113.

26. A. Bandura, *Self-Efficacy: The Exercise of Control* (New York: Freeman, 1997).

27. T. A. Judge, C. L. Jackson, J. C. Shaw, B. Scott, and B. L. Rich, "Is the Effect of Self-Efficacy on Job/Task Performance an Epiphenomenon?" 2005, working paper, University of Florida.

28. J. S. Adams, "Inequity in Social Exchanges," in L. Berkowitz (ed.), *Advances in Experimental Social Psychology* (New York: Academic Press, 1965), pp. 267–300.

29. C. T. Kulik and M. L. Ambrose, "Personal and Situational Determinants of Referent Choice," *Academy of Management Review*, April 1992, pp. 212–37.

30. Ostroff and L. E. Atwater, "Does Whom You Work with Matter? Effects of Referent Group Gender and Age Composition on Managers' Compensation," *Journal of Applied Psychology*, 88(4), 2003, pp. 725–40.

31. Ibid.

32. See, for example, E. Walster, G. W. Walster, and W. G. Scott, *Equity: Theory and Research* (Boston: Allyn & Bacon, 1978); and J. Greenberg, "Cognitive Reevaluation of Outcomes in Response to Underpayment Inequity," *Academy of Management Journal*, March 1989, pp. 174–84.

33. See, for example, R. C. Huseman, J. D. Hatfield, and E. W. Miles, "A New Perspective on Equity Theory: The Equity Sensitivity Construct," *Academy of Management Journal*, April 1987, pp. 222–34; and J. A. Colquitt, "Does the Justice of One Interact with the Justice of Many? Reactions to Procedural Justice in Teams," *Journal of Applied Psychology*, 89(4), 2004, pp. 633–46.

34. See, for instance, J. A. Colquitt, D. E. Conlon, M. J. Wesson, C. O. L. H. Porter, and K. Y. Ng, "Justice at the Millennium: A Meta-Analytic Review of the 25 Years of Organizational Justice Research," *Journal of Applied Psychology*, June 2001, pp. 425–45; and G. P. Latham and C. C. Pinder, "Work Motivation Theory and Research at the Dawn of the Twenty-First Century," *Annual Review of Psychology*, vol. 56 (2005), pp. 485–516.

35. D. P. Skarlicki and R. Folger, "Retaliation in the Workplace: The Roles of Distributive, Procedural, and Interactional Justice," *Journal of Applied Psychology*, 82(3), 1997, pp. 434–43.

36. R. Cropanzano, C. A. Prehar, and P. Y. Chen, "Using Social Exchange Theory to Distinguish Procedural from Interactional Justice," *Group & Organization Management*, 27(3), 2002, pp. 324–51.

37. J. A. Colquitt, D. E. Conlon, M. J. Wesson, C. O. L. H. Porter, and K. Y. Ng, "Justice at the Millennium," pp. 425–45.

38. V. H. Vroom, *Work and Motivation* (New York: John Wiley, 1964).

39. Vroom refers to these three variables as *expectancy*, *instrumentality*, and *valence*, respectively.

40. M. Muchinsky, "A Comparison of Within- and Across-Subjects Analyses of the Expectancy-Valence Model for Predicting Effort," *Academy of Management Journal*, March 1977, pp. 154–58; and C. W. Kennedy, J. A. Fossum, and B. J. White, "An Empirical Comparison of Within-Subjects and Between-Subjects Expectancy Theory Models," *Organizational Behavior and Human Decision Process*, August 1983, pp. 124–43.

41. R. J. House, H. J. Shapiro, and M. A. Wahba, "Expectancy Theory as a Predictor of Work Behavior and Attitudes: A Re-evaluation of Empirical Evidence," *Decision Sciences*, January 1974, pp. 481–506.

42. G. Hofstede, "Motivation, Leadership, and Organization: Do American Theories Apply Abroad?" *Organizational Dynamics*, Summer 1980, p. 55.

43. Ibid.

44. J. K. Giacobbe-Miller, D. J. Miller, and V. I. Victorov, "A Comparison of Russian and U.S. Pay Allocation Decisions, Distributive Justice Judgments, and Productivity Under Different Payment Conditions," *Personnel Psychology*, Spring 1998, pp. 137–63.

45. S. L. Mueller and L. D. Clarke, "Political-Economic Context and Sensitivity to Equity: Differences Between the United States and the Transition Economies of Central and Eastern Europe," *Academy of Management Journal*, June 1998, pp. 319–29.

46. I. Harpaz, "The Importance of Work Goals: An International Perspective," *Journal of International Business Studies*, First Quarter 1990, pp. 75–93.

47. G. E. Popp, H. J. Davis, and T. T. Herbert, "An International Study of Intrinsic Motivation Composition," *Management International Review*, January 1986, pp. 28–35.

CHAPTER 6

1. J. R. Hackman and G. R. Oldham, "Motivation Through the Design of Work: Test of a Theory," *Organizational Behavior and Human Performance*, August 1976, pp. 250–79; and J. R. Hackman and G. R. Oldham, *Work Redesign* (Reading, MA: Addison-Wesley, 1980).

2. See, for example, Y. Fried and G. R. Ferris, "The Validity of the Job Characteristics Model: A Review and Meta-Analysis," *Personnel Psychology*, Summer 1987, pp. 287–322; and T. A. Judge, "Promote Job Satisfaction Through Mental Challenge," in E. A. Locke (ed.), *Handbook of Principles of Organizational Behavior*, pp. 75–89.

3. T. A. Judge, S. K. Parker, A. E. Colbert, D. Heller, and R. Ilies, "Job Satisfaction: A Cross-Cultural Review," in N. Anderson and D. S. Ones (eds.), *Handbook of Industrial, Work and Organizational Psychology*, vol. 2 (Thousand Oaks, CA: Sage Publications, 2002), pp. 25–52.

4. C. A. O'Reilly and D. F. Caldwell, "Informational Influence as a Determinant of Perceived Task Characteristics and Job Satisfaction," *Journal of Applied Psychology*, April 1979, pp. 157–65; R. V. Montagno, "The Effects of Comparison to Others and Prior Experience on Responses to Task Design," *Academy of Management Journal*, June 1985, pp. 491–98; and P. C. Bottger and I. K.-H. Chew, "The Job Characteristics Model and Growth Satisfaction: Main Effects of Assimilation of Work Experience and Context Satisfaction," *Human Relations*, June 1986, pp. 575–94.

5. See, for instance, data on job enlargement described in M. A. Campion and C. L. McClelland, "Follow-up and Extension of the Interdisciplinary Costs and Benefits of Enlarged Jobs," *Journal of Applied Psychology*, June 1993, pp. 339–51.

6. See, for example, R. W. Griffin, "Effects of Work Redesign on Employee Perceptions, Attitudes, and Behaviors: A Long-Term Investigation," *Academy of Management Journal*, 34(2), 1991, pp. 425–35; and J. L. Cotton, *Employee Involvement* (Newbury Park, CA: Sage, 1993), pp. 141–72.

7. From the National Study of the Changing Workforce cited in S. Shellenbarger, "Number of Women Managers Rise," *Wall Street Journal*, September 30, 2003, p. D2.

8. Cited in "Flextime Gains in Popularity in Germany," *Manpower Argus*, September 2000, p. 4.

9. See, for example, D. R. Dalton and D. J. Mesch, "The Impact of Flexible Scheduling on Employee Attendance and Turnover," *Administrative Science Quarterly*, June 1990, pp. 370–87; and B. B. Baltes, T. E. Briggs, J. W. Huff, J. A. Wright, and G. A. Neuman, "Flexible and Compressed Workweek Schedules: A Meta-Analysis of Their Effects on Work-Related Criteria," *Journal of Applied Psychology*, 84(4), 1999, pp. 496–513.

10. Cited in S. Caminiti, "Fair Shares," *Working Woman*, November 1999, pp. 52–54.

11. Ibid., p. 54.

12. Dawson, "Japan: Work-Sharing Will Prolong the Pain," *Business Week*, December 24, 2001, p. 46.

13. See, for example, E. J. Hill, M. Ferris, and V. Martinson, "Does It Matter Where You Work? A Comparison of How Three Work Venues (Traditional Office, Virtual Office, and Home Office) Influence Aspects of Work and Personal/Family Life," *Journal of Vocational Behavior*, 63(2), 2003, pp. 220–41.

14. B. Kurland and D. E. Bailey, "Telework: The Advantages and Challenges of Working Here, There, Anywhere, and Anytime," *Organizational Dynamics*, Autumn 1999, pp. 53–68; and Wells, "Making Telecommuting Work," p. 34.

15. Huws, "Wired in the Country," *People Management*, November 1999, pp. 46–47.

16. Cited in R. W. Judy and C. D'Amico, *Workforce 2020* (Indianapolis: Hudson Institute, 1997), p. 58.

17. Wells, "Making Telecommuting Work."

18. See, for example, S. E. Seibert, S. R. Silver, and W. A. Randolph, "Taking Empowerment to the Next Level: A Multiple-Level Model of Empowerment, Performance, and Satisfaction," *Academy of Management Journal*, 47(3), 2004, pp. 332–49.

19. Robert, T. M. Probst, J. J. Martocchio, R. Drasgow, and J. J. Lawler, "Empowerment and Continuous Improvement in the United States, Mexico, Poland, and India: Predicting Fit on the Basis of the Dimensions of Power Distance and Individualism," *Journal of Applied Psychology*, October 2000, pp. 643–58.

20. Heller, E. Pusic, G. Strauss, and B. Wilpert, *Organizational Participation: Myth and Reality* (Oxford: Oxford University Press, 1998).

21. See, for instance, J. A. Wagner III, "Participation's Effects on Performance and Satisfaction: A Reconsideration of Research Evidence," *Academy of Management Review*, April 1994, pp. 312–30; J. A. Wagner III, C. R. Leana, E. A. Locke, and D. M. Schweiger, "Cognitive and Motivational Frameworks in U.S. Research on Participation: A Meta-Analysis of Primary Effects," *Journal of Organizational Behavior*, vol. 18, 1997, pp. 49–65; and J. A. Wagner III and J. A. LePine, "Effects of Participation on Performance and Satisfaction: Additional Meta-Analytic Evidence," *Psychological Reports*, June 1999, pp. 719–25.

22. Cotton, Employee Involvement, p. 114.

23. See, for example, M. Gilman and P. Marginson, "Negotiating European Works Council: Contours of Constrained Choice," *Industrial Relations Journal*, March 2002, pp. 36–51; and B. Keller, "The European Company Statute: Employee Involvement—and Beyond," *Industrial Relations Journal*, December 2002, pp. 424–45.

24. Cotton, *Employee Involvement*, pp. 129–30, 139–40.

25. Ibid., p. 140.

26. P. S. Goodman and P. P. Pan, "Chinese Workers Pay for Wal-Mart's Low Prices," *Washington Post*, February 8, 2004, p. A01.

27. W. Zellner, "Trickle-Down Is Trickling Down at Work," *Business Week*, March 18, 1996, p. 34; and "Linking Pay to Performance Is Becoming a Norm in the Workplace," *Wall Street Journal*, April 6, 1999, p. A1.

28. L. Wiener, "Paycheck Plus," *U.S. News & World Report*, February 24/March 3, 2003, p. 58.

29. Cited in "Pay Programs: Few Employees See the Pay-for-Performance Connection," *Compensation & Benefits Report*, June 2003, p. 1.

30. B. Wysocki Jr., "Chilling Reality Awaits Even the Employed," *Wall Street Journal*, November 5, 2001, p. A1.

31. S. L. Rynes, B. Gerhart, and L. Parks, "Personnel Psychology: Performance Evaluation and Pay for Performance," *Annual Review of Psychology*, 56(3), 2005, pp. 571–600.

32. C. M. DiMassa and J. Rubin, "Teachers Unions Blast Governor's Merit Pay Plan," *Los Angeles Times*, January 10, 2005. 2005, at http://www.latimes.com/news/local/la-me-merit10jan10.story.

33. L. Lavelle, "Executive Pay," *Business Week*, April 16, 2001, p. 77.

34. See, for instance, M. Reynolds, "A Cost-Reduction Strategy That May Be Back," *Healthcare Financial Management*, January 2002, pp. 58–64; and M. R. Dixon, L. J. Hayes, and J. Stack, "Changing Conceptions of Employee Compensation," *Journal of Organizational Behavior Management*, 23(2–3), 2003, pp. 95–116.

35. "U.S. Wage and Productivity Growth Attainable Through Gainsharing," Employment Policy Foundation. Accessed May 10, 2000, at http://www.epf.org.

36. "The Employee Ownership 100." Accessed July 2003 at http://www.nceo.org.

37. Cited in K. Frieswick, "ESOPs: Split Personality," *CFO*, July 7, 2003, p. 1.

38. A. A. Buchko, "The Effects of Employee Ownership on Employee Attitudes.

39. C. M. Rosen and M. Quarrey, "How Well Is Employee Ownership Working?" *Harvard Business Review*, September–October 1987, pp. 126–32.

40. Cited in "ESOP Benefits Are No Fables," *Business Week*, September 6, 1999, p. 26.

41. W. N. Davidson and D. L. Worrell, "ESOP's Fables: The Influence of Employee Stock Ownership Plans on Corporate Stock Prices and Subsequent Operating Performance," *Human Resource Planning*, January 1994, pp. 69–85.

42. See data in D. Stamps, "A Piece of the Action," *Training*, March 1996, p. 66.

43. M. Magnan and S. St-Onge, "Profit-Sharing and Firm Performance: A Comparative and Longitudinal Analysis," paper presented at the 58th Annual Meeting of the Academy of Management, San Diego, August 1998; and D. D'Art, and T. Turner, "Profit Sharing, Firm Performance, and Union Influence in Selected European Countries," *Personnel Review*, 33(3), 2004, pp. 335–50.

44. T. M. Welbourne and L. R. Gomez-Mejia, "Gainsharing: A Critical Review and a Future Research Agenda," *Journal of Management*, 21(3), 1995, pp. 559–609.

45. C. Lee, K. S. Law, and P. Bobko, "The Importance of Justice Perceptions on Pay Effectiveness: A Two-Year Study of a Skill-Based Pay Plan," *Journal of Management*, 25(6), 1999, pp. 851–73; A. Podolske, "Seven-Year Update on Skill-Based Pay Plans." Accessed July 1999, at http://www.ioma.com.

46. Lawler, Ledford, and Chang, "Who Uses Skill-Based Pay, and Why."

47. M. Rowland, "It's What You Can Do That Counts," *New York Times*, June 6, 1993, p. F17.

48. Ibid.

49. D. A. DeCenzo and S. P. Robbins, *Human Resource Management*, 7th ed. (New York: Wiley, 2002), pp. 346–48.

50. E. Unsworth, "U.K. Employers Find Flex Benefits Helpful: Survey," *Business Insurance*, May 21, 2001, pp. 19–20.

51. Our definition of a formal recognition system is based on S. E. Markham, K. D. Scott, and G. H. McKee, "Recognizing Good Attendance: A Longitudinal, Quasi-Experimental Field Study," *Personnel Psychology*, Autumn 2002, p. 641.

52. D. Drickhamer, "Best Plant Winners: Nichols Foods Ltd.," *Industry Week*, October 1, 2001, pp. 17–19.

53. M. Littman, "Best Bosses Tell All," *Working Woman*, October 2000, p. 54.

54. Cited in S. Caudron, "The Top 20 Ways to Motivate Employees," *Industry Week*, April 3, 1995, pp. 15–16. See also B. Nelson, "Try Praise," *INC.*, September 1996, p. 115.

55. Cited in K. J. Dunham, "Amid Shrinking Workplace Morale, Employers Turn to Recognition," *Wall Street Journal*, November 19, 2002, p. B8.

CHAPTER 7

1. See, for instance, N. M. Ashkanasy and C. S. Daus, "Emotion in the Workplace: The New Challenge for Managers," *Academy of Management Executive*, February 2002, pp. 76–86; and N. M. Ashkanasy, C. E. J. Hartel, and C. S. Daus, "Diversity and Emotion: The New Frontiers in Organizational Behavior Research," *Journal of Management*, 28(3), 2002, pp. 307–38.

2. See, for example, L. L. Putnam and D. K. Mumby, "Organizations, Emotion and the Myth of Rationality," in S. Fineman (ed.), *Emotion in Organizations* (Thousand Oaks, CA: Sage, 1993), pp. 36–57.

3. B. E. Ashforth and R. H. Humphrey, "Emotion in the Workplace: A Reappraisal," *Human Relations*, February 1995, pp. 97–125.

4. J. M. George, "Trait and State Affect," in K. R. Murphy (ed.), *Individual Differences and Behavior in Organizations* (San Francisco: Jossey-Bass, 1996), p. 145.

5. See N. H. Frijda, "Moods, Emotion Episodes and Emotions," in M. Lewis and J. M. Haviland (eds.), *Handbook of Emotions* (New York: Guilford Press, 1993), pp. 381–403.

6. H. M. Weiss and R. Cropanzano, "Affective Events Theory: A Theoretical Discussion of the Structure, Causes and Consequences of Affective Experiences at Work," in B. M. Staw and L. L. Cummings (eds.), *Research in Organizational Behavior*, vol. 18 (Greenwich, CT: JAI Press, 1996), pp. 17–19.

7. See P. Ekman and R. J. Davidson (eds.), *The Nature of Emotions: Fundamental Questions* (Oxford, England: Oxford University Press, 1994).

8. Frijda, "Moods, Emotion Episodes and Emotions," p. 381.

9. See Ekman and Davidson (eds.), *The Nature of Emotions*.

10. J. Nolte, *The Human Brain*, 5th ed. (St. Louis: Mosby, 2002).

11. D. M. Tucker, P. Luu, G. Frishkoff, J. Quiring, and C. Poulsen, "Frontolimbic Response to Negative Feedback in Clinical Depression," *Journal of Abnormal Psychology*, 112(4), November 2003, pp. 667–78.

12. R. C. Gur, F. Gunning-Dixon, W. B. Bilker, and R. E. Gur, "Sex Differences in Temporo-Limbic and Frontal Brain Volumes of Healthy Adults," *Cerebral Cortex*, 12(9), September 2002, pp. 998–1,003.

13. L. M. Poverny and S. Picascia, "There is No Crying in Business." Accessed June 2006, at http://www.womensmedia.com/new/Crying-at-Work.shtml.

14. L. P. Frankel, *Nice Girls Don't Get the Corner Office* (New York: Warner Books, 2004).

15. A. R. Damasio, *Descartes' Error: Emotion, Reason, and the Human Brain* (New York: Quill, 1994).

16. L. Cosmides and J. Tooby, "Evolutionary Psychology and the Emotions," in M. Lewis and J. M. Haviland-Jones (eds.), *Handbook of Emotions*, 2nd ed. (New York: Guilford Press, 2000), pp. 91–115.

17. D. M. Buss, "Cognitive Biases and Emotional Wisdom in the Evolution of Conflict Between the Sexes," *Current Directions in Psychological Science*, 10(6), December 2001, pp. 219–23.

18. K. N. Laland and G. R. Brown, *Sense and Nonsense: Evolutionary Perspectives on Human Behaviour* (Oxford, England: Oxford University Press, 2002).

19. R. J. Larsen and E. Diener, "Affect Intensity as an Individual Difference Characteristic: A Review," *Journal of Research in Personality*, vol. 21, 1987, pp. 1–39.

20. D. Watson, *Mood and Temperament* (New York: Guilford Publications, 2000).

21. Ibid.

22. Ibid., p. 100.

23. J. A. Fuller, J. M. Stanton, G. G. Fisher, C. Spitzmüller, S. S. Russell, and P. C. Smith, "A Lengthy Look at the Daily Grind: Time Series Analysis of Events, Mood, Stress, and Satisfaction," *Journal of Applied Psychology*, 88(6), December 2003, pp. 1,019–33.

24. A. M. Isen, "Positive Affect as a Source of Human Strength," in L.G. Aspinwall and U. Staudinger (eds.), *The Psychology of Human Strengths* (Washington, DC: American Psychological Association, 2003), pp. 179–195.

25. Watson, *Mood and Temperament*.

26. H. S. Friedman, J. S. Tucker, J. E. Schwartz, C. Tomlinson-Keasey, et al., "Psychosocial and Behavioral Predictors of Longevity: The Aging and Death of the 'Termites,'" *American Psychologist*, 50(2), February 1995, pp. 69–78.

27. *Sleep in America Poll* (Washington, DC: National Sleep Foundation, 2005).

28. M. Lavidor, A. Weller, and H. Babkoff, "How Sleep Is Related to Fatigue," *British Journal of Health Psychology*, vol. 8 (2003), pp. 95–105; and J. J. Pilcher and E. Ott, "The Relationships Between Sleep and Measures of Health and Well-Being in College Students: A Repeated Measures Approach," *Behavioral Medicine*, vol. 23 (1998), pp. 170–78.

29. E. K. Miller and J. D. Cohen, "An Integrative Theory of Prefrontal Cortex Function," *Annual Review of Neuroscience*, vol. 24 (2001), pp. 167–202.

30. B. A. Scott and T. A. Judge, "Tired and Cranky?: The Effects of Sleep Quality on Employee Emotions and Job Satisfaction," Working paper, Department of Management, University of Florida, 2005.

31. P. R. Giacobbi, H. A. Hausenblas, and N. Frye, "A Naturalistic Assessment of the Relationship Between Personality, Daily Life Events, Leisure-Time Exercise, and Mood," *Psychology of Sport & Exercise*, 6(1), January 2005, pp. 67–81.

32. L. L. Carstensen, M. Pasupathi, M. Ulrich, and J. R. Nesselroade, "Emotional Experience in Everyday Life Across the Adult Life Span," *Journal of Personality and Social Psychology*, 79(4), 2000, pp. 644–55.

33. K. Deaux, "Sex Differences," in M. R. Rosenzweig and L. W. Porter (eds.), *Annual Review of Psychology*, vol. 26 (Palo Alto, CA: Annual Reviews, 1985), pp. 48–82; and A. M. Kring and A. H. Gordon, "Sex Differences in Emotion: Expression, Experience, and Physiology," *Journal of Personality and Social Psychology*, March 1998, pp. 686–703.

34. M. Grossman and W. Wood, "Sex Differences in Intensity of Emotional Experience: A Social Role Interpretation," *Journal of Personality and Social Psychology*, November 1992, pp. 1,010–22.

35. J. A. Hall, *Nonverbal Sex Differences: Communication Accuracy and Expressive Style* (Baltimore, MD: Johns Hopkins Press, 1984).

36. A. Hochschild, *The Second Shift* (New York: Viking, 1989); and F. M. Deutsch, "Status, Sex, and Smiling: The Effect of Role on Smiling in Men and Women," *Personality and Social Psychology Bulletin*, September 1990, pp. 531–40.

37. L. W. Hoffman, "Early Childhood Experiences and Women's Achievement Motives," *Journal of Social Issues* 28(2), 1972, pp. 129–55.

38. Ashforth and Humphrey, "Emotion in the Workplace," p. 104.

39. M. Eid and E. Diener, "Norms for Experiencing Emotions in Different Cultures: Inter- and Intranational Differences," *Journal of Personality and Social Psychology*, 81(5), 2001, pp. 869–85.

40. Ibid.

41. Ibid.

42. B. Mesquita, "Emotions in Collectivist and Individualist Contexts," *Journal of Personality and Social Psychology*, 80(1), 2001, pp. 68–74.

43. R. I. Levy, *Tahitians: Mind and Experience in the Society Islands* (Chicago: University of Chicago Press, 1973).

44. D. Matsumoto, "Cross-Cultural Psychology in the 21st Century." Accessed at http://teachpsych.lemoyne.edu/teachpsych/faces/script/Ch05.htm.

45. See J. A. Morris and D. C. Feldman, "Managing Emotions in the Workplace," *Journal of Managerial Issues*, 9(3), 1997, pp. 257–74; and S. M. Kruml and D. Geddes, "Catching Fire Without Burning Out: Is There an Ideal Way to Perform Emotion Labor?" in N. M. Ashkansay, C. E. J. Hartel, and W. J. Zerbe, *Emotions in the Workplace* (New York: Quorum Books, 2000), pp. 177–88.

46. P. Ekman, W. V. Friesen, and M. O'Sullivan, "Smiles When Lying," in P. Ekman and E. L. Rosenberg (eds.), *What the Face Reveals: Basic and Applied Studies of Spontaneous Expression Using the Facial Action Coding System (FACS)* (London: Oxford University Press, 1997), pp. 201–16.

47. R. Cropanzano, D. E. Rupp, and Z. S. Byrne, "The Relationship of Emotional Exhaustion to Work Attitudes, Job

Performance, and Organizational Citizenship Behavior," *Journal of Applied Psychology*, February 2003, pp. 160–69.

48. A. R. Hochschild, "Emotion Work, Feeling Rules, and Social Structure," *American Journal of Sociology*, November 1979, pp. 551–75; and J. M. Diefendorff and E. M. Richard, "Antecedents and Consequences of Emotional Display Rule Perceptions," *Journal of Applied Psychology*, April 2003, pp. 284–94.

49. R. C. Solomon, "Back to Basics: On the Very Idea of Basic Emotions," *Journal for the Theory of Social Behaviour*, 32(2), June 2002, pp. 115–44.

50. C. M. Brotheridge and R. T. Lee, "Development and Validation of the Emotional Labour Scale," *Journal of Occupational & Organizational Psychology*, 76(3), September 2003, pp. 365–79.

51. A. A. Grandey, D. N. Dickter, and H. Sin, "The Customer Is Not Always Right: Customer Aggression and Emotion Regulation of Service Employees," *Journal of Organizational Behavior*, 25(3), May 2004, pp. 397–418.

52. A. Rafaeli and R. I. Sutton, "The Expression of Emotion in Organizational Life," in L. L. Cummings and B. M. Staw (eds.), *Research in Organizational Behavior*, vol. 11 (Greenwich, CT: JAI Press, 1989), p. 8.

53. A. Rafaeli, "When Cashiers Meet Customers: An Analysis of Supermarket Cashiers," *Academy of Management Journal*, June 1989, pp. 245–73.

54. D. Rubin, "Grumpy German Shoppers Distrust the Wal-Mart Style," *Seattle Times*, December 30, 2001, p. A15.

55. See, for example, Daniel Goleman, *Emotional Intelligence* (New York: Bantam, 1995); M. Davies, L. Stankov, and R. D. Roberts, "Emotional Intelligence: In Search of an Elusive Construct," *Journal of Personality and Social Psychology*, October 1998, pp. 989–1,015; and J. Ciarrochi, J. P. Forgas, and J. D. Mayer (eds.), *Emotional Intelligence in Everyday Life* (Philadelphia: Psychology Press, 2001).

56. F. I. Greenstein, *The Presidential Difference: Leadership Style from FDR to Clinton* (Princeton, NJ: Princeton University Press, 2001).

57. C. Cherniss, "The Business Case for Emotional Intelligence," Consortium for Research on Emotional Intelligence in Organizations. Accessed November 19, 2006, at http://www.eiconsortium.org/research/business_case_for_ei.pdf.

58. D. L. Van Rooy and C. Viswesvaran, "Emotional Intelligence: A Meta-Analytic Investigation of Predictive Validity and Nomological Net," *Journal of Vocational Behavior*, 65(1), August 2004, pp. 71–95.

59. R. Bar-On, D. Tranel, N. L. Denburg, and A. Bechara, "Exploring the Neurological Substrate of Emotional and Social Intelligence," *Brain*, 126(8), August 2003, pp. 1,790–1,800.

60. E. A. Locke, "Why Emotional Intelligence Is an Invalid Concept," *Journal of Organizational Behavior*, 26(4), June 2005, pp. 425–31.

61. J. M. Conte, "A Review and Critique of Emotional Intelligence Measures," *Journal of Organizational Behavior*, 26(4), June 2005, pp. 433–40.

62. T. Decker, "Is Emotional Intelligence a Viable Concept?" *Academy of Management Review*, 28, no. 2 (April 2003), pp. 433–40; and Davies, Stankov, and Roberts, "Emotional Intelligence."

63. F. J. Landy, "Some Historical and Scientific Issues Related to Research on Emotional Intelligence," *Journal of Organizational Behavior*, 26(4), June 2005, pp. 411–24.

64. L. M. J. Spencer, D. C. McClelland, and S. Kelner, *Competency Assessment Methods: History and State of the Art* (Boston: Hay/McBer, 1997).

65. L. B. Alloy and L. Y. Abramson, "Judgement of Contingency in Depressed and Nondepressed Students: Sadder but Wiser?" *Journal of Experimental Psychology: General*, vol. 108, 1979, pp. 441–85.

66. N. Ambady and H. M. Gray, "On Being Sad and Mistaken: Mood Effects on the Accuracy of Thin-Slice Judgments," *Journal of Personality and Social Psychology*, 83(4), 2002, pp. 947–61.

67. See, for example, A. M. Isen, "Positive Affect and Decision Making," in M. Lewis and J. M. Haviland-Jones (eds.), *Handbook of Emotions*, 2nd ed. (New York: Guilford, 2000), pp. 261–77.

68. J. Park and M. R. Banaji, "Mood and Heuristics: The Influence of Happy and Sad States on Sensitivity and Bias in Stereotyping," *Journal of Personality and Social Psychology*, 78(6), 2000, pp. 1,005–23.

69. See, for example, M. A. Mumford, "Where Have We Been, Where Are We Going? Taking Stock in Creativity Research," *Creativity Research Journal*, vol. 15, 2003, pp. 107–20.

70. M. J. Grawitch, D. C. Munz, and E. K. Elliott, "Promoting Creativity in Temporary Problem-Solving Groups: The Effects of Positive Mood and Autonomy in Problem Definition on Idea-Generating Performance," *Group Dynamics*, 7(3), September 2003, pp. 200–13.

71. N. Madjar, G. R. Oldham, and M. G. Pratt, "There's No Place Like Home? The Contributions of Work and Nonwork Creativity Support to Employees' Creative Performance," *Academy of Management Journal*, 45(4), 2002, pp. 757–67.

72. J. M. George and J. Zhou, "Understanding when Bad Moods Foster Creativity and Good Ones Don't: The Role of Context and Clarity of Feelings," *Journal of Applied Psychology*, 87(4), August 2002, pp. 687–97.

73. A. Erez and A. M. Isen, "The Influence of Positive Affect on the Components of Expectancy Motivation," *Journal of Applied Psychology*, 87(6), 2002, pp. 1,055–67.

74. Remus Ilies and T. A. Judge, "Goal Regulation Across Time: The Effect of Feedback and Affect," *Journal of Applied Psychology*, 90(3), May 2005, pp. 453–467.

75. K. M. Lewis, "When Leaders Display Emotion: How Followers Respond to Negative Emotional Expression of Male and Female Leaders," *Journal of Organizational Behavior*, March 2000, pp. 221–34.

76. George, "Trait and State Affect," p. 162.

77. Ashforth and Humphrey, "Emotion in the Workplace," p. 116.

78. N. Reynolds, "Whiz-Kids Gamble on TV Channel for Poker." Accessed april 16, 2005, at http://www.telegraph.co.uk/news/main.jhtml?xml=/news/2005/04/16/npoke16.xml.

79. See, for example, G. A. Van Kleef, C. K. W. De Dreu, and A. S. R. Manstead, "The Interpersonal Effects of Anger and Happiness in Negotiations," *Journal of Personality and Social Psychology*, 86(1), 2004, pp. 57–76.

80. K. M. O'Connor and J. A. Arnold, "Distributive Spirals: Negotiation Impasses and the Moderating Role of Disputant Self-Efficacy," *Organizational Behavior and Human Decision Processes*, 84(1), 2001, pp. 148–76.

81. B. Shiv, G. Loewenstein, A. Bechara, H. Damasio, and A. R. Damasio, "Investment Behavior and the Negative Side of Emotion," *Psychological Science*, 16(6), 2005, pp. 435–439.

82. G. F. Will, "Solidarity Isn't Forever," *Washington Post*, September 16, 2005, p. A31.

83. W-C. Tsai and Y-M. Huang, "Mechanisms Linking Employee Affective Delivery and Customer Behavioral Intentions," *Journal of Applied Psychology*, October 2002, pp. 1,001–08.

84. A. A. Grandey, "When 'The Show Must Go On': Surface Acting and Deep Acting as Determinants of Emotional Exhaustion and Peer-Rated Service Delivery," *Academy of Management Journal*, February 2003, pp. 86–96.

85. See E. Hatfield, J. T. Cacioppo, and R. L. Rapson, *Emotional Contagion* (Cambridge, England: Cambridge University Press, 1994).

86. W. Tasi and Y. Huang, "Mechanisms Linking Employee Affective Delivery and Customer Behavioral Intentions."

87. R. Ilies and T. A. Judge, "Understanding the Dynamic Relationships Among Personality, Mood, and Job Satisfaction: A Field Experience Sampling Study," *Organizational Behavior and Human Decision Processes*, vol. 89, 2002, pp. 1,119–39.

88. R. Rau and A. Triemer, "Overtime in Relation to Blood Pressure and Mood During Work, Leisure, and Night Time," *Social Indicators Research*, 67(1–2), June 2004, pp. 51–73.

89. T. A. Judge and R. Ilies, "Affect and Job Satisfaction: A Study of Their Relationship at Work and at Home," *Journal of Applied Psychology*, vol. 89, 2004) pp. 661–73.

90. A. G. Bedeian, "Workplace Envy," *Organizational Dynamics*, Spring 1995, p. 50; and A. Ben-Ze'ev, *The Subtlety of Emotions* (Cambridge, MA: MIT Press, 2000), pp. 281–326.

91. Bedeian, "Workplace Envy," p. 54.

92. T. A. Judge, B. A. Scott, and R. Ilies, "Hostility, Job Attitudes, and Workplace Deviance: Test of a Multilevel Model," *Journal of Applied Psychology*, vol. 91, 2006, pp. 126–138.

93. S. Nelton, "Emotions in the Workplace," *Nation's Business*, February 1996, p. 25.

94. See the Yerkes–Dodson law cited in D. O. Hebb, "Drives and the CNS (Conceptual Nervous System)," *Psychological Review*, July 1955, pp. 243–54.

CHAPTER 8

1. L. R. Sayles, "Work Group Behavior and the Larger Organization," in C. Arensburg, et al. (eds.), *Research in Industrial Relations* (New York: Harper & Row, 1957), pp. 131–45.

2. S. Lieberman, "The Effects of Changes in Roles on the Attitudes of Role Occupants," *Human Relations*, November 1956, pp. 385–402.

3. See D. M. Rousseau, *Psychological Contracts in Organizations: Understanding Written and Unwritten Agreements* (Thousand Oaks, CA: Sage, 1995); L. Sels, M. Janssens, and I. Van den Brande, "Assessing the Nature of Psychological Contracts: A Validation of Six Dimensions," *Journal of Organizational Behavior*, June 2004, pp. 461–88; and C. Hui, C. Lee, and D. M. Rousseau, "Psychological Contract and Organizational Citizenship Behavior in China: Investigating Generalizability and Instrumentality," *Journal of Applied Psychology*, April 2004, pp. 311–21.

4. See I. H. Settles, R. M. Sellers, and A. Damas Jr., "One Role or Two? The Function of Psychological Separation in Role Conflict," *Journal of Applied Psychology*, June 2002, pp. 574–82.

5. For a review of the research on group norms, see J. R. Hackman, "Group Influences on Individuals in Organizations," in M. D. Dunnette and L. M. Hough (eds.), *Handbook of Industrial & Organizational Psychology*, 2nd ed., vol. 3 (Palo Alto, CA: Consulting Psychologists Press, 1992), pp. 235–50. For a more recent discussion, see M. G. Ehrhart and S. E. Naumann, "Organizational Citizenship Behavior in Work Groups: A Group Norms Approach," *Journal of Applied Psychology*, December 2004, pp. 960–74.

6. E. Mayo, *The Human Problems of an Industrial Civilization* (New York: Macmillan, 1933); and F. J. Roethlisberger and W. J. Dickson, *Management and the Worker* (Cambridge, MA: Harvard University Press, 1939).

7. C. A. Kiesler and S. B. Kiesler, *Conformity* (Reading, MA: Addison-Wesley, 1969).

8. Ibid., p. 27.

9. S. E. Asch, "Effects of Group Pressure upon the Modification and Distortion of Judgments," in H. Guetzkow (ed.), *Groups, Leadership and Men* (Pittsburgh, PA: Carnegie Press, 1951), pp. 177–90; and S. E. Asch, "Studies of Independence and Conformity: A Minority of One Against a Unanimous Majority," *Psychological Monographs: General and Applied*, 70(9), 1956, pp. 1–70.

10. R. Bond and P. B. Smith, "Culture and Conformity: A Meta-Analysis of Studies Using Asch's (1952, 1956) Line Judgment Task," *Psychological Bulletin*, January 1996, pp. 111–37.

11. See S. L. Robinson and A. M. O'Leary-Kelly, "Monkey See, Monkey Do: The Influence of Work Groups on the Antisocial Behavior of Employees," *Academy of Management Journal*, December 1998, pp. 658–72; and R. J. Bennett and S. L. Robinson, "The Past, Present, and Future of Workplace Deviance," in J. Greenberg (ed.), *Organizational Behavior: The State of the Science*, 2nd ed. (Mahwah, NJ: Lawrence Erlbaum Associates, 2003), pp. 237–71.

12. S. L. Robinson and A. M. O'Leary-Kelly, "Monkey See, Monkey Do."

13. A. Erez, H. Elms, and E. Fong, "Lying, Cheating, Stealing: It Happens More in Groups," Paper presented at the European Business Ethics Network Annual Conference, Budapest, August 30, 2003.

14. See, for instance, D. G. Wagner and J. Berger, "Status Characteristics Theory: The Growth of a Program," in J. Berger and M. Zelditch (eds.), *Theoretical Research Programs: Studies in the Growth of a Theory* (Stanford, CA: Stanford University Press, 1993), pp. 23–63; and J. S. Bunderson, "Recognizing and Utilizing Expertise in Work Groups: A Status Characteristics Perspective," *Administrative Science Quarterly*, December 2003, pp. 557–91.

15. See R. S. Feldman, *Social Psychology*, 3rd ed. (Upper Saddle River, NJ: Prentice Hall, 2001), pp. 464–65.

16. Cited in Hackman, "Group Influences on Individuals in Organizations," p. 236.

17. J. A. Wiggins, F. Dill, and R. D. Schwartz, "On 'Status-Liability,'" *Sociometry*, April–May 1965, pp. 197–209.

18. O. J. Harvey and C. Consalvi, "Status and Conformity to Pressures in Informal Groups," *Journal of Abnormal and Social Psychology*, Spring 1960, pp. 182–87.

19. See, for example, J. M. Twenge, "Changes in Women's Assertiveness in Response to Status and Roles: A Cross-Temporal Meta-Analysis, 1931–1993," *Journal of Personality and Social Psychology*, July 2001, pp. 133–45.

20. J. Greenberg, "Equity and Workplace Status: A Field Experiment," *Journal of Applied Psychology*, November 1988, pp. 606–13.

21. See G. Hofstede, *Cultures and Organizations: Software of the Mind* (New York, McGraw-Hill, 1991).

22. This section is based on P. R. Harris and R. T. Moran, *Managing Cultural Differences*, 5th ed. (Houston, TX: Gulf Publishing, 1999).

23. E. J. Thomas and C. F. Fink, "Effects of Group Size," *Psychological Bulletin*, July 1963, pp. 371–84; A. P. Hare, *Handbook of Small Group Research* (New York: Free Press, 1976); and M. E. Shaw, *Group Dynamics: The Psychology of Small Group Behavior*, 3rd ed. (New York: McGraw-Hill, 1981).

24. G. H. Seijts and G. P. Latham, "The Effects of Goal Setting and Group Size on Performance in a Social Dilemma," *Canadian Journal of Behavioural Science*, 32(2), 2000, pp. 104–16.

25. Shaw, *Group Dynamics: The Psychology of Small Group Behavior*.

26. See, for instance, R. C. Liden, S. J. Wayne, R. A. Jaworski, and N. Bennett, "Social Loafing: A Field Investigation," *Journal of Management*, April 2004, pp. 285–304.

27. W. Moede, "Die Richtlinien der Leistungs-Psychologie," *Industrielle Psychotechnik* 4 (1927), pp. 193–207.

28. See, for example, J. A. Shepperd, "Productivity Loss in Performance Groups: A Motivation Analysis," *Psychological Bulletin*, January 1993, pp. 67–81; and S. J. Karau and K. D. Williams, "Social Loafing: A Meta-Analytic Review and Theoretical Integration," *Journal of Personality and Social Psychology*, October 1993, pp. 681–706.

29. For some of the controversy surrounding the definition of cohesion, see J. Keyton and J. Springston, "Redefining Cohesiveness in Groups," *Small Group Research*, May 1990, pp. 234–54.

30. See D. J. Beal, R. R. Cohen, M. J. Burke, and C. L. McLendon, "Cohesion and Performance in Groups: A Meta-Analytic Clarification of Construct Relations," *Journal of Applied Psychology*, December 2003, pp. 989–1,004.

31. Ibid.

32. Based on J. L. Gibson, J. M. Ivancevich, and J. H. Donnelly Jr., *Organizations*, 8th ed. (Burr Ridge, IL: Irwin, 1994), p. 323.

33. N. Foote, E. Matson, L. Weiss, and E. Wenger, "Leveraging Group Knowledge for High-Performance Decision-Making," *Organizational Dynamics*, 31(2), 2002, pp. 280–95.

34. See G. W. Hill, "Group Versus Individual Performance: Are N+1 Heads Better Than One?" *Psychological Bulletin*, May 1982, pp. 517–39; and R. F. Martell and M. R. Borg, "A Comparison of the Behavioral Rating Accuracy of Groups and Individuals," *Journal of Applied Psychology*, February 1993, pp. 43–50.

35. D. Gigone and R. Hastie, "Proper Analysis of the Accuracy of Group Judgments," *Psychological Bulletin*, January 1997, pp. 149–67.

36. See, for example, W. C. Swap and Associates, *Group Decision Making* (Newbury Park, CA: Sage, 1984).

37. I. L. Janis, *Groupthink* (Boston: Houghton Mifflin, 1982). See also W. W. Park, "A Comprehensive Empirical Investigation of the Relationships Among Variables of the Groupthink Model," *Journal of Organizational Behavior*, December 2000, pp. 873–87.

38. Janis, *Groupthink*.

39. Ibid.

40. G. Moorhead, R. Ference, and C. P. Neck, "Group Decision Fiascos Continue: Space Shuttle Challenger and a Revised Groupthink Framework," *Human Relations*, May 1991, pp. 539–50; E. J. Chisson, *The Hubble Wars* (New York: HarperPerennial, 1994); and C. Covault, "Columbia Revelations Alarming E-Mails Speak for Themselves. But Administrator O'Keefe Is More Concerned About Board Findings on NASA Decision-Making," *Aviation Week & Space Technology*, March 3, 2003, p. 26.

41. M. E. Turner and A. R. Pratkanis, "Mitigating Groupthink by Stimulating Constructive Conflict," in C. De Dreu and E. Van de Vliert (eds.), *Using Conflict in Organizations* (London: Sage, 1997), pp. 53–71.

42. See, for example, N. Kogan and M. A. Wallach, "Risk Taking as a Function of the Situation, the Person, and the Group," in *New Directions in Psychology*, vol. 3 (New York: Holt, Rinehart and Winston, 1967); and M. A. Wallach, N. Kogan, and D. J. Bem, "Group Influence on Individual Risk Taking," *Journal of Abnormal and Social Psychology*, vol. 65, 1962, pp. 75–86.

43. R. D. Clark III, "Group-Induced Shift Toward Risk: A Critical Appraisal," *Psychological Bulletin*, October 1971, pp. 251–70.

44. A. F. Osborn, *Applied Imagination: Principles and Procedures of Creative Thinking*, 3rd ed. (New York: Scribner, 1963). See also R. P. McGlynn, D. McGurk, V. S. Effland, N. L. Johll, and D. J. Harding, "Brainstorming and Task Performance in Groups Constrained by Evidence," *Organizational Behavior and Human Decision Processes*, January 2004, pp. 75–87.

45. N. L. Kerr and R. S. Tindale, "Group Performance and Decision-Making," *Annual Review of Psychology*, vol. 55 (2004), pp. 623–55.

46. C. Faure, "Beyond Brainstorming: Effects of Different Group Procedures on Selection of Ideas and Satisfaction with the Process," *Journal of Creative Behavior*, vol. 38 (2004), pp. 13–34.

47. See, for instance, A. B. Hollingshead and J. E. McGrath, "Computer-Assisted Groups: A Critical Review of the Empirical Research," in R. A. Guzzo and E. Salas (eds.), *Team Effectiveness*

and Decision Making in Organizations (San Francisco: Jossey-Bass, 1995), pp. 46–78.

48. B. B. Baltes, M. W. Dickson, M. P. Sherman, C. C. Bauer, and J. LaGanke, "Computer-Mediated Communication and Group Decision Making: A Meta-Analysis," *Organizational Behavior and Human Decision Processes*, January 2002, pp. 156–79.

49. T. P. Verney, "Role Perception Congruence, Performance, and Satisfaction," in D. J. Vredenburgh and R. S. Schuler (eds.), *Effective Management: Research and Application*, Proceedings of the 20th Annual Eastern Academy of Management, Pittsburgh, PA, May 1983, pp. 24–27.

50. Ibid.

51. A. G. Bedeian and A. A. Armenakis, "A Path-Analytic Study of the Consequences of Role Conflict and Ambiguity," *Academy of Management Journal*, June 1981, pp. 417–24; and P. L. Perrewe, K. L. Zellars, G. R. Ferris, A. M. Rossi, C. J. Kacmar, and D. A. Ralston, "Neutralizing Job Stressors: Political Skill as an Antidote to the Dysfunctional Consequences of Role Conflict," *Academy of Management Journal*, February 2004, pp. 141–152.

52. Shaw, *Group Dynamics*.

53. B. Mullen, C. Symons, L. Hu, and E. Salas, "Group Size, Leadership Behavior, and Subordinate Satisfaction," *Journal of General Psychology*, April 1989, pp. 155–70.

CHAPTER 9

1. Cited in C. Joinson, "Teams at Work," *HRMagazine*, May 1999, p. 30; and P. Strozniak, "Teams at Work," *Industry Week*, September 18, 2000, p. 47.

2. See, for example, E. Salas, C. A. Bowers, and E. Edens (eds.), *Improving Teamwork in Organizations: Applications of Resource Management Training* (Mahwah, NJ: Lawrence Erlbaum, 2002); and L. I. Glassop, "The Organizational Benefits of Teams," *Human Relations*, February 2002, pp. 225–50.

3. K. Kelly, "The New Soul of John Deere," *Business Week*, January 31, 1994, pp. 64–66.

4. G. Bodinson and R. Bunch, "AQP's National Team Excellence Award: Its Purpose, Value and Process," *The Journal for Quality and Participation*, Spring 2003, pp. 37–42.

5. See, for example, H. W. Lane and M. Brehm Brechu, "Taking Self-Managed Teams to Mexico," *Academy of Management Executive*, August 1999, pp. 15–27; and A. Erez, J. A. LePine, and H. Elms, "Effects of Rotated Leadership and Peer Evaluation on the Functioning and Effectiveness of Self-Managed Teams: A Quasi-experiment," *Personnel Psychology*, Winter 2002, pp. 929–48.

6. W. Royal, "Team-Centered Success," *Industry Week*, October 18, 1999, pp. 56–58.

7. See, for instance, R. A. Cook and J. L. Goff, "Coming of Age with Self-Managed Teams: Dealing with a Problem Employee," *Journal of Business and Psychology*, Spring 2002, pp. 485–496; and C. W. Langfred, "Too Much of a Good Thing? Negative Effects of High Trust and Individual Autonomy in Self-Managing Teams," *Academy of Management Journal*, June 2004, pp. 385–99.

8. J. R. Barker, "Tightening the Iron Cage: Concertive Control in Self-Managing Teams," *Administrative Science Quarterly*, September 1993, pp. 408–37; and C. Smith and D. Comer,

"Self-Organization in Small Groups: A Study of Group Effectiveness Within Non-Equilibrium Conditions," *Human Relations*, May 1994, pp. 553–81.

9. Lane and Brechu, "Taking Self-Managed Teams to Mexico."

10. Bodinson and Bunch, "AQP's National Team Excellence Award."

11. M. Brunelli, "How Harley-Davidson Uses Cross-Functional Teams," Purchasing Online. Accessed November 4, 1999, at www.manufacturing.net/magazine/purchasing/archives/1999.

12. S. Crock, "Collaboration: Lockheed Martin," *Business Week*, November 24, 2003, p. 85.

13. D. E. Hyatt and T. M. Ruddy, "An Examination of the Relationship Between Work Group Characteristics and Performance: Once More into the Breech," *Personnel Psychology*, Autumn 1997, p. 555.

14. This model is based on M. A. Campion, E. M. Papper, and G. J. Medsker, "Relations Between Work Team Characteristics and Effectiveness: A Replication and Extension," *Personnel Psychology*, Summer 1996, pp. 429–52; Hyatt and Ruddy, "An Examination of the Relationship Between Work Group Characteristics and Performance," pp. 553–85; S. G. Cohen and D. E. Bailey, "What Makes Teams Work: Group Effectiveness Research from the Shop Floor to the Executive Suite," *Journal of Management*, 23(3), 1997, pp. 239–90; L. Thompson, *Making the Team* (Upper Saddle River, NJ: Prentice Hall, 2000), pp. 18–33; and J. R. Hackman, *Leading Teams: Setting the Stage for Great Performance* (Boston: Harvard Business School Press, 2002).

15. Hyatt and Ruddy, "An Examination of the Relationship Between Work Group Characteristics and Performance," p. 577.

16. F. LaFasto and C. Larson, *When Teams Work Best: 6,000 Team Members and Leaders Tell What It Takes to Succeed* (Thousand Oaks, CA: Sage, 2002).

17. R. I. Beekun, "Assessing the Effectiveness of Sociotechnical Interventions: Antidote or Fad?" *Human Relations*, August 1989, pp. 877–97.

18. V. U. Druskat and J. V. Wheeler, "Managing from the Boundary: The Effective Leadership of Self-Managing Work Teams," *Academy of Management Journal*, August 2003, pp. 435–57.

19. D. Eden, "Pygmalion Without Interpersonal Contrast Effects: Whole Groups Gain from Raising Manager Expectations," *Journal of Applied Psychology*, August 1990, pp. 394–98.

20. J. M. George, "Leader Positive Mood and Group Performance: The Case of Customer Service," *Journal of Applied Social Psychology*, December 1995, pp. 778–94; and A. P. Brief and H. M. Weiss, "Organizational Behavior: Affect in the Workplace," *Annual Review of Psychology*, 2002, pp. 279–307.

21. M. Williams, "In Whom We Trust: Group Membership as an Affective Context for Trust Development," *Academy of Management Review*, July 2001, pp. 377–96.

22. See L. N. McClurg, "Team Rewards: How Far Have We Come?" *Human Resource Management*, Spring 2001, pp. 73–86.

23. For a more detailed breakdown on team skills, see M. J. Stevens and M. A. Campion, "The Knowledge, Skill, and Ability Requirements for Teamwork: Implications for Human Resource Management," *Journal of Management*, Summer 1994, pp. 503–30.

24. H. Moon, J. R. Hollenbeck, and S. E. Humphrey, "Asymmetric Adaptability: Dynamic Team Structures as One-Way Streets," *Academy of Management Journal*, 47(5), October 2004, pp. 681–95; J. A. LePine, J. R. Hollenbeck, and D. R. Ilgen, "Effects of Individual Differences on the Performance of Hierarchical Decision-Making Teams: Much More than g," *Journal of Applied Psychology*, 82(5), October 1997, pp. 803–11; C. L. Jackson and J. A. LePine, "Peer Responses to a Team's Weakest Link: A Test and Extension of LePine and Van Dyne's Model," *Journal of Applied Psychology*, 88(3), June 2003, pp. 459–75.

25. See, for instance, M. R. Barrick, G. L. Stewart, M. J. Neubert, and M. K. Mount, "Relating Member Ability and Personality to Work-Team Processes and Team Effectiveness," *Journal of Applied Psychology*, June 1998, pp. 377–91; and L. M. Moynihan and R. S. Peterson, "A Contingent Configuration Approach to Understanding the Role of Personality in Organizational Groups," in B. M. Staw and R. I. Sutton (eds.), *Research in Organizational Behavior*, vol. 23 (Oxford, England: JAI/Elsevier, 2001), pp. 332–38.

26. Barrick, Stewart, Neubert, and Mount, "Relating Member Ability and Personality to Work-Team Processes and Team Effectiveness."

27. Ibid., p. 388.

28. Ibid.

29. B. Beersma, J. R. Hollenbeck, and S. E. Humphrey, "Cooperation, Competition, and Team Performance: Toward a Contingency Approach," *Academy of Management Journal*, 46(5), October 2003, pp. 572–90; Ellis, Hollenbeck, and Ilgen, "Team Learning: Collectively Connecting the Dots," pp. 821–35; C. O. L. H. Porter, J. R. Hollenbeck, and D. R. Ilgen, "Backing Up Behaviors in Teams: The Role of Personality and Legitimacy of Need," *Journal of Applied Psychology*, 88(3), June 2003, pp. 391–403; J. R. Hollenbeck, H. Moon, and A. P. J. Ellis, "Structural Contingency Theory and Individual Differences: Examination of External and Internal Person-Team Fit," *Journal of Applied Psychology*, 87(3), June 2002, pp. 599–606; and J. A. Colquitt, J. R. Hollenbeck, and D. R. Ilgen, "Computer-Assisted Communication and Team Decision-Making Performance: The Moderating Effect of Openness to Experience," *Journal of Applied Psychology*, 87(2), April 2002, pp. 402–10.

30. C. Margerison and D. McCann, *Team Management: Practical New Approaches* (London: Mercury Books, 1990).

31. See, for example, S. E. Jackson, A. Joshi, and N. L. Erhardt, "Recent Research on Team and Organizational Diversity: SWOT Analysis and Implications," *Journal of Management*, 29(6), 2003, pp. 801–30; and D. van Knippenberg, C. K. W. De Dreu, and A. C. Homan, "Work Group Diversity and Group Performance: An Integrative Model and Research Agenda," *Journal of Applied Psychology*, December 2004, pp. 1,008–22.

32. J. A. LePine, J. R. Hollenbeck, and D. R. Ilgen, "Gender Composition, Situational Strength, and Team Decision-Making Accuracy: A Criterion Decomposition Approach," *Organizational Behavior & Human Decision Processes*, 88(1), May 2002, pp. 445–75.

33. W. E. Watson, K. Kumar, and L. K. Michaelsen, "Cultural Diversity's Impact on Interaction Process and Performance: Comparing Homogeneous and Diverse Task Groups," *Academy of Management Journal*, June 1993, pp. 590–602; and S. Mohammed and L. C. Angell, "Surface- and Deep-Level Diversity in Workgroups: Examining the Moderating Effects of Team Orientation and Team Process on Relationship Conflict," *Journal of Organizational Behavior*, December 2004, pp. 1,015–39.

34. Watson, Kumar, and Michaelsen, "Cultural Diversity's Impact on Interaction Process and Performance."

35. K. Y. Williams and C. A. O'Reilly III, "Demography and Diversity in Organizations: A Review of 40 Years of Research," in B. M. Staw and L. L. Cummings (eds.), *Research in Organizational Behavior*, vol. 20, pp. 77–140.

36. W. G. Wagner, J. Pfeffer, and C. A. O'Reilly, "Organizational Demography and Turnover in Top-Management Groups," *Administrative Science Quarterly*, 29(1), 1984, pp. 74–92.

37. J. Katzenbach, "What Makes Teams Work?" *Fast Company*, November 2000, p. 110.

38. The evidence in this section is described in Thompson, *Making the Team*, pp. 65–67. See also R. C. Liden, S. J. Wayne, and R. A. Jaworski, "Social Loafing: A Field Investigation," *Journal of Management*, 30(2), 2004, pp. 285–304.

39. J. D. Shaw, M. K. Duffy, and E. M. Stark, "Interdependence and Preference for Group Work: Main and Congruence Effects on the Satisfaction and Performance of Group Members," *Journal of Management*, 26(2), 2000, pp. 259–79; and S. A. Kiffin-Peterson and J. L. Cordery, "Trust, Individualism, and Job Characteristics of Employee Preference for Teamwork," *International Journal of Human Resource Management*, February 2003, pp. 93–116.

40. R. Wageman, "Critical Success Factors for Creating Superb Self-Managing Teams," *Organizational Dynamics*, Summer 1997, p. 55.

41. Campion, Papper, and Medsker, "Relations Between Work Team Characteristics and Effectiveness," p. 430; and D. C. Man and S. S. K. Lam, "The Effects of Job Complexity and Autonomy on Cohesiveness in Collectivist and Individualist Work Groups: A Cross-Cultural Analysis," *Journal of Organizational Behavior*, December 2003, pp. 979–1,001.

42. I. D. Steiner, *Group Processes and Productivity* (New York: Academic Press, 1972).

43. K. Blanchard, D. Carew, and E. Parisi-Carew, "How to Get Your Group to Perform Like a Team," *Training and Development*, September 1996, pp. 34–37.

44. E. Weldon and L. R. Weingart, "Group Goals and Group Performance," *British Journal of Social Psychology*, Spring 1993, pp. 307–34; see also R. P. DeShon, S. W. J. Kozlowski, A. M. Schmidt, K. R. Milner, and D. Wiechmann, "A Multiple-Goal, Multilevel Model of Feeback Effects on the Regulation of Individual and Team Performance," *Journal of Applied Psychology*, December 2004, pp. 1,035–56.

45. S. M. Gully, K. A. Incalcaterra, A. Joshi, and J. M. Beaubien, "A Meta-Analysis of Team-Efficacy, Potency, and Performance: Interdependence and Level of Analysis as Moderators of Observed Relationships," *Journal of Applied Psychology*, October 2002, pp. 819–32; and C. B. Gibson, "The Efficacy Advantage: Factors Related to the Formation of Group Efficacy," *Journal of Applied Social Psychology*, October 2003, pp. 2,153–86.

46. K. A. Jehn, "A Qualitative Analysis of Conflict Types and Dimensions in Organizational Groups," *Administrative Science Quarterly*, September 1997, pp. 530–57; see also R. S. Peterson and K. J. Behfar, "The Dynamic Relationship Between Performance Feedback, Trust, and Conflict in Groups: A Longitudinal Study," *Organizational Behavior and Human Decision Processes*, September–November 2003, pp. 102–12.

47. See, for instance, B. L. Kirkman and D. L. Shapiro, "The Impact of Cultural Values on Employee Resistance to Teams: Toward a Model of Globalized Self-Managing Work Team Effectiveness," *Academy of Management Review*, July 1997, pp. 730–57; and B. L. Kirkman, C. B. Gibson, and D. L. Shapiro, "'Exporting' Teams: Enhancing the Implementation and Effectiveness of Work Teams in Global Affiliates," *Organizational Dynamics*, 30(1), 2001, pp. 12–29.

48. D. Harrington-Mackin, *The Team Building Tool Kit* (New York: AMACOM, 1994), p. 53.

49. T. D. Schellhardt, "To Be a Star Among Equals, Be a Team Player," *Wall Street Journal*, April 20, 1994, p. B1.

50. Ibid.

51. "Teaming Up for Success," *Training*, January 1994, p. S41.

52. J. S. DeMatteo, L. T. Eby, and E. Sundstrom, "Team-Based Rewards: Current Empirical Evidence and Directions for Future Research," in B. M. Staw and L. L. Cummings (eds.), *Research in Organizational Behavior*, vol. 20, pp. 141–83.

53. B. Geber, "The Bugaboo of Team Pay," *Training*, August 1995, pp. 27, 34.

54. Kinlaw, *Developing Superior Work Teams*, p. 43.

55. B. Krone, "Total Quality Management: An American Odyssey," *The Bureaucrat*, Fall 1990, p. 37.

56. C. E. Naquin and R. O. Tynan, "The Team Halo Effect: Why Teams Are not Blamed for Their Failures," *Journal of Applied Psychology*, April 2003, pp. 332–40.

57. A. B. Drexler and R. Forrester, "Teamwork—Not Necessarily the Answer," *HR Magazine*, January 1998, pp. 55–58. See also R. Saavedra, P. C. Earley, and L. Van Dyne, "Complex Interdependence in Task-Performing Groups," *Journal of Applied Psychology*, February 1993, pp. 61–72; and K. A. Jehn, G. B. Northcraft, and M. A. Neale, "Why Differences Make a Difference: A Field Study of Diversity, Conflict, and Performance in Workgroups," *Administrative Science Quarterly*, December 1999, pp. 741–63.

CHAPTER 10

1. See, for example, K. W. Thomas and W. H. Schmidt, "A Survey of Managerial Interests with Respect to Conflict," *Academy of Management Journal*, June 1976, p. 317.

2. W. G. Scott and T. R. Mitchell, *Organization Theory: A Structural and Behavioral Analysis* (Homewood, IL: Richard D. Irwin, 1976).

3. D. K. Berlo, *The Process of Communication* (New York: Holt, Rinehart & Winston, 1960), pp. 30–32.

4. J. Langan-Fox, "Communication in Organizations: Speed, Diversity, Networks, and Influence on Organizational Effectiveness, Human Health, and Relationships," in N. Anderson, D. S. Ones, H. K. Sinangil, and C. Viswesvaran (eds.), *Handbook of Industrial, Work and Organizational Psychology*, vol. 2 (Thousand Oaks, CA: Sage, 2001), p. 190.

5. R. L. Simpson, "Vertical and Horizontal Communication in Formal Organizations," *Administrative Science Quarterly*, September 1959, pp. 188–96; and J. W. Smither and A. G. Walker, "Are the Characteristics of Narrative Comments Related to Improvement in Multirater Feedback Ratings Over Time?" *Journal of Applied Psychology*, 89(3), June 2004, pp. 575–81.

6. J. Fast, *Body Language* (Philadelphia: M. Evan, 1970), p. 7.

7. A. Mehrabian, *Nonverbal Communication* (Chicago: Aldine-Atherton, 1972).

8. N. M. Henley, "Body Politics Revisited: What Do We Know Today?" in P. J. Kalbfleisch and M. J. Cody (eds.), *Gender, Power, and Communication in Human Relationships* (Hillsdale, NJ: Lawrence Erlbaum, 1995), pp. 27–61.

9. Cited in "Heard It Through the Grapevine," *Forbes*, February 10, 1997, p. 22.

10. See, for instance, J. W. Newstrom, R. E. Monczka, and W. E. Reif, "Perceptions of the Grapevine: Its Value and Influence," *Journal of Business Communication*, Spring 1974, pp. 12–20; and S. J. Modic, "Grapevine Rated Most Believable," *Industry Week*, May 15, 1989, p. 14.

11. K. Davis, cited in R. Rowan, "Where Did That Rumor Come From?" *Fortune*, August 13, 1979, p. 134.

12. R. L. Rosnow and G. A. Fine, *Rumor and Gossip: The Social Psychology of Hearsay* (New York: Elsevier, 1976).

13. E. Morphy, "Study: Online Customer Service Is Dismal," June 8, 2005, *Yahoo! News* at http:// news.yahoo.com/s/nf/36133.

14. G. Anders, "Inside Job," *Fast Company*, September 2001, p. 178.

15. See P. R. Carlile, "Transferring, Translating, and Transforming: An Integrative Framework for Managing Knowledge Across Boundaries," *Organization Science*, 15(5), September–October 2004, pp. 555–68.

16. B. Roberts, "Pick Employees' Brains," *HR Magzine*, February 2000, pp. 115–16; B. Fryer, "Get Smart," *INC. Technology 1999*, no. 3, p. 65; and D. Zielinski, "Have You Shared a Bright Idea Today?" *Training*, July 2000, p. 65.

17. B. Fryer, "Get Smart," p. 63.

18. D. Mason and D. J. Pauleen, "Perceptions of Knowledge Management: A Qualitative Analysis," *Journal of Knowledge Management*, 7(4), 2003, pp. 38–48.

19. J. Gordon, "Intellectual Capital and You," *Training*, September 1999, p. 33.

20. J. C. McCroskey, J. A. Daly, and G. Sorenson, "Personality Correlates of Communication Apprehension," *Human Communication Research*, Spring 1976, pp. 376–80.

21. See, for instance, S. K. Opt and D. A. Loffredo, "Rethinking Communication Apprehension: A Myers-Briggs Perspective," *Journal of Psychology*, September 2000, pp. 556–70.

22. See, for example, T. L. Rodebaugh, "I Might Look OK, but I'm Still Doubtful, Anxious, and Avoidant: The Mixed Effects of

Enhanced Video Feedback on Social Anxiety Symptoms," *Behaviour Research & Therapy*, 42(12), December 2004, pp. 1,435–51.

23. J. A. Daly and J. C. McCroskey, "Occupational Desirability and Choice as a Function of Communication Apprehension," *Journal of Counseling Psychology*, 22(4), 1975, pp. 309–313.

24. J. A. Daly and M. D. Miller, "The Empirical Development of an Instrument of Writing Apprehension," *Research in the Teaching of English*, Winter 1975, pp. 242–49.

25. See D. Tannen, *You Just Don't Understand: Women and Men in Conversation* (New York: Ballantine Books, 1991); and D. Tannen, *Talking from 9 to 5* (New York: William Morrow, 1995).

26. L. M. Kyl-Heku and D. M. Buss, "Tactics as Units of Analysis in Personality Psychology: An Illustration Using Tactics of Hierarchy Negotiation," *Personality & Individual Differences*, 21(4), October 1996, pp. 497–517.

27. D. Tannen, "Talking Past One Another: 'But What Do You Mean?' Women and Men in Conversation," in J. M. Henslin (ed.), *Down to Earth Sociology: Introductory Readings*, 12th ed. (New York: Free Press, 2003), pp. 175–81.

28. Cited in J. Leo, "Falling for Sensitivity," *U.S. News & World Report*, December 13, 1993, p. 27.

29. R. E. Axtell, *Gestures: The Do's and Taboos of Body Language Around the World* (New York: Wiley, 1991).

30. See M. Munter, "Cross-Cultural Communication for Managers," *Business Horizons*, May–June 1993, pp. 75–76.

31. See E. T. Hall, *Beyond Culture* (Garden City, NY: Anchor Press/Doubleday, 1976); E. T. Hall, "How Cultures Collide," *Psychology Today*, July 1976, pp. 67–74; E. T. Hall and M. R. Hall, *Understanding Cultural Differences* (Yarmouth, ME: Intercultural Press, 1990); R. E. Dulek, J. S. Fielden, and J. S. Hill, "International Communication: An Executive Primer," *Business Horizons*, January–February 1991, pp. 20–25; D. Kim, Y. Pan, and H. S. Park, "High- Versus Low-Context Culture: A Comparison of Chinese, Korean, and American Cultures," *Psychology and Marketing*, September 1998, pp. 507–21; M. J. Martinko and S. C. Douglas, "Culture and Expatriate Failure: An Attributional Explication," *International Journal of Organizational Analysis*, July 1999, pp. 265–93; and W. L. Adair, "Integrative Sequences and Negotiation Outcome in Same- and Mixed-Culture Negotiations," *International Journal of Conflict Management*, 14(3–4), 2003, pp. 1,359–92.

32. N. Adler, *International Dimensions of Organizational Behavior*, 4th ed. (Cincinnati, OH: Southwestern, 2002), p. 94.

33. See, for example. R. S. Schuler, "A Role Perception Transactional Process Model for Organizational Communication-Outcome Relationships," *Organizational Behavior and Human Performance*, April 1979, pp. 268–91.

34. J. P. Walsh, S. J. Ashford, and T. E. Hill, "Feedback Obstruction: The Influence of the Information Environment on Employee Turnover Intentions," *Human Relations*, January 1985, pp. 23–46.

35. S. A. Hellweg and S. L. Phillips, "Communication and Productivity in Organizations: A State-of-the-Art Review," in *Proceedings of the 40th Annual Academy of Management Conference*, Detroit, Michigan, 1980, pp. 188–92; see also B. A. Bechky,

"Sharing Meaning Across Occupational Communities: The Transformation of Understanding on a Production Floor," *Organization Science*, 14(3), May–June 2003, pp. 312–30.

36. R. R. Reilly, B. Brown, M. R. Blood, and C. Z. Malatesta, "The Effects of Realistic Previews: A Study and Discussion of the Literature," *Personnel Psychology*, Winter 1981, pp. 823–34; see also J. M. Phillips, "Effects of Realistic Job Previews on Multiple Organizational Outcomes: A Meta-Analysis," *Academy of Management Journal*, 41(6), December 1998, pp. 673–90.

CHAPTER 11

1. J. P. Kotter, "What Leaders Really Do," *Harvard Business Review*, May–June 1990, pp. 103–11; and J. P. Kotter, *A Force for Change: How Leadership Differs from Management* (New York: Free Press, 1990).

2. J. G. Geier, "A Trait Approach to the Study of Leadership in Small Groups," *Journal of Communication*, December 1967, pp. 316–23.

3. S. A. Kirkpatrick and E. A. Locke, "Leadership: Do Traits Matter?" *Academy of Management Executive*, May 1991, pp. 48–60; and S. J. Zaccaro, R. J. Foti, and D. A. Kenny, "Self-Monitoring and Trait-Based Variance in Leadership: An Investigation of Leader Flexibility Across Multiple Group Situations," *Journal of Applied Psychology*, April 1991, pp. 308–15.

4. Judge, Bono, Ilies, and Gerhardt, "Personality and Leadership."

5. J. Champy, "The Hidden Qualities of Great Leaders," *Fast Company*, vol. 76 (November 2003), p. 135.

6. J. Antonakis, "Why 'Emotional Intelligence' Does Not Predict Leadership Effectiveness: A Comment on Prati, Douglas, Ferris, Ammeter, and Buckley (2003)," *International Journal of Organizational Analysis*, vol. 11, 2003, pp. 355–361. See also M. Zeidner, G. Matthews, and R. D. Roberts, "Emotional Intelligence in the Workplace: A Critical Review," *Applied Psychology: An International Review*, vol. 53, 2004, pp. 371–399.

7. Ibid.; R. G. Lord, C. L. DeVader, and G. M. Alliger, "A Meta-Analysis of the Relation Between Personality Traits and Leadership Perceptions: An Application of Validity Generalization Procedures," *Journal of Applied Psychology*, August 1986, pp. 402–10; and J. A. Smith and R. J. Foti, "A Pattern Approach to the Study of Leader Emergence," *Leadership Quarterly*, Summer 1998, pp. 147–60.

8. See S. Hansen, "Stings Like a Bee," *INC.*, November 2002, pp. 56–64; and J. Greenbaum, "Is Ghengis on the Hunt Again?" Accessed January 14, 2005, at www. internetnews.com/commentary/article.php/3459771.

9. H. Yen, "Richard Parsons, AOL Time Warner's New CEO, Known as Consensus-Builder." Accessed December 6, 2001, at www.tbo.com.

10. R. R. Blake and J. S. Mouton, *The Managerial Grid* (Houston: Gulf, 1964).

11. F. E. Fiedler, *A Theory of Leadership Effectiveness* (New York: McGraw-Hill, 1967).

12. F. E. Fiedler, M. M. Chemers, and L. Mahar, *Improving Leadership Effectiveness: The Leader Match Concept* (New York: John Wiley, 1977).

13. Cited in R. J. House and R. N. Aditya, "The Social Scientific Study of Leadership," p. 422.

14. L. H. Peters, D. D. Hartke, and J. T. Pohlmann, "Fiedler's Contingency Theory of Leadership: An Application of the Meta-Analysis Procedures of Schmidt and Hunter," *Psychological Bulletin*, March 1985, pp. 274–85; C. A. Schriesheim, B. J. Tepper, and L. A. Tetrault, "Least Preferred Coworker Score, Situational Control, and Leadership Effectiveness: A Meta-Analysis of Contingency Model Performance Predictions," *Journal of Applied Psychology*, August 1994, pp. 561–73; and R. Ayman, M. M. Chemers, and F. Fiedler, "The Contingency Model of Leadership Effectiveness: Its Levels of Analysis," *Leadership Quarterly*, Summer 1995, pp. 147–67.

15. D. Duchon, S. G. Green, and T. D. Taber, "Vertical Dyad Linkage: A Longitudinal Assessment of Antecedents, Measures, and Consequences," *Journal of Applied Psychology*, February 1986, pp. 56–60; Liden, Wayne, and Stilwell, "A Longitudinal Study on the Early Development of Leader-Member Exchanges"; R. J. Deluga and J. T. Perry, "The Role of Subordinate Performance and Ingratiation in Leader-Member Exchanges," *Group & Organization Management*, March 1994, pp. 67–86; T. N. Bauer and S. G. Green, "Development of Leader-Member Exchange: A Longitudinal Test," *Academy of Management Journal*, December 1996, pp. 1,538–67; S. J. Wayne, L. M. Shore, and R. C. Liden, "Perceived Organizational Support and Leader-Member Exchange: A Social Exchange Perspective," *Academy of Management Journal*, February 1997, pp. 82–111; and M. Uhl-Bien, "Relationship Development as a Key Ingredient for Leadership Development," in S. E. Murphy and R. E. Riggio (eds.), *Future of Leadership Development* (Mahwah, NJ: Lawrence Erlbaum, 2003), pp. 129–47.

16. O. Janssen and N. W. Van Yperen, "Employees' Goal Orientations, the Quality of Leader-Member Exchange, and the Outcomes of Job Performance and Job Satisfaction," *Academy of Management Journal*, 47(3), June 2004, pp. 368–384.

17. K. M. Kacmar, L. A. Witt, and S. Zivnuska, "The Interactive Effect of Leader-Member Exchange and Communication Frequency on Performance Ratings," *Journal of Applied Psychology*, 88(4), August 2003, pp. 764–72.

18. A. Stensgaard, "What Happens to the Inner Circle of the Ousted CEO?" AME Info. Accessed April 27, 2003, at http://www.ameinfo.com/news/Detailed/23359.html.

19. See, for instance, C. R. Gerstner and D. V. Day, "Meta-Analytic Review of Leader-Member Exchange Theory: Correlates and Construct Issues," *Journal of Applied Psychology*, December 1997, pp. 827–44; C. Gomez and B. Rosen, "The Leader-Member Exchange as a Link Between Managerial Trust and Employee Empowerment," *Group & Organization Management*, March 2001, pp. 53–69; J. M. Maslyn and M. Uhl-Bien, "Leader-Member Exchange and Its Dimensions: Effects of Self-Effort and Other's Effort on Relationship Quality," *Journal of Applied Psychology*, August 2001, pp. 697–708; M. L. Kraimer, S. J. Wayne, and R. A. Jaworski, "Sources of Support and Expatriate Performance: The Mediating Role of Expatriate Adjustment," *Personnel Psychology*, vol. 54, Spring 2001, pp. 71–99; and note 42.

20. D. Eden, "Leadership and Expectations: Pygmalion Effects and Other Self-Fulfilling Prophecies in Organizations," *Leadership Quarterly*, Winter 1992, pp. 278–79.

21. J. C. Wofford and L. Z. Liska, "Path-Goal Theories of Leadership: A Meta-Analysis," *Journal of Management*, Winter 1993, pp. 857–76; and P. M. Podsakoff, S. B. MacKenzie, and M. Ahearne, "Searching for a Needle in a Haystack: Trying to Identify the Illusive Moderators of Leadership Behaviors," *Journal of Management*, vol. 21, 1995, pp. 423–70.

22. J. R. Villa, J. P. Howell, and P. W. Dorfman, "Problems with Detecting Moderators in Leadership Research Using Moderated Multiple Regression," *Leadership Quarterly*, vol. 14, 2003, pp. 3–23; C. A. Schriesheim, and L. Neider, "Path-Goal Leadership Theory: The Long and Winding Road," *Leadership Quarterly*, vol. 7, 1996, pp. 317–21; and M. G. Evans, "R. J. House's 'A Path-Goal Theory of Leader Effectiveness,'" *Leadership Quarterly*, vol. 7, 1996, pp. 305–309.

23. M. Weber, *Max Weber: The Theory of Social and Economic Organization*, A. M. Henderson and T. Parsons (trans.) (New York: Free, Press, 1947).

24. J. A. Conger and R. N. Kanungo, *Charismatic Leadership in Organizations* (Thousand Oaks, CA: Sage, 1998); and R. Awamleh and W. L. Gardner, "Perceptions of Leader Charisma and Effectiveness: The Effects of Vision Content, Delivery, and Organizational Performance," *Leadership Quarterly*, Fall 1999, pp. 345–73.

25. B. Shamir, R. J. House, and M. B. Arthur, "The Motivational Effects of Charismatic Leadership: A Self-Concept Theory," *Organization Science*, November 1993, pp. 577–94.

26. C. H. Schmitt, "The Confidence Game," *U.S. News & World Report*, September 13, 2004, pp. EE4–EE8; and S. Levy, "iPod, Therefore i Am," *Newsweek*, July 26, 2004, pp. 44–50.

27. B. Kark, R. Gan, and B. Shamir, "The Two Faces of Transformational Leadership: Empowerment and Dependency," *Journal of Applied Psychology*, April 2003, pp. 246–55; and P. D. Cherlunik, K. A. Donley, T. S. R. Wiewel, and S. R. Miller, "Charisma Is Contagious: The Effect of Leaders' Charisma on Observers' Affect," *Journal of Applied Social Psychology*, October 2001, pp. 2,149–59.

28. H. L. Tosi, V. Misangyi, A. Fanelli, D. A. Waldman, and F. J. Yammarino, "CEO Charisma, Compensation, and Firm Performance," *Leadership Quarterly*, June 2004, pp. 405–20.

29. J. Collins, "Level 5 Leadership: The Triumph of Humility and Fierce Resolve," *Harvard Business Review*, January 2001, pp. 67–76; J. Collins, "Good to Great," *Fast Company*, October 2001, pp. 90–104; J. Collins, "The Misguided Mix-Up," *Executive Excellence*, December 2002, pp. 3–4; and H. L. Tosi, V. Misangyi, A. Fanelli, D. A. Waldman, and F. J. Yammarino, "CEO Charisma, Compensation, and Firm Performance," *Leadership Quarterly*, June 2004, pp. 405–20.

30. See, for instance, B. M. Bass, *Leadership and Performance Beyond Expectations* (New York: Free Press, 1985); B. M. Bass, "From Transactional to Transformational Leadership: Learning to Share the Vision," *Organizational Dynamics*, Winter 1990, pp. 19–31; F. J. Yammarino, W. D. Spangler, and B.M. Bass, "Transformational Leadership and Performance: A Longitudinal Investigation," *Leadership Quarterly*, Spring 1993, pp. 81–102; J. C. Wofford, V. L. Goodwin, and J. L. Whittington, "A Field Study of a Cognitive Approach to Understanding Transformational and Transactional Leadership," *Leadership Quarterly*, 9(1), 1998, pp. 55–84; B. M. Bass, B. J. Avolio, D. I. Jung, and

Y. Berson, "Predicting Unit Performance by Assessing Transformational and Transactional Leadership," *Journal of Applied Psychology*, April 2003, pp. 207–18; J. Antonakis, B. J. Avolio, and N. Sivasubramaniam, "Context and Leadership: An Examination of the Nine-Factor Full-Range Leadership Theory Using the Multifactor Leadership Questionnaire," *Leadership Quarterly*, June 2003, pp. 261–95; and T. A. Judge, and R. F. Piccolo, "Transformational and Transactional Leadership: A Meta-Analytic Test of Their Relative Validity," *Journal of Applied Psychology*, October 2004, pp. 755–68.

31. D. Baum, "Battle Lessons: What the Generals Don't Know," *The New Yorker*, January 17, 2005, pp. 42–48.

32. J. R. Baum, E. A. Locke, and S. A. Kirkpatrick, "A Longitudinal Study of the Relation of Vision and Vision Communication to Venture Growth in Entrepreneurial Firms," *Journal of Applied Psychology*, February 2000, pp. 43–54.

33. B. J. Avolio, W. Zhu, W. Koh, and P. Bhatia, "Transformational Leadership and Organizational Commitment: Mediating Role of Psychological Empowerment and Moderating Role of Structural Distance," *Journal of Organizational Behavior*, December 2004, pp. 951–68; T. Dvir, N. Kass, and B. Shamir, "The Emotional Bond: Vision and Organizational Commitment Among High-Tech Employees," *Journal of Organizational Change Management*, 17(2), 2004, pp. 126–43; and D. I. Jung and B. J. Avolio, "Opening the Black Box: An Experimental Investigation of the Mediating Effects of Trust and Value Congruence on Transformational and Transactional Leadership," *Journal of Organizational Behavior*, December 2000, pp. 949–64.

34. Cited in B. M. Bass and B. J. Avolio, "Developing Transformational Leadership: 1992 and Beyond," *Journal of European Industrial Training*, January 1990, p. 23.

35. T. A. Judge and R. F. Piccolo, "Transformational and Transactional Leadership: A Meta-Analytic Test of Their Relative Validity," *Journal of Applied Psychology*, October 2004, pp. 755–68.

36. See, for instance, J. Barling, T. Weber, and E. K. Kelloway, "Effects of Transformational Leadership Training on Attitudinal and Financial Outcomes: A Field Experiment," *Journal of Applied Psychology*, December 1996, pp. 827–32; and T. Dvir, D. Eden, and B. J. Avolio, "Impact of Transformational Leadership on Follower Development and Performance: A Field Experiment," *Academy of Management Journal*, August 2002, pp. 735–44.

37. R. J. House and P. M. Podsakoff, "Leadership Effectiveness: Past Perspectives and Future Directions for Research," in J. Greenberg (ed.), *Organizational Behavior: The State of the Science* (Hillsdale, NJ: Lawrence Erlbaum, 1994), pp. 45–82; and B. M. Bass, *Leadership and Performance Beyond Expectations* (New York: Free Press, 1985).

38. B. J. Avolio and B. M. Bass, "Transformational Leadership, Charisma and Beyond," working paper, School of Management, State University of New York, Binghamton, 1985, p. 14.

39. See B. J. Avolio, W. L. Gardner, F. O. Walumbwa, F. Luthans, and D. R. May, "Unlocking the Mask: A Look at the Process by Which Authentic Leaders Impact Follower Attitudes and Behaviors," *Leadership Quarterly*, December 2004, pp. 801–23; W. L. Gardner and J. R. Schermerhorn Jr., "Performance Gains Through Positive Organizational Behavior and Authentic Leadership," *Organizational Dynamics*, August 2004, pp. 270–81;

and D. R. May, A. Y. L. Chan, T. D. Hodges, and B. J. Avolio, "Developing the Moral Component of Authentic Leadership," *Organizational Dynamics*, August 2003, pp. 247–60.

40. R. G. Lord, C. L. DeVader, and G. M. Alliger, "A Meta-Analysis of the Relation Between Personality Traits and Leadership Perceptions: An Application of Validity Generalization Procedures," *Journal of Applied Psychology*, August 1986, pp. 402–10.

41. B. M. Staw and J. Ross, "Commitment in an Experimenting Society: A Study of the Attribution of Leadership from Administrative Scenarios," *Journal of Applied Psychology*, June 1980, pp. 249–60; and J. Pfeffer, *Managing with Power* (Boston: Harvard Business School Press, 1992), p. 194.

42. S. D. Dionne, F. J. Yamarino, L. E. Atwater, and L. R. James, "Neutralizing Substitutes for Leadership Theory: Leadership Effects and Common-Source Bias," *Journal of Applied Psychology*, 87, 2002, pp. 454–64; and J. R. Villa, J. P. Howell, P. W. Dorfman, and D. L. Daniel, "Problems with Detecting Moderators in Leadership Research Using Moderated Multiple Regression," *Leadership Quarterly*, 14, 2002, pp. 3–23.

43. B. M. Bass, "Cognitive, Social, and Emotional Intelligence of Transformational Leaders," in R. E. Riggio, S. E. Murphy, and F. J. Pirozzolo (eds.), *Multiple Intelligences and Leadership* (Mahwah, NJ: Lawrence Erlbaum, 2002), pp. 113–114.

44. See, for instance, R. Lofthouse, "Herding the Cats," *EuroBusiness*, February 2001, pp. 64–65; M. Delahoussaye, "Leadership in the 21st Century," *Training*, September 2001, pp. 60–72; and K. Ellis, "Making Waves," *Training*, June 2003, pp. 16–21.

45. See, for instance, J. Barling, T. Weber, and E. K. Kelloway, "Effects of Transformational Leadership Training on Attitudinal and Financial Outcomes: A Field Experiment; and D. V. Day, "Leadership Development: A Review in Context," *Leadership Quarterly*, Winter 2000, pp. 581–613.

46. M. Sashkin, "The Visionary Leader," in J. A. Conger, R. N. Kanungo and Associates (eds.), *Charismatic Leadership* (San Francisco: Jossey-Bass, 1988), p. 150.

47. M. Conlin, "CEO Coaches," *Business Week*, November 11, 2002, pp. 98–104.

48. Howell and Frost, "A Laboratory Study of Charismatic Leadership."

49. T. Dvir, D. Eden, and B. J. Avolio, "Impact of Transformational Leadership on Follower Development and Performance: A Field Experiment," *Academy of Management Journal*, August 2002, pp. 735–44; B. J. Avolio and B. M. Bass, *Developing Potential Across a Full Range of Leadership: Cases on Transactional and Transformational Leadership* (Mahwah, NJ: Lawrence Erlbaum, 2002); A. J. Towler, "Effects of Charismatic Influence Training on Attitudes, Behavior, and Performance," *Personnel Psychology*, Summer 2003, pp. 363–81; and Barling, Weber, and Kelloway, "Effects of Transformational Leadership Training on Attitudinal and Financial Outcomes."

CHAPTER 12

1. Ilies, Hauserman, Schwochau, and Stibal, "Reported Incidence Rates of Work-Related Sexual Harassment in the United States"; A. B. Malamut and L. R. Offermann, "Coping with Sexual Harassment: Personal, Environmental, and

Cognitive Determinants," *Journal of Applied Psychology*, December 2001, pp. 1,152–66; L. M. Cortina and S. A. Wasti, "Profiles in Coping: Responses to Sexual Harassment Across Persons, Organizations, and Cultures," *Journal of Applied Psychology*, February 2005, pp. 182–92; J. H. Wayne, "Disentangling the Power Bases of Sexual Harassment: Comparing Gender, Age, and Position Power," *Journal of Vocational Behavior*, December 2000, pp. 301–25; and F. Wilson and P. Thompson, "Sexual Harassment as an Exercise of Power," *Gender, Work & Organization*, January 2001, pp. 61–83.

2. P. M. Podsakoff and C. A. Schriesheim, "Field Studies of French and Raven's Bases of Power: Critique, Reanalysis, and Suggestions for Future Research," *Psychological Bulletin*, May 1985, pp. 387–411; T. R. Hinkin and C. A. Schriesheim, "Development and Application of New Scales to Measure the French and Raven (1959) Bases of Social Power," *Journal of Applied Psychology*, August 1989, pp. 561–67; and P. P. Carson, K. D. Carson, and C. W. Roe, "Social Power Bases: A Meta-Analytic Examination of Interrelationships and Outcomes," *Journal of Applied Social Psychology*, 23(14), 1993, pp. 1,150–69.

3. See, for example, D. Kipnis, S. M. Schmidt, C. Swaffin-Smith, and I. Wilkinson, "Patterns of Managerial Influence: Shotgun Managers, Tacticians, and Bystanders," *Organizational Dynamics*, Winter 1984, pp. 58–67; D. Kipnis and S. M. Schmidt, "Upward-Influence Styles: Relationship with Performance Evaluations, Salary, and Stress," *Administrative Science Quarterly*, December 1988, pp. 528–42; G. Yukl and J. B. Tracey, "Consequences of Influence Tactics Used with Subordinates, Peers, and the Boss," *Journal of Applied Psychology*, August 1992, pp. 525–35; G. Blickle, "Influence Tactics Used by Subordinates: An Empirical Analysis of the Kipnis and Schmidt Subscales," *Psychological Reports*, February 2000, pp. 143–54; and G. Yukl, "Use Power Effectively," pp. 249–52.

4. G. Yukl, *Leadership in Organizations*, 5th ed. (Upper Saddle River, NJ: Prentice Hall, 2002), pp. 141–74; G. R. Ferris, W. A. Hochwarter, C. Douglas, F. R. Blass, R. W. Kolodinksy, and D. C. Treadway, "Social Influence Processes in Organizations and Human Resource Systems," in G. R. Ferris and J. J. Martocchio (eds.), *Research in Personnel and Human Resources Management*, vol. 21 (Oxford, UK: JAI Press/Elsevier, 2003), pp. 65–127; and C. A. Higgins, T. A. Judge, and G. R. Ferris, "Influence Tactics and Work Outcomes: A Meta-Analysis," *Journal of Organizational Behavior*, March 2003, pp. 89–106.

5. C. M. Falbe and G. Yukl, "Consequences for Managers of Using Single Influence Tactics and Combinations of Tactics," *Academy of Management Journal*, July 1992, pp. 638–53.

6. Yukl, *Leadership in Organizations*.

7. Ibid.

8. Falbe and Yukl, "Consequences for Managers of Using Single Influence Tactics and Combinations of Tactics."

9. Yukl, "Use Power Effectively," p. 254.

10. J. K. Murnighan and D. J. Brass, "Intraorganizational Coalitions," in M. H. Bazerman, R. J. Lewicki, and B. H. Sheppard (eds.), *Research on Negotiation in Organizations* (Greenwich, CT: JAI Press, 1991).

11. S. B. Bacharach and E. J. Lawler, "Political Alignments in Organizations," in R. M. Kramer and M. A. Neale (eds.), *Power and Influence in Organizations* (Newbury Park, CA: Sage Publications, 1988), pp. 68–69.

12. D. Farrell and J. C. Petersen, "Patterns of Political Behavior in Organizations," *Academy of Management Review*, July 1982, p. 405. For analyses of the controversies underlying the definition of organizational politics, see A. Drory and T. Romm, "The Definition of Organizational Politics: A Review," *Human Relations*, November 1990, pp. 1,133–54; and R. S. Cropanzano, K. M. Kacmar, and D. P. Bozeman, "Organizational Politics, Justice, and Support: Their Differences and Similarities," in R. S. Cropanzano and K. M. Kacmar (eds.), *Organizational Politics, Justice and Support: Managing Social Climate at Work* (Westport, CT: Quorum Books, 1995), pp. 1–18.

13. See, for example, G. Biberman, "Personality and Characteristic Work Attitudes of Persons with High, Moderate, and Low Political Tendencies," *Psychological Reports*, October 1985, pp. 1,303–10; R. J. House, "Power and Personality in Complex Organizations," in B. M. Staw and L. L. Cummings (eds.), *Research in Organizational Behavior*, vol. 10 (Greenwich, CT: JAI Press, 1988), pp. 305–57; G. R. Ferris, G. S. Russ, and P. M. Fandt, "Politics in Organizations," in R. A. Giacalone and P. Rosenfeld (eds.), *Impression Management in the Organization* (Hillsdale, NJ: Lawrence Erlbaum, 1989), pp. 155–56; and W. E. O'Connor and T. G. Morrison, "A Comparison of Situational and Dispositional Predictors of Perceptions of Organizational Politics," *Journal of Psychology*, May 2001, pp. 301–12.

14. K. M. Kacmar and R. A. Baron, "Organizational Politics"; M. Valle and L. A. Witt, "The Moderating Effect of Teamwork Perceptions on the Organizational Politics–Job Satisfaction Relationship," *Journal of Social Psychology*, June 2001, pp. 379–88; and W. A. Hochwarter, C. Kiewitz, S. L. Castro, P. L. Perrewe, and G. R. Ferris, "Positive Affectivity and Collective Efficacy as Moderators of the Relationship Between Perceived Politics and Job Satisfaction," *Journal of Applied Social Psychology*, May 2003, pp. 1,009–35.

15. G. R. Ferris, D. D. Frink, M. C. Galang, J. Zhou, K. M. Kacmar, and J. L. Howard, "Perceptions of Organizational Politics: Prediction, Stress-Related Implications, and Outcomes," *Human Relations*, February 1996, pp. 233–66; and E. Vigoda, "Stress-Related Aftermaths to Workplace Politics: The Relationships Among Politics, Job Distress, and Aggressive Behavior in Organizations," *Journal of Organizational Behavior*, August 2002, pp. 571–91.

16. C. Kiewitz, W. A. Hochwarter, G. R. Ferris, and S. L. Castro, "The Role of Psychological Climate in Neutralizing the Effects of Organizational Politics on Work Outcomes," *Journal of Applied Social Psychology*, June 2002, pp. 1,189–207; J. M. L. Poon, "Situational Antecedents and Outcomes of Organizational Politics Perceptions"; and M. C. Andrews, L. A. Witt, and K. M. Kacmar, "The Interactive Effects of Organizational Politics and Exchange Ideology on Manager Ratings of Retention," *Journal of Vocational Behavior*, April 2003, pp. 357–69.

17. S. Aryee, Z. Chen, and P. S. Budhwar, "Exchange Fairness and Employee Performance: An Examination of the Relationship Between Organizational Politics and Procedural Justice," *Organizational Behavior & Human Decision Processes*, May 2004, pp. 1–14; and Kacmar, Bozeman, Carlson, and Anthony, "An Examination of the Perceptions of Organizational Politics Model."

18. Ibid., p. 389.

19. Ibid., p. 409.

20. B. E. Ashforth and R. T. Lee, "Defensive Behavior in Organizations: A Preliminary Model," *Human Relations*, July 1990, pp. 621–48.

21. M. Valle and P. L. Perrewe, "Do Politics Perceptions Relate to Political Behaviors? Tests of an Implicit Assumption and Expanded Model," *Human Relations*, March 2000, pp. 359–86.

22. See T. Romm and A. Drory, "Political Behavior in Organizations: A Cross-Cultural Comparison," *International Journal of Value Based Management*, vol. 1, 1988, pp. 97–113; and E. Vigoda, "Reactions to Organizational Politics: A Cross-Cultural Examination in Israel and Britain," *Human Relations*, November 2001, pp. 1,483–518.

23. Vigoda, "Reactions to Organizational Politics," p. 1,512.

24. Ibid., p. 1,510.

25. M. R. Leary and R. M. Kowalski, "Impression Management: A Literature Review and Two-Component Model," *Psychological Bulletin*, January 1990, pp. 34–47.

26. See, for instance, B. R. Schlenker, *Impression Management: The Self-Concept, Social Identity, and Interpersonal Relations* (Monterey, CA: Brooks/Cole, 1980); W. L. Gardner and M. J. Martinko, "Impression Management in Organizations," *Journal of Management*, June 1988, pp. 321–38; Leary and Kowalski, "Impression Management," pp. 34–47; P. R. Rosenfeld, R. A. Giacalone, and C. A. Riordan, *Impression Management in Organizations: Theory, Measurement, and Practice* (New York: Routledge, 1995); C. K. Stevens and A. L. Kristof, "Making the Right Impression: A Field Study of Applicant Impression Management During Job Interviews," *Journal of Applied Psychology*, October 1995, pp. 587–606; D. P. Bozeman and K. M. Kacmar, "A Cybernetic Model of Impression Management Processes in Organizations," *Organizational Behavior and Human Decision Processes*, January 1997, pp. 9–30; M. C. Bolino and W. H. Turnley, "More than One Way to Make an Impression: Exploring Profiles of Impression Management," *Journal of Management*, 29(2), 2003, pp. 141–60; S. Zivnuska, K. M. Kacmar, L. A. Witt, D. S. Carlson, and V. K. Bratton, "Interactive Effects of Impression Management and Organizational Politics on Job Performance," *Journal of Organizational Behavior*, August 2004, pp. 627–40; and W.-C. Tsai, C.-C. Chen, and S.-F. Chiu, "Exploring Boundaries of the Effects of Applicant Impression Management Tactics in Job Interviews," *Journal of Management*, February 2005, pp. 108–25.

27. M. Snyder and J. Copeland, "Self-Monitoring Processes in Organizational Settings," in Giacalone and Rosenfeld (eds.), *Impression Management in the Organization*, p. 11; E. D. Long and G. H. Dobbins, "Self-Monitoring, Impression Management, and Interview Ratings: A Field and Laboratory Study," in J. L. Wall and L. R. Jauch (eds.), *Proceedings of the 52nd Annual Academy of Management Conference*, Las Vegas, August 1992, pp. 274–78; A. Montagliani and R. A. Giacalone, "Impression Management and Cross-Cultural Adaptation," *Journal of Social Psychology*, October 1998, pp. 598–608; and W. H. Turnley and M. C. Bolino, "Achieved Desired Images While Avoiding Undesired Images: Exploring the Role of Self-Monitoring in Impression Management," *Journal of Applied Psychology*, April 2001, pp. 351–60.

28. R. A. Baron, "Impression Management by Applicants During Employment Interviews: The 'Too Much of a Good Thing' Effect," in R. W. Eder and G. R. Ferris (eds.), *The Employment Interview: Theory, Research, and Practice* (Newbury Park, CA: Sage Publications, 1989), pp. 204–15.

29. Ferris, Russ, and Fandt, "Politics in Organizations."

30. A. P. J. Ellis, B. J. West, A. M. Ryan, and R. P. DeShon, "The Use of Impression Management Tactics in Structural Interviews: A Function of Question Type?" *Journal of Applied Psychology*, December 2002, pp. 1,200–08.

31. Baron, "Impression Management by Applicants During Employment Interviews"; D. C. Gilmore and G. R. Ferris, "The Effects of Applicant Impression Management Tactics on Interviewer Judgments," *Journal of Management*, December 1989, pp. 557–64; Stevens and Kristof, "Making the Right Impression"; L. A. McFarland, A. M. Ryan, and S. D. Kriska, "Impression Management Use and Effectiveness Across Assessment Methods," *Journal of Management*, 29(5), 2003, pp. 641–61; and Tsai, Chen, Chiu, "Exploring Boundaries of the Effects of Applicant Impression Management Tactics in Job Interviews."

32. Gilmore and Ferris, "The Effects of Applicant Impression Management Tactics on Interviewer Judgments."

33. Stevens and Kristof, "Making the Right Impression."

34. C. A. Higgins, T. A. Judge, and G. R. Ferris, "Influence Tactics and Work Outcomes: A Meta-Analysis," *Journal of Organizational Behavior*, March 2003, pp. 89–106.

35. Ibid.

CHAPTER 13

1. L. L. Putnam and M. S. Poole, "Conflict and Negotiation," in F. M. Jablin, L. L. Putnam, K. H. Roberts, and L. W. Porter (eds.), *Handbook of Organizational Communication: An Interdisciplinary Perspective* (Newbury Park, CA: Sage Publications, 1987), pp. 549–99.

2. See K. A. Jehn, "A Multimethod Examination of the Benefits and Detriments of Intragroup Conflict," *Administrative Science Quarterly*, June 1995, pp. 256–82; K. A. Jehn, "A Qualitative Analysis of Conflict Types and Dimensions in Organizational Groups," *Administrative Science Quarterly*, September 1997, pp. 530–57; K. A. Jehn and E. A. Mannix, "The Dynamic Nature of Conflict: A Longitudinal Study of Intragroup Conflict and Group Performance," *Academy of Management Journal*, April 2001, pp. 238–51; K. A. Jehn and C. Bendersky, "Intragroup Conflict in Organizations: A Contingency Perspective on the Conflict-Outcome Relationship," in R. M. Kramer and B. M. Staw (eds.), *Research in Organizational Behavior*, vol. 25 (Oxford, England: Elsevier, 2003), pp. 199–210; and C. K. W. De Dreu and L. R. Weingart, "Task Versus Relationship Conflict, Team Performance, and Team Member Satisfaction: A Meta-Analysis," *Journal of Applied Psychology*, August 2003, pp. 741–49.

3. J. Yang and K. W. Mossholder, "Decoupling Task and Relationship Conflict: The Role of Intragroup Emotional Processing," *Journal of Organizational Behavior*, 25(5), August 2004, pp. 589–605.

4. See S. P. Robbins, *Managing Organizational Conflict: A Nontraditional Approach* (Upper Saddle River, NJ: Prentice Hall,

1974), pp. 31–55; and Wall and Callister, "Conflict and Its Management," pp. 517–23.

5. M. J. Gelfand, M. Higgins, L. H. Nishii, et al., "Culture and Egocentric Perceptions of Fairness in Conflict and Negotiation," *Journal of Applied Psychology*, October 2002, pp. 833–45.

6. L. R. Pondy, "Organizational Conflict: Concepts and Models," *Administrative Science Quarterly*, September 1967, p. 302.

7. Ibid.

8. See, for instance, R. A. Cosier and C. R. Schwenk, "Agreement and Thinking Alike: Ingredients for Poor Decisions," *Academy of Management Executive*, February 1990, pp. 69–74; K. A. Jehn, "Enhancing Effectiveness: An Investigation of Advantages and Disadvantages of Value-Based Intragroup Conflict," *International Journal of Conflict Management*, July 1994, pp. 223–38; R. L. Priem, D. A. Harrison, and N. K. Muir, "Structured Conflict and Consensus Outcomes in Group Decision Making," *Journal of Management*, 21(4), 1995, pp. 691–710; and K. A. Jehn and E. A. Mannix, "The Dynamic Nature of Conflict: A Longitudinal Study of Intragroup Conflict and Group Performance," *Academy of Management Journal*, April 2001, pp. 238–51.

9. See, for instance, C. J. Loomis, "Dinosaurs?" *Fortune*, May 3, 1993, pp. 36–42.

10. K. Swisher, "Yahoo! May Be Down, But Don't Count It Out," *Wall Street Journal*, March 9, 2001, p. B1; and M. Mangalindan and S. L. Hwang, "Coterie of Early Hires Made Yahoo! A Hit but an Insular Place," *Wall Street Journal*, March 9, 2001, p. A1.

11. J. Hall and M. S. Williams, "A Comparison of Decision-Making Performances in Established and Ad-Hoc Groups," *Journal of Personality and Social Psychology*, February 1966, p. 217.

12. R. L. Hoffman, "Homogeneity of Member Personality and Its Effect on Group Problem-Solving," *Journal of Abnormal and Social Psychology*, January 1959, pp. 27–32; R. L. Hoffman and N. R. F. Maier, "Quality and Acceptance of Problem Solutions by Members of Homogeneous and Heterogeneous Groups," *Journal of Abnormal and Social Psychology*, March 1961, pp. 401–07; and P. Pitcher and A. D. Smith, "Top Management Team Heterogeneity: Personality, Power, and Proxies," *Organization Science*, January–February 2001, pp. 1–18.

13. For example, see J. A. Wall Jr., and R. R. Callister, "Conflict and Its Management," pp. 523–26 for evidence supporting the argument that conflict is almost uniformly dysfunctional. See also P. J. Hinds, and D. E. Bailey, "Out of Sight, Out of Sync: Understanding Conflict in Distributed Teams," *Organization Science*, November–December 2003, pp. 615–32.

14. M. Geyelin and E. Felsenthal, "Irreconcilable Differences Force Shea & Gould Closure," *Wall Street Journal*, January 31, 1994, p. B1.

15. This section is based on F. Sommerfield, "Paying the Troops to Buck the System," *Business Month*, May 1990, pp. 77–79; W. Kiechel III, "How to Escape the Echo Chamber," *Fortune*, June 18, 1990, pp. 129–30; E. Van de Vliert and C. De Dreu, "Optimizing Performance by Stimulating Conflict," *International Journal of Conflict Management*, July 1994, pp. 211–22; E. Van de Vliert, "Enhancing Performance by Conflict-Stimulating

Intervention," in C. De Dreu and E. Van de Vliert (eds.), *Using Conflict in Organizations* (Newbury Park, CA: Sage Publications), pp. 208–22; K. M. Eisenhardt, J. L. Kahwajy, and L. J. Bourgeois III, "How Management Teams Can Have a Good Fight," *Harvard Business Review*, July–August 1997, pp. 77–85; S. Wetlaufer, "Common Sense and Conflict," *Harvard Business Review*, January–February 2000, pp. 114–24; and G. A. Okhuysen and K. M. Eisenhardt, "Excel Through Group Process," in E. A. Locke (ed.), *Handbook of Principles of Organizational Behavior* Malden, MA: Blackwell, 2004, pp. 216–18.

16. J. A. Wall Jr., *Negotiation: Theory and Practice* (Glenview, IL: Scott, Foresman, 1985).

17. This model is based on R. J. Lewicki, "Bargaining and Negotiation," *Exchange: The Organizational Behavior Teaching Journal*, 6(2), 1981, pp. 39–40.

18. J. Lee, "The Negotiators," *Forbes*, January 11, 1999, pp. 22–24.

19. B. Barry and R. A. Friedman, "Bargainer Characteristics in Distributive and Integrative Negotiation," *Journal of Personality & Social Psychology*, February 1998, pp. 345–59.

20. J. B. White, R. Tynan, A. D. Galinsky, and L. Thompson, "Face Threat Sensitivity in Negotiation: Roadblock to Agreement and Joint Gain," *Organizational Behavior & Human Decision Processes*, July 2004, pp. 102–24.

21. C. Watson and L. R. Hoffman, "Managers as Negotiators: A Test of Power Versus Gender as Predictors of Feelings, Behavior, and Outcomes," *Leadership Quarterly*, Spring 1996, pp. 63–85.

22. A. E. Walters, A. F. Stuhlmacher, and L. L. Meyer, "Gender and Negotiator Competitiveness: A Meta-Analysis," *Organizational Behavior and Human Decision Processes*, October 1998, pp. 1–29; and A. F. Stuhlmacher and A. E. Walters, "Gender Differences in Negotiation Outcome: A Meta-Analysis," *Personnel Psychology*, Autumn 1999, pp. 653–77.

23. Stuhlmacher and Walters, "Gender Differences in Negotiation Outcome," p. 655.

24. L. J. Kray, A. D. Galinsky, and L. Thompson, "Reversing the Gender Gap in Negotiations: An Exploration of Stereotype Regeneration," *Organizational Behavior & Human Decision Processes*, March 2002, pp. 386–409.

25. C. K. Stevens, A. G. Bavetta, and M. E. Gist, "Gender Differences in the Acquisition of Salary Negotiation Skills: The Role of Goals, Self-Efficacy, and Perceived Control," *Journal of Applied Psychology*, 78(5), October 1993, pp. 723–35.

26. See N. J. Adler, *International Dimensions of Organizational Behavior*, 4th ed. (Cincinnati, OH: Southwestern, 2002), pp. 208–56; W. L. Adair, T. Okurmura, and J. M. Brett, "Negotiation Behavior when Cultures Collide: The United States and Japan," *Journal of Applied Psychology*, June 2001, pp. 371–85; M. J. Gelfand, M. Higgins, L. H. Nishii, et al., "Culture and Egocentric Perceptions of Fairness in Conflict and Negotiation," *Journal of Applied Psychology*, October 2002, pp. 833–45; and X. Lin and S. J. Miller, "Negotiation Approaches: Direct and Indirect Effect of National Culture," *International Marketing Review*, 20(3), 2003, pp. 286–303.

27. K. D. Schmidt, *Doing Business in France* (Menlo Park, CA: SRI International, 1987).

28. S. Lubman, "Round and Round," *Wall Street Journal,* December 10, 1993, p. R3.

29. Adair, Okumura, and Brett, "Negotiation Behavior When Cultures Collide."

30. P. R. Harris and R. T. Moran, *Managing Cultural Differences,* 5th ed. (Houston: Gulf Publishing, 1999), pp. 56–59.

31. E. S. Glenn, D. Witmeyer, and K. A. Stevenson, "Cultural Styles of Persuasion," *Journal of Intercultural Relations,* Fall 1977, pp. 52–66.

32. J. Graham, "The Influence of Culture on Business Negotiations," *Journal of International Business Studies,* Spring 1985, pp. 81–96.

33. K. W. Thomas, "Toward Multidimensional Values in Teaching: The Example of Conflict Behaviors," *Academy of Management Review,* July 1977, p. 487.

34. Based on R. Fisher and W. Ury, *Getting to Yes: Negotiating Agreement Without Giving In* (Boston: Houghton Mifflin, 1981); Wall and Blum, "Negotiations," pp. 295–96; and Bazerman and Neale, *Negotiating Rationally.*

CHAPTER 14

1. See, for instance, R. L. Daft, *Organization Theory and Design,* 8th ed. (Cincinnati, OH: Southwestern, 2004).

2. See, for instance, S. M. Davis and P. R. Lawrence, "Problems of Matrix Organization," *Harvard Business Review,* May–June 1978, pp. 131–42; and T. Sy and S. Cote, "Emotional Intelligence: A Key Ability to Succeed in the Matrix Organization," *Journal of Management Development,* 23(5), 2004, pp. 437–55.

3. See, for instance, R. E. Miles and C. C. Snow, "The New Network Firm: A Spherical Structure Built on Human Investment Philosophy," *Organizational Dynamics,* Spring 1995, pp. 5–18; M. A. Schilling and H. K. Steensma, "The Use of Modular Organizational Forms: An Industry-Level Analysis," *Academy of Management Journal,* December 2001, pp. 1,149–68; K. R. T. Larsen and C. R. McInerney, "Preparing to Work in the Virtual Organization," *Information and Management,* May 2002, pp. 445–56; J. Gertner, "Newman's Own: Two Friends and a Canoe Paddle," *New York Times,* November 16, 2003, p. 4BU; and Y. Shin, "A Person-Environment Fit Model for Virtual Organizations," *Journal of Management,* October 2004, pp. 725–43.

4. J. Bates, "Making Movies and Moving On," *Los Angeles Times,* January 19, 1998, p. A1.

5. "GE: Just Your Average Everyday $60 Billion Family Grocery Store," *Industry Week,* May 2, 1994, pp. 13–18.

6. H. C. Lucas Jr., *The T-Form Organization: Using Technology to Design Organizations for the 21st Century* (San Francisco: Jossey-Bass, 1996).

7. This analysis is referred to as a *contingency approach* to organization design. See, for instance, J. M. Pennings, "Structural Contingency Theory: A Reappraisal," in B. M. Staw and L. L. Cummings (eds.), *Research in Organizational Behavior,* vol. 14 (Greenwich, CT: JAI Press, 1992), pp. 267–309; J. R. Hollenbeck, H. Moon, A. P. J. Ellis, et al., "Structural Contingency Theory and Individual Differences: Examination

of External and Internal Person-Team Fit," *Journal of Applied Psychology,* June 2002, pp. 599–606; and H. Moon, J. R. Hollenbeck, S. E. Humphrey, et al., "Asymmetric Adaptability: Dynamic Team Structures as One-Way Streets," *Academy of Management Journal,* October 2004, pp. 681–95.

8. See R. E. Miles and C. C. Snow, *Organizational Strategy, Structure, and Process* (New York: McGraw-Hill, 1978); D. Miller, "The Structural and Environmental Correlates of Business Strategy," *Strategic Management Journal,* January–February 1987, pp. 55–76; D. C. Galunic and K. M. Eisenhardt, "Renewing the Strategy-Structure-Performance Paradigm," in B. M. Staw and L. L. Cummings (eds.), *Research in Organizational Behavior,* vol. 16 (Greenwich, CT: JAI Press, 1994), pp. 215–55; and I. C. Harris and T. W. Ruefli, "The Strategy/Structure Debate: An Examination of the Performance Implications," *Journal of Management Studies,* June 2000, pp. 587–603.

9. See, for instance, P. M. Blau and R. A. Schoenherr, *The Structure of Organizations* (New York: Basic Books, 1971); D. S. Pugh, "The Aston Program of Research: Retrospect and Prospect," in A. H. Van de Ven and W. F. Joyce (eds.), *Perspectives on Organization Design and Behavior* (New York: John Wiley, 1981), pp. 135–66; R. Z. Gooding and J. A. Wagner III, "A Meta-Analytic Review of the Relationship Between Size and Performance: The Productivity and Efficiency of Organizations and Their Subunits," *Administrative Science Quarterly,* December 1985, pp. 462–81; and A. C. Bluedorn, "Pilgrim's Progress: Trends and Convergence in Research on Organizational Size and Environments," *Journal of Management,* Summer 1993, pp. 163–92.

10. See J. Woodward, *Industrial Organization: Theory and Practice* (London: Oxford University Press, 1965); C. Perrow, "A Framework for the Comparative Analysis of Organizations," *American Sociological Review,* April 1967, pp. 194–208; J. D. Thompson, *Organizations in Action* (New York: McGraw-Hill, 1967); J. Hage and M. Aiken, "Routine Technology, Social Structure, and Organizational Goals," *Administrative Science Quarterly,* September 1969, pp. 366–77; C. C. Miller, W. H. Glick, Y. Wang, and G. P. Huber, "Understanding Technology-Structure Relationships: Theory Development and Meta-Analytic Theory Testing," *Academy of Management Journal,* June 1991, pp. 370–99; and K. H. Roberts and M. Grabowski, "Organizations, Technology, and Structuring," in S. R. Clegg, C. Hardy, and W. R. Nord (eds.), *Managing Organizations: Current Issues* (Thousand Oaks, CA: Sage Publications, 1999), pp. 159–71.

11. See F. E. Emery and E. Trist, "The Causal Texture of Organizational Environments," *Human Relations,* February 1965, pp. 21–32; P. Lawrence and J. W. Lorsch, *Organization and Environment: Managing Differentiation and Integration* (Boston: Harvard Business School, Division of Research, 1967); M. Yasai-Ardekani, "Structural Adaptations to Environments," *Academy of Management Review,* January 1986, pp. 9–21; Bluedorn, "Pilgrim's Progress"; and M. Arndt and B. Bigelow, "Presenting Structural Innovation in an Institutional Environment: Hospitals' Use of Impression Management," *Administrative Science Quarterly,* September 2000, pp. 494–522.

12. See, for instance, L. W. Porter and E. E. Lawler III, "Properties of Organization Structure in Relation to Job Attitudes and Job

Behavior," *Psychological Bulletin*, July 1965, pp. 23–51; L. R. James and A. P. Jones, "Organization Structure: A Review of Structural Dimensions and Their Conceptual Relationships with Individual Attitudes and Behavior," *Organizational Behavior and Human Performance*, June 1976, pp. 74–113; D. R. Dalton, W. D. Todor, M. J. Spendolini, G. J. Fielding, and L. W. Porter, "Organization Structure and Performance: A Critical Review," *Academy of Management Review*, January 1980, pp. 49–64; W. Snizek and J. H. Bullard, "Perception of Bureaucracy and Changing Job Satisfaction: A Longitudinal Analysis," *Organizational Behavior and Human Performance*, October 1983, pp. 275–87; and D. B. Turban and T. L. Keon, "Organizational Attractiveness: An Interactionist Perspective," *Journal of Applied Psychology*, April 1994, pp. 184–93.

CHAPTER 15

1. This seven-item description is based on C. A. O'Reilly III, J. Chatman, and D. F. Caldwell, "People and Organizational Culture: A Profile Comparison Approach to Assessing Person-Organization Fit," *Academy of Management Journal*, September 1991, pp. 487–516; and J. A. Chatman and K. A. Jehn, "Assessing the Relationship Between Industry Characteristics and Organizational Culture: How Different Can You Be?" *Academy of Management Journal*, June 1994, pp. 522–53.

2. S. Hamm, "No Letup—and No Apologies," *Business Week*, October 26, 1998, pp. 58–64; and C. Carlson, "Former Intel Exec Slams Microsoft Culture." Accessed November 25, 2006, at www.eweek.com/article2/0,1895,94976,00.asp.

3. R. T. Mowday, L. W. Porter, and R. M. Steers, *Employee-Organization Linkages: The Psychology of Commitment, Absenteeism, and Turnover* (New York: Academic Press, 1982); and C. Vandenberghe, "Organizational Culture, Person-Culture Fit, and Turnover: A Replication in the Health Care Industry," *Journal of Organizational Behavior*, March 1999, pp. 175–84.

4. See N. J. Adler, *International Dimensions of Organizational Behavior*, 4th ed. (Cincinnati, OH: Southwestern, 2002), pp. 67–69.

5. T. E. Deal and A. A. Kennedy, "Culture: A New Look Through Old Lenses," *Journal of Applied Behavioral Science*, November 1983, p. 501.

6. J. Case, "Corporate Culture," *INC.*, November 1996, pp. 42–53.

7. Sorensen, "The Strength of Corporate Culture and the Reliability of Firm Performance."

8. See, for instance, P. L. Moore, "She's Here to Fix the Xerox," *Business Week*, August 6, 2001, pp. 47–48; and C. Ragavan, "FBI Inc.," *U.S. News & World Report*, June 18, 2001, pp. 15–21.

9. S. Cartwright and C. L. Cooper, "The Role of Culture Compatibility in Successful Organizational Marriages," *Academy of Management Executive*, May 1993, pp. 57–70; E. Krell, "Merging Corporate Cultures," *Training*, May 2001, pp. 68–78; and R. A. Weber and C. F. Camerer, "Cultural Conflict and Merger Failure: An Experimental Approach," *Management Science*, April 2003, pp. 400–12.

10. P. Gumbel, "Return of the Urge to Merge," *Time Europe Magazine*. Accessed November 25, 2003, at

www.time.com/time/europe/magazine/article/0,13005,90103072 1-464418,00.html.

11. S. F. Gale, "Memo to AOL Time Warner: Why Mergers Fail—Case Studies," *Workforce*. Accessed November 25, 2006, at www.workforce.com; and W. Bock, "Mergers, Bubbles, and Steve Case," *Wally Bock's Monday Memo*. Accessed January 20, 2003, at www.mondaymemo.net/030120feature.htm.

12. E. H. Schein, "Leadership and Organizational Culture," in F. Hesselbein, M. Goldsmith, and R. Beckhard (eds.), *The Leader of the Future* (San Francisco: Jossey-Bass, 1996), pp. 61–62.

13. L. Grensing-Pophal, "Hiring to Fit Your Corporate Culture," *HR Magazine*, August 1999, pp. 50–54.

14. J. S. Lublin, "Cheap Talk," *Wall Street Journal*, April 11, 2002, p. B14.

15. K. Rhodes, "Breaking in the Top Dogs," *Training*, February 2000, pp. 67–74.

16. J. Van Maanen and E. H. Schein, "Career Development," in J. R. Hackman and J. L. Suttle (eds.), *Improving Life at Work* (Santa Monica, CA: Goodyear, 1977), pp. 58–62.

17. G. Chen and R. J. Klimoski, "The Impact of Expectations on Newcomer Performance in Teams as Mediated by Work Characteristics, Social Exchanges, and Empowerment," *Academy of Management Journal*, vol. 46, 2003, pp. 591–607; C. R. Wanberg and J. D. Kammeyer-Mueller, "Predictors and Outcomes of Proactivity in the Socialization Process," *Journal of Applied Psychology*, vol. 85, 2000, pp. 373–85; J. D. Kammeyer-Mueller and C. R. Wanberg, "Unwrapping the Organizational Entry Process: Disentangling Multiple Antecedents and Their Pathways to Adjustment," *Journal of Applied Psychology*, vol. 88, 2003, pp. 779–94; E. W. Morrison, "Longitudinal Study of the Effects of Information Seeking on Newcomer Socialization," *Journal of Applied Psychology*, vol. 78, 2003, pp. 173–83.

18. E. Ransdell, "The Nike Story? Just Tell It!" *Fast Company*, January–February 2000, pp. 44–46.

19. See K. Kamoche, "Rhetoric, Ritualism, and Totemism in Human Resource Management," *Human Relations*, April 1995, pp. 367–85.

20. V. Matthews, "Starting Every Day with a Shout and a Song," *Financial Times*, May 2, 2001, p. 11; and M. Gimein, "Sam Walton Made Us a Promise," *Fortune*, March 18, 2002, pp. 121–30.

21. "DCACronyms," April 1997, Rev. D, published by The Boeing Co.

22. See R. H. Kilmann, M. J. Saxton, and R. Serpa (eds.), *Gaining Control of the Corporate Culture* (San Francisco: Jossey-Bass, 1985); T. H. Fitzgerald, "Can Change in Organizational Culture Really Be Managed?" *Organizational Dynamics*, Autumn 1988, pp. 5–15; B. Dumaine, "Creating a New Company Culture," *Fortune*, January 15, 1990, pp. 127–31; J. P. Kotter and J. L. Heskett, *Corporate Culture and Performance* (New York: Free Press, 1992), pp. 83–106; and H. M. Trice and J. M. Beyer, *The Cultures of Work Organizations* (Upper Saddle River, NJ: Prentice Hall, 1993), pp. 393–428.

23. See B. Victor and J. B. Cullen, "The Organizational Bases of Ethical Work Climates," *Administrative Science Quarterly*, March 1988, pp. 101–25; L. K. Trevino, "A Cultural Perspective on

Changing and Developing Organizational Ethics," in W. A. Pasmore and R. W. Woodman (eds.), *Research in Organizational Change and Development*, vol. 4 (Greenwich, CT: JAI Press, 1990); M. W. Dickson, D. B. Smith, M. W. Grojean, and M. Ehrhart, "An Organizational Climate Regarding Ethics: The Outcome of Leader Values and the Practices That Reflect Them," *Leadership Quarterly*, Summer 2001, pp. 197–217; and R. L. Dufresne, "An Action Learning Perspective on Effective Implementation of Academic Honor Codes," *Group & Organization Management*, April 2004, pp. 201–18.

24. J. A. Byrne, "The Environment Was Ripe for Abuse," *Business Week*, February 25, 2002, pp. 118–20; A. Raghavan, K. Kranhold, and A. Barrionuevo, "How Enron Bosses Created a Culture of Pushing Limits," *Wall Street Journal*, August 26, 2002, p. A1; and S. Pasha and J. Seid, "Lay and Skilling's Day of Reckoning," *CNN Money*. Accessed May 25, 2006, at money.cnn.com/2006/05/25/news/newsmakers/enron_verdict.

25. S. Daley, "A Spy's Advice to French Retailers: Politeness ⌐ays," *New York Times*, December 26, 2000, p. A4.

26. Based on M. L. Lengnick-Hall and Cynthia A. Lengnick-Hall, "Expanding Customer Orientation in the HR Function," *Human Resource Management*, Fall 1999, pp. 201–14; B. Schneider, D. E. Bowen, M. G. Ehrhart, and K. M. Holcombe, "The Climate for Service: Evolution of a Construct," in N. M. Ashkanasy, C. P. M. Wilderom, and M. F. Peterson (eds.), *Handbook of Organizational Culture and Climate* (Thousand Oaks, CA: Sage, 2000), pp. 21–36; M. D. Hartline, J. G. Maxham III, and D. O. McKee, "Corridors of Influence in the Dissemination of Customer-Oriented Strategy to Customer Contact Service Employees," *Journal of Marketing*, April 2000, pp. 35–50; L. A. Bettencourt, K. P. Gwinner, and M. L. Meuter, "A Comparison of Attitude, Personality, and Knowledge Predictors of Service-Oriented Organizational Citizenship Behaviors," *Journal of Applied Psychology*, February 2001, pp. 29–41; and A. M. Sussking, K. M. Kacmar, and C. P. Borchgrevink, "Customer Service Providers' Attitudes Relating to Customer Service and Customer Satisfaction in the Customer-Service Exchange," *Journal of Applied Psychology*, February 2003, pp. 179–87.

27. M. D. Hartline and O. C. Ferrell, "The Management of Customer-Contact Service Employees: An Empirical Investigation," *Journal of Marketing*, vol. 60, p. 56; and R. C. Ford and C. P. Heaton, "Lessons from Hospitality That Can Serve Anyone," *Organizational Dynamics*, Summer 2001, pp. 41–42.

28. A. Taylor, "Driving Customer Satisfaction," *Harvard Business Review*, July 2002, pp. 24–25.

29. M. Clendenin, "UMC's New CEO Brings Customer Focus," *EBN*, July 21, 2003, p. 4.

30. See, for instance, E. Anderson and R. L. Oliver, "Perspectives on Behavior-Based Versus Outcome-Based Salesforce Control Systems," *Journal of Marketing*, October 1987, pp. 76–88; W. R. George, "Internal Marketing and Organizational Behavior: A Partnership in Developing Customer-Conscious Employees at Every Level," *Journal of Business Research*, January 1990, pp. 63–70; and K. K. Reardon and B. Enis, "Establishing a Company-Wide Customer Orientation Through Persuasive Internal Marketing," *Management Communication Quarterly*, February 1990, pp. 376–87.

CHAPTER 16

1. See K. H. Hammonds, "Practical Radicals," *Fast Company*, September 2000, pp. 162–74; and P. C. Judge, "Change Agents," *Fast Company*, November 2000, pp. 216–26.

2. These similes were developed by P. B. Vaill, *Managing as a Performing Art: New Ideas for a World of Chaotic Change* (San Francisco: Jossey-Bass, 1989).

3. K. Lewin, "Group Decision and Social Change," in G. E. Swanson, T. M. Newcome, and E. L. Hartley (eds.), *Readings in Social Psychology*, 2nd ed. (New York: Holt, 1952), pp. 459–73.

4. T. Peters, *Thriving on Chaos* (New York: Alfred A. Knopf, 1987), p. 3.

5. J. E. Dutton, S. J. Ashford, R. M. O'Neill, and K. A. Lawrence, "Moves That Matter: Issue Selling and Organizational Change," *Academy of Management Journal*, August 2001, pp. 716–36.

6. Q. N. Huy, "Emotional Balancing of Organizational Continuity and Radical Change: The Contribution of Middle Managers," *Administrative Science Quarterly*, March 2002, pp. 31–69.

7. J. A. LePine, J. A. Colquitt, and A. Erez, "Adaptability to Changing Task Contexts: Effects of General Cognitive Ability, Conscientiousness, and Openness to Experience," *Personnel Psychology*, Fall, 2000, pp. 563–93; T. A. Judge, C. J. Thoresen, V. Pucik, and T. M. Welbourne, "Managerial Coping with Organizational Change: A Dispositional Perspective," *Journal of Applied Psychology*, February 1999, pp. 107–22; and S. Oreg, "Resistance to Change: Developing an Individual Differences Measure," *Journal of Applied Psychology*, August 2003, pp. 680–93.

8. For a sampling of various OD definitions, see N. Nicholson (ed.), *Encyclopedic Dictionary of Organizational Behavior* (Malden, MA: Blackwell, 1998), pp. 359–61; G. Farias and H. Johnson, "Organizational Development and Change Management," *Journal of Applied Behavioral Science*, September 2000, pp. 376–79; and H. K. Sinangil and F. Avallone, "Organizational Development and Change," in N. Anderson, D. S. Ones, H. K. Sinangil, and C. Viswesvaran (eds.), *Handbook of Industrial, Work and Organizational Psychology*, vol. 2 (Thousand Oaks, CA: Sage, 2001), pp. 332–35.

9. See W. A. Pasmore and M. R. Fagans, "Participation, Individual Development, and Organizational Change: A Review and Synthesis," *Journal of Management*, June 1992, pp. 375–97; T. G. Cummings and C. G. Worley, *Organization Development and Change*, 7th ed. (Cincinnati: Southwestern, 2001); and R. Lines, "Influence of Participation in Strategic Change: Resistance, Organizational Commitment and Change Goal Achievement," *Journal of Change Management*, September 2004, pp. 193–215.

10. S. Highhouse, "A History of the T-Group and Its Early Application in Management Development," *Group Dynamics: Theory, Research, & Practice*, December 2002, pp. 277–90.

11. J. E. Edwards and M. D. Thomas, "The Organizational Survey Process: General Steps and Practical Considerations," in P. Rosenfeld, J. E. Edwards, and M. D. Thomas (eds.), *Improving Organizational Surveys: New Directions, Methods, and Applications* (Newbury Park, CA: Sage Publications, 1993), pp. 3–28.

12. E. H. Schein, *Process Consultation: Its Role in Organizational Development*, 2nd ed. (Reading, MA: Addison-Wesley, 1988), p. 9. See also E. H. Schein, *Process Consultation Revisited: Building Helpful Relationships* (Reading, MA: Addison-Wesley, 1999).

13. Ibid.

14. See, for example, E. H. Neilsen, "Understanding and Managing Intergroup Conflict," in J. W. Lorsch and P. R. Lawrence (eds.), *Managing Group and Intergroup Relations* (Homewood, IL: Irwin-Dorsey, 1972), pp. 329–43.

15. R. R. Blake, J. S. Mouton, and R. L. Sloma, "The Union–Management Intergroup Laboratory: Strategy for Resolving Intergroup Conflict," *Journal of Applied Behavioral Science*, no. 1 (1965), pp. 25–57.

16. See, for example, G. R. Bushe, "Advances in Appreciative Inquiry as an Organization Development Intervention," *Organizational Development Journal*, Summer 1999, pp. 61–68; D. L. Cooperrider and D. Whitney, *Collaborating for Change: Appreciative Inquiry* (San Francisco: Berrett-Koehler, 2000); R. Fry, F. Barrett, J. Seiling, and D. Whitney (eds.), *Appreciative Inquiry & Organizational Transformation: Reports from the Field* (Westport, CT: Quorum, 2002); J. K. Barge and C. Oliver, "Working with Appreciation in Managerial Practice," *Academy of Management Review*, January 2003, pp. 124–42; and D. van der Haar and D. M. Hosking, "Evaluating Appreciative Inquiry: A Relational Constructionist Perspective," *Human Relations*, August 2004, pp. 1,017–36.

17. J. Gordon, "Meet the Freight Fairy," *Forbes*, January 20, 2003, p. 65.

18. See, for example, H. S. Gitlow, *Quality Management Systems: A Practical Guide for Improvement* (Boca Raton, FL: CRC Press, 2001); and J. W. Cortada, *The Quality Yearbook 2001* (New York: McGraw-Hill, 2001).

19. M. Hammer and J. Champy, *Reengineering the Corporation: A Manifesto for Business Revolution* (New York: Harper-Business, 1993).

20. See K. Slobogin, "Many U.S. Employees Feel Overworked, Stressed, Study Says." Accessed May 16, 2001, at www.cnn.com; and S. Armour, "Rising Job Stress Could Affect Bottom Line," *USA Today*, July 29, 2003, p. 1B.

21. Adapted from R. S. Schuler, "Definition and Conceptualization of Stress in Organizations," *Organizational Behavior and Human Performance*, April 1980, p. 189. For an updated review of definitions, see C. L. Cooper, P. J. Dewe, and M. P. O'Driscoll, *Organizational Stress: A Review and Critique of Theory, Research, and Applications* (Thousand Oaks, CA: Sage, 2002).

22. See M. A. Cavanaugh, W. R. Boswell, M. V. Roehling, and J. W. Boudreau, "An Empirical Examination of Self-Reported Work Stress Among U.S. Managers," *Journal of Applied Psychology*, February 2000, pp. 65–74.

23. J. A. LePine, M. A. LePine, and C. L. Jackson, "Challenge and Hindrance Stress: Relationships with Exhaustion, Motivation to Learn, and Learning Performance," *Journal of Applied Psychology*, October 2004, pp. 883–91; and M. A. Cavanaugh, W. R. Boswell, M. V. Roehling, and J. W. Boudreau, "An Empirical Examination of Self-reported Work Stress Among U.S. Managers," *Journal of Applied Psychology*, February 2000, pp. 65–74.

24. E. Demerouti, A. B. Bakker, F. Nachreiner, and W. B. Schaufeli, "The Job Demands-Resources Model of Burnout," *Journal of Applied Psychology*, June 2001, pp. 499–512; N. W. Van Yperen and O. Janssen, "Fatigued and Dissatisfied or Fatigued but Satisfied? Goal Orientations and Responses to High Job Demands," *Academy of Management Journal*, December 2002, pp. 1,161–71; and N. W. Van Yperen and M. Hagedoorn, "Do High Job Demands Increase Intrinsic Motivation or Fatigue or Both? The Role of Job Control and Job Social Support," *Academy of Management Journal*, June 2003, pp. 339–48.

25. See, for example, the special edition on organizational learning in *Organizational Dynamics*, Autumn 1998; P. Senge, *The Dance of Change: The Challenges to Sustaining Momentum in Learning Organizations* (New York: Doubleday/Currency, 1999); A. M. Webber, "Will Companies Ever Learn?" *Fast Company*, October 2000, pp. 275–82; R. Snell, "Moral Foundations of the Learning Organization," *Human Relations*, March 2001, pp. 319–42; M. M. Brown and J. L. Brudney, "Learning Organizations in the Public Sector? A Study of Police Agencies Employing Information and Technology to Advance Knowledge," *Public Administration Review*, January/February 2003, pp. 30–43; and T. B. Lawrence, M. K. Mauws, B. Dyck, and R. F. Kleysen, "The Politics of Organizational Learning: Integrating Power into the 4I Framework," *Academy of Management Review*, January 2005, pp. 180–91.

26. D. H. Kim, "The Link Between Individual and Organizational Learning," *Sloan Management Review*, Fall 1993, p. 37.

27. C. Argyris and D. A. Schon, *Organizational Learning* (Reading, MA: Addison-Wesley, 1978).

28. B. Dumaine, "Mr. Learning Organization," *Fortune*, October 17, 1994, p. 148.

29. F. Kofman and P. M. Senge, "Communities of Commitment: The Heart of Learning Organizations," *Organizational Dynamics*, Autumn 1993, pp. 5–23.

30. Dumaine, "Mr. Learning Organization," p. 154.

31. See S. Shane, S. Venkataraman, and I. MacMillan, "Cultural Differences in Innovation Championing Strategies," *Journal of Management*, 21(5), 1995, pp. 931–52.

Glindex (Combined Glossary and Index)

Definitions are shown in *italics*.

3M Co., 243

A

A.T. Kearney, 252
Ability, 14–15
   an individual's capacity to perform
      the various tasks in a job
Absenteeism, 26
Absolutes, 6
Achievement, need for, 74
Adams, J. Stacy, 80
Adobe Systems, 2
Affect, 108
Affect intensity, 112
   individual differences in the strength
      with which individuals experience
      their emotions
Affective commitment, 20
   an emotional attachment to the organization
      and a belief in its values
Affective component, 16, 17
Affiliation, needs for, 74
Alcoa, 11, 232, 258
Alternative work arrangements, 94–97
Amazon.com, 10
American Express, 2, 96, 176, 195
American Safety Razor, 101
American Steel & Wire, 102
Amgen, 2
Anchoring bias, 61
   tendency to fixate on initial information
Anheuser-Busch, 219
Anthropology, 6
   the study of societies for the purpose
      of learning about human beings
      and their activities
Anticapitalism backlash, 7
Antisocial behavior, 129
AOL Technologies, 151, 178, 252
Apex Digital, 240, 241
Apple Computer, 101, 176, 186, 242, 243
Applebee's, 104
Appreciative inquiry (AI), 273–274
Arousal, 80

Asch, Solomon, 128, 129
Ash, Mary Kay, 186
Assertiveness, 46
AT&T, 34, 96, 155, 241, 242
Attentional processes, 28
Attitude-behavior relationship, 18–19
Attitudes
   evaluative statements, either favorable
      or unfavorable, concerning objects,
      people, or events
   affective component, 16, 17
   attitude-behavior relationship, 18–19
   behavioral component, 16, 17
   cognitive component, 16, 17
   cognitive dissonance, 17–18
   components of, 16, 17
   consistency of, 16–17
   job attitudes, 19–22
   moderating variables, 18
   self-perception theory, 19
Attribution theory, 53–54
Attribution theory of leadership, 192–193
   leadership is merely an attribution
      that people make about other
      individuals
Authentic leadership, 191–192
Authority, 233
   rights inherent in a managerial position
      to give orders and expect the orders
      to be obeyed
Automatic Data Processing, 232
Autonomy, role of, 90
Availability bias, 61
   tendency for people to base their judgments
      on information that is readily available
      to them
Avon, 188

B

Bandura, Albert, 80
Bargaining strategies, 220–222

X

Y